MW00811361

THE STRUGGLE TO RESHAPE THE MIDDLE EAST
IN THE 21ST CENTURY

For Omar and Mariam

THE STRUGGLE TO RESHAPE THE MIDDLE EAST IN THE 21ST CENTURY

Edited by Samer S. Shehata

EDINBURGH
University Press

Edinburgh University Press is one of the leading university presses in the UK. We publish academic books and journals in our selected subject areas across the humanities and social sciences, combining cutting-edge scholarship with high editorial and production values to produce academic works of lasting importance. For more information visit our website: edinburghuniversitypress.com

© editorial matter and organisation Samer S. Shehata, 2023, 2024
© the chapters their several authors, 2023, 2024

Edinburgh University Press Ltd
The Tun – Holyrood Road
12 (2f) Jackson's Entry
Edinburgh EH8 8PJ

First published in hardback by Edinburgh University Press 2023

Typeset in 11/14pt EB Garamond by
Cheshire Typesetting Ltd, Cuddington, Cheshire, and
printed and bound by CPI Group (UK) Ltd,
Croydon, CR0 4YY

A CIP record for this book is available from the British Library

ISBN 978 1 3995 1822 2 (hardback)
ISBN 978 1 3995 1823 9 (paperback)
ISBN 978 1 3995 1824 6 (webready PDF)
ISBN 978 1 3995 1825 3 (epub)

The right of Samer S. Shehata to be identified as editor of this work has been asserted in accordance with the Copyright, Designs and Patents Act 1988 and the Copyright and Related Rights Regulations 2003 (SI No. 2498).

CONTENTS

NOTES ON CONTRIBUTORS

Cole Bunzel is a research fellow at the Hoover Institution, Stanford University, where he studies the history and politics of the modern Middle East with a particular focus on militant Islamism and the Arabian Peninsula. The editor of the website Jihadica, he has written widely on the ideology of Sunni jihadism and is the author of the forthcoming book *Wahhabism: The History of a Militant Islamic Movement* (2023).

Francesco Cavatorta is Professor of Political Science and Director of the Centre Interdisciplinaire de Recherche sur l'Afrique et le Moyen Orient (CIRAM) at Laval University, Quebec, Canada. He has published several journal articles and books on the politics of the Arab world. His current research projects deal with party politics and the role of political parties in the region.

Nader Entessar is Professor Emeritus of Political Science at the University of South Alabama, where he was the Chair of the Department of Political Science and Criminal Justice from 2006 to 2017. His research areas are Iran's foreign policy, US–Iran relations, security issues in West and Central Asia, and the regional dimensions of Kurdish politics in the Middle East. He has published more than 100 articles and policy papers in academic journals and popular publications in the United States, Europe and the Middle East. His most recent books are *Iran Nuclear Negotiations: Accord and Détente since the Geneva Agreement of 2013* (2015), *Iran Nuclear Accord and the Remaking* *of the Middle East* (2018) and *Trump and Iran: From Containment to Confrontation* (2020).

Waleed Hazbun is Richard L. Chambers Professor of Middle Eastern Studies in the Department of Political Science at the University of Alabama, where he teaches international relations and US foreign policy in the Middle East. He holds a PhD in political science from MIT and previously taught at the American University of Beirut. He is author of *Beaches, Ruins, Resorts: The Politics of Tourism in the Arab World* (2008), and co-editor of *New Conflict Dynamics: Between Regional Autonomy and Intervention in the Middle East and North Africa* (2017) and 'Exit Empire – Imagining New Paths for US Policy', *Middle East Report* No. 294 (spring 2020).

Marc Lynch is Professor of Political Science and International Affairs at The George Washington University, where he directs the Middle East Studies Programme. He is the founding director of the Project on Middle East Political Science, and a contributing editor to the Washington Post's Monkey Cage blog. His books include *The Political Science of the Middle East: Theory and Research After the Arab Uprisings* (2002), *The New Arab Wars: Uprisings and Anarchy in the Middle East* (2016), *The Arab Uprisings: The Unfinished Revolutions of the New Middle East* (2012) and *The Arab Uprisings Explained: New Contentious Politics in the Middle East* (2014). He writes frequently for publications such as *Foreign Affairs*, hosts the Middle East Political Science Podcast, and blogs at Abu Aardvark's MENA Academy.

Waleed Mahdi is an Associate Professor at the University of Oklahoma with expertise in US–Arab cultural politics. He conducts research at the intersection of area studies and ethnic studies as he explores issues of cultural representation and identity politics in American, Arab and Arab American contexts. His recent book *Arab Americans in Film: From Hollywood and Egyptian Stereotypes to Self-Representation* (2020) examines how Arab American belonging is constructed, defined and redefined across Hollywood, Egyptian and Arab American cinemas. Mahdi is a recipient of several national and international awards, and his peer-reviewed work appears in various venues including *American Quarterly*, *Journal of Cinema and Media Studies*, *International Journal of Cultural Studies* and *Mashriq and Mahjar*. His current book project engages with Yemeni and Yemeni American creative expressions of agency in the twenty-first century.

Gencer Özcan is Professor of International Relations at Istanbul Bilgi University. He has taught at Marmara University's Department of Politics and International Relations (1983–99) and Yıldız Technical University's Department of Politics and International Relations (1999–2009). His research concentrates on Turkish foreign and security policy, foreign policy analysis and the Middle East. He has published widely on Turkish foreign policy in the Middle East, the role of the security sector in decision making and the development of the national security concept in Turkish political history. He graduated from the Faculty of Political Sciences at Ankara University and received his PhD from Boğaziçi University.

Soli Özel is currently a senior lecturer at Istanbul Kadir Has University. He is also a non-resident senior fellow at Institut Montaigne in Paris. He has taught at Johns Hopkins SAIS, University of Washington, Northwestern and Yale in the US, at Sciences-Po in France and at Hebrew University in Israel. His articles have been published in various journals, most recently in *Social Research*, and his commentaries have appeared in the *Financial Times*, *New York Times*, *Le Monde*, *The Guardian*, *Ha'aretz*, *International Herald Tribune* and *Wall Street Journal*. He is a regular contributor to the blog of Institut Montaigne. He is working on a book with Michael T. Rock on the trajectories of democracy and development in four Muslim countries: Egypt, Malaysia, Indonesia and Turkey.

Valeria Resta is an Adjunct Professor at the Catholic University of the Sacred Heart (Italy). Her research deals with the functioning of political parties in authoritarian and transitional settings of the Arab World. She is the author of *Tunisia and Egypt after the Arab Spring: Party Politics in Transitions from Authoritarian Rule* (forthcoming) and co-editor of the *Routledge Handbook on Political Parties in the Middle East and North Africa* (2023). Her latest works have appeared in the *British Journal of Middle Eastern Studies*, *Politics and Religion* and *Italian Political Science Review*.

Noa Schonmann is Assistant Professor at Leiden University's Institute for Area Studies (LIAS) in the Netherlands. Previously she was Lecturer in Politics and International Relations at the University of Oxford and a fellow of Pembroke College. She completed her DPhil at Oxford's Oriental Institute and holds a Master's in Modern Middle East History from Tel Aviv University. A historian of international relations, her research focuses on conflict and regional order in the Middle East, Israeli foreign policy, and the influence of societal factors on authoritarian states' foreign policies in the region. Her monograph is titled *Israel's Phantom Pact: Foreign Policy on the Periphery of the Middle East*.

Samer S. Shehata is the Colin Mackey and Patricia Molina de Mackey Associate Professor of Middle East Studies at the University of Oklahoma. He has taught at the American University in Cairo, Columbia, Georgetown, New York University, and the Doha Institute for Graduate Studies. He is the author of *Shop Floor Culture and Politics in Egypt* (2009), and editor of *Islamist Politics in the Middle East: Movements and Change* (2012). His articles have appeared in the *International Journal of Middle East Studies*, *Current History*, *MERIP*, *Georgetown Journal of International Affairs*, *Middle East Policy*, *Folklore*, and as book chapters and encyclopedia articles. Shehata has received fellowships from the Social Science Research Council, American Research Center in Egypt, the Woodrow Wilson International Center for Scholars, the Carnegie Corporation and the Council on Foreign Relations. He has been a visiting scholar at the University of California at Berkeley and, most recently, the United States Institute of Peace.

Kristian Coates Ulrichsen is a Fellow for the Middle East at Rice University's Baker Institute for Public Policy. His research spans the history, political and international political economy, and international relations of the Gulf States and their changing position within the global order. Coates Ulrichsen is the author of five monographs and the editor of three volumes about the Gulf States, including *Insecure Gulf: The End of Certainty and the Transition to the Post-Oil Era* (2011), *The Gulf States in International Political Economy* (2015) and, most recently, *Qatar and the Gulf Crisis* (2020). Prior to joining the Baker Institute in 2013, Coates Ulrichsen co-directed the Kuwait Programme on Development, Governance and Globalisation in the Gulf States at the London School of Economics and Political Science and was also an associate fellow with the Middle East North Africa Programme at Chatham House between 2012 and 2021.

ACKNOWLEDGEMENTS

This volume emerged out of a symposium at the University of Oklahoma in 2019. Each year the University's Department of International and Area Studies organises an academic symposium led by one or more of its faculty members. This annual event is the department's signature research undertaking. In 2019 I organised the symposium around the theme of the turbulent state of Middle East regional politics following the 2003 Iraq war and the 2010–11 Arab uprisings.

Organising a multi-day conference that includes a dozen scholars from different parts of the world requires tremendous financial and organisational resources. The symposium was generously supported by the University of Oklahoma's Department of International and Area Studies, the Center for Middle East Studies, and the Farzaneh Family Center for Iranian and Persian Gulf Studies. Financial support was also provided from the Office of the Vice President for Research and Partnerships and the Office of the Provost, University of Oklahoma. I am deeply appreciative of all of this support.

My colleagues in the Department of International and Area Studies also played a critical role supporting the symposium and this volume. The department chair at the time, Mitchell Smith, and the subsequent chair, Eric Heinze, believed in the project from the beginning. Beth Young, Stephanie Hohmann Sager and Marjaneh Seirafi-Pour worked tirelessly arranging the logistics of travel, meals, lodging, local transportation, and much else. It was primarily because of their efforts that the symposium was successful. Other departmental colleagues graciously chaired sessions, participated in panels and welcomed symposium participants to the department and the University of Oklahoma.

Of course, the contributors to this volume deserve the greatest credit. Edited volumes are a collective endeavour and without their sustained effort, dedication and patience this project would not have materialised. Not only did they accept the original symposium invitation, each committed to the overall project, including revising and rewriting chapters, and in one case, writing an entirely new chapter to more closely match the volume's theme. Waleed Hazbun also provided valuable suggestions on the Introduction and more general guidance about the regional and international relations of the Middle East. Two other Oklahoma-based colleagues, Mohamed Daadaoui and Joshua Landis, also made valuable contributions to the symposium. I thank all these scholars for their work and support.

Several other institutions and individuals also deserve special thanks. I held a Council on Foreign Relations fellowship during the 2021–2 academic year as I completed the final revisions to the manuscript. I was fortunate to be a visiting scholar at the US Institute of Peace (USIP) at the time. I thank Michael Yaffe, the Vice President of the Middle East North Africa Center at USIP, and the entire USIP MENA team for their warm welcome and for providing temporary workspace in one of the most beautiful buildings in Washington DC. I also thank Hesham Youssef for carefully reading the Introduction and providing incisive insights about regional politics. Needless to say, the views expressed in the following chapters are those of the individual contributors and do not reflect any of the individuals or institutions named above.

It was an absolute pleasure working with Emma House and Louise Hutton at Edinburgh University Press. I could not have hoped for more dedicated and professional editors. Two anonymous reviewers provided valuable comments on the entire manuscript as well as helpful suggestions on individual chapters. I also thank Lel Gillingwater for her outstanding and meticulous copy-editing, and Julie Witmer who designed a map of the Middle East and North Africa specifically for this volume.

Ahmed Morsy and Hesham Youssef provided numerous opportunities to discuss developments in the Middle East while I was finalising the Introduction. I thank them for their intellectual engagement and delightful company. Noureddine Jebnoun meticulously read the Introduction and provided invaluable suggestions which improved the chapter and the entire volume considerably. I thank him for this and, more importantly, for his continuing friendship.

Finally, this project would not have been possible without the support of my family. I will never be able to adequately acknowledge the support my parents, Said and Soraya Shehata, have provided over the course of a lifetime. I hope their knowledge of my love for them is sufficient. Above all, my partner, Riem El-Zoghbi, and our children Omar and Mariam, have contributed more to this project, and to every aspect of my life, than they will ever know. They are the loves of my life and the sources of endless joy, constant support and unwavering encouragement – all without even trying.

Strait of Gibraltar

Ceuta Melilla
(SPAIN)

Algiers

Mediterranean Sea

Tunis

Casablanca   Rabat

Oran   Constantine

Fes

Marrakesh

Tripoli

Benghazi

Laayoune

MOROCCO

W. SAHARA

ALGERIA

TUNISIA

LIBYA

MAURITANIA

Tamanrasset

Nouakchott

INTRODUCTION

Samer S. Shehata

This volume examines different dimensions of the turbulent regional politics of the Middle East from the 2003 US invasion and occupation of
Iraq to the decade after the 2010–11 Arab uprisings. This period has been
among the most turbulent and politically unstable in the region's contemporary history. Turbulence during this period included the 2003 US invasion
and occupation of Iraq and the resulting civil war and political instability, and
the 2010–11 Arab uprisings and the civil wars, proxy warfare, regime breakdown, state collapse and the refugee flows that followed. This critical period
also entailed intense regional rivalry, competition, and shifting alliances in
addition to different forms of regional and international intervention.[1] All of
this contributed to widespread insecurity for a number of states and societies
in the region, prompting some states to attempt to reshape the region in ways
more favourable to their interests. This volume traces and seeks to explain the
dynamics of the struggle to shape a new Middle East regional order during this
period through detailed case studies of regional turbulence.

A Violent Era in Transition

The 2003 Iraq war produced greater insecurity within Iraq and destabilised
the surrounding region. It altered the balance of power in the Middle East,
activated sectarian identities and inflamed sectarian tensions. The war also
intensified the rivalry between two regional powers, Saudi Arabia and Iran,
while dramatically reducing the US appetite for further military intervention
in the region.

The 2010–11 Arab uprisings then fractured the old regional order which was primarily organised around Middle Eastern states' relationship with the US. The previous order was characterised by a division between so-called 'moderate Arab states' aligned with the US and the so-called 'axis of resistance', states and non-state actors opposed to US and Israeli regional hegemony: Iran, Syria, Hezbollah and Hamas.[2] Ironically, the common characteristic of states in both camps was that they were authoritarian. In fact, the region was frequently described by some scholars as consisting of 'stable authoritarian' regimes.[3]

The uprisings, and then the armed conflicts and devastating civil wars that developed in Syria, Libya and Yemen, and earlier in Iraq, also weakened these states, in some cases resulting in their collapse. The weakening of states and the breakdown of regimes had profound consequences for these societies. But it also affected other states in the region. Regional powers such as Turkey, Iran, Saudi Arabia and Israel, as well as smaller states with oversized ambitions such as the United Arab Emirates (UAE) and Qatar, perceived these changes as both threats and opportunities and, in some cases, as both simultaneously.

Autocratic leaders in Riyadh, Abu Dhabi and elsewhere viewed political instability across the region, the ascendency of Islamist movements and the social forces pushing for democracy as existential threats to their survival. The ensuing political struggles in countries affected by the Arab uprisings thus had both security and political implications for Middle Eastern states near and far.

As a result, over the last two decades, the regional environment has been characterised by unprecedented levels of intervention and violence, including by powerful regional states attempting to influence politics in other states in the region. Moreover, the uprisings and the subsequent civil wars heightened the vulnerability of these states to different forms of external intervention, not simply military intervention. This has included funding and arming proxies in addition to cross-border financial flows, propaganda and disinformation campaigns, and political and diplomatic support – all different modes of influence – in competing efforts to shape the 'domestic' politics of other states in the region and ultimately to reshape the Middle East based on different sets of competing interests, often with quite deadly and disastrous consequences.

The resulting regional landscape has been among the most violent and unstable in the region's history. In addition to the 2003 Iraq war, multiple and devastating civil wars following the 2011 uprisings produced millions of refugees and internally displaced people, in the region and beyond.[4] This period also witnessed the emergence of new and horrifically violent non-state actors that have challenged states for sovereignty, intense regional competition, shifting alliances and resurgent authoritarianism.

Although the eight-year Iran–Iraq war (1980–8) was devastating for both Iran and Iraq, and possibly resulted in greater numbers of deaths, the fighting during that conflict was primarily confined to the countries at war, and occasionally the surrounding region.[5] In contrast, the last two decades have witnessed four civil wars across two continents, multiple proxy wars and millions of refugees crossing multiple borders, in addition to six 'presidents for life' deposed as a result of popular mobilisation and protest.[6]

The human costs of this level of instability and violence have been horrific, particularly in Syria and Yemen. In 2016, the UN Special Envoy for Syria, Staffan de Mistura, estimated that 400,000 people had been killed in the country since 2011, the vast majority by the Syrian regime.[7] By 2022, the Syrian Observatory for Human Rights put the figure at over 600,000.[8] In 2021, the UN Refugee Agency estimated that 6.6 million Syrians had become refugees as a result of the conflict, making it the largest refugee crisis in the world at the time. Another 6.7 million Syrians had become internally displaced.[9]

The Yemen war has also had catastrophic human costs with UNICEF declaring it the worst humanitarian crisis in 2021.[10] Reported numbers of deaths from the war vary even more widely than in Syria, with the UN estimating that more than 370,000 Yemenis have died since 2015, including from 'indirect causes' such as deteriorating health systems and lack of food and critical infrastructure.[11] Civil war in Libya and continued violence and instability in Iraq have also caused tremendous human suffering.[12]

While all of this was taking place, none of the underlying causes of the 2011 Arab uprisings – poor economic conditions, high unemployment, corruption, abysmal governance, political oppression and authoritarianism – were adequately addressed by governments in the region.[13] In fact, economic and political conditions have worsened in many countries since the uprisings. The global COVID-19 pandemic followed by the 2022 Russian invasion of Ukraine, and its consequences on global food and oil prices, have further exacerbated the economic situation in much of the region.[14]

Overlapping Conflicts

This volume examines different aspects of the turbulent regional politics of the Middle East over the last two decades through detailed case studies by leading

Middle East scholars. Collectively it examines the drivers of regional change and turbulence; the foreign policies of Iran and Turkey towards the Syrian crisis; the role of Israel in the Middle East regional order; violent and non-violent Islamist actors that emerged following the 2003 Iraq war and the 2011 Arab uprisings (that is, al-Qaida in Iraq and Salafi political parties); and the impact of regional turbulence following the 2011 Arab uprisings on Egypt and Yemen, and relations between the Gulf Cooperation Council (GCC) states and the GCC as an organisation. Three intersecting and at times overlapping conflicts have produced much, although not all, of the regional instability and violence during this period. The first conflict, briefly mentioned above, is the rivalry between Saudi Arabia and Iran.

The 2003 US invasion of Iraq was devastating for the millions of Iraqis killed, injured or who became refugees because of the war and its aftermath. The war also dramatically shifted the regional balance of power in the Middle East in favour of Iran. It eliminated Iran's historical regional adversary and increased Iranian influence in Iraq and beyond. The war's aftermath also heightened sectarian tensions between Shi'as and Sunnis within the country and the wider region, with significant repercussions for other states in the Middle East.[15]

The Saudi regime perceived these developments with great concern. Since the 1979 Iranian Revolution, Saudi Arabia has viewed Iran as an adversary, a rival and, at times, an existential threat. The Iranian Revolution overthrew a monarchy and established an Islamic republic in its place. Both revolution and the form of political Islam supposedly embodied by the Islamic Republic are perceived as profoundly threatening to the Saudi monarchy, which bases its own legitimacy, in part, on Islam. The Saudis have long accused Iran of 'exporting revolution' and working to undermine Arab Gulf monarchies. And as a Shi'a majority state, Iran is also said to support fellow Shi'as across the region, many of whom are marginalised, including in Saudi Arabia and the Arab Gulf monarchies. Tehran and Riyadh also find themselves in adversarial regional and international alliances, further exacerbating tense relations.

Thus, the shift in the balance of power and the expansion of Iranian influence was deeply troubling for the Saudi regime and led to a series of direct and indirect conflicts in Syria, Yemen, Lebanon and elsewhere in the region, including a number of proxy wars, with deadly and destabilising consequences.

The second conflict that has fuelled regional turbulence in the Middle

East over the last decade has been the struggle between democracy and authoritarianism or, stated differently, between revolution and counter-revolution.[16] The 2010–11 Arab uprisings were inspiring for millions across the region who hoped the protests would bring about an era of freedom, social justice and democracy. The uprisings simultaneously motivated autocrats across the region to respond aggressively to the increased threats they faced, even in states that did not experience widespread protests. Regimes responded immediately as a result of increased threat perception, both inside and outside of their borders. The unwillingness of the Obama administration to forcefully support autocratic allies during the protests, such as Egypt's Hosni Mubarak, also demonstrated to rulers that they could no longer depend on Washington in the face of such crises.[17]

The lesson for US-backed autocrats was that they needed to act aggressively both at home and abroad in order to maintain power. The heightened threat perception as a result of the uprisings and the realisation that the US could not be relied upon in the face of domestic protests produced increasingly aggressive behaviour by some regimes, including a willingness to interfere in neighbouring states and the wider region, including militarily, in pursuit of regime security.[18]

Bahrain provides an obvious example of direct intervention during the uprisings as well as the intersection of two of the conflicts mentioned above: the rivalry between Saudi Arabia and Iran, and the struggle between democracy and authoritarianism. Peaceful protests began on the small island kingdom on 14 February 2011, following the success of the Tunisian and Egyptian revolutions. Thousands of Bahrainis demonstrated, calling for the release of political prisoners, a new constitution, freedom of expression and other political reforms.[19] Although the protests were met with repression, the uprising gained strength over the following weeks to include hundreds of thousands of citizens peacefully demanding change.

The struggle for democracy in Bahrain threatened the country's ruling monarchy, but it also threatened other Gulf autocrats. In response, on 14 March 2011, approximately 1,500 Saudi and Emirati troops from the Gulf Cooperation Council's Peninsula Shield forces crossed the 25-kilometre King Fahd causeway into the island nation in support of the regime. Although the Peninsula Shield Force did not directly put down the uprising, the importance of their deployment cannot be overstated. It signalled to protesters, regional adversaries and international actors that Bahrain's autocratic Arab neighbours would not tolerate the overthrow of an Arab Gulf monarchy or the establishment of a democracy on the Arabian Peninsula.[20]

Over the next few days, more than 5,000 Bahraini security forces, aided by tanks and military helicopters, violently dispersed protests in Manama and other cities and towns across the country. More than a thousand people were arrested, including opposition leaders, and a number of people were killed. Dozens were disappeared. Government forces also entered hospitals, detained patients with protest-related injuries and arrested many of the health care professionals treating them. A few days later, the government demolished the Pearl Monument in central Manama, the epicentre and symbol of the uprising. A harsh crackdown on opposition and civil society in the country has continued.[21]

The 2011 Bahraini uprising and the GCC intervention illustrate the intersection and at times overlapping character of two of the conflicts that have produced much of the regional turbulence in the Middle East in the post-2003 and post-2011 periods. The uprising was about democracy (at least initially) while the government's response and the GCC intervention was about maintaining an authoritarian regime. The Bahraini uprising was also simultaneously intertwined with the Saudi–Iranian conflict.

Bahrain was part of the Persian Empire for several hundred years and Iran continued to make territorial claims on the island at least until 1970. With an economically and politically disenfranchised Shi'a majority living under an autocratic Sunni monarchy, Bahrain has long been a point of contention across Gulf waters. Saudi Arabia and Bahrain have repeatedly alleged Iranian interference in the country's domestic affairs. And the Bahraini government has frequently questioned the loyalty of Shi'a Bahraini activists and opposition movements.

Riyadh and Manama accused Tehran of fomenting opposition during the uprising with the aim of overthrowing an Arab Sunni regime. In this sense, the 2011 Bahraini uprising and the GCC intervention simultaneously reflect the conflict between democracy and authoritarianism and that between Saudi Arabia and Iran.

The third conflict that has produced significant turbulence in the Middle East over the last decade revolves around political Islam and Islamist movements.[22] Like democracy, some regimes in the region are profoundly threatened by political Islam. These regimes have reacted with great alarm to the rise and, at times, increasing power of Islamist movements, particularly after the 2011 uprisings. To a large extent, these fears reflect regime anxieties about Islamist movements as domestic challengers. Saudi Arabia, and particularly the UAE, have deep anxieties about Islamist movements, with Abu Dhabi almost hysterical in its fear and opposition to political Islam.[23]

Popular, mass-based Islamist movements like Egypt's Muslim Brotherhood and Tunisia's al-Nahda represent a profoundly different understanding of the relationship between Islam and politics than that supposedly practised in Saudi Arabia. For these movements, Islam is compatible with mass politics, political participation and electoral democracy. Many such movements have been the primary challengers to autocratic rule in the region, decrying corruption and promising better governance. These movements are often premised on ideas of social justice, resistance to oppression and Western domination, and championing ordinary people's interests rather than those of the elites. In this sense, mass-based Islamist movements represent an ideational and political challenge to regimes in Riyadh, Abu Dhabi, and elsewhere.

The conflict surrounding political Islam has pitted regimes supportive of Islamist movements in Qatar and Turkey against those opposed to such movements in the UAE, Saudi Arabia and Egypt under Abdel Fattah al-Sisi. Egypt after the 2011 uprising was the main, although not the only, battleground in this conflict. While Ankara, and especially Doha, supported Mohamed Morsi and Egypt's Muslim Brotherhood government, Abu Dhabi and Riyadh actively worked to undermine Morsi's rule.[24] These states also found themselves supporting different sides of political contests in Tunisia, Libya, and elsewhere. And the 2017 Qatar or GCC crisis, in which Saudi Arabia, the UAE and Bahrain, along with Egypt, severed diplomatic ties and imposed a blockade on Qatar, also reflected this divide, among others.[25]

Mapping the Struggle over a New Regional Order

Taken together, these three intersecting and at times overlapping regional conflicts have generated tremendous turbulence in the Middle East in the nearly two decades following the 2003 Iraq war. The chapters in this volume explore specific cases of turbulence during this period through detailed case studies based on original research and analysis.

In Chapter One, Marc Lynch provides an analytical overview of the main drivers of turbulence in the Middle East at the global, regional and domestic levels. Lynch argues that the Middle East regional order has fundamentally changed and that proxy warfare has become the dominant mode of power politics since 2003. One reason for this is because the George W. Bush administration's 'global war on terror' and the 2003 Iraq war brought an end to the US's unipolar dominance in the region. The consequences of these catastrophic misadventures have been multiple, as mentioned above, including the unanticipated shift in the regional balance of power in favour of Iran and the US's unwillingness for further military involvement or deeper political entanglements in the region.

These changes, in addition to the dramatic 2011 Arab uprisings and their consequences, unleashed a set of regional dynamics that have led to increased intervention, further instability and violence, and new opportunities for Russian and Chinese influence. Lynch concludes by noting that 'profound changes at the global, regional and domestic levels have created a new regional structure which is not amenable to the restoration of an American-led unipolar system.'

This macro analytical overview of regional politics since 2011 provides the wider context for the chapters that follow.

Following this overview, in Chapter Two, Waleed Hazbun examines US policy towards the Middle East under the Obama and Trump administrations. Hazbun complements Lynch's analysis by focusing in greater detail on US policy and its disastrous consequences during this period. Hazbun agrees that the US's unquestioned dominance in the region is over and that US policies significantly contributed to the region's turbulence, particularly the 2003 war and the global war on terror. 'The current geopolitical "disorder" is . . . rooted in repeated US efforts to attempt to order the region through coercive force with little concern for the interests and security of the peoples of the region.' Hazbun demonstrates how both US military and non-military policies generated dynamics that intensified competition between states and produced greater instability. The deeper problem, according to this analysis, lies not with the particular policies pursued by different administrations but with how American interests in the region have been understood. The 'construction of American interests in the Middle East produces contradictory, often self-defeating policies that produce tragic outcomes'. Hazbun calls this 'the tragedy of American interests'.

Although Obama recognised the contradictions of US interests, his policies also had tragic consequences in the form of 'unleashing . . . a militarised Saudi and Emirati counter-revolution', the Yemen war, and the expansion of less visible and unaccountable US military action, including the increased use of drone warfare. While Hazbun characterises Obama's approach to the Middle East as 'tragic', he describes Trump's policies as 'melodramatic', because Trump was both unaware of these contradictions and viewed the region, and the world, in moral dichotomies of good and evil. Hazbun's is an original and creative critique of US policy that exposes the limits of both Obama's and Trump's approaches to the region.

In Chapter Three, Noa Schonmann examines Israel's role within the Middle East regional order and assesses the extent of change within or beyond that order in the post-2003 and post-2011 period. She persuasively demonstrates that although Middle East international relations scholars readily acknowledge Israel as part of a Middle East regional order, frequently referring to Israel's 'hard' military power, few scholars pay more than scant attention to Israel's role within that order. This has remained the case despite the conflicts, uprisings and violence in the region since the 2003 Iraq war and the 2011 Arab uprisings. Although scholars have analysed the shifting fortunes of Iran, Turkey, Egypt, Syria, Iraq and other states during this period, Israel's role in the regional order continues to be neglected.

This lack of attention should not lead to the conclusion that Israel is outside of, or unimportant to, the regional order or 'order making', Schonmann argues. Using the analogy of a society, as is done in certain schools of international relations theory, Schonmann posits that Israel is best understood as an 'outside-member' of the regional order, 'the perennial outsider', but one that is nonetheless an integral part of that order and not external to it.

Schonmann also posits that it is impossible to accurately assess the extent of change, or lack thereof, within the Middle East regional order as a result of events since 2003 without understanding Israel's role within that order. There have been significant changes in the balance of power, fortunes of states and regional alliances in the Middle East over the last two decades, especially since the 2003 Iraq war and the 2011 Arab uprisings. 'The [American] invasion at once brought Iran back into the regional power game and started the countdown to US retreat from the region.' Another outcome of the Iraq war and the aftermath of the 2011 Arab uprisings, according to Schonmann and others, is the relative decline in salience of the Palestinian–Israeli conflict in Arab and Middle East politics. This, coupled with the increasing perceived threat from Iran, allowed some Arab states to normalise relations with Israel without a resolution to the Palestinian–Israeli conflict, something previously unimaginable. Schonmann interprets this not as the collapse of the old regional order, or the emergence of a new order, but as an attempt by these states to counter-balance Iran's growing power. Overall, Schonmann offers an original perspective on Israel's role in a changing Middle East regional order and a caution against the idea that the old order has entirely collapsed and a completely new one has fully emerged.

The Middle East conflict that has witnessed the most regional and international intervention over the last two decades has been the Syrian crisis. The Syrian civil war produced enormous devastation and suffering within Syria and significant turbulence in the wider region. Iran, Turkey, Saudi Arabia, the UAE, Qatar, Hezbollah and Israel have all been either directly involved militarily or have supported proxies in this protracted and multidimensional conflict. The US, and even more so Russia, have also been drawn into the conflict. Chapters Four and Five of this volume examine Iran and Turkey's strategic orientation and policies towards Syria: the two Middle Eastern regional powers that have been most deeply involved in the crisis.

In Chapter Four, Nader Entessar analyses Iran's policy towards Syria from the perspective of Tehran's regional security calculus. Entessar describes the history of the Iranian–Syrian alliance from the beginning of the Iran–Iraq war in 1980, arguing that Syria has been critical in the Islamic Republic's thinking about its 'strategic depth' as its 'first line of defence'. Syria is simultaneously the other pillar, along with Iran, in the so-called 'axis of resistance': those states and non-state actors, including Hezbollah and Hamas, that stand opposed to US and Israeli hegemony in the region.[26]

For these reasons, Iran supported the Assad regime from the very beginning of the Syrian civil war and also played a role in persuading Russia to support Assad militarily in 2015. A number of regional and international factors including the Iran nuclear negotiations, the rise of the so-called Islamic State and other Sunni extremist groups in Iraq and Syria, Turkey's involvement in the conflict, and the escalating 'cold war' with Saudi Arabia, also impacted Iran's strategic considerations. Entessar traces how progress in the Iranian nuclear negotiations impacted both Tehran's inclusion in the Astana talks, aimed at ending the fighting in Syria, as well as the positions it took in negotiations about how to resolve the Syria crisis. Entessar also assesses how Russia's military involvement in Syria and Russian–Iranian cooperation in the country's civil war could affect the 'axis of resistance' in the future.

Gencer Özcan and Soli Özel continue the discussion of Syria in Chapter Five through a detailed analysis of the evolution of Turkey's Syria policy after 2011. At the outset of the Arab uprisings, Ankara's position towards Damascus reflected its 'zero problems with neighbours' policy.[27] This changed as the uprisings swept across the region producing the belief in Ankara that major changes were also likely to take place in Damascus that would benefit Turkey's regional standing.

In order to understand the evolution of Turkey's Syria policy, Özcan and Özel argue that it is necessary to analyse both Turkish domestic politics and 'the regional dynamics set in motion by the Arab uprisings' simultaneously. They do this by carefully examining the interplay between Turkey's domestic political scene (for example, the ruling Justice and Development Party's (AKP) rivalry with the Gülenist movement, electoral competition and party alignments, efforts at reaching a peace with the Kurdish Workers' Party (PKK), and President Erdoğan's attempts to amend the Turkish constitution) and regional developments (for example, the rise of the Islamic State and its impact on US and European views of the Syrian conflict, the growing refugee crisis, Russian military intervention, and the success of Kurdish Democratic Union Party (YKP) forces fighting the Islamic State). Only such an analysis of both domestic and regional political dynamics can fully explain the dramatic changes in Turkey's Syria policy from 'zero problems', to regime change, to accommodation with Russia and Iran after the rise of the Islamic State, to one of primarily seeking to prevent the emergence of a Kurdish political entity on Turkey's southern border.

Both the 2003 Iraq war and the 2011 Arab uprisings, including the Syrian crisis, had significant consequences for the Arab Gulf states. The Iraq war changed the balance of power in favour of Iran, while the wave of popular mobilisation against Arab autocrats in 2011 heightened the threat perception of authoritarian monarchies in the Gulf.

In Chapter Six, Kristian Coates Ulrichen examines how the 2011 uprisings and the different reactions to regional turbulence by Gulf states impacted the GCC and relations between its members. Ulrichsen focuses on the 2017 'GCC crisis': the severing of diplomatic ties and boycott of Qatar by three other GCC states, Saudi Arabia, the UAE and Bahrain, along with Egypt. Although tensions within the GCC existed previously and had occasionally surfaced, the 2017 crisis was unprecedented in its scope and intensity. Saudi Arabia closed its border with Qatar, the small peninsula nation's only land crossing, and also closed its skies to Qatari air traffic, along with the UAE, Bahrain and Egypt. The four countries accused Doha of supporting terrorism and interfering in their domestic politics – accusations Doha vehemently denied.

The crisis had substantial economic and human costs for Qatar and, to a lesser extent, the other countries involved in the dispute. Ulrichsen argues that latent tensions between GCC states existed from the beginning of the organisation's founding in 1981. The great disparity in size and economic and political power between Saudi Arabia and other member states meant there had always been concerns that Riyadh could attempt to exert influence or pressure its smaller GCC neighbours. These latent concerns, as well as other tensions, were significantly exacerbated by the 2011 wave of popular protests and the radically divergent ways Abu Dhabi, Riyadh and Doha perceived and then reacted to these events. While Qatar was open to, and in some cases actively supported, the uprisings, Saudi Arabia and Abu Dhabi perceived them and the associated rising power of Islamist parties as profoundly threatening. These differences manifested themselves in Qatar and Abu Dhabi and Riyadh supporting competing sides in political and sometimes military conflicts in Libya, Syria and, most importantly, in Egypt. Ulrichsen also analyses how the GCC continued to operate until the crisis was eventually 'resolved' as a result of Kuwaiti and American mediation in January 2021. His analysis contributes to our understanding of how regional turbulence generated by the Arab uprisings impacted relations between GCC member states, the GCC as an organisation, and the possible longer-term consequences of the crisis on Arab Gulf state relations.

The post-2003 and 2011 periods, as stated above, have been characterised by unprecedented levels of regional and international intervention.[28] Chapters Seven and Eight examine how different types of international and regional interventions have impacted two states in the region: Yemen and Egypt. In Chapter Seven, Waleed Mahdi investigates how powerful international and regional actors repeatedly employed discourses of security and state fragility to intervene in Yemen in pursuit of their own national security interests. Such actions, first by the US in its 'war on terror', then through the GCC initiative, ostensibly intended to guide Yemen's political transition and prevent it from becoming a 'failed state', through the Saudi and Emirati military intervention beginning in 2015, simultaneously denied Yemenis their sovereignty while producing even greater instability in the country. The Saudi and Emirati military intervention not only constitutes an egregious violation of Yemeni sovereignty, it also produced tremendous devastation and profound suffering.

Mahdi problematises the idea of 'sovereignty' in his discussion of US drone strikes in Yemen. Yemen's ousted president, Ali Abdullah Saleh, allowed the US to conduct drone operations as part of its 'war on terror' without informing the country's citizens. Saleh then lied about the drone strikes, which killed scores of civilians, when they were discovered, claiming they were Yemeni government operations, a falsehood that functioned to deny that the country's sovereignty had been violated. Mahdi's chapter powerfully demonstrates how discourses about promoting stability and security and the dangers of 'fragile' and 'failed states' were repeatedly deployed to justify political and military intervention by powerful international and regional actors. Such actions, however, produced neither stability nor security, and had disastrous consequences for millions of Yemenis, further denying them the ability to create a future by and for themselves.

Chapter Eight investigates another case of regional intervention after the Arab uprisings. Based on original research including interviews with Egyptian officials from both the Mohamed Morsi and Abdel Fattah al-Sisi governments, American officials, and others, Samer Shehata argues that the UAE, Saudi Arabia and, to a lesser extent, Israel, played significant roles in undermining Egypt's short-lived democratic experiment. All three states perceived Mubarak's removal, the rise of Egypt's Muslim Brotherhood and the possibility of Egyptian democracy as profoundly threatening. For Israel, the threat concerned national security. For Saudi Arabia and the UAE, it had to do with regime survival.

Shehata first details how Riyadh, Abu Dhabi and Tel Aviv supported Mubarak immediately after the 25 January 2011 protests began. All three states intensively lobbied the US to continue backing Mubarak and not pressure the beleaguered autocrat to resign, despite the growing protests, in addition to their own diplomatic and media efforts to support their ally. Shehata then examines how Saudi Arabia and the UAE attempted to influence the trajectory of Egyptian politics post-Mubarak by supporting Egypt's Salafi parties as a check against the growing power of the Muslim Brotherhood. The oil-rich Gulf states also effectively used economic aid and investment to further their political aims, first limiting economic flows to Cairo after Mubarak's ouster and then virtually ending all aid and investment after Morsi's election.

Then, when Morsi was ousted in 2013, the UAE, Saudi Arabia and Israel immediately, forcefully and generously supported the coup. In addition to diplomatic support (and alleged Saudi and Emirati involvement in the coup itself), all three states intensively lobbied the international community, including the US and European countries, not to view the removal of Egypt's first democratically elected president as a coup. Shehata also documents the massive and unprecedented amounts of economic aid and investment that immediately poured into the country from the Gulf to consolidate the Sisi regime. While not discounting domestic political factors, Shehata argues that any account of Egypt's political trajectory after 2011 cannot ignore the role regional actors played, particularly Saudi Arabia and the UAE, in influencing the trajectory of Egyptian politics and contributing to the country's 'failed democratic transition'.

The emergence and growth of violent Islamist groups has been another major development in regional politics over the last two decades. Al-Qaida and its many affiliates and offshoots, and the so-called Islamic State of Iraq and Syria, are the two best-known Islamist extremist groups that have operated in the region during this period. Their growth and expansion greatly benefitted from the 2003 Iraq war, the resulting insecurity and the conflicts that developed in the aftermath of the 2011 Arab uprisings. Both groups took full advantage of state breakdown, rising sectarianism and civil wars to advance their aims.

In Chapter Nine, Cole Bunzel assesses the extent of al-Qaida's success in taking advantage of the security vacuum caused by the 2003 Iraq war and the 2011 Syrian civil war to establish a presence in Iraq and Syria. Although Osama bin Laden, Abu Mus'ab al-Zarqawi and Omar al-Baghdadi dreamed of expelling the US from the Middle East and creating a new regional order, Bunzel demonstrates how and why al-Qaida was far less successful in gaining a foothold in the Fertile Crescent than is widely believed.

Based on careful analysis of Arabic primary sources, including correspondence between bin Laden, Ayman al-Zawahiri and others, and leading Sunni jihadists in Iraq and Syria, video recordings and official statements, Bunzel reveals significant differences and disagreements in both ideology and tactics between 'al-Qaida central' in Afghanistan and Pakistan and the various groups that emerged in Iraq after 2003 and Syria in 2011, including al-Qaida in Mesopotamia and the various iterations of the Islamic State. Differences in ideology (that is, the centrality of anti-Shi'a sentiment), and disagreements in strategy and tactics (for example, the attempt to foment sectarian war and the gruesome practice of beheading), in addition to more mundane disputes over control, reveal that 'al-Qaida central' had very limited authority or influence over the various jihadi groups that operated in Iraq and Syria during this period. Bunzel also highlights how opportunism characterised many of these relationships. When it appeared advantageous for groups in Iraq and Syria to claim affiliation with al-Qaida because of prestige, legitimacy or financial backing, they did. But when this was no longer beneficial, these groups willingly distanced themselves, disavowed, or in the case of the Islamic State, even challenged al-Qaida for leadership. Bunzel's chapter also serves as a corrective to those who have emphasised al-Qaida's 'enduring strength', 'organisational coherence' or reach into Iraq and Syria.

Valeria Resta and Francesco Cavatorta continue the discussion of Salafi politics in Chapter Ten. Their focus, however, is not on radical Jihadi Salafis but the Salafi political parties that emerged across the region after the 2011 uprisings. Having previously existed only in Kuwait, Salafi parties were established in Tunisia, Egypt and Yemen following the uprisings. The authors correctly note that although scholars have increasingly focused on political Salafism, the foreign policy agendas of these parties have largely been neglected.

By analysing the political platforms and party agendas of Salafi parties in Tunisia, Egypt and Kuwait, Resta and Cavatorta argue that Salafi parties are less radical in their foreign policy thinking than what many assume and, that unlike Jihadi Salafis, they accept the idea of the nation state and the international system. All the parties Resta and Cavatorta examine have reconciled pan-Arabist and pan-Islamist sentiment and notions of Islamic unity with an acceptance of the nation state and the international system. Although they find variation among the foreign policy agendas of Salafi political parties on several issues, the authors conclude that political Salafis are 'pragmatic political entrepreneurs' that are also affected by 'inclusion-moderation' dynamics.

The Beginnings of a New Era?

As the chapters described above demonstrate, the last two decades have been among the most tumultuous, violent and unstable in Middle Eastern regional politics. Although many of the conflicts that generated the unprecedented turbulence are ongoing and are unlikely to be resolved, there are indications that this period of intense regional turbulence has come to an end. Daily levels of violence in Syria, Yemen and Libya are significantly lower than in previous years, and efforts are underway to manage, if not resolve, all three conflicts. Regional intervention has also decreased, although it continues, and the intensity of competition between regional powers has noticeably declined. In several cases relations between former rivals have also noticeably improved.

The Syrian conflict has now settled into a protracted stalemate and the Assad regime has not only survived but has managed to regain much of the territory it previously lost, thanks to Russian and Iranian backing.[29] Fighting in Yemen and Libya has also declined as a result of the inability of any side to decisively vanquish their opponents and the exhaustion of the warring parties, despite the continued involvement of regional and international actors. Although both conflicts are unresolved, there have been renewed efforts by the international community to achieve a political settlement in Libya and to end the civil war in Yemen.[30]

Saudi Arabia and the UAE have also scaled back some of their aggressive and interventionist regional policies after a series of failures. The Saudi-led military campaign in Yemen has been tremendously costly, particularly for Saudi Arabia (it has been even more devastating for Yemenis). It has also failed to achieve its military or political objectives. While both Riyadh and Abu Dhabi are likely to remain involved in Yemen for years to come, they now appear more interested in a negotiated settlement to the conflict.[31]

Changes in the UAE's regional policies are another indication of declining regional turbulence. The UAE embarked on unprecedented and aggressive policies in response to the 2011 Arab uprisings that were intended to reshape the region in ways favourable to its interests and safeguard it from the wave of protests calling for democratic change. Abu Dhabi reacted more aggressively to the uprisings and the resulting regional instability than any other capital. This entailed funding armed groups fighting Bashar al-Assad's regime in Syria (like other Gulf states), supporting the counter-revolution in Egypt in 2013, financial and military support for Khalifa Haftar's Libyan National Army fighting the internationally recognised Libyan government in Tripoli, and direct military intervention in Libya beginning in 2014 and in Yemen beginning in 2015.[32] These interventions put the UAE on opposite sides of conflicts with Qatar, Turkey and Iran.[33]

Since 2019, there has been a noticeable shift in UAE policy towards all of these conflicts, with the exception of Egypt, where the Emirati and Saudi counter-revolution succeeded. As a result of the failure of some of these more aggressive policies to produce the desired results, the election of Joe Biden, whose administration was expected to be less accommodating of UAE and Saudi regional interventions, and the reputational and financial costs of its actions, Abu Dhabi has significantly altered course in Yemen and Libya and has also attempted to improve relations with Qatar, Turkey and Iran.

In July 2019, the UAE announced the phased withdrawal of most of its ground forces from Yemen. Although it remains heavily involved in the country through its support for the Southern Transitional Council and other armed groups, and its control of the Yemeni islands of Socotra in the Gulf of Aden and Mayun (also known as Perim) in the Bab al-Mandib strait, the UAE is now attempting to safeguard its interests in Yemen without redeploying troops to the country, even in the face of occasional escalations such as the January 2022 Ansar Allah drone and missile strikes on Abu Dhabi in apparent retaliation for earlier attacks on Ansar Allah positions by UAE-backed groups. (The Ansar Allah movement is commonly referred to as the Houthis.) The UAE will continue to maintain a presence and project power over the strategically important sea routes off Yemen's coasts, but it is reluctant to deepen its own military's footprint in the country.[34] This does not mean that the Yemen war will soon end or that the horrific suffering of the Yemeni people will soon be over. It does appear, however, that the period of most intense and violent UAE intervention in Yemen is over.

The UAE's orientation towards Iran has also changed. As mentioned above, the UAE and Iran found themselves on opposite sides of conflicts in Syria and Yemen after the 2011 uprising against the Assad regime and the 2014 Ansar Allah takeover of Sanaa. The Emirates also openly supported Donald Trump's withdrawal from the Iran nuclear agreement in May 2018 and his 'maximum pressure' policy against Iran.[35]

Abu Dhabi's approach to Tehran began to change in 2019, however, as tensions between Washington and Tehran ratcheted up. After a series of attacks on ships in the Persian Gulf and the Gulf of Oman in the summer of 2019, including an Emirati vessel, and the downing of a US drone by Iran which was not met with a military response, the UAE sought to reduce tensions with Tehran.[36] Two Emirati delegations travelled to Iran in July 2019 while Emirati officials spoke of 'de-escalation'.[37] (The UAE also announced its partial troop withdrawal from Yemen at this time.)[38] The UAE's national security adviser Sheikh Tahnoun bin Zayed, who is also Crown Prince Mohamed bin Zayed's younger brother, visited Tehran in October 2019, and Abu Dhabi released US$700 million in frozen Iranian funds shortly thereafter.[39] The UAE also delivered multiple shipments of medical supplies to Iran in 2020 as the country was dealing with the COVID-19 pandemic.[40] The exchange of visits continued with Iran's top nuclear negotiator and deputy foreign minister, Ali Bagheri Kani, travelling to Dubai in November 2021, and Tahnoun bin Zayed visiting Tehran the following month.[41] Thus, as tensions between the US and Iran increased and with the election of the Biden administration, the UAE recalibrated its policy to reduce tensions with its much larger Gulf neighbour.[42]

UAE–Qatari relations have also improved in a further sign that the intensity of regional competition has declined.[43] The UAE-led blockade of Qatar, which began in 2017 and included Saudi Arabia, Bahrain and Egypt, failed to achieve its goal of 'regime change' or pressuring Doha to change its regional policies. This, along with the expectation that the incoming Biden administration would be less tolerant of the blockade, facilitated the end of the 'GCC crisis' (Kristian Ulrichsen examines this in Chapter Six). The UAE, Saudi Arabia, Bahrain and Egypt restored diplomatic relations with Qatar after the signing of the Al-Ula agreement at the 2021 GCC conference in Saudi Arabia. Although significant differences between these countries remain, relations have noticeably improved.[44]

The 'resolution' of the 'GCC crisis' also facilitated warming UAE–Turkish relations. Ankara is Doha's main regional ally, and Abu Dhabi and Ankara found themselves on opposite sides of regional conflicts following the Arab uprisings. Turkey and Qatar supported Muslim Brotherhood-type movements across the region which the UAE considered a threat to its national security. Ankara accused Abu Dhabi of supporting the 2016 coup attempt in Turkey and working against its interests elsewhere in the Middle East and North Africa.[45]

For reasons similar to those discussed above (for example, the failure of aggressive regional policies to produce their intended results and other geopolitical and economic considerations), both the UAE and Turkey found it advantageous to mend relations.[46] The UAE's national security adviser visited Ankara in August 2021 followed by Crown Prince Mohamed bin Zayed's visit three months later.[47] Mohamed bin Zayed came with billions of dollars of investment funds and commercial agreements which President Recep Tayyip Erdoğan hoped would boost Turkey's faltering lira and the country's battered economy. Erdoğan reciprocated in February 2021, travelling to Dubai, in a sign of continued warming relations.[48] (Erdoğan also visited Saudi Arabia in April 2022 and then hosted Saudi's Crown Prince Mohammed bin Salman in Turkey in June 2022, further indicating the extent to which previous regional rifts have mended.)[49]

There has also been a noticeable shift in the UAE's orientation towards Libya.[50] After supporting Khalifa Haftar's Libyan National Army (along with Egypt) financially, diplomatically and militarily against the internationally recognised government in Tripoli, including through hundreds of drone and missile strikes and by funding the Russian Wagner Group and other mercenaries fighting in support of Haftar, Abu Dhabi began to shift its position shortly after the Biden administration took office.[51] The UAE signalled its willingness to support international efforts to achieve peace in Libya in January 2021 and the interim Libyan prime minister visited Abu Dhabi to meet with Mohamed bin Zayed in April 2021.[52]

Meanwhile, there have also been efforts in the region to address some of the structural drivers of regional instability, although it is uncertain whether these efforts will succeed. Iran and Saudi Arabia, for example, began direct talks in 2021 with the goal of improving relations, five years after Riyadh had severed ties with Tehran.[53] As outlined above (and explored further in Chapter One), the Saudi–Iranian rivalry has fuelled multiple proxy wars. Although it is far from certain that relations between Riyadh and Tehran will improve, reduced Saudi–Iranian tensions would likely have positive regional repercussions, including by dampening sectarian antagonisms. And although conflicts in Yemen, Syria, Iraq and Lebanon each have their own internal dynamics, improved Saudi–Iranian relations could also have salutary consequences on the management of these conflicts.

Progress has also been made against the Islamic State, the violent non-state actor that benefitted from and contributed to turbulence and insecurity in Iraq and Syria. The US-led international coalition against the Islamic State has had considerable success. Although the group remains active and capable of carrying out violent operations in Syria and Iraq, since 2019 the Islamic State no longer controls significant territory in either country and the group's financial resources and organisational capabilities have been severely degraded.[54]

Other recent developments have had a mixed impact on regional turbulence. The Palestinian–Israeli conflict remains unresolved and capable of generating significant regional turbulence despite the much-heralded 2020 normalisation agreements between the UAE, Bahrain and Israel brokered by the Trump administration. This conflict, and the wider Arab–Israeli conflict, have been among the most destabilising regional issues from 1948 to date, having produced six major wars, two intifadas, four 'Gaza wars', and massive destruction, displacement and upheaval.

Rather than viewing the Abraham Accords as an achievement towards Arab–Israeli peace, as governments in Washington, Tel Aviv, Abu Dhabi and Manama have claimed, they are better understood as regime balancing against a common adversary. Israel, Bahrain and the UAE each perceive Iran as the primary regional security threat. The accords, therefore, are more about establishing a new regional security alliance against Tehran than halting the further Israeli annexation of Palestinian land or achieving a 'two-state solution', as initially claimed.[55] The agreements also opened new opportunities for economic trade and technology and cyber cooperation between the UAE and Israel.[56]

The fact that the Palestinian–Israeli conflict was eclipsed in the post-2003 and post-2011 period by new and more destructive regional issues is an indication of the unprecedented turbulence witnessed during this period and not the end of this conflict's ability to generate upheaval.[57] The Palestinian issue remains unresolved and continues to be important for Arab publics and Arab states (although less so for Arab states), despite successive Israeli governments showing no interest in resolving the conflict. The continuing occupation of the West Bank, further settlement expansion, including in East Jerusalem, and the continued Israeli blockade of Gaza (with Egyptian complicity) will inevitably produce future violent eruptions. Although the status quo may be tolerable for many in Israel, it has increasingly been described as a form of apartheid.[58] Such conditions, coupled with a dysfunctional, authoritarian and corrupt Palestinian Authority and an impoverished Gaza governed by an Islamist movement struggling to reconcile both resistance and ideology with sound governance, are unsustainable and will produce neither peace nor security.

The propensity of the conflict to generate turbulence became apparent in May 2021 when fighting broke out between Israel and Hamas following the announced evictions of Palestinian families from their homes in East Jerusalem and the violent storming of al-Aqsa Mosque by Israeli forces, which injured hundreds of Palestinian worshippers. Subsequent fighting between Israel and Hamas resulted in 256 Palestinian deaths and thirteen deaths in Israel.[59] This conflict will continue to produce intermittent regional turbulence for years to come.

The conflict over political Islam is also unresolved and will likely remain so for the foreseeable future. In fact, this conflict is interrelated to the struggle between democracy and authoritarianism in the region. Regardless of how much the region's autocratic rulers, and supposedly 'secular' and 'liberal' elites, would wish otherwise, political Islam remains a significant and organic part of the fabric of Arab societies. Without peacefully integrating Islamist parties and movements into functioning political systems, therefore, democracy will remain unachievable. This is no easy task and as a result this conflict will continue to generate turbulence in the domestic and regional politics of the region.

Finally, the struggle between democracy and authoritarianism in the Middle East also remains unresolved and will remain so for the foreseeable future. A decade after the 2011 uprisings, it would be impossible to deny the resurgence of authoritarianism globally and in the region. Despite the initial 'success' of democratisation in Tunisia, democratic consolidation has proven challenging. Tunisia's President Kais Saied's July 2021 suspension of parliament and other anti-democratic measures were made possible by deteriorating economic conditions and a feeling among many Tunisians that democracy had failed to deliver any economic dividends. Such feelings were aggravated by the COVID-19 pandemic, infighting among political elites and dysfunctional governance.

Hopes for democratisation in Sudan after the 2019 ouster of Omar al-Bashir were also shaken by the military takeover in October 2021. The suspension of the civilian government and continuing repression against peaceful protesters provides no clear path back to the previously planned transition to fully civilian and democratic rule. Elsewhere in the region, authoritarianism has been resurgent in Egypt following the 2013 coup, and counter-revolutionary states, particularly Saudi Arabia and the UAE, remain aggressively committed to maintaining a regional authoritarian status quo.

Although the period of intense regional turbulence that is the focus of this volume has come to an end, this conflict and the others described above and in the following pages will continue to generate instability and turbulence at both the domestic and regional levels in the Middle East and North Africa for years to come.

Notes

1   In his contribution to this volume, Waleed Hazbun defines 'turbulence' conceptually as 'a system with a proliferation of heterogeneous actors below and above the state level with expanded capabilities that disrupt and complicate the dynamics of regional politics'.

2   It should be noted that there was little that was 'moderate' about the so-called

'moderate Arab states'. They were all thoroughly authoritarian, had little regard for human rights or the rule of law and were not particularly 'moderate' regarding women's rights or religious freedoms. The primary distinguishing quality between the supposedly 'moderate' states and the 'axis of resistance' was their alliance with the US and their acceptance of Israel.

3 Explaining the 'persistence' of authoritarianism and the 'durability' or 'stability' of authoritarian regimes was arguably the primary focus of most political scientists studying the region. For a discussion of the 'stable authoritarian regime' literature about the Middle East before the 2011 uprisings see, F. Gregory Gause III, 'The Middle East Academic Community and the "Winter of Arab Discontent": Why Did We Miss It?' in Ellen Laipson ed., *Seismic Shift: Understanding Change in the Middle East* (Washington DC: Stimson Center, 2011). For a critique of this literature, see Noureddine Jebnoun, 'Rethinking the Paradigm of "Durable" and "Stable" Authoritarianism in the Middle East', in Noureddine Jebnoun et al., eds, *Modern Middle East Authoritarianism: Roots, Ramifications, and Crisis* (Abingdon: Routledge, 2014), 1–24.

4 Maha Yahya, 'Refugees in the Making of an Arab Regional Disorder', Carnegie Middle East Center, November 2015. Available at <https://carnegieendowment.org/files/CMEC57_Yahya_final.pdf> (last accessed 7 October 2022); Phillip Connor, 'Middle East's Migrant Population More than Doubles Since 2005', Pew Research Center, October 2016. Available at <https://www.pewresearch.org/global/2016/10/18/middle-easts-migrant-population-more-than-doubles-since-2005/> (last accessed 7 October 2022).

5 Although both Iraq and Iran received external support from regional allies, the fighting did not extend to those countries. Iraq was generously supported by the Arab Gulf monarchies and Egypt while Syria and Libya supported Iran. The fighting did extend to the Persian Gulf, however, as both countries attacked each other's oil tankers and, in some cases, other countries' tankers carrying Iraqi and Iranian oil.

6 Another head of state, Saddam Hussein, was deposed in 2003 as a result of military invasion.

7 'Note to Correspondents: Transcript of Press Stakeout by United Nations Special Envoy for Syria, Mr. Staffan de Mistura', United Nations Secretary-General, 22 April 2016. Available at <https://www.un.org/sg/en/content/sg/note-correspondents/2016-04-22/note-correspondents-transcript-press-stakeout-united> (last accessed 7 October 2022).

8 Syrian Observatory for Human Rights, 1 June 2021. Available at <https://www.syriahr.com/en/217360/> (last accessed 7 October 2022).

9 'Syria Emergency', UN Refugee Agency, modified 15 March 2021. Available at

<https://www.unhcr.org/en-us/syria-emergency.html> (last accessed 7 October 2022).

10 "'Shameful Milestone" in Yemen as 10,000 Children Killed or Maimed Since Fighting Began', UNICEF, 19 October 2021. Available at <https://www.unicef .org/press-releases/shameful-milestone-yemen-10000-children-killed-or-maimed -fighting-began> (last accessed 7 October 2022).

11 Taylor Hanna, David K. Bohl and Jonathan D. Moyer, *Assessing the Impact of War in Yemen: Pathways for Recovery*, United Nations Development Programme, 2021, 32.

12 These figures do not include deaths, injuries or refugees from the 2003 Iraq war, the insurgency that followed, or subsequent war-related violence and other 'indirect causes'. Nor do these figures include deaths, injuries and refugee flows from the Libyan civil war or the uprisings and political repression in Egypt, Bahrain and other countries.

13 Some of the factors that contributed to regional turbulence continue to shape both domestic and regional politics. Algeria and Sudan in 2019 demonstrate that the story of the Arab uprisings is ongoing. That year witnessed the ouster of Abdel Aziz Bouteflika, who had been in power in Algeria for two decades, and Omar al-Bashir, who was Sudan's president for thirty years. Both leaders were ousted in large part due to popular mobilisation and protests, during which demonstrators voiced similar grievances against incumbent regimes. Although the struggles in Algiers and Khartoum are not over, we have already seen regional states attempt to influence the trajectories of political change in these countries.

14 According to the UN, 'High dependence on oil resources, tourism and remittances – sectors that are negatively impacted by the pandemic, in addition to protracted conflict, further aggravate the impact of COVID-19 on the Arab region.' According to my calculations, gross domestic product fell by 10 per cent in the Arab region and 9.6 per cent in the Middle East and North Africa between 2019 and 2020 based on World Bank data, while the IMF 'lowered its Middle East and North Africa economic forecast to its lowest in 50 years'. See <https://data.world bank.org/> (last accessed 7 October 2022); and 'The Impact of COVID-19 on the Arab Region', United Nations, July 2020, p. 8. Available at <https://unsdg.un .org/sites/default/files/2020-07/sg_policy_brief_covid-19_and_arab_states_en glish_version_july_2020.pdf> (last accessed 7 October 2022). The human and political costs of the pandemic have also been severe. More than 90,000 Iranians died from COVID-19 up to July 2021, according to the Iranian government, while many believe the actual number of deaths is multiple times higher. See Dan De Luce and Leila Gharagozlou, 'Iran's Covid Death Toll May Be Four Times the Government's Official Tally, Says Top Doctor', *NBC News*, 28 October 2020.

Available at <https://www.nbcnews.com/health/health-news/iran-s-covid-de ath-toll-may-be-four-times-government-n1245028> (last accessed 7 October 2022). The pandemic also contributed to Tunisia's political crisis in July 2021, when President Kais Saied sacked the head of government and cabinet, froze parliament and invoked emergency powers. The country's staggering number of COVID-19 deaths relative to its population and poor vaccination rollout, are widely believed to have contributed to the crisis. See Jihed Abidellaoui, 'Anger over Tunisia's pandemic failures fuels political crisis', *Reuters*, 1 August 2021. Available at <https://www.reuters.com/world/africa/anger-over-tunisias-pan demic-failures-fuels-political-crisis-2021-08-01/> (last accessed 7 October 2022).

15 Several Arab leaders voiced concerns about Iran's growing regional influence after the 2003 Iraq war, revealing their anxieties about Shiʻa Arabs in the process. Jordan's King Abdullah warned of regional instability if a pro-Iranian regime emerged following Iraq's first post-invasion elections in 2005. He described Iraq as a 'battleground' in the war between the West and Iran and warned that 'a new "crescent" of dominant Shiʻite movements or governments stretching from Iran into Iraq, Syria and Lebanon could emerge' if Tehran gained influence over Baghdad. A few months later, Egyptian president Hosni Mubarak claimed that Shiʻa Arabs were more loyal to Iran than the countries where they lived, in an interview with Al Arabiya Television. His remarks were immediately criticised. See Robin Wright and Peter Baker, 'Iraq, Jordan See Threat to Election from Iran', *Washington Post*, 8 December 2004. Available at <https://www.washing tonpost.com/archive/politics/2004/12/08/iraq-jordan-see-threat-to-election -from-iran/7e0cc1bc-aeb3-447a-bc9e-cfa5499699bc/> (last accessed 7 October 2022); and Edward Wong, 'Iraqis Denounce Mubarak's Remarks on Strife', *New York Times*, 10 April 2006. Available at <https://www.nytimes.com/2006/04 /10/world/middleeast/iraqis-denounce-mubaraks-remarks-on-strife.html> (last accessed 7 October 2022).

16 To avoid confusion about what I mean by the struggle between democracy and authoritarianism (or revolution and counter-revolution), I need to make several points explicit. First, I do not mean by this that politics across the entire region, from Mauritania to Iran, was the same before 2011. There was, of course, significant diversity in terms of regime type, levels of freedom of speech, press, assembly and political contestation before, and after, the 2011 uprisings. My point is only that the entirety of the Arab region before 2011 can be characterised as 'authoritarian' while the 2011 uprisings were attempts to bring about fundamental political change, including democracy. Second, by characterising the conflict in this way I also do not mean that politics was absent before the uprisings. Different forms of politics, resistance and contestation occurred throughout the region,

even in those states considered most repressive. Third, I also do not mean by this characterisation that people in the Middle East were, or are, somehow incapable of practising democracy or that the Middle East is somehow 'exceptional' in this regard. Nor do I assume that 'democratisation' is inevitable or that there is a singular transition process from authoritarianism to democracy.

17 See Nawaf Obaid, 'Amid the Arab Spring, a U.S.-Saudi Split', *New York Times*, 15 May 2011. Available at <https://www.washingtonpost.com/opinions/amid -the-arab-spring-a-us-saudi-split/2011/05/13/AFMy8Q4G_story.html> (last accessed 7 October 2022). Obaid, a Saudi analyst, harshly criticises a litany of US policies towards the region and writes of a 'tectonic shift in the U.S.-Saudi relationship'. The American response to the 9/11 attacks, 'an ill-conceived response to the Arab protest movement', and US policy towards Israel and Iran has led the kingdom to view the US as 'an unwilling and unreliable partner', according to Obaid.

18 See Anoushiravan Ehteshami, 'Saudi Arabia as a Resurgent Regional Power', *The International Spectator* 53, no. 4 (2018), 75–94; Karen E. Young, 'The Interventionist Turn in Gulf States' Foreign Policies', Issue Paper 4, The Arab Gulf States Institute in Washington, 1 June 2016. Available at <https://agsiw .org/wp-content/uploads/2016/06/Young_Interventionist_ONLINE.pdf> (last accessed 7 October 2022); Lina Khatib, 'Syria, Saudi Arabia, the U.A.E. and Qatar: The "Sectarianization" of the Syrian Conflict and Undermining of Democratization in the Region', *British Journal of Middle Eastern Studies* 46, no. 3 (2019): 385–403.

19 See 'Report of the Bahrain Independent Commission of Inquiry', 23 November 2011, p. 66, Available at <http://www.bici.org.bh/BICIreportEN.pdf> (last accessed 30 October 2022).

20 See Neil MacFarquhar, 'Saudi Arabia Scrambles to Limit Region's Upheaval', *New York Times*, 27 May 2011. Available at <https://www.nytimes.com/2011 /05/28/world/middleeast/28saudi.html> (last accessed 7 October 2022).

21 Marc Owen Jones and Ala'a Shehabi, eds, *Bahrain's Uprising: Resistance and Repression in the Gulf* (London: Zed Books, 2015); Marc Owen Jones, *Political Repression in Bahrain* (Cambridge: Cambridge University Press, 2020).

22 It is important to make clear that the conflict about political Islam or Islamist groups described here is primarily about counter-revolutionary regimes in the UAE, Saudi Arabia and Egypt aggressively opposing Islamist movements for political reasons, often characterising these groups as 'extremists' or 'terrorists' because they are their primary challengers. This does not mean that political Islam or Islamist politics is somehow 'incompatible' with democracy, as was debated in an earlier generation of scholarship. See Asef Bayat, 'Islam and Democracy: The

Perverse Charm of an Irrelevant Question', in *Making Islam Democratic: Social Movements and the Post-Islamist Turn* (Stanford: Stanford University Press, 2007), 1–15.

23   Peter Salisbury, 'Risk Perception and Appetite in UAE Foreign and National Security Policy', Chatham House, July 2020, 4, 16; Wikileaks, 'Strong words in private from MBZ at IDEX – Bashes Iran, Qatar, Russia', 25 February 2009. Available at <https://wikileaks.org/plusd/cables/09ABUDHABI193_a.html> (last accessed 7 October 2022); Robert F. Worth, 'Mohammed bin Zayed's Dark Vision of the Middle East's Future', *New York Times Magazine*, 9 January 2020.

24   See Chapter Eight in this volume and David D. Kirkpatrick, *Into the Hands of the Soldiers: Freedom and Chaos in Egypt and the Middle East* (New York: Viking, 2018).

25   See Chapter Six in this volume and Andreas Krieg, ed., *Divided Gulf: The Anatomy of a Crisis* (Singapore: Palgrave Macmillan), 2018.

26   Tensions developed between Hamas, Syria and Iran as a result of the Assad regime's response to the Syrian uprising. Hamas criticised the regime's response, its leaders left Damascus and the group's offices were closed in 2012. Iran, as Syria and Hamas's largest backer, has tried to reconcile both parties, along with Hezbollah, since at least 2017.

27   As the policy's name implied, 'zero problems with neighbours', attempted to establish positive, cooperative and mutually beneficial relations between Ankara and all its neighbours, despite differences in ideology, political orientation or alliance membership.

28   Matthew Petti and Trita Parsi, 'No Clean Hands: The Interventions of Middle Eastern Powers, 2010–2020', Quincy Paper No. 8, July 2021.

29   Ellie Geranmayeh and Kadri Liik, 'The New Power Couple: Russia and Iran in the Middle East', European Council on Foreign Relations, September 2016, pp. 4–6.

30   The Second Berlin Conference on Libya held in June 2021 focused on implementing terms agreed at the 2020 Berlin Conference, including holding national elections and the departure of foreign troops and fighters from the country. Although the scheduled 2021 presidential elections in Libya were postponed, the ceasefire in place since October 2020 has remained. Libya's future, however, is far from certain. See 'Fleshing Out the Libya Ceasefire Agreement', International Crisis Group, 4 November 2020. Available at <https://www.crisisgroup.org/middle-east-north-africa/north-africa/libya/b80-fleshing-out-libya-ceasefire-agreement> (last accessed 30 October 2022); and the UN Support Mission in Libya's statement, Second Berlin Conference on Libya, 23 June 2021. Available at

<https://unsmil.unmissions.org/sites/default/files/2021_berlin_2_conclusions_final_-_eng.pdf> (last accessed 7 October 2022). The UN, Oman and the US have all been involved in peace efforts in Yemen. See Abdullah Baabood, 'Omani Perspectives on the Peace Process in Yemen', Berghof Foundation, 7 June 2021. Available at <https://berghof-foundation.org/library/omani-perspectives-on-the-peace-process-in-yemen> (last accessed 7 October 2022); and Aziz Yaakoubi, 'End of Yemen Quagmire? Saudi-led Coalition, Houthis Near Peace Deal', *Reuters*, 21 June 2021. Available at <https://www.reuters.com/world/middle-east/end-yemen-quagmire-saudi-led-coalition-houthis-near-peace-deal-2021-06-21/> (last accessed 7 October 2022).

31 A two-month truce began in Yemen at the beginning of Ramadan in April 2022. It was subsequently extended but came to an end in October 2022. Although the truce was not renewed, at the time of writing significant fighting has not resumed. See Ben Hubbard, 'Yemen's Warring Parties Begin First Cease-fire in Six Years', *New York Times*, 2 April 2022. Available at <https://www.nytimes.com/2022/04/02/world/middleeast/yemen-cease-fire.html> (last accessed 7 October 2022). See also Jon Gambrell and Isabel Debre, 'Saudi Arabia Offers Cease-fire Plan to Yemen Rebels', *AP*, 22 March 2021. Available at <https://apnews.com/article/saudi-arabia-cease-fire-plan-yemen-rebels-5bb3778d54227f77beea2bd017cd7554> (last accessed 7 October 2022).

32 UAE involvement in Egypt's counter-revolution is discussed in Chapter Eight. The UAE, like other Gulf states, also funded anti-Assad militias in Syria after the start of the Syrian civil war in addition to participating militarily in the US-led anti-Islamic State coalition.

33 The severing of diplomatic ties and the blockade of Qatar in 2017, led by the UAE, along with Saudi Arabia, Bahrain and Egypt, is another example of the unprecedented and aggressive policies undertaken by Abu Dhabi in response to the Arab uprisings.

34 Both Socotra and Mayun are located in strategic waterways. Mayun's significance is that it lies in the Bab al-Mandib strait, an important chokepoint linking the Gulf of Aden to the Red Sea and then onto the Mediterranean through the Suez Canal. The strait is critical for international shipping, including Abu Dhabi's oil exports and commercial economy, and in the context of regional competition, control of the islands allows the UAE to project power in the region and monitor important maritime routes off Yemen's coasts. If the strait were blocked it would cause major disruptions for energy flows and global trade, requiring vessels headed through the Suez Canal to make the much longer and more expensive journey around the southern tip of Africa. See Eleonora Adremagni, 'UAE Foreign Policy: From Militias in the Rimland to Straits Diplomacy', Carnegie

Endowment for International Peace, 28 October 2021. Available at <https://car negieendowment.org/sada/85676> (last accessed 7 October 2022).

35 Joyce Karam, 'UAE, Saudi Arabia and Bahrain Welcome Trump's Exit from Iran Nuclear Deal', *The National*, 9 May 2018. Available at <https://www.th enationalnews.com/world/mena/uae-saudi-arabia-and-bahrain-welcome-trump -s-exit-from-iran-nuclear-deal-1.728557> (last accessed 7 October 2022).

36 Tensions increased further in September 2019 after a sophisticated drone attack against a Saudi oil installation in Abqaiq which processes the majority of Saudi Arabia's crude oil output. Although the Trump administration denounced the attack it did not respond militarily. This was followed by an attack on an Iranian oil tanker off the coast of Saudi Arabia in the Red Sea in October 2019. See Ben Hubbard, Palko Karasz and Stanley Reed, 'Two Major Saudi Oil Installations Hit by Drone Strike, and U.S. Blames Iran', *New York Times*, 14 September 2019. Available at <https://www.nytimes.com/2019/09/14/world/middleeast /saudi-arabia-refineries-drone-attack.html> (last accessed 7 October 2022). See also 'Gulf tanker Attacks: Iran Releases Photos of "Attacked" Ship', *BBC News*, 14 October 2019. Available at <https://www.bbc.com/news/world-middle-east -50040670> (last accessed 7 October 2022).

37 Giorgio Cafiero and Khalid al-Jaber, 'The UAE and Iran's Maritime Talks', *Lobe Log*, 6 August 2019. Available at <https://lobelog.com/the-uae-and-irans-ma ritime-talks/> (last accessed 7 October 2022); Liz Sly, 'The UAE's Ambitions Backfire as It Finds Itself on the Front Line of U.S.–Iran Tensions', *The Washington Post*, 11 August 2019. Available at <https://www.washingtonpo st.com/world/the-uaes-ambitions-backfire-as-it-finds-itself-on-the-front-line-of -us-iran-tensions/2019/08/11/d3ee41a0-509d-11e9-bdb7-44f948cc0605_story .html> (last accessed 7 October 2022). See also *Reuters*, 'Rivals Iran and UAE to Hold Maritime Security Talks', 30 July 2019. Available at <https://www.re uters.com/article/uk-mideast-iran-emirates-idUKKCN1UP18P> (last accessed 7 October 2022).

38 Mohamad Ali Harissi, 'UAE Says Reducing Troops in War-torn Yemen', *AFP*, 8 July 2019. Available at <https://news.yahoo.com/uae-says-reducing-troops -war-torn-yemen-144623157.html> (last accessed 7 October 2022). See also Imad Harb, 'Why the United Arab Emirates is Abandoning Saudi Arabia in Yemen', *Foreign Policy*, 1 August 2019. Available at <https://foreignpolicy.com/2019 /08/01/why-the-united-arab-emirates-is-abandoning-saudi-arabia-in-yemen/> (last accessed 7 October 2022); Jeremy Binnie, 'UAE Announces Withdrawal from Aden', Janes, 31 October 2019. Available at <https://www.janes.com/de fence-news/news-detail/uae-announces-withdrawal-from-aden> (last accessed 7 October 2022).

39 David Hearst, 'Exclusive: UAE's Secret Mission to Iran', *Middle East Eye*, 13 October 2019. Available at <https://www.middleeasteye.net/news/exclusive-uaes-secret-mission-iran> (last accessed 7 October 2022). See also 'UAE Releases $700 Million in Frozen Iranian Funds "in Return for Security"', *The New Arab*, 20 October 2019. Available at <https://english.alaraby.co.uk/news/uae-releases-700-million-frozen-iranian-funds> (last accessed 7 October 2022).

40 'UAE Sends Additional Aid to Iran in Fight against COVID-19', *Reliefweb*, 27 June 2020. Available at <https://reliefweb.int/report/iran-islamic-republic/uae-sends-additional-aid-iran-fight-against-covid-19> (last accessed 7 October 2022).

41 'Iran's Top Nuclear Negotiator Holds Talks in the UAE – State News Agency', *Reuters*, 24 November 2021. Available at <https://www.reuters.com/world/middle-east/irans-top-nuclear-negotiator-holds-talks-uae-state-news-agency-2021-11-24> (last accessed 7 October 2022). Kani later tweeted that the countries had agreed 'to open a new chapter' in bilateral relations.

42 The UAE also restored relations with Syria in 2018 and the UAE foreign minister visited Damascus to meet with Bashar al-Assad in November 2021. The UAE's relationship with Syria exemplifies the complicated character of relations in the region as it is, in part, an effort by Abu Dhabi to reduce Iranian influence on Damascus, something that will likely prove extremely difficult as Iran has been Syria's most important ally in the region, particularly during the country's civil war, since the 1979 Iranian Revolution.

43 The severing of relations and blockade of Qatar by Saudi Arabia, the UAE, Bahrain and Egypt produced neither a change of leadership in Doha nor a significant change in Qatar's regional policies. See Chapter Six in this volume and Kristian Coates Ulrichsen, *Qatar and the Gulf Crisis* (Oxford: Oxford University Press, 2020).

44 The UAE's national security adviser Sheikh Tahnoun bin Zayed visited Qatar in August 2021, the first Emirati official to visit the country since relations were broken. See 'Senior UAE Official Meets Qatar's Emir in Rare Visit', *Reuters*, 26 August 2021. Available at <https://www.reuters.com/world/middle-east/senior-uae-official-meets-qatars-emir-rare-visit-2021-08-26/> (last accessed 7 October 2022).

45 Asli Aydıntaşbaş and Cinzia Bianco, 'Useful Enemies: How Turkey–UAE Rivalry is Remaking the Middle East', European Council on Foreign Relations, 15 March 2021, 7. Available at <https://ecfr.eu/publication/useful-enemies-how-the-turkey-uae-rivalry-is-remaking-the-middle-east/> (last accessed 7 October 2022).

46 Hamdullah Baycar, 'Rapprochement Spree: Abu Dhabi Recalibrates Relations

with Ankara', *Sada* (Carnegie Endowment for International Peace), 16 December 2021. Available at <https://carnegieendowment.org/sada/86025> (last accessed 7 October 2022).

47   Suzan Fraser and Aya Batrawy, 'Top UAE Security Chief Visits Turkey after Years of Tension', *AP*, 19 August 2021. Available at <https://apnews.com/artic le/europe-middle-east-business-turkey-059bc288038fd6c46b1c444319f9f683> (last accessed 7 October 2022).

48   Aya Batrawy, 'Turkey's Flag Flies High as Erdogan's Dubai Trip Marks Reset', *ABC News*, 15 February 2022. Available at <https://abcnews.go.com/Intern ational/wireStory/turkeys-flag-flies-high-erdogans-dubai-trip-marks-82900810> (last accessed 7 October 2022). Improved UAE–Turkish relations also hold out the possibility, although not the certainty, of reducing tensions in conflicts where both countries are supporting opposing sides, such as in Libya.

49   Ahmed Maher, 'Turkish President Erdogan's Visit to Saudi Arabia Seeks to Restore Strained Relations', *The National*, 28 April 2022. Available at <https:// www.thenationalnews.com/gulf-news/saudi-arabia/2022/04/28/turkish-presi dent-erdogans-visit-to-saudi-arabia-seeks-to-restore-strained-relations/>   (last accessed 7 October 2022); Kareem Fahim and Zeynep Karatas, 'Turkey's Erdogan Hosts Saudi Crown Prince, Ending Rift over Khashoggi Murder', *Washington Post*, 22 June 2022. Available at <https://www.washingtonpost.com/world/20 22/06/22/turkey-saudi-mbs-khashoggi/> (last accessed 7 October 2022).

50   The UAE's position towards Syria has also evolved during this period from supporting elements in the Syrian opposition after the 2011 uprising, along with other Gulf states, to restoring diplomatic relations with Damascus in 2018 and subsequently leading efforts to reintegrate the Assad regime back into Arab politics. See Joseph Daher, 'The Dynamics and Evolution of UAE–Syria Relations: Between Expectations and Obstacles', European University Institute, 25 October 2019.

51   For an outstanding account of some aspects of the UAE's involvement in Libya, see Candace Rondeaux, Oliver Imhof and Jack Margolin, 'The Abu Dhabi Express: Analyzing the Wagner Group's Libya Logistics Pipeline & Operations', *New America*, November 2021. See also Samuel Ramani, 'The UAE in Libya: A Power Broker or Spoiler?' Gulf International Forum, 24 June 2021. Available at <https://gulfif.org/the-uae-in-libya-a-power-broker-or-spoiler/> (last accessed 7 October 2022). See also, 'UAE Says Will Cooperate with UN, US on Libya Conflict', *France 24*, 29 January 2021. Available at <https://www.france24.com /en/live-news/20210129-uae-says-will-cooperate-with-un-us-on-libya-conflict> (last accessed 7 October 2022).

52   'UAE Pledges Support for Libya's New Unity Government', *The Arab Weekly*,

8 April 2021. Available at <https://thearabweekly.com/uae-pledges-support-lib yas-new-unity-government> (last accessed 7 October 2022).

53 Ben Hubbard, Farnaz Fassihi and Jane Arraf, 'Fierce Foes, Iran and Saudi Arabia Secretly Explore Defusing Tensions', *New York Times*, 1 May 2021. Available at <https://www.nytimes.com/2021/05/01/world/middleeast/Saudi-Iran-talks .html> (last accessed 7 October 2022).

54 Although degraded, the Islamic State remains a global network with affiliates capable of undertaking deadly operations and producing instability in multiple regions. See 'Averting an ISIS Resurgence in Iraq and Syria', International Crisis Group, 11 October 2019. Available at <https://www.crisisgroup.org/middle-east-north-africa/eastern-mediterranean/syria/207-averting-isis-resurgence-iraq-and-syria> (last accessed 30 October 2022); and 'Twelfth Report of the Secretary-General on the Threat Posed by ISIL (Da'esh) to International Peace and Security and the Range of United Nations Efforts in Support of Member States in Countering the Threat', United Nations, 29 January 2021. Available at <https://www.securitycouncilreport.org/atf/cf/%7B65BFCF9B-6D27-4E9C-8CD3-CF6E4FF96FF9%7D/s_2021_98.pdf> (last accessed 7 October 2022). Both reports emphasise the continuing dangers the Islamic State poses and the possibility that the group will reconstitute itself, as it has done in the past.

55 Elham Fakhro, 'Selling Normalization in the Gulf', *Middle East Report Online*, 23 June 2021. Available at <https://merip.org/2021/06/selling-normalization-in -the-gulf/> (last accessed 7 October 2022). It should also be noted that Israel, the UAE and Bahrain also view Arab democracy and political Islam as common security threats. The accords were also a way for the UAE and Bahrain to improve their standing with the US.

56 Patrick Kingsley, 'Israel Signs Trade Deal with U.A.E.', *New York Times*, 31 May 2022. Available at <https://www.nytimes.com/2022/05/31/world/middleeast/israel-emirates-uae-trade.html> (last accessed 7 October 2022); Mohammed Soliman, 'How Tech is Cementing the UAE–Israel Alliance', Middle East Institute, 11 May 2021. Available at <https://www.mei.edu/publications/how -tech-cementing-uae-israel-alliance> (last accessed 7 October 2022).

57 The Iraq war and the ensuing instability within Iraq, and the Arab uprisings and the resulting Syrian, Yemeni and Libyan civil wars, in addition to massive refugee flows, the emergence of the Islamic State and intense regional competition, generated horrific levels of violence that overshadowed the Palestinian–Israeli conflict during this period.

58 Amnesty International, 'Israel's Apartheid Against Palestinians: Cruel System of Domination and Crime Against Humanity', 2022. Available at <https://www

.amnesty.org/en/wp-content/uploads/2022/02/MDE1551412022ENGLISH
.pdf> (last accessed 7 October 2022).

59 Israel–Gaza Conflict: UN Body to Investigate Violence, *BBC News*, 27 May
2021. Available at <https://www.bbc.com/news/world-middle-east-5727
0053> (last accessed 7 October 2022); and 'Response to the Escalation in the
oPt Situation Report No.1: 21–27 May 2021', UN Office for the Coordination
of Humanitarian Affairs. Available at <https://www.ochaopt.org/content
/response-escalation-opt-situation-report-no-1-21-27-may-2021> (last accessed
7 October 2022).

1

POWER POLITICS IN THE
POST-UPRISINGS MIDDLE EAST

Marc Lynch

P roxy warfare has been the signature mode of power politics in the post-uprisings Middle East.[1] Competing regional powers have intervened in the political affairs and the civil wars of weaker states around the Middle East by supporting local allies with arms, money and media. At the heart of the post-2011 decade, active proxy wars were being waged by more than half a dozen different powers in Iraq, Libya, Syria and Yemen. In several cases, proxy war evolved over time into more direct intervention – overt intervention by Saudi Arabia and the UAE, with the support of multiple partners, in Yemen; covert intervention by Egypt and the UAE in support of their struggling proxies in Libya; Turkey taking control of parts of northern Syria and sending forces into Libya. Proxy competition and interventionism could be observed in numerous other countries in the form of political parties, the media, and the cultivation of networks within regimes and militaries. Why did proxy warfare become so prevalent after 2011? What effects did this proxy warfare have? Will it prove an enduring feature of the landscape?

These questions point towards deeper assessments of the conceptualisation of structure in the regional order, the fundamentally international nature of the uprisings and their aftermath, and the nature and degree of change.[2] More than ten years after the 2011 Arab uprisings, it would be easy to conclude that nothing of significance in the international relations of the Middle East had changed. The Trump administration's approach to the Middle East, consolidating an alliance with Israel and key Arab states against Iran, recreated that of the Bush administration in key dimensions. Trump's indifference to human rights and democracy aligned well with the preferences of those Arab regimes to restore autocratic rule. The Biden administration, for its part, came into office determined to reduce US involvement in the region in order to focus on Asia – just like the Trump and Obama administrations had done. The surface similarity between regional order in 2009 and 2020, despite the enormous upheaval of the previous decade, is indeed a striking testament to the power of structure to replicate itself.

Those surface similarities are misleading, however. The Middle Eastern regional order has transformed in fundamental ways, changing the meaning and the practice of regional politics. The Arab–Israeli confrontation with Iran plays out today across different theatres, is fought with different weapons, and is underlay by a very different global and regional configuration of power. The Israeli–Palestinian situation is rapidly changing from below, as the two-state solution fades from view and the UAE leads a push for normalisation with Israel in its absence. The Arab states are riven by deep differences, with the competition between Qatar and the Saudi–Emirati front, even if formally resolved in early 2021, still affecting politics across the region and beyond. The devastation of Syria and Iraq has left a gaping wound at the heart of the Middle East, while power and authority has shifted eastward towards the Gulf. Structuring all of these regional developments are fundamental shifts in the global balance of power, hastened by the choices of the Trump administration, which have ended the age of American unipolar dominance without yet clarifying a new global order. As Paul Salem put it:

> In an unstable regional order, countries' internal and external conflicts are mutually exacerbating: internal tensions in one country draw in external alignments and contribute to regional proxy conflict, and regional conflict is more likely to impose itself onto domestic contests and push states toward failure and civil war.[3]

The new ways and means of regional power politics are rooted in these structural changes.[4] There has been a proliferation of both the opportunities for competitive interventions and the threats emerging from them. The Arab uprisings decisively weakened many states in the region, at least temporarily, while proliferating the number and types of relevant actors able to meaningfully impact politics. This created new opportunities for regional powers to expand their influence and power in states previously closed to them, through means never before available. At the same time, the lesson of the uprisings was that even seemingly stable, powerful regimes could fall victim to sudden popular mobilisation. This perceived vulnerability was compounded by the sudden and rapid emergence of the Islamic State, by the Trump administration's non-response to the late 2019 Iranian drone attack on the Abqaiq oil facility in Saudi Arabia, and by the Biden administration's sudden withdrawal from Afghanistan. The decline of American unipolar authority exacerbated this combination of opportunity and threat by weakening belief in US security guarantees and encouraging regional allies to diversify their alliance options and to act unilaterally in pursuit of their interests. The Trump administration's special enthusiasm for escalation of proxy wars with Iran loosened even the meagre external constraints on aggressive regional actions which Obama had attempted to impose. Biden's push for de-escalation around the region, and the related rapprochements between the UAE and both Qatar and Turkey, has reined in some of the most extreme interventionism, but has yet to address the underlying structural drivers.

The pressure to engage in interventionism was intense, rooted in familiar security dilemma dynamics. In a logic familiar from the Cold War, the fortunes of local proxies became an index for the broader balance of power. If Qatari proxies gained the upper hand in Libya, that became a symbol of broader Qatari rising power even if the actual material significance of those gains was minimal. Houthi advances in Yemen were taken as a signal of growing Iranian power, inevitably inviting an escalation in Saudi bombing campaigns in response. The nature of this competition meant that it was virtually impossible for states to decipher whether the moves by their rivals were offensive or defensive in nature.[5] While some regimes no doubt simply wanted to take advantage of opportunities to expand their influence, even less ambitious regimes understood that their rivals would likely take advantage of such opportunities. Not intervening, from this perspective, would simply mean ceding the field to their rivals in dangerous ways. This security dilemma logic helps to explain why interventions in lost causes such as Yemen and Libya typically continued long after the initial logic had faded.

This chapter surveys the new ways and means of power politics in the Middle East through the lens of change at the global level. It begins with the new global structure, showing how the rise of Russian and Chinese agency in the region, along with American–European tensions over Iran, has created new opportunities for local powers while limiting American options. It then examines the structure of power within the Middle East. Finally, it looks at how actors have sought to mobilise power within these rapidly changing global and regional structures. The era of proxy warfare could prove transient, should states reconsolidate in ways which reduce both opportunity and threat, if competing regional powers can agree on de-escalation strategies, and if the US restores some element of restraint. While such de-escalation has been seen in various forms in the reconciliation between the UAE and Turkey, the end of the boycott of Qatar, attempted international mediation in Libya and Yemen, and the accession to Syrian regime victory, such progress has been fragile and transient. It will likely continue to be so until a new regional order consolidates.

Global Political Order

The US is no longer the unipolar power in the Middle East.[6] This represents a striking change from the conditions which have prevailed since the 1991 end of the Cold War. It is fitting that the Middle East would be the locale for the revealed structural decline of the US. For some twenty years, American global unipolarity was most visible in practice in the Middle East. The American practice of power under unipolarity changed dramatically after the 2001 terrorist attacks by al-Qaida, but it is often forgotten that this was the second, not the first, such radical structural change. The transformation of the American regional position after 1991 was in some ways more dramatic than that of 2001 – on a par with those of 2011.

The American Middle East was established through the 1990–1 military campaign to liberate Kuwait from Iraqi occupation. Operation Desert Storm was fought as a genuine coalition, with the Soviet agreement to UN Security Council authorisation symbolising the new possibilities of a post-Cold War global order. Following the end of the war, the US left in place a substantial military capability, building an archipelago of bases and infrastructure in the Gulf to facilitate the exercise of its power in the form of the 'dual containment' of Iran and Iraq. It also launched the new phase of peace talks between Israel and Arab states, taking on the lead role in mediating and underwriting those negotiations. The Israeli–Arab peace talks were only secondarily about achieving peace. More important, structurally speaking, was that the ongoing talks established the US as the sole interlocutor in Arab–Israeli relations, and the active pursuit of peace allowed Arab regimes to justify their ongoing alliance with the US.

The year 2001 ushered in a second radical shift in the practice of American unipolarity. In 1991, the US had focused on consolidating a favourable status quo. In 2001, the US decided that its regional power depended on a radical change in the status quo. Revisionism from the top is an unusual structural move from the perspective of international relations (IR) theory, precisely because it tends to have such destabilising effects. The key practices of this shift were the global war on terror, the Bush administration's Freedom Agenda and the invasion of Iraq. This involved a massive expansion of the US military footprint in the region, the radical destabilisation of the balance of regional power in favour of Iran, and the unleashing of potent new ideational waves of sectarianism and jihadist extremism. The occupation of Iraq proved an enormous military and fiscal burden on the US, turning public opinion against military interventions and largely pre-empting possibilities for further interventions. The global financial crisis which struck in 2008 further undermined the foundations of American power.

The 2011 disruption was on a par with 1991 and 2001. The Arab uprisings challenged the American-led regional order directly and indirectly. The Obama administration's efforts to support but contain the uprisings, directing them towards moderate democratic reforms while avoiding more radical change, largely failed. Rhetorical support for democratisation put the US at odds with Arab regimes and protest movements alike, all of whom wanted full throated support rather than hedging on possible outcomes. This represented a deep political disruption of the post-1991 unipolar American order in the Middle East which accelerated pre-existing trends towards global rebalancing.

The Obama administration experienced profound resistance from its key regional allies towards several of its most important strategic priorities. Israel resisted Obama's efforts to restart negotiations with the Palestinians towards a two-state solution. It also, along with Saudi Arabia and the UAE, fiercely opposed the effort to negotiate a nuclear agreement with Iran. Many Arab regimes, as well as their publics, complained bitterly over American refusal to get more openly involved in the campaign to overthrow Bashar al-Assad in Syria. Almost all regimes complained about even modest American efforts to support democratic transitions, with the counter-revolutionary states openly backing the 2013 military coup which ended the rocky transition in Egypt.

The Trump administration sought to rebuild America's position in the region by reversing the Obama administration's key policies in favour of full-throated alignment with Israel and the counter-revolutionary Gulf states. It worked closely with Israel's right-wing government, pushing for a normalisation of relations with the Arab world while eliminating pressure towards a two-state solution for the Palestinians. It adopted a much more aggressive position towards Iran, abandoning the Joint Comprehensive Plan of Action (JCPOA), assassinating Islamic Revolutionary Guard Corps (IRGC) leader Qassem Soleimani in Baghdad, and escalating covert action against Tehran. It prioritised the Abraham Accords, normalising relations between Israel, the UAE and other Arab states without progress on the Palestinian issue, while abandoning democracy and human rights in its dealings with Arab autocrats, turning a blind eye towards the 2018 murder of Saudi journalist Jamal Khashoggi. Symbolic airstrikes against Syria were meant to draw a contrast with Obama, but did not signal a broader interventionism; instead, Trump preferred to give a green light to allies such as Israel and the UAE to undertake such military actions.

Trump's personal relationships with Gulf leaders created a new dimension in the nature of the US presence in the Middle East. The Trump administration maintained very close personal networks, particularly through his son-in-law Jared Kushner's relationship with Mohamed bin Zayed of the UAE and Mohammed bin Salman of Saudi Arabia. This relationship created opportunities for those counter-revolutionary regimes to extend their influence into Washington. The near capture of US policy by the Israel–Saudi–Emirati alignment only went so far, however. The blockade of Qatar proved so disruptive to the US military posture in the region that it never received the American support which the UAE and Saudi Arabia had likely anticipated; it quietly ended in 2021 on the eve of the transition to Biden having achieved none of its goals. Arab regimes found themselves still limited in their cooperation with Israel by popular opposition to normalising such relations in the absence of a Palestinian state. Congress grew increasingly hostile to Saudi Arabia and the UAE over the war in Yemen and the Khashoggi assassination. In short, even a full effort by the Trump administration to restore a regional order based on a 'no daylight' alliance with Israel and its key Arab allies fell far short of rebuilding the shattered foundations of regional order.

The Biden administration, while ostensibly seeking a return to pre-Trump foreign policy orthodoxy, maintained many of those policies. Campaign rhetoric about pressuring Saudi Arabia over its human rights abuses and the war in Yemen quietly faded away once Biden took office. The Biden administration continued to push for regional normalisation with Israel, did not reverse Trump's provocative decisions in Jerusalem and the Golan Heights, and to date has not advanced any new plans for Israeli–Palestinian negotiations. Its primary regional policy objective, a return to the Iran nuclear agreement, proved difficult and ultimately failed. Neither Trump's close alignment nor Biden's limited course correction restored America's standing with its regional allies, however. Gulf doubts about the value of US security guarantees especially spiralled when it did not respond to the Iranian attack on the Abqaiq oil refineries. Biden's withdrawal from Afghanistan exacerbated those perceptions of declining US interest and presence in the region.

This dissatisfaction with Washington provided openings for rivals such as Russia and China. Regional regimes found it useful to entertain offers from Russia as a way to demonstrate to Washington that they had alternatives as a way of generating bargaining power within the alliance. The threat of defection, especially with regard to the Iran nuclear agreement, was a potent mechanism for extracting concessions from the US, such as unprecedented levels of arms sales and security guarantees. Saudi Arabia and the UAE even leveraged American fear of their interference with the Iran nuclear deal to win support for the intervention in Yemen.

Russia took full advantage of these opportunities, while engaging in creatively disruptive diplomacy of its own.[7] While not a true peer competitor even by its own estimation, it did not need to be in order to advance its goals of undermining the American dominated regional order and breaking the US monopoly on diplomacy. Its 2015 military intervention in Syria succeeded in saving the Assad regime, at great human cost, proving to many in the region the greater value of its military commitments to those of a US which hesitated to intervene. It is fascinating that Russia reaped dividends from an intervention which went against, not with, the regional powers with which it hoped to build better relations. In the years after 2011, and especially after 2015 (with the Syria intervention and the nuclear deal with Iran), more and more close American regional allies met with Putin at home or in Moscow. Gulf states such as the UAE and Saudi Arabia held high profile meetings, while even regimes highly dependent on the US such as Jordan began to coordinate with Moscow. Russia even offered military aid to General Khalifa Hiftar in Libya, in conjunction with close American allies UAE and Egypt against the US preference for a negotiated agreement.

China's increased involvement took a less overtly political form, but arguably had greater long-term implications. As it incorporated the Gulf and North Africa into its Belt and Road Initiative, China became more and more deeply involved in the infrastructural development of the region. Its leading position as a purchaser of Gulf oil and gas gave it strong material interests in stability, and especially a preference to avoid a war with Iran which could significantly disrupt those vital energy supplies. Almost every Gulf state, as well as Iran, has signed long-term strategic partnership agreements with Beijing over the last few years, significantly upgrading cooperation and interdependence across a wide range of sectors. While China has not yet mounted any overt bid to challenge US primacy in the Middle East, its rapidly growing economic, political and security presence – especially in the Gulf – show its steady erosion.

Regional Order

What were the foundations of regional order, and how precisely were they shattered? The global changes outlined above established the structural conditions, but local dynamics distinct to the region also shaped the turn to proxy warfare. These conditions include shifts in the regional balance of power, changes in the relative internal strength and cohesion of states, shifts in the ideational lines of struggle, and changes in the perception of primary threat. This created a profound disruption in established regional hierarchies, an unusual uncertainty which invited both challengers and established powers to take revisionist moves in hopes of locking in a new, favourable order before conditions again stabilised.[8]

First, the regional balance of power: the Arab uprisings severely weakened several key actors, creating dramatic new lines of influence as regional power shifted decisively towards the Gulf.[9] The core powers of the Arab centre – Egypt, Syria, Iraq, Libya – were all consumed by internal conflict and largely reduced to takers rather than makers of regional policy. In their place, the small, wealthy Gulf states such as Qatar and the UAE joined Saudi Arabia as key regional powers. Their ability to project power through special forces, high tech weapons purchases and financial support to local allies proved far more adaptable to the new regional politics than the large, unwieldy mass armies of traditional powers such as Egypt. The effects of the destruction of Syria and the internal problems of Egypt were comparable to the destabilising effects of the devastation of Iraq in 2003. Just as after 2003, Iran moved to strengthen its regional position through the building up of local proxy forces; where those proxies had previously been concentrated in Iraq and Lebanon, they now expanded into Syria and Yemen. The steady increase in Houthi missile and drone attacks against Saudi Arabia and the UAE show Iran's ability to translate these alliances and proxy relationships into offensive power projection.

Second, the Arab uprisings caused significant changes in the relative internal strength and cohesion of states.[10] Some states, particularly those in the Gulf, were able to use their extreme levels of wealth and state domination of society to prevent any meaningful challenges. Others proved highly vulnerable to popular mobilisation, even if they avoided regime changes. The distribution of state strength and weakness became as critical as the military balance of power in terms of the contours of the new regional order. States which could prevent others from intervening in their affairs were relatively more powerful, while those which could not became relatively weaker and more vulnerable.

Third, important shifts in the ideational lines of struggle created new opportunities and drivers for proxy warfare. An anti-Islamist push led by the UAE and Saudi Arabia forced the Muslim Brotherhood and its related networks into new terrain, polarising politics along religious lines where such conflicts had not previously been highly salient. The sectarian dimension of the conflicts in Iraq and Syria, especially, created opportunities for the mobilisation of sectarian proxies. Conflating democratic activism with either Islamism (Egypt) or Shiʻite activism (Bahrain) was a frequent tactic of the counter-revolutionary regimes.

Fourth, beyond these identity conflicts, regional norms governing intervention and sovereignty had clearly evolved through practice and justificatory strategy. What was at stake in the battles over hierarchy and security was not simply material power or institutional dominance, but rather power over the ideational justifications for legitimacy in the emergent regional order. In previous eras, overt military intervention in other Arab countries was something of a taboo, with conflict sublimated into earlier versions of proxy political warfare. In the years after 2011, many leading Arab states called for and participated in the military intervention in Libya, openly justified support for rebel movements in Syria, and intervened in Yemen directly. Each of these was articulated in a discourse of legitimacy through which the competing powers battled through the media and through regional institutions to establish a consensus on their standard for legitimacy. Thus, the same language of legitimacy was used by Egypt's Muslim Brotherhood to protest the forcible removal of President Morsi in 2013 and by Saudi Arabia to justify the military intervention in Yemen to restore the ousted President Hadi. Media platforms, social media campaigns and the support of influential individuals and movements became critical elements of national power in the struggle over a reconstituted regional order.

Finally, the Arab uprisings drove profound changes in the perception of primary threat by regimes and publics. Regimes keenly interested in their own survival now saw that popular uprisings anywhere in the region might spark imitation protests in their own country. The rapid, forceful diffusion of the Arab uprisings in 2011 fundamentally changed the way most regional regimes understood their own internal security. Preventing uprisings in other countries became not only a way to project power abroad, but also a way to protect regime survival at home. In such a context, popular Islamist movements such as the Muslim Brotherhood or mass-based democracy movements could be seen as greater threats to the survival of autocratic regimes than ostensible external enemies such as Iran. Many activists, by contrast, viewed those strong states themselves as the primary source of threat.

These developments led to the crystallisation of several cross-cutting lines of cooperation and conflict. Along one axis, the Sunni Arab states, tacitly aligned with Israel and Turkey, competed with Iran. This competition structured much of the American, Israeli and global strategy towards the region, and in proxy warfare terms played out most prominently in Syria, Iraq and Yemen. It involved a strongly sectarian dimension, with the geopolitical competition often manifesting on the ground as a Sunni–Shiʿa divide.[11] A secondary axis pitted Saudi Arabia and the UAE against Qatar and Turkey, in a divide expressed along lines of Islamism and anti-Islamism. This conflict played out across North Africa, especially in Egypt, Libya and Tunisia, and then erupted to the forefront of regional politics with the 2017 boycott of Qatar. The intensity of this ideological conflict waned in 2021, with the ending of the Qatar blockade and a rapprochement between Turkey and the UAE, but the conditions for its rapid rekindling remained.

Saudi Arabia represents something of a special case for the interaction of domestic and international dynamics.[12] While it did not face profound regime security threats from external forces, the hotly contested rise to power of Crown Prince Mohammed bin Salman had profound and direct implications for regional order. Mohammed bin Salman had a distinctively reckless and aggressive policy style, which delighted in overturning regional and international norms and practices. While these initiatives were intended to build support at home, they consistently failed to accomplish their goals, generating chaos but rarely solving problems. Moves such as the murder of Jamal Khashoggi, the temporary detention of Lebanese prime minister Saad Hariri, the intervention in Yemen, and the blockade of Qatar generated growing doubts about Mohammed bin Salman and about Saudi Arabia's reliability as an ally. The interaction effects between erratic Saudi foreign policy moves and the domestic political turbulence generated considerable turbulence in the already unsettled regional environment.

This regional landscape placed Iran within a distinctive combination of both increased power and increased threat. The fragmentation of states and distribution of insurgencies allowed Iran to expand and build its infrastructure of proxies and allies. The sectarianisation of these conflicts justified and facilitated Iran's mobilisation of Shi'a communities and networks into powerful militias. The IRGC took on a leading role in Iran's regional policies. The rise of the Islamic State in Iraq led to the activation of the Hashd (the Popular Mobilisation Units) building on pre-existing Shi'a militias and political parties to create an institutionalised network of powerful militias as the heart of the Iraqi state. The IRGC, Hezbollah and a range of Shi'a militias became key military actors in the survival of the Assad regime in Syria. Where the Houthi movement in Yemen had always kept Iran at arm's length, the exigencies of the war pushed it ever closer to Tehran.

As Iran's regional power grew, though, so too did the threats it faced. Initially, its response had been to enter into negotiations over its nuclear programme, culminating in the JCPOA. This agreement had begun to build a process of Iran's reintegration into the international community, relieving sanctions while restraining its nuclear programme. Continuing regional competition from Syria to Yemen had largely emptied these very real material accomplishments (sanctions relief and the dismantlement of the nuclear programme) of their social purpose, however. Even the direct and highly significant cooperation by Iran's Shi'ite proxies with the US in the campaign against the Islamic State in Iraq did little to change the broader regional dynamic. The JCPOA redefined the regional competition but did not hearken significant moves towards establishing Iran's place within the regional order. The Trump administration's abrogation of the JCPOA in 2018 and its campaign of maximum pressure, along with barely veiled regime change aspirations, created dramatic new threats to Iran's external and internal security. This combination of greater regional power than ever before with greater externally driven insecurity than ever before empowered hardliners within the Iranian regime and encouraged more provocative regional policies. This made the consolidation of regional order less likely, and the escalation of indirect and direct conflict across multiple theatres more likely.

Proxy Warfare

How did these structural trends at the global and regional levels manifest in the specific proxy wars of the post-2011 period? In general, the direct and indirect interventionism by the regional powers tended to exacerbate the conflicts, extend their duration, increase their human and material costs, and intensify polarisation. In each of the major cases, external intervention contributed to the fragmentation of states and the undermining of regional order. It is difficult to exaggerate the human cost paid for the regional proxy wars in the post-2011 period by Syrians, Yemenis, Libyans or even Egyptians following the coup: millions of people killed, many times that internally displaced or driven into exile, physical infrastructure devastated, identities polarised, an entire generation deprived of education, safety and community. The gap between human security and regime conceptions of security has rarely been more glaringly clear than in these regional proxy wars.

These negative effects took distinctive forms in each of the major cases, of course. In Libya, for instance, the intervention to overthrow Qaddafi was fought in such a way that it left behind a configuration of power in which externally supported militias overshadowed the capabilities of the central state.[13] Qatar, Turkey and the UAE each maintained a regular flow of financial and military support to their local proxies. The ongoing fragmentation and collapse of the Libyan state took on a new dimension with the campaign by General Khalifa Hiftar to militarily establish central control. Hiftar's move received the backing of Egypt and the UAE, which was met by support from Qatar and Turkey to the competing coalition. Proxy warfare in Libya, then, sustained the civil war and blocked the consolidation of the state.

In Yemen, the 2015 Saudi–UAE intervention followed upon the dramatic military moves by the Houthi movement, aligned with former president Ali Abdullah Saleh, to capture the capital Sana'a and overthrow the GCC-backed President Hadi.[14] The Houthi move was largely generated by internal dynamics, set in motion by the impending release of a UN-brokered constitutional plan which would have threatened their local power. The direct Saudi–UAE intervention, supported by a diverse Arab coalition, transformed the war in fundamental ways. In the south, the UAE established a base for the ousted government, while setting about to methodically carve out a potentially permanent set of bases and control. In the north, the Saudi-led bombing campaign largely failed to significantly impede Houthi control but did push the

Houthis into ever-closer dependence on Iran for weapons and support and invited ever-escalating Houthi attacks on Saudi Arabia itself. The divergence between Saudi and UAE goals in Yemen led to inconsistent strategies within the same putative alliance, which prolonged the war even further; the UAE eventually ended its participation in the war even as Saudi Arabia struggled to find some exit from its quagmire. As the war continued to grind on, the Houthis increasingly internationalised the conflict with drone and missile strikes aimed at Saudi Arabia and the UAE, showing their ability to impose real and potential costs on adversaries which had for years bombed and blockaded them with impunity.

In Syria, by contrast, years of proxy warfare which utterly devastated the country ultimately wound down with the pyrrhic victory for the Assad regime. The insurgency against Assad had been fundamentally compromised by the internal struggles among its primary external backers. Saudi Arabia, Qatar and Turkey each sought to promote their own allies within the Syrian opposition leadership and on the ground. The problems were compounded by the role of private supporters, especially Islamist ones across the Gulf, who funnelled huge amounts of money to like-minded groups on the ground. The US spent much of the post-2011 period covertly backing the Syrian opposition, but also struggling to coordinate the efforts of its allies. Efforts to control the flow of sophisticated weaponry and to limit external support to more moderate fighting groups consumed American policy, putting it at odds with its allies and with groups on the ground. Assad and his external backers, for their part, proved willing to inflict a literally unlimited amount of damage on the Syrian people in order to ensure his hold on power at any cost.

One of the key implications of the competitive nature of these processes is that the destructive outcomes have little to do with any single choice or strategy employed by any single actor. Obama choosing not to intervene in Syria in 2013 is often presented as the cause for many of the negative trends in the region, but this is largely untrue. Earlier US intervention would simply have attracted an earlier Russian countermove, escalating the conflict sooner but not fundamentally changing the outcome. More Saudi intervention in Yemen would simply have increased the Iranian countermoves; more Emirati intervention in Libya would simply have accelerated Qatari or Turkish countermoves. The logic of competitive interventions means that once embarked upon, these wars were inevitably going to descend into precisely the interminable, highly destructive quagmires which they have become.

Conclusion

Obama, Trump and Biden have all struggled with the alliance politics of the post-uprisings era. This is unlikely to change because the transformations unleashed by the Arab uprisings are fundamental. Profound changes at the global, regional and domestic levels have created a new regional structure which is not amenable to the restoration of an American-led unipolar system. The Biden administration hoped to restore the pre-Trump status quo under American leadership but found this a high hurdle to clear.

While such an end to American-led unipolarity may be mourned – or, more likely, denied – in Washington, it is not necessarily a bad thing for the region as a whole. The US-led order has been persistently wracked by turbulence across the region and entrenched autocracy domestically. Since the US established its unipolar order in 1991, it has been at war with or in Iraq virtually continuously; Israel has fought multiple wars with Palestinians and Hezbollah, while getting no closer to a two-state solution or an enduring peace; jihadist movements such as al-Qaida and the Islamic State have proliferated and evolved; and multiple states, including Syria, Yemen and Libya, have collapsed into protracted civil war. The US-led regional order depended on alliances with autocratic regimes, which in turn enabled and entrenched the patterns of authoritarianism, repression and corruption which gave fuel to the Arab uprisings. In short, the American-led order has not been particularly stable and has not produced positive outcomes for Arab citizens.

The chaos and turbulence which has afflicted the region since 2011 is often portrayed as the cost of American retrenchment, with the implication being that restoring US leadership would be better for the region. But this too seems misguided. The vast majority of the violence and repression following 2011 came at the hands of regimes allied with the US which were desperate to either prevent democratic changes or to exploit state breakdowns. The transition from a unipolar to a multipolar order, like any international power transition, generates profound uncertainty and risk. But since those changes are structurally driven, rather than based in the agency of any American (or other) political actor, the imperative is to find better ways to adapt and to facilitate the emergence of a new regional order.

The US will not be the primary driver of whatever regional order emerges from this period of contention. Regional powers will need to find some equilibrium which allows for de-escalation and the consolidation of some order which reduces their perception of threat. This will only happen when those powers perceive the costs of their interventionism as too high to sustain and believe that their rivals have arrived at a similar calculus. Even the most destructive proxy wars of the post-2011 period had relative limited impact on the intervening powers themselves, which allowed them to continue their policies at what seemed to be low cost. The dangerous escalation of attacks on shipping in the Gulf in the summer of 2019, by contrast, may have demonstrated to Iran and the Arab Gulf states that the escalatory spiral could risk imposing too high costs. Such a mutual recognition could presumably shift the logic of the new regional politics from escalation to de-escalation. But even such a shift is unlikely to allow the states of the region to overcome the logic of regional competition under uncertainty – especially with the prospects of renewed popular mobilisation against autocratic rule and economic failure looming.

Notes

1 Marc Lynch, 'The New Arab Order', *Foreign Affairs* 97, no. 5 (October 2018); Marc Lynch, *The New Arab Wars: Uprisings and Anarchy in the Middle East* (New York: Public Affairs, 2016).

2 Marc Lynch and Curtis Ryan, 'The Arab Uprisings as International Relations', *PS: Political Science and Politics* 50, no. 3 (2017): 643–6.

3 Paul Salem, 'Working Toward a Stable Regional Order', *Annals of the American Academy of Political and Social Sciences* 668 (2016): 36–52.

4 Stacie Goddard and Daniel Nexon, 'The Dynamics of Global Power Politics: A Framework for Analysis', *Journal of Global Security Studies* 1, no. 1 (2016): 4–18.

5 For the classic discussion of these dynamics, see Robert Jervis, *Perception and Misperception in International Politics* (Princeton: Princeton University Press, 1976).

6 On the theoretical implications of unipolarity, see Steven Walt, 'Alliances in a Unipolar World', *World Politics* 61, no. 1 (2009): 86–120; G. John Ikenberry, ed., *America Unrivaled: The Future of the Balance of Power* (Ithaca: Cornell University Press, 2001); William Wohlforth, 'The Stability of a Unipolar World', *International Security* 24, no. 1 (1999): 5–41; Ethan Kapstein and Michael Mastanduno, eds, *Unipolar Politics: Realism and State Strategies After the Cold War* (New York: Columbia University Press, 1999); Robert Jervis, 'Unipolarity: A Structural Perspective', *World Politics* 61, no. 1 (2009): 188–213.

7 Dmitri Trenin, *What is Russia Up To in the Middle East?* (Cambridge: Polity Press, 2018); Aron Lund, 'From Cold War to Civil War: 75 Years of Russian–Syrian Relations', Swedish Institute of International Affairs, July 2019; Marlene

Laurelle, ed., 'Russia's Policy in Syria and the Middle East', Central Asia Program and Project on Middle East Political Science, January 2019.

8   David A. Lake, 'Regional Hierarchy: Authority and Local International Order', *Review of International Studies* 35 (2009): 35–58.

9   F. Gregory Gause III, 'Beyond Sectarianism: The New Middle East Cold War', Brookings Doha Center Analysis Paper, 22 July 2014; Bülent Aras and Emirhan Yorulmalzlar, 'Mideast Geopolitics: The Struggle for a New Order', *Middle East Policy* 24, no. 2 (2015): 57–69.

10 Bassel Salloukh, 'Overlapping Contests and Middle East International Relations: The Return of the Weak Arab State', *PS: Political Science and Politics* 50, no. 3 (2017): 660–3.

11 Christopher Phillips, *The Battle for Syria: International Rivalry in the New Middle East* (New Haven, CT: Yale University Press, 2018).

12 Kristian Ulrichsen, ed., *The Changing Security Dynamics of the Persian Gulf* (Oxford: Oxford University Press, 2018); Madawi Al-Rasheed, ed., *Salman's Legacy: The Dilemmas of a New Era in Saudi Arabia* (Oxford: Oxford University Press, 2018).

13 Frederic Wehrey, *The Burning Shores: Inside the Battle for the New Libya* (New York: Farrar, Straus and Giroux, 2018); Jalal Harchaoui and Mohamed-Essaïd Lazib, 'Proxy War Dynamics in Libya', PWP Conflict Studies, 2019.

14 Adam Baron, 'Foreign and Domestic Influences in the War in Yemen', PWP Conflict Studies, 2019.

2

BETWEEN TRAGEDY AND CHAOS: US POLICY IN A TURBULENT MIDDLE EAST UNDER OBAMA AND TRUMP

Waleed Hazbun

On 10 January 2019, US Secretary of State Michael Pompeo delivered a speech at the American University in Cairo (AUC) rebutting President Barack Obama's 2009 'A New Beginning' address. Speaking at Egypt's public Cairo University while addressing the broader Muslim world, Obama sought to turn a page in US–Middle East relations after George W. Bush's destructive, over militarised interventionist post-9/11 policies. In contrast, Pompeo boldly declared that 'the United States under President Trump has reasserted its traditional role as a force for good in this region.'[1] He outlined the recommitment of US support for its 'traditional' allies, including Egypt under the increasingly authoritarian President Abdel Fattah al-Sisi, Israel and the Arab Gulf states. Pompeo identified the regional menaces the US sought to confront, including Iran, Syria, Hezbollah and 'radical Islamist terrorism'. In seeking to justify continuing US force projection in the region, Pompeo noted: 'For those who fret about the use of American power, remember this: America has always been, and always will be, a liberating force, not an occupying power.' Pompeo concluded his remarks by declaring that institutions such as the American University in Cairo and the one in Beirut, both founded by American Protestant missionaries in the nineteenth century, were 'symbols of America's innate goodness, of our hopes for you, and of the better future we desire for all nations of the Middle East'.

Unfortunately, Pompeo's simplistic and superficial view of these hybrid Arab-American institutions erases any suggestion of how they might serve as models for a more effective and less destructive US policy in the Middle East.

At their best, the cosmopolitan faculty and diverse students at these institutions strive to support multiple ways of doing things, such as creating knowledge and accommodating cultural and political difference.[2] Such norms, under threat from university administrators,[3] could suggest an alternative model for US policy in the Middle East. Rather than seeking to impose and sustain an US-dominated order, the US could work to repair the damage inflicted by past policies, help resolve regional conflicts, and build regional and global institutions that allow states and societies to mitigate the sources of insecurity they experience in an increasingly multipolar global system. Steering such a course, however, would require not only a redefinition of US interests in the region but, more critically, to sustain such a shift would require a reimagining of America's deeply rooted self-identity and understanding of the US's role in the world. Obama attempted to redefine what counted as an American 'vital interest' in the Middle East and tried to redirect US policy accordingly, but he failed to reshape how Americans and other US policymakers understood the US's relationship with the peoples and states of the Middle East. President Donald Trump, in contrast, largely used foreign policy for domestic purposes as a tool to redefine the US's global identity in terms of an aggressively nationalist, America First vision, which allowed regional conflicts and humanitarian crises to worsen and pose additional challenges to any future efforts to redirect the US's approach to the Middle East.

The Tragedies of US Policy in the Middle East

Any effort to reimagine US policy in the Middle East would need to confront what I refer to as the 'tragedy' of American interests in the Middle East. In his revisionist history of US foreign policy, William Appleman Williams argues that 'American diplomacy contained the fundamental elements of tragedy' as US policymaker pursued goals that contradicted each other and often through means that contradicted America's avowed ideals.[4] Many thoughtful US policymakers and observers of US foreign policy have recognised how the construction of American interests in the Middle East produces contradictory, often self-defeating policies that produce tragic outcomes.

John S. Badeau, a former AUC president who served as US ambassador to Egypt under President John F. Kennedy later wrote: 'How to define general American interest in the Arab world, yet allow for the reality of specific short-term interests, is a constant problem.'[5] In the 1950s and 1960s, Badeau and other US policymakers struggled to cultivate broad Arab support for closer ties with the US. Many American policymakers and scholars viewed the process of 'modernisation' as leading to Arab societies with interests more closely aligned with the US and called for the US to support modernisation efforts even in states the US did not have strong ties to.[6] At the same time, however, these Americans understood that modernisation could lead to the overthrowing of strongly anti-communist, conservative regimes that depended on Western states for their security. Badeau explained the dilemma:

> It can be argued . . . that the Western interest in stability and progress should result in a policy of supporting progressive – in some cases radical – move-ments throughout the Arab world, so that the West may be identified with the emerging future rather than the decaying past. Yet in some Arab coun-tries where particular American and Western interests are strong, the pas-sage from traditionalism to modernity may wreck the stability of the existing order in which American interest is set.[7]

Eventually, the US abandoned its efforts to accommodate Arab nationalism and became, some would add tragically, closely tied to conservative, repressive regimes that at the time for many Arabs represented 'the decaying past'.

In the 1970s, peacemaking came to replace modernisation as a tool for resolving the contradictions of US interests. William Quandt outlines the com-monly accepted parameters of US policy during the Cold War: 'Managing the relationship with the Soviet Union in the Middle East, access to inexpensive oil, and support for Israel.'[8] These interests, however, often suggested contra-dictory policies, as closer ties to an Arab state might be useful to contain Soviet influence or protect oil flows but created tensions with Israel (and its sup-porters in the US). Quandt, who previously served on the National Security Council, explains that US policymakers understood that 'a way to resolve the potential conflict among American interests in the Middle East . . . was by promoting the Arab–Israeli peace process', allowing the US to cultivate Arab allies without creating tensions with Israel.[9]

With the end of the Cold War, the US no longer needed to pursue the containment of the Soviet Union, but its geopolitical dominance in an era of 'unipolarity' allowed it to outline and pursue ambitious goals. The US sought to resolve the remaining contradictions in American interests in the Middle East through, on the one hand, promoting Arab–Israel peace and, on the other hand, projecting military power throughout the Persian Gulf to contain the regional influence of the so-called 'rogue states' Iran and Iraq. US reliance on the unilateral use of force and the backing of authoritarian regimes, however, contradicted the broader US strategy of building a multilateral, rules-based liberal international order. Thomas Wright observes 'the Middle East is an exception in the U.S.-led liberal order' as 'there was nothing liberal about the U.S.-led regional order in the Middle East.'[10]

The contradiction between US claims to support democracy globally and its long-standing backing of repressive, authoritarian regimes in the Middle East was recognised in US policy debates following the 9/11 attacks and in the wake of the disastrous US invasion of Iraq. In her 2005 address to AUC, Secretary of State Condoleezza Rice declared:

> For 60 years, my country, the United States, pursued stability at the expense of democracy . . . here in the Middle East – and we achieved neither. Now, we are taking a different course. We are supporting the democratic aspirations of all people.[11]

The administration of President George W. Bush, however, failed to recognise the contradiction of promoting democratisation through regime change wars. It also refused to recognise the legitimacy of elections in Egypt, Palestine and Lebanon in which parties opposed to US regional policy gained strength.

Obama's 2009 'A New Beginning' speech in Cairo was an effort to begin to address these and other contradictions. In contrast, Pompeo's Cairo speech declared that the US 'is a force for good' in the Middle East with little sense of the contractions the US must navigate. Pompeo argued that under Obama, 'We learned that when America retreats chaos often follows.' Such a statement relies on an exaggerated sense of American leverage and capacity to impose political order on the region. In the wake of the 2003 US-led invasion of Iraq, the American ability to shape the behaviour of diverse, highly mobilised actors and determine political outcomes in the Middle East shrank. Moreover, Pompeo failed to consider how the US might have helped produce through its interventions the very 'chaos' he blames on Obama's supposed retreat. Instead, the Trump administration redefined its own contribution to regional chaos as progress, seemingly dissolving the contradictions and dilemmas faced by past administrations. Worse, it sought to erase any awareness of the contradictions of American interests and how their simultaneous pursuit risks tragedy.

To reframe our understanding of the challenges of US policy in the region, I suggest that the post-Arab uprisings 'chaos' in the region should be viewed not as a resurgence of regional forces exploiting the retreat of the US, but rather as a reflection of the structural transformation of Middle East geo-politics over the past two decades marking the decline of the 'American era' in the Middle East. This transformation was not a consequence of any so-called 'power vacuum'. Neither can we explain it as driven by Iran's alleged quest for regional domination, sectarian differences, or even the rise of reckless leader-ship in Saudi Arabia or the US. Rather, I argue the current geopolitical 'dis-order' is a product of the contradictions of US policy. It is rooted in repeated US efforts to attempt to order the region through coercive force with little concern for the interests and security of the peoples of the region.

With regional Middle East states lacking a shared understanding of threats, US post-9/11 interventions failed to establish a stable regional security archi-tecture. On the contrary, these policies generated intense insecurity for both rival and allied states – as well as within their societies – while facilitating the proliferation of armed non-state actors and weapons flows. As the regional system became more complex and multipolar, continued US reliance on coer-cion rather than accommodation and compromise only intensified the forces of regional instability that the US is unable to control.

With the decline of US leverage in the Middle East, Obama came to recog-nise the contradictions of US interests in the region and struggled to navigate a path between them. By the end of his second term, Obama often expressed a tragic understanding of politics in which any order is fragile, efforts to control geopolitical dynamics fraught with risk, and even wise leaders are forced to choose between bad options in their effort to avoid the worst outcomes.[12] In almost all of his policy moves, his efforts were frustrated. Obama embraced the emerging democratic and Islamist forces during the Arab uprisings, but they failed to consolidate power and faced a harsh backlash. Obama's attempt to establish a higher threshold for US intervention led to inconsistent policies that failed to prevent political fragmentation and humanitarian disasters in Libya, Syria and Yemen. His effort to restart the Arab–Israeli peace process, faced strident Israeli opposition, while even his successful negotiation of a nuclear deal with Iran helped launch the destructive regional policies of Saudi Arabia.

In each case, US initiatives faced both domestic and regional opposition while the US lacked the leverage to shape the course of events. The resulting disorder facilitated the emergence of Trump's America First approach to US foreign policy. Trump abandoned any efforts to address the multiple contrac-tions of US interests and forged what we might term a more 'melodramatic' approach to foreign policy defined by moral dichotomies between good and evil. Viewing regional politics in this melodramatic way, devoid of contradictions (and blind to potential tragedies), enabled Trump to take a definitive side in regional conflicts that wilfully drove the region further into the abyss of conflict and chaos. Alternative policy options would require not only that US policymakers and the public recognise the tragic contradictions of US interests but also take responsibility for the consequences and commit to defining a new approach to the Middle East devoid of the enduring contradictions of US policy.

Regional Turbulence and the Decline of the 'American Era'

At the heart of the current geopolitical challenges the US faces in the Middle East is the widespread insecurity experienced by regimes and societies. While most of the ongoing fighting is conducted by regional states and sub-state militias, the dynamics of the geopolitical system must be viewed, to a large degree, as a product of repeated American deployments of military force and its failure to engage in the necessary accommodations to promote balancing between regional rivalries.

In the early 1990s, US policymakers boasted a bold vision for building a regional security architecture based on progress towards Arab–Israeli peace, the containment of Iran and Iraq, and economic and military support for US-allied regimes making, at times, hesitant steps towards political and economic liberalisation.[13] Even before the collapse of this strategy around 2000, countercurrents to it emerged due to the continuing US military presence in the Persian Gulf, declining support for the coercive containment of Iraq and Iran, failed peacemaking efforts, and as a consequence of disruptive neoliberal economic policies.[14]

The Middle East system was most radically impacted by the 2003 US-led invasion of Iraq, the US's strategy of regional transformation and, more broadly, its global war on terror. The collapse of the Iraqi state and the rise of a domestic insurgency that mobilised transnational jihadists – along with a massive US military presence and its disregard for international law and norms – generated heightened insecurity among US rivals, including Iran and Syria. Normative restraints on the aggressive behaviour of regional states were also diminished. Iran and other US rivals sought to challenge American power by supporting armed militias and insurgent networks and by acquiring new military capabilities through local manufacturing and imports.

By the early 2010s, the long-standing American vision for a US-dominated post-Cold War regional security architecture in the Middle East was clearly in disarray. Amid this turmoil, the 'American era' in the region came to an end.[15] Middle East states no longer mostly looked to the US to provide regional security or order. In this new context, Iran, Qatar, Turkey, UAE and Saudi Arabia have all sought, to different degrees, to project power beyond their proximate neighbours and reshape the regional system to meet their own interests.[16] They deployed military force and armed non-state militias, enabling the rapid militarisation of several uprisings and the outbreak of multiple civil wars leading to the fragmentation of territorial control in Iraq, Syria, Libya and Yemen. In this process, the immediate security and regional interests of several US-allied states began to take priority over US regional policy preferences. While the US refused to constrain the behaviour of Qatar and Turkey, as well as its Saudi and Emirati allies, the US was also unable to contain Iran's expanding influence. The efforts of these states to project coercive power directly and indirectly at the regional level led to a new level of destructive civil wars, weapons proliferation, state fragmentation and ongoing humanitarian crises. Meanwhile, the emergence of multipolarity at the global level – with Russia, and to a lesser degree China, seeking to gain leverage in the Middle East – together with the rise of multiple regional powers with rival goals, meant that the Middle East was no longer either a unipolar system organised around US dominance or a bipolar system defined by Saudi–Iranian rivalry.

To understand the decline of US leverage in the region, I suggest we view the Middle East regional system in terms of a model of turbulence. By turbulence I mean a system with a proliferation of heterogenous actors below and above the state level with expanded capabilities that disrupt and complicate the dynamics of regional politics. States remain the most powerful actors, but the definition of their interests and the capacity of their actions to achieve desired goals is diminished as these states must negotiate a multidimensional geography of rival forces and actors within the context of increasingly multipolar global politics.

The inefficiency of balancing, breakdown of regulatory norms and increased capacities for self-organisation by armed non-state actors all helped sustain the regional environment of turbulence in the Middle East. The result has been a regional system in which the interests of states, including that of the US, are often hard to discern and shift in complex ways. This regional environment fostered the emergence of ISIS and complicated regional politics as states have to navigate a hyper-polar environment that gives greater leverage to smaller actors and makes the alignment of interests between states more contingent and fragile. As a result, regardless of the degree of US intervention, US policymakers are forced to operate with limited political leverage and capacity to achieve strategic goals. Not only does this turbulence frustrate efforts to increase US intervention through diplomacy and military force, but it also poses challenges to strategies that seek to reduce direct US involvement in the region. Regional turbulence makes navigating the contradictions of US interests more challenging as it makes the consequences and risks more dangerous.

The Tragedy of the Obama Doctrine

What is striking about American diplomacy under President Obama, especially in contrast to the administrations preceding and following his, is that Obama recognised the challenge of navigating the contradictions of US interests in the Middle East. Obama also understood the US's responsibility for fostering the turbulence engulfing the region that exacerbated those challenges. In 2002, as an Illinois state senator considering a run for the Senate, Obama spoke out against a US invasion of Iraq:

> I know that an invasion of Iraq without a clear rationale and without strong international support will only fan the flames of the Middle East, and encourage the worst, rather than best, impulses of the Arab world, and strengthen the recruitment arm of al-Qaida. I am not opposed to all wars. I'm opposed to dumb wars.[17]

In the same speech Obama also questioned the US's relationship with its traditional allies, declaring:

> Let's fight to make sure our so-called allies in the Middle East, the Saudis and the Egyptians, stop oppressing their own people, and suppressing dissent, and tolerating corruption and inequality, and mismanaging their economies.[18]

As Marc Lynch observes, 'Obama came to office with a conviction that reducing the United States' massive military and political investment in the Middle East was a vital national security interest in its own right.'[19] Within a broader strategy seeking to 'pivot to Asia', Obama sought to drawdown the massive US military footprint in the Middle East and encourage regional states to take greater responsibility for managing regional security.

As reflected in his 2009 'A New Beginning' speech at Cairo University, Obama did not redefine US regional goals or security commitments, but outlined a desire to pursue US interests through a renewed effort at diplomatic engagement and a search for mutual interests.[20] For a brief while in the spring of 2011, witnessing the aspirations for internally driven political change in the Arab world, Obama might have glimpsed the possibilities of an unravelling of some of the contractions within American Middle East interests. In responding to the uprising in Egypt, Obama and some of his younger advisors sought to craft a policy that was supportive of change and sympathetic to the protestors while most senior cabinet-level members of the National Security Council were hesitant.[21] Once the Egyptian president Hosni Mubarak had stepped aside, Obama could more actively express support for change, even as he faced pushback from other US allies such as the Arab leaders in the Gulf.

In his 19 May 2011 speech 'A Moment of Opportunity', Obama attempted to craft a new narrative of American relations with the Arab world. He referred to the ongoing events as a 'story of self-determination' that would 'mark a new chapter in American diplomacy'.[22] Obama claimed that the US would now 'have a chance to pursue the world as it should be'. Obama, however, defended the US posture in the region by restating American 'core interests' that included 'countering terrorism and stopping the spread of nuclear weapons; securing the free flow of commerce and safe-guarding the security of the region; standing up for Israel's security and pursuing Arab–Israeli peace'.[23] These interests, however, continued to pose contradictions for US policy. In a 7 November 2011 speech to the National Democratic Institute (NDI), US Secretary of State Hillary Clinton reiterated US support for democratic change in the Arab world and noted the closest US allies globally are democracies, but also sought to respond to criticism of continuing US support for authoritarian regimes in the Arab world and the dilemmas posed by elections that bring to power foes of US policy.[24] Echoing the concerns of Badeau from decades before, she declared that 'the risks posed by transitions will not keep us from pursuing positive change', but noted US support for change is decided on a case by case basis shaped by US interests, including 'defense of our allies, and a secure supply of energy'. She recognised that 'there will be times when not all of our interests align.' She considered these contradictions 'just reality' and assured her audience that 'as a country with many complex interests, we'll always have to walk and chew gum at the same time.'

Between these aspirations for change and the existing US commitments in the region, the Obama administration struggled to manage the challenge of accommodating the rise of the Muslim Brotherhood in Egypt and Tunisia along with the rising regional powers Qatar and Turkey, who sought to expand their influence by identifying with these new regimes viewed with hostility by other US regional allies. Obama reluctantly agreed to intervene in Libya in 2011, supported by the Gulf states, as part of an effort to foster the emergence of a new regional order. Instead, however, this effort only opened the door to state collapse, civil war and regional geopolitical conflict between rival visions of regional order. Then, as the efforts of Islamist parties in Egypt and Tunisia to establish stable political orders faltered, US commitments to democratic change eroded. Soon an authoritarian-conservative countermovement led by Saudi Arabia and the UAE, fearing both popular political mobilisation and the growth of Iran's regional influence, asserted its financial, diplomatic and military power, and came to displace the US as a force seeking to reshape regional order.

By the end of his first term, due to declining political leverage and the rise of new sources of instability in the region, Obama downsized US goals and expectations in the Middle East. In his extensive survey of Obama's foreign policy published in 2016 under the title of 'The Obama Doctrine', Jeffrey Goldberg remarks that Obama had 'grown steadily more fatalistic about the constraint on America's ability to direct global events'.[25] This recognition of the limits of US power reflects Obama's embrace of a tragic vision of US policy in the Middle East in which he feels his options are limited to bad choices. Obama's goal became to avoid the worst possible catastrophes. Goldberg notes Obama

> has also been eager to question some of the long-standing assumptions under-girding traditional U.S. foreign-policy thinking. To a remarkable degree, he is willing to question why America's enemies are its enemies, or why some of its friends are its friends.[26]

This questioning did not amount to a new regional strategy but rather reflected a rejection of what a former senior US diplomat referred to as the 'magical thinking' that animated much of US post-Cold War policy in the Middle East.[27] At the same time, however, these actions put the US at odds with its traditional allies, making the effort to reshape US goals and regional strategy more challenging and dangerous.

While the security of Israel and Saudi Arabia had long been central to US regional strategy, these states were becoming obstacles to Obama's policy initiatives to contain Iran, promote an end to the Israeli–Palestinian conflict, and limit the fallout of regional civil wars. Meanwhile, both US allies and rivals in the region came to feel more insecure. Increased rivalry and conflict between regional states led to interventions, the militarisation of several uprisings, and deployments of military force resulting in what Marc Lynch terms the 'new Arab wars'.[28] In the process, Obama sought to redefine the US's relationship with the Middle East, suggesting that while terrorism and Iran's regional role were strategic challenges, the US did not otherwise face pressing strategic security threats that required the large-scale projection of military force in the region.[29] This recognition allowed Obama to begin to reconsider to what degree the US needed to risk being committed to contradictory interests.

In the past, the US defined its core regional goals to include an end to the Arab–Israeli conflict and the rollback of Iranian regional influence. During the course of Obama's presidency, it became increasingly clear the US did not have the capacity to fully achieve either goal. Early in his administration, with a limited Israeli freeze on settlement activity, Obama attempted to relaunch Israeli–Palestinian peace talks. He soon faced stiff resistance and unilateral actions from Israeli prime minister Benjamin Netanyahu and his right-wing government. The Palestinians continued to face harsher economic conditions, military assaults, policing of their territory and Israeli settlement building. Obama was more successful in his second term, following the use of expanded economic sanctions, in opening talks with Iran and working with the P5+1 to craft an agreement on limiting Iranian progress towards a nuclear weapons programme. Obama's effort to replace US–Iran confrontation with limited cooperation was met with strong opposition from Arab Gulf allies and Israel. While US–Israeli strategic ties remained strong, it was less clear to Obama how Israel was serving to advance other US regional interests. Israeli military dominance, US domestic energy sources and the Iran nuclear deal made the US – under Obama at least – more willing to live with its failure to achieve its long-standing strategic goals of Arab–Israeli peace and the rollback of Iranian regional influence. At the same time, any broader hopes or concern for political reform and democratisation were taken off the table.

Within this context, Obama sought new ways to unwind the contractions of American interests by adjusting how US interests and threats were understood and addressed. These efforts, however, traded one set of tragic consequences for another.

In the case of Syria, Obama redefined and narrowed US interests while recognising the limits of US capacity to determine outcomes. Having already called for Assad to step down in 2011 when many thought the regime would fall, Obama would offer only limited support to the armed opposition. He publicly suggested that US vital interests in Syria were mostly limited to concern about Syrian use of banned weapons, but in 2013 when the Syrian regime seemed to cross a 'red line', deploying chemical weapons against civilians, Obama chose to work with Russia to implement the destruction of Syria's chemical weapon stockpiles rather than engage in punitive airstrikes. Obama's hesitancy was shaped by the experience in Libya and the broader structural dynamics of the Syrian conflict. He argued: 'The notion that we could have – in a clean way that didn't commit U.S. military forces – changed the equation on the ground there was never true.'[30] In limiting US concerns to the proliferation of banned weapons, he dashed the hopes of those who sought to use the conflict as a means to tip the regional geopolitical balance against Syria's ally Iran. Obama's refusal to engage US forces more directly against the Syrian regime, or in support of the opposition, frustrated policymakers inside and outside the administration as well as regional US allies who felt the US had the capacity to topple the regime, end the war and advance the rollback of Iranian regional influence.

At the same time, however, Obama was unwilling to seek a negotiated settlement that might have ended the conflict but require the rehabilitation of Assad and recognition of Russian and Iranian influence. Instead, the US worked with its regional allies to facilitate the militarisation of the opposition and according to many 'bears real responsibility for the humanitarian tragedy' in Syria and the rise of ISIS.[31] While Obama could keep the US out of direct military conflict against Syria by declaring that US vital interests were not at stake in the Syrian civil war, many Americans came to view the Syrian conflict as a product of sectarian divisions the US was unable to resolve and in terms of the securitisation of the refugee flows and the rise of ISIS. These effects would later allow Trump to implement a 'Muslim ban', supported by the anti-immigrant xenophobia of his support base but justified in the face of legal challenges as serving a national security interest.

Obama's most potentially transformative policy was boldly opening negotiations with Iran and establishing a multilateral agreement to limit and monitor Iran's nuclear programme. For Obama, the agreement addressed an issue, nuclear proliferation, that rose to the level of US vital interests and avoided expanding US military engagements in the region. But like his Syria policy, carefully navigating a path between the contradictions of US interests, Obama failed to escape tragic consequences. In pursuing an agreement with Iran limited to the nuclear programme while calling on regional allies to take more responsibility for their own security, Obama enabled the unleashing of a militarised Saudi and Emirati counter-revolution. The Saudi-led efforts to suppress the Islamist and democratic forces behind the uprisings and to impose a Saudi vision for a new regional order have been destabilising. Saudi distrust of Washington's role in the region spiked when in 2011 Obama acquiesced to the fall of Mubarak. From that point Saudi and US approaches to regional politics diverged. Not only did Riyadh seek to derail the democracy-oriented struggles of the Arab uprisings, it also reversed any democratic gains they could have made by crushing the protests in Bahrain, managing an elite transition in Yemen, and supporting the 2013 coup in Egypt against the democratically elected President Mohamed Morsi. At the same time, Saudi Arabia struggled to maintain its regional influence in the face of expanding Iranian power and the rising influence of Turkey and Qatar.

Obama inadvertently encouraged these Saudi policies as the P5+1 pursued a nuclear deal with Iran in the face of strong Saudi and Israeli opposition. Saudi Arabia and the UAE opposed any accommodation with Iran and prevented regional discussions that might have helped stabilise the regional order. Having long been sheltered under the US security umbrella, the UAE and Saudi Arabia committed their resources, enabled by strategic ties with the US, to develop and deploy military power at the regional level. Most tragically, the Obama administration played a critical role in enabling the Saudi-led campaign in Yemen launched in 2015 and offering massive arms packages to Saudi Arabia and the UAE, even as many US officials believed the US had little interest in the conflict other than showing support to Gulf allies in the wake of differences over the Iran nuclear deal.

The least visible but most tragic and long-lasting outcome of Obama's effort to negotiate a path through the contraction of US interests is Obama's shift towards a 'light footprint' military posture. As Andrew Bacevich notes: 'While his administration jettisoned the phrase "Global War on Terror" upon taking office, the war itself continued and has even expanded.'[32] Obama clearly wanted to shift the US away from the large, land-based military forces that drove the 2003 invasion and occupation, but nevertheless still sought means to project coercive power in pursuit of remaining regional goals. While US goals were now narrower, focusing particularly on what were viewed as extremist and terrorist groups such as ISIS, Obama effectively expanded the scope and intensity of US military deployments in less visible and less politically accountable ways.

The transformation of the US military force posture and tactics was already underway during the Bush administration. The development of new organisational structures in the US military evolved from the ground up as a consequence of US forces fighting on the frontlines of the so-called 'war on terror' in Afghanistan and Iraq. In the process, the Joint Special Operations Command (or JSOC) became an organisational hub for US commands and agencies that developed new networked forms of military operations.[33] These include the use of small units of elite special forces, reliance on high tech operations using drones, electronic tracking, cyber war, and closer military-to-military cooperation with often US-trained or backed militias and special units within the militaries of the region. This evolving form of networked warfare mirrors the networked forms of self-organised militias and fighters that have come to control large areas of Syria, Iraq, Yemen and Libya.

As a result, many US forces came to operate within a largely autonomous command structure while engaging in a shadow war of targeted killing that Steve Niva notes 'resembles a global and possibly permanent policing operation in which targeted operations are used to manage populations and threats in lieu of addressing the social and political problems that produce the threats in the first place'.[34] Bacevich also observes that Obama's approach to war has had the effect of

> desensitizing the American public to war's perpetuation. Reducing US casualties and moderating financial costs, as Obama has done, drains war itself of domestic political significance. That US forces are more or less permanently engaged in active combat on the far side of the planet has become one of those things that Americans today simply accept, like persistent budget deficits or periodic mass shootings.[35]

Using these tools, the continuing post-uprisings deployment of US military power in Iraq, Syria, Yemen and elsewhere accommodated the decline of US popular support for American wars in the Middle East and uncertainty about core strategic interests but also risked sustaining a form of perpetual warfare with limited political accountability.

Overall, the deep tragedy of Obama's approach to US policy in the Middle East was a certain awareness of the remaining contradictions of US interests. While George W. Bush often pursued policies such as a 'forward strategy of freedom' and 'democracy promotion' that only made sense within an ideological worldview defined in large measure by a reaction to the 9/11 attacks, Obama sought to strip US strategy of that ideological faith and came to define a more limited set of vital interests. This more realist approach often reflected an awareness of the structural conditions the US faced in the Middle East, recognising the limits of each policy move, but that awareness facilitated a complacency with tragedy. While Americans, for a range of different reasons, felt disappointed by US policy in the Middle East under his administration, Obama and his closest advisors remained secure in their view that there were no better options given the structural logic of the region's politics and domestic political considerations.[36]

Trump and the Melodramatic

For all the heightened rhetoric and Obama bashing, there were some 'surprising continuities' in US policy towards the Middle East under Donald Trump.[37] The continuities, sometimes contradicted by Trump's speeches and tweets, were to a large degree a product of the regional turbulence that dampened US leverage as well as wider recognition of the declining nature of threats from the region to US interests.[38] While US forces remained deployed against ISIS, the US otherwise had limited ability to effectively pursue goals beyond Obama's modest one. Donald Trump's approach to US foreign policy shared some elements with Obama, especially in terms of limiting American security commitments abroad and seeking to accommodate the structure shift from unipolarity to multipolarity.[39] Trump, like Obama, agreed that the US invasion of Iraq was a mistake and said he wanted to bring US troops home and end 'endless wars'. Trump also echoed sentiments Obama had expressed about some US allies being 'free-riders' who should be forced to take over from the US the burdens of maintaining regional security. At the same time, however, Trump fixated on rejecting aspects of Obama's approach, most notably pulling out of the multilateral Iran nuclear deal and implementing a 'maximum pressure' strategy against Iran, while nevertheless seeking to avoid war. He also reversed US policy towards Saudi Arabia and Israel, unabashedly aligning very closely with the interests and policies of these states, allowing their interests to effectively define US policy.

A key to making sense of the contrast between the Obama and Trump approaches to the Middle East is not the definition of US interests, but Trump's abandonment of Obama's self-awareness of tragedy. Trump does not embrace a tragic vision of politics. Trump gave little heed to the structural conditions of regional politics in the Middle East and refused to recognise the forces that limit US options to a choice between various tragic outcomes. Obama was aware of these conditions and recognised the constraints they imposed, but his careful efforts to navigate through them did not resonate with public sentiment or the US policymaking community. In fact, Obama's second-term average approval rating on foreign affairs was 39 per cent, among the lowest since the Carter administration.[40] Obama, however, viewed this lack of approval as due, on the one hand, to his effort to challenge the 'Washington playbook' of the policy elite who overuse military force and, on the other hand, due to his failure to connect with the American public on foreign policy. He reflected: 'There is no doubt that there are times where I have not been attentive enough to feelings and emotions and politics in communicating what we're doing and how we're doing it.'[41]

While Obama notes 'feelings and emotions' in reference to communicating with the public, Trump defined much of his foreign policymaking in terms of feeling and emotions more than in terms of strategic interests. Trump aimed his policies and speeches to resonate with the affect of his populist-nationalist followers and used this framework to guide his policymaking. For example, Trump's securitisation of issues of trade, immigration and global institutions represented them not as threats to American interests abroad, but rather as threats to the identity and wellbeing of Americans domestically. He was sensitive to the fears of what Walter Russell Mead refers to as 'Jacksonian America', consisting of self-identified white Americans who feel they have not benefitted from the globalisation of the US economy and are fearful of its growing ethnic and cultural diversity.[42] He suggested that the 'threats' America faced could be addressed by building walls, banning travellers, maintaining a large military, pulling out of multilateral agreements, and restructuring transnational flows with tariffs and bilateral trade deals, or else targeting uncowed 'bad actors',[43] such as Iran, through coercive sanctions, military swagger and arms deals enabling allies (such as Saudi Arabia) to engage in regional wars.

Thus, where there was a major shift in US foreign policy between Obama and Trump was in Trump's abandonment of the tragic realist approach of Obama that recognised the downsides of all options and the limits of US capabilities. Trump did not try to navigate the contradictions of US interests; rather, he followed what might be called a melodramatic script, defined by stark moral dichotomies. As Elisabeth Anker notes: 'Melodrama is a genre form that tells stories about people besieged by overwhelming forces, deploying heightened emotions, moral binaries of good and evil, characterizations of people as villains, victims or heroes, and stories that end with the triumph of virtue.'[44]

In this reading, I follow the work of my University of Alabama colleague Daniel Levine who suggests that contemporary politics is increasingly experienced as melodrama rather than tragedy.[45] A shift in narrative frame from tragedy to melodrama is useful when analysing the shift from Obama to Trump. It also suggests a logic for Trump's approach to foreign affairs and his effort to further redefine the US's sense of itself and role in the region.

Most of Trump's speeches displayed strong, even vulgar, melodramatic expressions, tropes and narratives. When celebrating policies such as the assassination of Iranian general Qassem Soleimani in January 2020, the strategic rationale was often poorly articulated and drowned out by the melodramatic language saturated in references to 'evil' and 'monster' and 'ruthless'.[46] While Obama sought to routinise (outside of public view) American deployment of violence through drones, special operations and cyber attacks, Trump has not only expanded the use of these techniques, lifting the limited restraints Obama imposed, but treated such events as excuses for press conferences or celebratory tweets.

Many of Trump's foreign policies, such as banning Syrian and other refugees from entering the US, appealed to the fears of his support base rather than serving any strategic interest. The highly vetted Syrian asylum seekers were never shown to pose a security threat to the US. Trump also lavished praise and deadly weapons on repressive autocrats. He gave strong military support and diplomatic backing to Saudi Arabia, the UAE, Egypt and Israel, while launching a 'maximum pressure' strategy against Iran. Trump even weaponised COVID-19 by continuing brutal economic sanctions as Iran struggled to respond to the pandemic. This approach abandoned any concern for democratic reform, resolving Arab–Israeli conflict and preventing the worsening of humanitarian disasters. It only accelerated Saudi Arabia's attempts to expand its regional influence and develop closer strategic cooperation with Israel. Together, Saudi Arabia, the UAE and Israel seemed to offer the Trump administration an (illusory) vision for regional order organised around the containment of Iran. This approach included the absurd notion of resolving the Israeli–Palestinian conflict by coercing the weakened Palestinian Authority into accepting the Israeli-dominated territorial status quo as represented by the 2020 Trump peace plan. Trump's backing of Israeli annexations of Syrian and Palestinian territory also led to a total breakdown of efforts to resolve the Arab–Israeli conflict in the face of opposition from most regional Arab states and societies. At the same time, the growing regional influence of Iran and the military assertiveness of Hezbollah have led to more aggressive Israeli actions, including attacks on Hezbollah assets in Syria, drone activity over Lebanon and the suspected sabotage of Iran's nuclear programme. These actions risked the escalation of conflict. At the same time, they eroded the domestic foundations and transnational connections that would be needed to build a new vision for US foreign policy based on global interdependence and common security to address the ongoing crises and regional Middle East insecurity.

In the Path of Tragedy

In *Notes on a Foreign Country*, Suzy Hansen, an American living in Istanbul, tries to diagnose the anxiety and confusion felt by Americans living in an era when aspects of American exceptionalism and global hegemony are waning.[47] She draws on the writings of James Baldwin, penned while he was living in Paris watching the French deal with the 'loss' of Algeria and notes Baldwin suggested that 'Americans have no sense of "tragedy".'[48] Many scholars of international relations (IR), such as John Mearsheimer, argue that the tragic elements embedded in realist IR theory clash with the basic values of most Americans who wish to view the US as always a 'benevolent force in world politics'.[49] US foreign policy towards the Middle East has always been driven as much by American self-identity as different conceptions of strategic interest. During and after the Cold War, policymakers viewed US policies in the Middle East as critical to the US's role as a global hegemon providing public goods such as the flow of oil to the global economy, containing revisionist states that challenge global order and defeating violent non-state actors. This role was sustained by popular ideas of American exceptionalism and of the US as the 'indispensable nation' for protecting global security and the openness of the global economy. Many Americans also supported these policies as they assumed that access to Middle East oil was vital to their own economic wellbe-ing, identified with Israelis and their military prowess, and feared the threats posed by what the US government identified as terrorist organisations.

Obama's effort to redefine how Americans understood US interests in the Middle East failed in part because the tragic framework he embraced rec-ognised the limits of US capabilities. He understood that the US would never again be able to pursue such ambitious goals in the region. This view did not resonate with American self-identity, especially in the era of Trump. In her dis-cussion of the meaning of American identity in an era of US decline, Hansen writes:

> It is also perhaps the first time Americans are confronting a powerlessness
> that the rest of the world has always felt, not only within their own borders
> but as pawns in a larger international game. Globalization, it turns out, has
> not meant the Americanization of the world; it has made Americans, in some
> ways, more like everyone else.[50]

Trump's mobilisation of popular support for America First represented a response to this seeming powerlessness that sought to embrace an American self-identity defined by populist-nationalism viewed through a melodramatic lens.

In rejecting the tragic framework, Trump disrupted the progress Obama had made in seeking to rebalance the US's approach to the Middle East.[51] In the run up to the 2020 election, much of the mainstream debate about the future of US policy in the Middle East by those opposed to Trump, including those who would come to serve in the Biden administration, was framed in terms of the need to find a balance that involved rebuilding US diplomatic leverage while embracing more limited interests and goals.[52]

The risk of these efforts is in how they have sought to rewrite the tragic narrative of the US's experience in the Middle East and allow policymakers such as those in the Biden administration to avoid returning to address the contradictions of US policy that Obama began to struggle with. They often frame the US's invasion of Iraq as a war with tragic consequences, rather than as product of hubris. They warn of the risks of the US abandoning the Middle East. When surveying the state of political chaos and humanitarian disasters in the region, they view this story as an Arab tragedy, a product of a region rife with age-old conflicts rather than a product of a consistent pattern of US poli-cies before and after 9/11. These policymakers fail to understand struggles for agency and political change unleashed by the Arab uprisings. Sadly, the only other major perspective in US policy debates seems to be those who argue that the US should simply abandon the region, suggesting the US would bear no responsibly for or suffer no consequences from future conflicts and humanitarian disasters.

While Obama's Middle East policy came to recognise the limited US capacity for resolving regional conflicts, let alone instigating regime change and rolling back Iran's regional influence, the dynamics of regional turbulence only grew more chaotic afterwards. That is to say, tragedy will only become more difficult to avoid in the future. Nevertheless, US policymakers still frame US options in terms of equations that likely have no solutions, for example, 'reducing an outdated U.S. military footprint without creating fresh insecurity, while maintaining deterrence and influence where needed to address those key U.S. interests that remain'.[53]

Due to the existing structural forces and the nature of regional turbulence, such efforts risk producing yet more tragedies when the US pursues conflicting and unrealistic interests. The effort to envision an alternative US role in the Middle East requires refashioning the debate about the US's role in the world so Americans come to view the insecurities experienced by societies abroad as counterparts to the challenges Americans face at home. To address common global problems such as human insecurity, political instability and socio-economic welfare requires not isolation from or leverage over other states but collective solutions based on transnational collaboration between diverse states and societies. The essence of the tragic narrative is that disasters can result from supposedly good intentions. But only by replacing a focus on 'US interests' and 'maintaining deterrence and influence' with a concern for the security and well-being of the peoples of the region can the US attempt to unwind the dynamics of turbulence that it has played a central role in creating.[54]

Notes

1   Secretary of State Michael Pompeo, 'A Force for Good: America Reinvigorated in the Middle East', speech at the American University in Cairo (AUC), 10 January 2019. Available at <https://2017-2021.state.gov/a-force-for-good-america-reinvigorated-in-the-middle-east/index.html> (last accessed 12 October 2022).

2   As former AUC president Lisa Anderson has noted, the faculty reaction to Pompeo reflected these norms. See Lisa Anderson, 'Is There a Future for American

Universities in the Middle East? Why the U.S. Model Is More Important Than Ever', *Foreign Affairs*, 22 March 2019. Available at <https://www.foreign affairs.com/articles/egypt/2019-03-22/there-future-american-universities-mid dle-east> (last accessed 12 October 2022).

3　One sign of the shrinking space for open exchange was the refusal of the American University of Beirut to allow the BBC to host a panel with an Iranian scholar on its campus. See Victoria Yan, 'Controversy Bubbles as BBC Event Canceled at AUB', *The Daily Star* (Lebanon), 5 March 2018.

4　William Appleman Williams, *The Tragedy of American Diplomacy* (New York: Delta Books, 1962), 2–3.

5　John S. Badeau, *The American Approach to the Arab World* (New York: Harper & Row, 1968), 16.

6　See Waleed Hazbun, 'The Uses of Modernization Theory: American Foreign Policy and Mythmaking in the Arab World', in Marwan Kraidy and Alex Lubin, eds, *American Studies Encounters the Middle East* (Chapel Hill: University of North Carolina Press, 2016), 175–206.

7　Badeau, *The American Approach to the Arab World*, 16.

8　William B. Quandt, *Peace Process: American Diplomacy and the Arab–Israeli Conflict Since 1967* (Berkeley: University of California Press, 2005), 14.

9　Ibid.

10　Thomas Wright, *All Measures Short of War* (New Haven, CT: Yale University Press, 2017), 99.

11　Secretary of State Condoleezza Rice, 'Remarks at the American University in Cairo', 20 June 2005. Available at <https://2001-2009.state.gov/secretary/rm /2005/48328.htm> (last accessed 12 October 2022).

12　On the notion of a tragic sense of politics, see Richard Ned Lebow, *The Tragic Vision of Politics* (Cambridge: Cambridge University Press, 2003).

13　Martin Indyk, 'The Clinton Administration's Approach to the Middle East', speech to the Washington Institute for Near East Policy, 18 May 1993. Available at <https://www.washingtoninstitute.org/policy-analysis/view/the-clinton-ad ministrations-approach-to-the-middle-east> (last accessed 12 October 2022).

14　Nadia El-Shazly and Raymond Hinnebusch, 'The Challenge of Security in the Post-Gulf War Middle East System', in Raymond A. Hinnebusch and Anoushiravan Ehteshami, eds, *The Foreign Policies of Middle East States* (Boulder, CO: Lynne Rienner, 2002), 71–90.

15　Stephen M. Walt, 'The End of the American Era', *National Interest* 16 (November/December 2011): 6–16.

16　Waleed Hazbun, 'Regional Powers and the Production of Insecurity in the Middle East', Middle East and North Africa Regional Architecture (MENARA)

Working Papers No. 11, September 2018. Available at <https://www.iai.it/sites /default/files/menara_wp_11.pdf> (last accessed 6 November 2022).

17 Barack Obama, 'Transcript: Obama's Speech Against the Iraq War', Chicago, IL, *NPR*, 2 October 2002. Available at <https://www.npr.org/templates/story/sto ry.php?storyId=99591469> (last accessed 12 October 2022).

18 Ibid.

19 Marc Lynch, 'Obama and the Middle East: Rightsizing the U.S. Role', *Foreign Affairs* 94, no. 5 (September/October 2015): 18.

20 President Barack Obama, 'A New Beginning', Remarks at Cairo University, 4 June 2009. Available at
<https://obamawhitehouse.archives.gov/the-press-office/remarks-president-cairo -university-6-04-09> (last accessed 12 October 2022).

21 See Ben Rhodes, *The World as It Is: A Memoir of the Obama White House* (New York: Random House, 2018), Chapter 9.

22 President Barack Obama, 'A Moment of Opportunity', remarks at the Department of State, 19 May 2011. Available at <https://obamawhitehouse.ar chives.gov/the-press-office/2011/05/19/remarks-president-middle-east-and-nor th-africa> (last accessed 12 October 2022).

23 Ibid.

24 Hillary Rodham Clinton, 'Keynote Address at the National Democratic Institute's 2011 Democracy Awards Dinner', Washington DC, 7 November 2011. Available at <https://www.ndi.org/sites/default/files/Keynote%20Addre ss%20at%20the%20National%20Democratic%20Institute%27s%202011%20De mocracy%20Awards%20Dinner.pdf> (last accessed 12 October 2022).

25 Jeffrey Goldberg, 'The Obama Doctrine', *The Atlantic* (April 2016), 77.

26 Ibid. 79.

27 William J. Burns, 'An End to Magical Thinking in the Middle East', *The Atlantic*, 8 December 2019. Available at <https://www.theatlantic.com/ideas/archive/20 19/12/end-magical-thinking-middle-east/602953/> (last accessed 12 October 2022).

28 Marc Lynch, *The New Arab Wars: Uprising and Anarchy in the Middle East* (New York: Public Affairs, 2016).

29 See also Sean L. Yom, 'US Foreign Policy in the Middle East: The Logic of Hegemonic Retreat', *Global Policy* 11 no. 1 (2020): 75–83.

30 Quoted in Goldberg, 'The Obama Doctrine', 73.

31 Asli Bali and Aziz Rana, 'Remember Syria?' *The Boston Review*, 18 July 2018. Available at <http://bostonreview.net/war-security/asli-bali-aziz-rana-trump-pu tin-syria> (last accessed 12 October 2022).

32 Andrew Bacevich, 'An Education in Statecraft', *The Nation*, 2 January 2017, 30.

33 Steve Niva, 'Disappearing Violence: JSOC and the Pentagon's New Cartography of Networked Warfare', *Security Dialogue* 44, no. 3 (2013): 185–202.

34 Ibid. 185.

35 Bacevich, 'An Education in Statecraft', 30.

36 See Ben Rhodes, *The World as It Is*.

37 F. Gregory Gause, III. 'Donald Trump and the Middle East', in Robert Jervis et al., eds, *Chaos in the Liberal Order: The Trump Presidency and International Politics in the Twenty-first Century* (New York: Columbia University Press, 2018), 273–286.

38 Yom, 'US Foreign Policy in the Middle East'; Andrew Miller, 'The End of the Middle East's Primacy in U.S. Foreign Policy', *Texas National Security Review*, Policy Roundtable: The Future of the Middle East, 13 February 2020. Available at <https://tnsr.org/roundtable/policy-roundtable-the-future-of-the-middle-east/#essay2> (last accessed 12 October 2022).

39 Randall Schweller, 'Why Trump Now: A Third-image Explanation', in Robert Jervis et al., *Chaos in the Liberal Order: The Trump Presidency and International Politics in the Twenty-first Century* (New York: Columbia University Press, 2018), 22–39.

40 Justin McCarthy, 'Americans' Approval of Obama on Foreign Affairs Rises', *Gallup*, 15 August 2016. Available at <https://news.gallup.com/poll/194624/americans-approval-obama-foreign-affairs-rises.aspx> (last accessed 12 October 2022). As of June 2020, Donald Trump maintained an average of 40 per cent, slightly higher than Obama's second term average. See <https://news.gallup.com/poll/1726/presidential-ratings-issues-approval.aspx> (last accessed 29 July 2020).

41 Quoted in Goldberg, 'The Obama Doctrine', 85.

42 Walter Russell Mead, 'The Jacksonian revolt: American Populism and the Liberal Order', *Foreign Affairs* 96, no. 2 (March/April 2017): 2–7.

43 Robin Emmott, 'Trump Shaping New "Liberal" Order to Block Russia, China, Iran, says Pompeo', *Reuters*, 4 December 2018. Available at <https://www.reuters.com/article/us-usa-eu/trump-shaping-new-liberal-order-to-block-russia-china-iran-says-pompeo-idUSKBN1O3102> (last accessed 12 October 2022).

44 Elisabeth Anker, 'New Texts Out Now: Elisabeth Anker, Orgies of Feeling: Melodrama and the Politics of Freedom', *Jadaliyya E-zine*, 11 February 2015. Available at <https://www.jadaliyya.com/Details/31777/New-Texts-Out-Now-Elisabeth-Anker,-Orgies-of-Feeling-Melodrama-and-the-Politics-of-Freedom> (last accessed 12 October 2022).

45 Daniel J. Levine, 'After Tragedy: Melodrama and the Rhetoric of Realism', *Journal of International Political Theory* 15, no. 3 (2018): 316–31.

46 See President Donald Trump, 'State of the Union Address', 4 February 2020. Available at<https://www.cnn.com/2020/02/04/politics/trump-2020-state-of -the-union-address/index.html> (last accessed 12 October 2022).

47 Suzy Hansen, *Notes on a Foreign Country: An American Abroad in a Post-American World* (New York: Farrar, Straus & Giroux, 2017).

48 Ibid. 20.

49 John Mearsheimer, *The Tragedy of Great Power Politics* (New York: W. W. Norton & Co., 2001), 25.

50 Hansen, *Notes on a Foreign Country*, 23–4.

51 Robert Malley, 'The Unwanted Wars: Why the Middle East is More Combustible Than Ever', *Foreign Affairs* 98, no. 6 (November/December 2019), 45.

52 Burns, 'An End to Magical Thinking in the Middle East'; Daniel Benaim and Jake Sullivan, 'America's Opportunity in the Middle East: Diplomacy Could Succeed Where Military Force Has Failed', *Foreign Affairs*, 22 May 2020. Available at <https://www.foreignaffairs.com/articles/middle-east/2020-05-22/americas-opportunity-middle-east> (last accessed 12 October 2022).

53 Benaim and Sullivan, 'America's Opportunity in the Middle East'.

54 See Waleed Hazbun, 'Reimagining US Engagement with a Turbulent Middle East', *Middle East Report* 294 (Spring 2020). Available at <https://merip.org/20 20/06/reimagining-us-engagement-with-a-turbulent-middle-east/> (last accessed 12 October 2022).

3

THE PERENNIAL OUTSIDER: ISRAEL AND REGIONAL ORDER CHANGE POST-2011

Noa Schonmann

A series of popular protests broke out across the Middle East and North Africa (MENA) a decade ago. The uprisings were quickly hailed a game changer for MENA politics and dubbed the 'Arab Spring', but the vision of authoritarian regimes collapsing in rapid succession proved a mirage.[1] If the uprisings' effect on intrastate politics has been overestimated, their impact on the region's interstate politics is still considered deeply transformative. Raymond Hinnebusch asserted that the uprisings have 'wrought major change in the . . . regional order'.[2] Louise Fawcett observed that 'the entire fabric of the regional system has been rocked by the consequences of the popular uprisings', throwing MENA's fragile order into sharp relief.[3] Marc Lynch argued that regional politics were reshaped to the point that 'the new order is fundamentally one of disorder.'[4]

Observers tend to agree on the downhill direction of change, but opinions diverge over its extent: are we witnessing major change *within* regional order, or a change *of* the order itself? A consortium of fourteen research institutes from Europe, the Middle East and North Africa collaborated between 2016 and 2019 under the framework of the MENARA project to answer this question.[5] They concluded that shifts in the region's geopolitical dynamics amount to changes *within* order, and suggested that researchers tend to overestimate order change because they focus on regional and global levels of analysis while 'ignoring important changes at the intersection between domestic and regional politics'.[6]

MENARA's project is unprecedented for its comprehensive approach, but I find this explanation overstates the case and misses the point.[7] Disagreement over the extent of order change is better explained, in the first place, by the cross-wired nature of the conversation. Assessments vary primarily because scholars diverge in conceiving the object of inquiry: 'international order'.[8] Fundamental as the concept of 'order' is to social inquiry, it is inherently diffuse,[9] and scholars' tendency to employ it intuitively and offhandedly goes a long way to explain their differences over order change.[10] My argument goes a step further: studies of MENA order tend to misestimate change in the aftermath of the Arab uprisings because they systematically disregard an important actor in regional order-making and a key driver of order change: Israel.

The following section surveys the post-2011 literature to demonstrate the wide variation among studies in approach to 'regional order' and point to one commonality: none seriously factors Israel into their analyses. The difficulty in taking Israel into account is explained, and the ways in which Israel partakes in shaping regional order are explored. The chapter argues that Israel's role is by no means negligible: Israel offers more than an external or a mere bystander perspective on regional order. The paper defines Israel as an outsider-member of the regional society of states, and its primary social boundary marker at that. As such, Israel plays a unique and essential role in constituting both the region and its social order. In general terms, I posit that to fully grasp social order change we must turn our gaze to relations evolving with society's liminal members. In the context of social order, societal outsiders offer more than just peripheral perspectives on core affairs. They are not merely passive objects of threat and opportunity beheld by core members; they are interactants that meaningfully partake in the ongoing process of societal order-making, and their relations of amity or enmity shape that order in a singular and significant way.

Cross-wired Conversation over Regional Order Post-2011

The debate over international order muddies rather quickly when conversation carries across theoretical schools of thought. Working from an IR-realist approach, Erzsébet Rózsa highlights the proliferation of 'weak states' in the region and US withdrawal from the region in the aftermath of the Arab Spring. In consequence, she observes, Saudi Arabia and Egypt assumed 'a leadership role', positioning themselves alongside three regional power centres whose ascent pre-dated 2011: the non-Arab states of Israel, Iran and Turkey. Rózsa concludes that 'the post-colonial regional order in the Middle East', which has been eroding since the end of the Cold War, is now 'finally and definitively reshaping' into a five-power multipolar system.[11] Rózsa's analysis boils 'order' down to the power structure among interdependent units in a geopolitical state system. She sees order change in terms of the consolidation and disintegration of units, and shifting distribution of relative power among them. Rózsa uses the concept descriptively, assigning order as such no particular functional end or normative value. Order as power structure matters insofar as it gives rise to (transiently) converging interests that shape regional patterns of rivalry and alliance among states.

Rózsa's unit of analysis, 'the Middle East', takes into account both Arab and non-Arab states. Israel factors into the relative power analysis but is quickly set apart from the region's other four emerging power poles on account of its cultural and economic disconnect from neighbouring states. Rózsa urges us to understand Israel's regional relevance only in terms of 'its capacity [to militarily] defend itself, rather than as a "core-state" in any political or civilizational (à la Huntington) sense'. Whereas other regional powers are analysed in terms of their interaction patterns (that is, leadership bids, axes of alliance and expanding spheres of influence), Israel matters only as a counterweight object. Rózsa explores how Israel's own threat perception shifted in light of the uprisings but precludes it from engaging in geostrategic relations that interactively shape regional order.[12] This leads her to conclude that Israel's increased isolation and disinterest in solving the Palestine issue make it 'impossible for the Gulf Arab states to join Israel in its attempt to curb the perceived Iranian threat of the nuclear program'.[13]

Lynch, too, approaches the question of regional order in realist terms. He observes that the uprisings' 'fallout fundamentally altered the regional balance of power':[14] while traditional powers such as Egypt and Syria, consumed with domestic conflict, were no longer able to project power abroad, wealthy Gulf states successfully employed their robust repressive capacity and central position in transnational networks of business, media and ideology to expand their regional influence.[15] As profound regime insecurity afflicted all Arab regimes, classic 'security dilemmas' proliferated, and regional dynamics grew ever more turbulent:[16] 'formal alliances and conventional conflicts between major states' gave way to a disarray of destructive proxy conflicts among 'influence peddling' regional powers, sowing chaos throughout the region.[17] The region's 'new order is fundamentally one of disorder',[18] Lynch concludes: the power balance among Arab states post-2011 can no longer sustain order from within the region, while the United States had lost its hegemonic 'power or the standing to impose a regional order' from the outside.[19]

Whereas for Rózsa order denotes the structure of *power* among units of a state system, Lynch conceives order as a pattern of *interaction* among them. For him, order signifies specifically a *settled* dynamic, a modicum of stability in the inescapable anarchy of international relations. Insofar as Lynch associates order with a particular pattern of interaction, his concept is not merely descriptive, but functional.[20] In his framework, balanced distributions of power are sources of order; they are of interest as solutions to the problem of turbulent interaction dynamics. How does Israel factor into the settling or unsettling of regional interaction dynamics post-2011? Lynch refers to 'Middle Eastern order'[21] as his object of inquiry. In practice, however, he focuses on interactions among, and the balance of power between, Arab states. Turkey and Iran are mentioned as partaking in regional interaction dynamics,[22] but ultimately Lynch brings analysis to the conclusion that the upheaval gave rise to 'a new *Arab* order'[23] (my emphasis). Non-Arab Turkey and Iran factor tangentially, insofar as Arab states perceive them as objects of threat and opportunity. When it comes to the dynamics of interstate relations, Israel entirely falls off Lynch's analytical radar.

Helle Malmvig calls for analyses of regional order to move beyond 'realist perspectives based on materialist understanding of power'.[24] In her assessment, the Arab uprisings have not changed the system's material power structure: the balance of power remains multipolar. Therefore, she argues, 'If we are to capture how regional order is changing as a result of the Arab Uprisings', our understanding of power must 'broaden to include normative power'.[25] Employing a constructivist securitisation approach, Malmvig concludes that regional order has changed insofar as the substance of regional norms and the balance of normative power have shifted since 2011. She observes that regional politics post-2011 revolve less around 'traditional issues of Palestine, Israel and the West', while the Sunni–Shi'a sectarian divide has deepened, broadened and grown securitised by multiple state and non-state actors. Furthermore, the Resistance Front (Iran, Syria, Hezbollah, Hamas) that had gained 'widespread popularity in Arab societies' at the turn of the century saw its normative power diminish following the war in Syria.[26] Malmvig's approach mirrors Rózsa's in using order to describe the system's power structure, though she stirs ideational power resources into the analytical mix, together with material ones.

Non-Arab Iran factors prominently in Malmvig's analysis of the changing 'Middle East' normative order, but neither Israel nor Turkey is mentioned in this context. This may well be due to the brevity of her think piece; nonetheless, it indicates she does not consider Israel as holding a notable stake in the region's normative power structuring process. Israel is not analysed as a securitising actor, only as an object of other actors' securitisation acts.

Hinnebusch's theoretically eclectic approach is, in some ways, close to Malmvig's.[27] His engagement with the question of regional order is longer ranging and more elaborate, but underlying it is a similar premise that 'what order exists in MENA rests largely on a power balance' that hinges as much on ideational as on material factors.[28] Historically, he writes, Arab state interactions 'approximated a Lockean order' that was built on a sense of shared identity and Egyptian near-hegemony. 'Nasser's pan-Arab regime' (1955–70) cultivated identity-based norms that effectively constrained the use of violence in inter-Arab power struggles: conflicts were mostly limited to ideological rivalry, discourse wars and regime subversion in a period that came to be known as the 'Arab Cold War'. Though counterbalancing swiftly curtailed Egypt's hegemonic bid,[29] pan-Arab norms still worked to confine the use of military means primarily to conflicts across the Arab–non-Arab fault line (vis-à-vis Israel and Iran). The 1990 Gulf War established American hegemony in the region, which temporarily muted military conflicts. But in the long run, Washington failed to impose pax-Americana in the region. Its interventions gave rise to a new discourse war between the anti-imperialist, anti-Zionist 'resistance axis', and the Western-aligned 'moderate bloc'.[30]

According to Hinnebusch, the uprisings profoundly altered the distribution of power among states, transforming in consequence the regional identity field wherein the interstate power struggle plays out. Hinnebusch describes how the uprisings debilitated the historically central secular Arab republics (Egypt, Iraq, Syria), draining power 'away to the periphery of the Gulf, especially Saudi Arabia, and to the non-Arab powers, Turkey and Iran . . .'.[31] The region remained as insecure and multipolar as ever, but the proliferation of weak and failed states 'forced [people] to fall back on their primordial [identity] communities for protection'.[32] The Islamism of the periphery states, increasingly fractured along Sunni–Shi'a sectarian lines, came to displace the long-wounded Arabism as the primary trans-state identity out of which shared norms can be constructed.[33] Hinnebusch argues that whereas secular pan-Arab identity gave rise to a set of norms that constrained the use of violence in inter-Arab power struggles, religious sectarian identities 'prescribed uncompromising jihad *within* the Islamic umma against heresy', intense enmity that demonises opponents as infidels, and intractable conflict.[34] Consequently, the interstate power struggle 'has taken new, more violent and intense forms',[35] shifting from discourse wars and financial backing of clients to massively violent proxy wars through the provision of arms, fighters and even military incursions.[36] By 2014, regional conflict came to assume 'features of an unrestrained Hobbesian struggle for power'.[37]

Like Lynch, Hinnebusch speaks of order as a pattern of interaction among states locked in a perpetual power struggle.[38] Both scholars place value on a particular pattern, though Lynch associates order with a settled, stable dynamic, whereas Hinnebusch associates order with restrained violence (in terms of its intensity and means). Hinnebusch offers an elaborate narrative of a Middle Eastern 'slide towards a Hobbesian order'[39] of unrestrained violence post-2011, which he lays out with barely a reference to Israel. At the outset, he identifies the MENA[40] as his unit of analysis: a system of states bound together by security interdependence and a conflictual pattern of interaction. Formally, Israel is considered 'an integral part of the region's conflicts and its balance of power'.[41] Yet, as his impressively wide-ranging narrative unfolds, it systematically overlooks Israel as an actor with the potential to shape regional order, even in the most rudimentary, 'realist' of ways: the distribution of power among states. When discussing shifts in the regional system post-2011, Hinnebusch counts Israel only once among the relative power-gainers.[42] As he proceeds to consider how the 'peripheral' power-gainers could shape regional order, in terms of expanding or protecting their spheres of influence and launching hegemonic bids, he refers to Saudi Arabia, Iran and Turkey; Israel drops off the list.[43] Hinnebusch brings Israel into his account of regional order only through the eyes of other regional actors: as a source of chronic grievance that galvanises the masses and as an object of threat against which states counterbalance. Israel is not seriously considered as a social inter-actant whose relations, above and beyond its power position and unilateral actions, may play a role in constructing and shaping the MENA regional order.

The Misfit: Shoehorning Israel into Regional Society

The studies reviewed are diverse in terms of their theoretical approaches and conceptual frameworks. Interestingly, even though each conceives 'international order' differently, all converge in concluding that the MENA region is dramatically less ordered post-2011. The literature survey highlights a further (and I propose, related) commonality, a consistent blindspot: none of the studies takes Israel seriously into account when examining processes of regional ordering.[44] All identified the ME(NA) state system as their unit of analysis and demarcated it primarily by degree of security interdependence among states. In principle, therefore, all see Israel as part of this state system. In fact, they generally recognise it as one of the system's most powerful units, continually and even increasingly so. None is likely to contest the claim that Israel regularly interacts with other states in the system, albeit in limited spheres of activity and often on adversarial terms. Yet, explicitly or implicitly, studies end up treating Israel as an external factor rather than an integral actor in regional order-making. Is it reasonable to think that a regional power of Israel's magnitude would have but a negligible, incidental effect on regional order? Is it reasonable to think we could fully grasp MENA regional order, let alone assess its shifting state, while overlooking a key stakeholder in it?

It is worth mentioning here that even studies that focus on Israel and set out to explore its foreign relations post-2011 are disinclined to consider it a regional order-shaper. Studies describe how the uprisings changed Israel's geostrategic environment and thereby heightened the country's threat perception, affected its domestic politics and shaped its foreign policy reaction.[45] The few who undertake to locate 'Israel's Place in a Changing Regional Order' do not in fact go far beyond the aspects above: they too are interested in Israel's perspective on the region, essentially in isolated, non-relational terms.[46] Israel remains a bystander, an 'external actor' whose 'posture' and (unilateral) actions are 'essentially designed to insulate itself from the regional upheaval'.[47] Left unasked are questions of whether and how Israel's interactions and relations of amity and enmity are shaping regional order.

Why is Israel omitted from analyses of regional ordering? The difficulty could be traced to the classic conception of 'international order' that was put forward in the most widely cited work on the subject: *The Anarchical Society*, published by Hedley Bull in 1977. For Bull, order entails society; indeed, Bull conceptualised international order as the property that distinguishes state societies from state systems. This fundamental distinction underlies the difficulty in analysing MENA order: recognising Israel as a unit of the regional state system is straightforward, the challenge lies in coming to terms with it as a member of the regional society of states.

Bull defines 'international system' as a group of states (or more generally a group of independent political communities) wherein 'the behaviour of each is a necessary factor in the calculations of the others.'[48] Such a group of interdependent states can come to form a society when they 'perceive common interests in a structure of coexistence' among them, and on that basis 'conceive themselves to be bound by a common set of rules in their relations with one another and share in the working of common institutions'.[49] In other words, Bull posits that when a preponderance of a system's states recognises coexistence as a common interest,[50] these states may 'tacitly or explicitly . . . consent to common rules and institutions' that prescribe how their 'interaction should proceed',[51] and thereby form a society. Bull defines 'international order' as a societal state of affairs wherein interdependent states tend to conform to the rules and institutions that sustain their coexistence,[52] and the emergence of such a pattern of conduct among states constitutes them as a *functioning* society.

Thus conceived, order is potential, functional and intentional. Potential in that it is a condition that emerges if and when states' behaviour towards one another overall conforms to rules and institutions that sustain their primary goal of coexistence.[53] Importantly, Bull recognises here that order is inherently precarious, and requires only that 'most states at most times pay some respect to the basic rules of coexistence in international society.'[54] Functional in that order is a pattern of social activity that (at least to some degree) enables states to attain common goals, primary and secondary.[55] Often overlooked is the point that Bull's concept of 'order' is also intentional: pattern is not any regularity discerned in the aggregated behaviour of society's members towards one another; Bull emphasises that such regularity must be 'brought about at least partly by contrivance', as opposed to emerging spontaneously, in a purely fortuitous way.[56] Thus, states bound into the social form of a system might feature 'some elements of order' derived from a haphazardly balanced distribution of power (as distinguished from the deliberate adherence to the evolved institution of power-balancing that is the provenance of state societies). Ultimately, he writes, 'An international system of this kind would be disorderly in the extreme, and would in fact exemplify the Hobbesian state of nature.'[57] Finally, Bull's conception of order does *not* require peaceful, amicable or even dialogic relations among the states, only a pattern of activity undertaken *deliberately* in pursuit of a coexistence structure. Indeed, enemy states can just as well see themselves as bound by a common set of rules and effectively cooperate in the working of common institutions in a conscious effort to sustain an international structure of coexistence (even if they contest the legitimacy of any particular state's claim to exist). Nor does Bull's conception of order presuppose ties of identity and shared culture binding interstate societies. Bull conceived international societies as bound together only by common consent to rules and institutions that sustain a structure of coexistence, and while he recognised that affinities of value, identity, or culture may enhance states' commitment to coexistence, for him 'the role of culture is an empirical question to be investigated, not an analytic assumption.'[58]

Bull's conceptual framework allows us to think of the MENA system of states, Israel included, as a society wherein states' conduct can sustain a degree of order that shifts across time. Hinnebusch is one of the many scholars who explicitly builds on Bull's work when analysing the MENA regional order.[59] All MENA states, he writes, 'tied together by conflict . . . constitute a "security complex" but only the thinnest of international societies';[60] the MENA is a state system 'embraced by a rather dysfunctional [and fractured] form of international society'.[61] Hinnebusch recognises a minimal set of global institutions, 'understood practices such as sovereignty, diplomacy and power-balancing', as operating in this regional society, and concludes that what order exists in MENA rests largely on power-balancing, an institution that can preserve pluralism in systems of states, but not durable peace among them. But, he hastens to add, one of the region's 'enduring and distinctive features' is that balancing is as much against legitimacy threats as military ones.[62] This is explained by the arbitrary borders imposed on Arab states by European imperialism. As a result, citizen loyalty is continually undercut by allegiance to Arab and Islamic 'supra-state communities', leaving Arab states 'debilitated by enduring legitimacy deficits'.[63] Consequently, Hinnebusch argues, the MENA interstate power struggle is particularly prone to being 'muted or exacerbated' by norms constructed out of 'powerful' identities that are widely shared at the region's inter-human relational domain. Hinnebusch ascribes to such identity-based norms a very strong, even primary, effect in shaping the MENA regional order overall and across time. Specifically, he brings his analysis to the conclusion that

insofar as the Arab states enjoyed a common Arab identity, the system approximated a Lockean order in which shared norms muted conflict. The change in the normative structure since the Arab uprising, in which Arabism has been displaced by Sunni–Shia sectarianism, has precipitated a slide toward a Hobbesian order [of unrestrained interstate violence].[64]

This is the move that leaves Israel largely outside the frame of Hinnebusch's regional order analysis. Israel is the only state in the region that belongs to neither identity-based 'supra-state community'; indeed, antagonism towards it is the key issue that traditionally unites the two, largely overlapping, communities. As ordering principles, both pan-Arabism and pan-Islamism have precluded collaborating with Israel so long as there is no just solution to the Palestinian plight. In this sense working with Israel is a critical liability to the legitimacy claims of states in the region. Insofar as Hinnebusch sees the MENA as a region where 'the most typical balancing dynamic has been "soft balancing"',[65] Israel – an actor endowed with ample military 'hard power' but singularly devoid of 'soft ideational power' – is rendered largely irrelevant to the regional institution of power-balancing. Much to the same effect, Malmvig foregrounds 'normative power'[66] structuring as key to understanding regional order change. Rózsa follows this line of thought when she explicitly rules Israel out as partaker in MENA balancing: Israel's cultural disconnect from neighbouring states and its hardline stance towards the Palestinians, she writes, make it 'impossible for the Gulf Arab states to join Israel in its attempt to curb the perceived Iran threat of the nuclear program'.[67]

First, I question Hinnebusch's assumption that an enduring feature of the MENA as a whole is that states balance against legitimacy/ideational threats as much as against military/material ones. The generalisation certainly holds for some states, some of the time, but as Hinnebusch's own narrative makes clear, it does not easily extend beyond the Arab states' society 'nested' within the MENA, and properly only applies there up to the 1980s.[68] Second, to the extent that domestic legitimacy considerations do factor into MENA states' balancing conduct, pan-Arabism/-Islamism principles did not altogether prevent the practice of sharing with Israel in the common institution of power-balancing. Hinnebusch rightly notes that Arab alliances with Israel 'tend to be excluded by ideological norms . . . even if these would serve the security interests of regimes/states . . .'[69] But, short of forging open alliances, many regional states have long coordinated and collaborated with Israel in shaping regional order away from the public eye, by way of informal alignments, tacit security regimes and implicit understandings. Examples abound of significant and long-term security coordination and cooperation between Israel and Arab states, such that is non-contractual and comes into existence when 'signals and subtleties are exchanged more often than not behind the scenes, between the lines, and under the table, via back channels involving indirect but also direct communication.'[70] Among them we find Israel's relations with Jordan, Egypt and the Gulf states in the decades prior to the signing of peace treaties.[71] Another notable example is the consolidation of a Periphery Pact grouping of the non-Arab regional states around Israel in the late 1950s and 1960s, which yielded close if covert relations with Turkey, Iran and Ethiopia.[72] At times, some Arab states' need to balance against external legitimacy threats certainly accounts for key regional ordering practices, but too much is overlooked if we therefore altogether rule Israel out of partaking in the regional institution of power-balancing.

Fawcett too sees Israel as a state 'that has not, so far, contributed to a viable regional order'.[73] In her analysis, order can be brought about from within the region either through frameworks of regionalist security governance (that is, formal and multilateral 'secondary institutions'[74]) or regional power leadership (order as a public good provided by an authoritative hegemon employing both hard and soft power resources).[75] Insofar as these two paths to order are premised on legitimacy, they are effectively foreclosed to Israel. Fawcett and others are, of course, right to observe that Israel has long been excluded from the MENA's 'secondary institutions' – those formal regionalist frameworks that bring order-making interactions aboveground and to the fore.[76] However, we should not overestimate the role such frameworks play in regional ordering. As Simon Murdon put it when reviewing the proliferation of secondary institutions in the region since 1945: 'The "thickening" of international society in the Middle East would ultimately embody a great deal of insubstantial frothing.'[77] Mark Heller rightly proceeds to point out that Israel's exclusion from regional organisations, which 'of course . . . do not have a truly significant impact on developments in the Middle East . . . has not, in the past, precluded interaction with other regional parties to promote interests that converge with theirs'.[78]

Beyond forging open alliances and membership in regionalist organisations, regional power leadership is another conspicuous mode of regional ordering through the workings of the power-balancing institution. Studies broadly concur that Israel stands among five 'potential regional powers' post-2011 (along with Saudi Arabia, Egypt, Iran and Turkey), but that it is far from attaining hegemonic leadership status.[79] Leadership entails acceptance –

cross-regional appeal and the ability to 'instrumentalize trans-state legitimacy discourses'.[80] Heller reflects a common stance when he writes that

> as the quintessential 'other' in an environment increasingly dominated by identity politics . . . [Israel] lacks the ability to translate its [hard] power assets into usable political currency . . . As a result, it cannot reasonably aspire to a leadership role in the region, even if it were inclined to do so.[81]

Again, we must not overwork this limitation: in the MENA, order was never really sustained by a regional hegemonic power, and presently no other regional power aspirants stands a chance of attaining such status.[82] As Fawcett herself concludes: the MENA 'has been, and still is, effectively closed to aspiring regional powers', and their overall absence 'provides a useful explanatory variable . . . to current regional [dis]order'.[83]

A final reason why studies often overlook Israel as a member of the MENA society can be linked to the fact that Israel's own policymakers tend to see the state as external to the region. In public discourse the prevailing notion that 'Israel may be in the region but not of the region' comes across in common expressions that self-identify the Jewish state as 'a villa in the jungle' or 'an island of democratic stability in a sea of instability'.[84] Avi Shlaim identifies a persistent streak of aloofness and isolationism in the attitude of Israeli policymakers towards the region.[85] Indeed, while Israel long pursued a qualitative military edge (QME) over its environment, it never sought a leadership role in regional affairs, and though 'the goal of ending the conflict with the Arab world has been a permanent feature of Israel's foreign policy, integration within the Middle East was never an appealing objective'.[86] Yet, self-understanding is not necessarily the most insightful. Israel's record of engagement with the regional society of states is not one of an external 'bystander' actor, a non-member located outside the realm of regional society. Rather, I posit, it is one of an outsider: a member of the MENA society of states that is engaged in a gamut of social relations of amity and enmity and has a clear stake in a structure of societal coexistence, yet one who deviates from core social norms.

Drawing on Social Psychology, 'outsider' is used here as a status category *within* the social structure: it marks those who occupy an outcast or alienated position to (some or all of) society's rules, norms, institutions, rather than occupying an external position to the entire complex of social relations (a position marking non-members of society itself).[87] Unbound by society's norms, deviants and rule breakers are nonetheless integral members of any society. On the one hand, they are curtailed actors: outsiders are excluded from directly participating in the process of societal rule-making (those rules that define them as outsiders). On the other hand, they play a crucial role in societal change. Their structural non-conformity challenges and undermines societal norms, and in so doing they continually demarcate the edges of social appropriateness. Often, the effect of such challenge is to uphold and reinforce the established social order, but they can also stretch and shape it.

The studies cited above conclude that Israel's lack of 'normative/soft power' renders it largely irrelevant to regional ordering. They overlook the counterpoint: though Israel's scope for order-shaping interactions is curtailed, it is uniquely and exceptionally empowered to affect change through the modes of interaction that are open to it. Insofar as Israel has no legitimacy to confer it also has none to lose, and while identity-based norms do not buttress it from 'hot wars', nor is it constrained by them. In these respects, Israel has exceptional and unique freedom of (inter)action in the region, which, alongside its prominent hard power position (both militarily and economically) and strong partnership with the region's long-standing external great power, the United States, renders it an exceptionally agile and valuable strategic (inter) actor. Israel's reputation for unleashing its military power, uninhibited by the identity-based norms that constrain its tacit allies, is a major factor in regional balancing. Notable in this regard, of course, is Israel's practice of raids that destroy or set back the nuclear aspirations of Iraq, Iran and Syria.

Heller's study concluded that, without soft power at its disposal, Israel only has the 'power to block, not to shape' regional order.[88] In certain respects, Israel is a highly curtailed regional order-shaper, but by no means an irrelevant one, and as a perennial outsider it is uniquely empowered to influence the regional order. Rather than striving to 'fit in', Israel has traditionally sought for itself the position of outsider to the regional society of states, and was long content to remain its outsider. This 'perennial outsider' position, adopted by choice as much as by circumstance, frees Israel from the costly demands of conforming to regional identity-based norms, and leaves it immune to the region's fierce regime-subverting 'discourse wars'. Of course it also excludes it from the insider practices of rule-making and formal institution-building. In consequence, Israel does not seek to 'manage' regional order nor lead regional society, but rather successfully works to shape the regional order to its needs. Like all other regional society members, Israel is both an actor (whose power stance and unilateral moves are taken into strategic account by other actors in the system) and an interactant, engaged in relations of amity and enmity. In both respects, Israel has the capacity to shape regional order.

The Perennial Outsider in Regional Ordering Post-2011

Does our assessment of regional order change once we factor Israel into our analysis? I argue that only when we take Israel into account, recognising its societal role as a perennial outsider, can we properly grasp regional order change post-2011. What then comes into view is a picture of greater, not lesser, degree of order in the aftermath of the uprisings. In what follows I advance this argument by focusing on power-balancing. Following Bull, I consider it a fundamental ordering mechanism that works to sustain a societal structure of coexistence by protecting the plurality of membership against the threat of hegemony. Insofar as states' practice of balancing remains deliberate while growing more elaborate and binding, we can say that the degree of order within their international society has increased in a key respect. In this context, I will trace Israel's interactions with Gulf states, showing that the parties have been working together, with increasing vigour and visibility since the turn of the century, to effectively bolster the region's master institution: power-balancing.

Relations between Israel and several Gulf states have developed slowly but surely and essentially out of sight over the past two decades to the point that by 2019 Ian Black asserted: 'They have transformed the geopolitical land-scape of the Middle East.'[89] While the 2011 uprisings did not bring this tectonic shift about, they were among the factors that brought that shift to light. Sporadic contacts between Israel and Gulf states can be traced back decades, but up to the 1990s they were bare minimal, strictly indirect and clandestine in nature.[90] Publicly committed to the Palestinian cause, the Saudis seem to have made a rare exception for tacit coordination with Israel when a critical shared security interest was at stake: in 1964–6, during the Yemen civil war, Saudi Arabia overlooked occasional encroachments into its airspace, as Israel airlifted weapons and supplies to royalist forces fighting the republicans, who were sustained by an Egyptian military intervention. Such tacit coordination, facilitated through British mediation, was brought about by a strong shared interest in blocking Nasser's expansionism in the region.[91] Yet, when a similar occasion arose during Iraq's invasion of Kuwait in 1990, the Saudis refused to allow Israeli use of their airspace for a preventive strike that would batter their shared enemy Saddam Hussein. King Fahd let Washington know that Saudi Arabia 'would remain stalwart if Israel struck back after being attacked first by Saddam', but the Americans had little interest in sharing such information with the Israelis, whom they were keen to restrain.[92]

In the long run, 1990 did emerge as a turning point in the Gulf states' approach towards Israel.[93] The morning after the Gulf War, Saudi Arabia stepped out into a post-Cold War world. Yielding to American pressure, it sent Prince Bandar bin Sultan, the Saudi ambassador to Washington, as Gulf Cooperation Council (GCC) observer to the Madrid Peace Conference. The 1991 conference occasioned the first public meeting of Israeli and Saudi officials, opening the door to further informal meetings, private and public, with Gulf officials.[94] The Saudis have long played a significant role, mostly behind the scenes, in promoting efforts to peacefully resolve the Israeli–Palestinian conflict. While in 1979 they condemned Egypt's bilateral peace treaty with Israel that sidelined the Palestinians, they continued to offer quiet support for peace efforts on the Palestinian and Syrian channels throughout the 1990s, working on the expectation that the Oslo process would lead to the establishment of a Palestinian state.[95] By 1994, along with their GCC colleagues, the Saudis were ready to lift the secondary economic boycott against Israel. Later that year Bahrain received an official delegation headed by the Israeli minister of environment, while Sultan Qaboos of Oman received an official visit by the Israeli prime minister. In 1996 Oman and Qatar allowed Israel to open trade missions in their capitals. Such developments – consisting of open and formal, if mostly low-level, relations essentially in the realm of trade – remained explicitly contingent on expected realisation of full statehood for Palestinians and fluctuated with the periodic outbreak of violence in the Israeli–Palestinian conflict. But the Oslo Accords did not create a Palestinian state, and the outbreak of the al-Aqsa intifada in September 2000 brought matters to a head. Two months later Qatar shut the Israeli trade mission. Public connections were severed, though some discreet ties continued.[96]

The collapse of the Oslo process and the second intifada marked but a setback in the development of Israel–Gulf relations. The American invasion of Iraq in 2003 reshuffled the regional deck of cards: it created a power vacuum at the heart of the region, drawing Iran into the regional power game and significantly strengthening its position. Iran's growing influence in the region clearly manifested in 2006, when it backed its Hezbollah proxy in the Lebanon war against Israel. In this context, 2006 marked a step change in Israel–Gulf relations: shared concern over Iran's regional ambitions brought Israel and the Gulf states to consider treading a common strategic path. Before the war,

Podeh observes, 'Arab leaders expressed their concerns about Iran's expansionist policy only behind closed doors, [in its aftermath] they were . . . willing to openly admit their desire to see Israel cause a painful blow to Hizbullah so as to damage Iranian prestige.'[97] Behind the scenes, meetings between Israeli and Saudi officials secretly commenced in an effort to set up a framework for intelligence exchanges. The highly clandestine nature of such contacts makes it impossible to trace them in full, but it is clear that a significant shift has taken place towards direct, high-level and routine contacts. According to foreign reports, shortly after the war Prince Bandar bin Sultan, now head of Saudi National Security Council, met in Jordan with Israeli prime minister Ehud Olmert and/or with Meir Dagan, head of the Mossad.[98] The reports were strongly denied by Riyadh. During Operation Cast Lead in December 2008, Israel is reported to have given Saudi Arabia prior notification before carrying out air raids along the Red Sea in an effort to block arms delivery to Gaza through Sudan. By 2009 'senior professionals in the intelligence and security fields from Israel and Gulf countries were collaborating', according to the deputy head of Israel's National Security Council.[99] A report in *The Times* claimed that a secret meeting in early 2009 between Dagan and Saudi officials resulted in Saudi tacit consent 'to the Israel air force flying through their airspace on a mission which is supposed to be in the common interests of both Israel and Saudi Arabia'.[100] The reports were denied by both Riyadh and Jerusalem. At the same time Israeli foreign minister Tzipi Livni was said to have developed a 'good and personal relationship' with UAE foreign minister Abdullah Ibn Zayed, sustaining quiet periodic dialogue between the two governments. Documents made public through Wikileaks also exposed regular contacts with Qatar up to early 2009.[101] At the close of the decade Israeli presence in Gulf markets was growing noticeable. In the absence of official relations, business operated under the thin veil of second passports and EU-registered companies, active primarily in the export of communication and irrigation, as well as civilian and national security technologies, diamond trade and real estate deals. Links with the UAE were the most extensive, with bilateral trade between 2006 and 2009 reportedly exceeding US$1 billion.[102]

Over the next decade, relations between Israel and Gulf states continued to develop 'in light of what both parties considered to be a feeble American response to the Iranian challenge'.[103] Gulf leaders were equally unimpressed by the Obama administration's hesitant and ultimately acquiescent response to the 2011 uprisings. Obama's years in office finally brought home the message that Washington was now ready to carry out its long-standing intention of pivoting away from the Middle East. For years both Israel and the Gulf states had founded their separate security strategies on the premise of American willingness to exercise leadership in the region.[104] Left to their own devices they now gravitated towards each other in an effort to undercut Iran's regional aspirations. Different sources confirm that Saudi and Emirati cooperation with Israel in the fields of intelligence-sharing and strategic analysis increased markedly during Obama's second term in office, while the Joint Comprehensive Plan of Action (JCPOA) nuclear deal was negotiated and later signed with Iran in 2015.[105] Relations with Israel were certainly boosted also by the change of guard in Saudi Arabia, as King Salman ascended the throne in 2015, bringing Crown Prince Mohammed bin Salman into an unprecedented position of power.

High-level contacts became routine from 2006, but early on they were almost entirely clandestine. The Obama years cemented and substantiated strategic cooperation. At the same time, contacts began to cautiously shift above ground: in late 2013 the Israeli president Shimon Peres addressed via satellite the Gulf Security Conference in Abu Dhabi; in 2014 Israel's energy minister visited Abu Dhabi; a series of secret meetings between former Saudi general Anwar Eshki and Dore Gold, director general of Israel's Foreign Affairs Ministry, was capped in June 2015 by a public meeting in Washington. The following year Eshki was accompanied by a delegation of Saudi businessmen and academics on a visit to Israel; by 2016 Emirati and Israeli forces were openly participating in joint military exercises in the US.[106]

The trend of shifting Israel–Gulf relations above ground was clearly boosted by the entry of President Donald Trump into the White House in January 2017, followed six months later by Washington's withdrawal from the JCPOA. Social media analysts observe that since 2017 the Saudi 'regime has embarked on an aggressive media campaign that is paving the way for the normalisation of ties with Israel, using the country's most renowned cult producers'.[107] In November 2017 Israeli chief of staff Gadi Eizenkot gave an unprecedented interview to Saudi media, where he noted that both countries were 'in complete agreement about Iran's intentions'. With President Trump, he added:

There is an opportunity to build a new international coalition in the region. We need to carry out a large and inclusive strategic plan to stop the Iranian danger. We are willing to exchange information with moderate Arab countries, including intelligence information in order to deal with Iran.[108]

The following year, it was reported that Saudi Arabia's top intelligence officer Khalid bin Ali al-Humaidan met in Jordan with his Israeli, Egyptian and Jordanian counterparts, as well as Trump's envoys Jason Greenblatt and Jared Kushner, to discuss regional security.[109] By October 2018 Eizenkot had met with his Saudi counterpart, General Fayyad bin Hamid al-Ruwayli, on the sidelines of the Counter Violent Extremist Organizations Conference in Washington DC, making it 'the first-ever publicized meeting between high-ranking Israeli and Saudi officials'.[110] Shortly thereafter Israel's prime minister Benjamin Netanyahu was accompanied by the Mossad head on a visit to Oman where he held talks with Sultan Qaboos bin Said, while opposition leader Avi Gabbay, chairman of the Labor Party, held talks with senior officials in Abu Dhabi.[111] The US-sponsored Middle East conference in Warsaw, organised to focus attention on 'Iran's influence and terrorism in the region',[112] offered Netanyahu the opportunity to share a stage with leaders and ministers from the Gulf states and Arab world at large.

In the past, the periodic convergence of security interests between Israel and the Gulf states gave rise only to limited episodes of tacit coordination, but the impasse over the question of Palestine long stood as an insurmountable block to strategic cooperation, let alone the forging of alliances. In the 1990s we see such episodes of tacit coordination articulating into a more regular modicum of tentative engagement, one that is now premised on commitment to progress towards a Palestinian state. At the turn of the century, from 2006 onwards, a strategic relationship progressively begins to emerge between Israel and the Gulf states. In terms of the regional order, if hitherto Israel was regarded by the Gulf states as contributing to the system's equilibrium merely by virtue of its existence, in 2006 it came to be seen 'as a possible partner in the Middle East balance of power'.[113]

It is important to realise that this ground-breaking shift comes about despite the fact that in 2006 prospects for the resolution of the Israeli–Palestinian conflict were as slim as ever, if not slimmer. Indeed, to make sense of this shift we must see it in light of another long-term process: the long-term marginalisation of the Palestinian question in Arab political discourse. Most observers agree that 'regional events have detracted attention from the Palestinian issue.'[114] From the perspective of Arab state elites, the salience of the

Palestinian cause has been steadily declining since the 1970s. In Gulf politics in particular, the year 1990 again marks a key turning point: PLO Chairman Yasser Arafat's decision to come out in support of Iraq's occupation of Kuwait was received with incredulity and outrage in the Gulf states.[115] The move constituted a blow from which Palestinian–Gulf relations never fully recovered. In the short term, through the Oslo years, support for the Palestinian cause remained the key obstacle for progression in Gulf–Israeli relations. In the long run, the sting of betrayal absolved Gulf elites from the burden of responsibility for the Palestinians, allowing them to prioritise the looming Iranian threat over Palestine. Indeed, Secretary of State Condoleezza Rice noted with surprise that when she brought up the Israeli–Palestinian conflict in a meeting with the GCC ministers in January 2007, 'The GCC ministers were pleased, but there wasn't a lot of discussion. This is pretty interesting, I thought. The Israeli–Palestinian issue has fallen down the list of priorities. Iran is number one, two, three, and four.'[116]

While in practice the Palestine question was no longer a hindrance to security collaborations with Israel, Gulf leaders insisted the relationship remained tacit and kept away from the public eye. This began to change following the outbreak of the uprisings in 2011. As many studies point out, the immediate effect of the uprisings was a shifting of the power structure in the system: draining power away from the historically central secular Arab republics (Egypt, Iraq, Syria), onto 'the periphery of the Gulf, especially Saudi Arabia, and to the non-Arab powers, Turkey and Iran . . .'[117] From this relatively stronger power position, the Gulf states enjoyed greater leeway to reassert and reinvent themselves. Those state elites that clung to power after 2011 – largely those in the conservative and pro-Western camp – found themselves in need of external sources of support to buttress them from domestic upheaval. Unbridled by the region's societal norms, Israel proved a willing and able partner to such endeavours.

In 2020 these long-term processes came to an axiom-shattering point: the absence of a just solution for the Palestinian plight is no longer a hindrance to normalisation of Israeli–Arab state relations. In August and September, the UAE and Bahrain formally committed themselves to full normalisation of relations with Israel under the framework of the US-sponsored 'Abraham Accords'. In this phase, Israel completed the shift from balancing object to interactant, fully and openly engaged in the regional institution of power-balancing: working through coalition-building moves to the emergence of overt counter-balancing alignments with core members of the system – Arab states in the Gulf and beyond – in which Israel is key, but not lynchpin.

News of Israel's quietly budding relations with a host of Gulf Arab states that hitherto refused to openly engage with it began breaking not long after the uprisings. Over the next few years, a steady news trickle informed us of relations proliferating, deepening and increasingly coming to light. Today, Israel is welcomed openly into regional power-balancing alignments, the way to which is paved by the signing of normalisation accords, in rapid succession. Israel as a societal boundary marker plays a key ordering role, as its hitherto tacit security collaborations progressively grow in scope, depth and visibility, recently reaching the ground-breaking point of diplomatic formalisation. It is tempting to look at recent normalisation accords and argue that we are now seeing Israel shifting from an external actor to an integral member of MENA society. In my view, Israel has long been and remains an integral society member. It is not in the process of shifting from outsider to insider. From Israel's perspective, the aim of rapprochement with Gulf states was not to craft a new regional order, but to sustain the old, with an Israel content to remain its perennial outsider.

Notes

1 The term 'Arab Spring' is now widely regarded a misnomer. Asher Susser, 'The "Arab Spring": Competing Analytical Paradigms', *Bustan: The Middle East Book Review* 3, no. 2 (2012): 109–30; Michael Totten, David Schenker, and Hussain Abdul-Hussain, 'Arab Spring or Islamist Winter? Three Views', *World Affairs* 174, no. 5 (2012): 23–42; Richard Falk, 'Rethinking the Arab Spring: Uprisings, Counterrevolution, Chaos and Global Reverberations', *Third World Quarterly* 37, no. 12 (2016): 2322–34. The term 'Arab Spring' is used hereon only when citing other authors. I prefer the term 'Arab uprisings'.

2 Raymond Hinnebusch, 'The Arab Uprising and Regional Power Struggle', in Shahram Azbarzadeh, ed., *Routledge Handbook of International Relations in the Middle East* (London: Routledge, 2019), 110.

3 Louise Fawcett, 'Regionalizing Security in the Middle East: Connecting the Regional and the Global', in Elizabeth Monier, ed., *Regional Insecurity after the Arab Uprisings: Narratives of Security and Threat* (London: Palgrave Macmillan, 2015), 42, 47.

4 Marc Lynch, 'The New Arab Order: Power and Violence in Today's Middle East', *Foreign Affairs* 97, no. 5 (2018): 116–17, 132. Paul Salem, too, saw 'the collapse of regional order': if hitherto the Middle East enjoyed a 'stable and

less conflictual regional order', post-2011 there is no longer 'regional order in any positive sense'. Paul Salem, 'Working Toward a Stable Regional Order', *The Annals of the American Academy of Political and Social Science* 668, no. 1 (2016): 45; Paul Salem, 'The Middle East in 2015 and Beyond: Trends and Drivers', The Middle East Institute (MEI) Policy Focus Series (2014): 6. See also Bülent Aras and Emirhan Yorulmazlar, 'Mideast Geopolitics: The Struggle for a New Order', *Middle East Policy* 24, no. 2 (2017): 57–69; Philipp Amour, 'Israel, the Arab Spring, and the Unfolding Regional Order in the Middle East: A Strategic Assessment', *British Journal of Middle Eastern Studies* 44, no. 3 (2017): 293, 294; Martin Beck and Thomas Richter, 'Fluctuating Regional (Dis-) Order in the Post-Arab Uprising Middle East', *Global Policy* 11, no. 1 (2020): 68; Christina Lassen, 'A Changing Regional Order: The Arab Uprisings, the West and the BRICS', Issam Fares Institute for Public Policy and International Affairs Working Paper Series 18 (2013): 16; Erzsébet Rózsa, 'Geo-Strategic Consequences of the Arab Spring', *PapersIEMed* 19 (2013): 16. For the minority view, assessing the uprisings' effect on regional order in more subtle or tentative terms, see Rasmus Boserup et al., 'Introduction', in Rasmus Boserup et al., eds, *New Conflict Dynamics: Between Regional Autonomy and Intervention in the Middle East and North Africa* (Copenhagen: Danish Institute for International Studies, 2017), 7; William Zartman, 'States, Boundaries and Sovereignty in the Middle East: Unsteady but Unchanging', *International Affairs* 93, no. 4 (2017): 947–8; Steven Heydemann and Emelie Chace-Donahue, 'Sovereignty versus Sectarianism: Contested Norms and the Logic of Regional Conflict in the Greater Levant', *Uluslararası İlişkiler* 15, no. 60 (2018): 19.

5 The three-year EU-funded MENARA Project ('Middle East and North Africa Regional Architecture: Mapping Geopolitical Shifts, Regional Order and Domestic Transformations', available at <http://menara.iai.it/menara-pr oject/> (last accessed 13 October 2022)), led by Eduard Soler i Lecha of the Barcelona Center for International Affairs (CIDOB), assessed the quality, extent and intensity of geopolitical shifts in the region over the past decade, and their implications for the regional order, seeking to account for 'fragmentation or integration dynamics in this region' and so capture 'geopolitical order in the making'. Eduard Soler i Lecha et al., 'Re-conceptualizing Orders in the MENA Region: The Analytical Framework of the MENARA Project' (2016), 4–5, 42; Raffaella Del Sarto et al., 'Interregnum: The Regional Order in the Middle East and North Africa after 2011' MENARA Final Reports 1 (February 2019).

6 The region has 'entered a period in which the existing order is increasingly challenged while an alternative one is still to be framed'. Del Sarto et al., 'Interregnum', 3, 5, 11, 42.

7   Most analyses seriously engage with domestic-level factors (though perhaps less
    comprehensively than the studies produced by the MENARA consortium).
    For example Ewan Stein, 'Ideological Codependency and Regional Order:
    Iran, Syria, and the Axis of Refusal', *Political Science* 50, no. 3 (2017): 676–80;
    Hinnebusch, 'The Arab Uprising'; Lynch, 'The New Arab Order'; Salem, 'The
    Middle East'; Mohammed Ayoob, 'Subaltern Realism Meets the Arab World',
    in Shahram Akbarzadeh, ed., *Routledge Handbook of International Relations in
    the Middle East* (London: Routledge, 2019), 59–68; Fawcett, 'Regionalizing
    Security'. Studies focusing on the nexus of the domestic and international in
    regional order pre-2011 include: Imad Mansour, 'The Domestic Sources of
    Regional Orders: Explaining Instability in the Middle East' (PhD Dissertation,
    McGill University, 2009); Benjamin Miller, *States, Nations, and the Great
    Powers: The Sources of Regional War and Peace* (Cambridge: Cambridge
    University Press, 2007).
8   The term 'international' in this context indicates interstate, as well as supra- and
    trans-state phenomena. It does not imply global scope, and in this text indeed
    refers mostly to phenomena whose scope is regional.
9   See Dennis Wrong, *The Problem of Order: What Unites and Divides Society*
    (New York: The Free Press, 1994); Nicholas Rengger, *International Relations,
    Political Theory and the Problem of Order: Beyond International Relations
    Theory?* (London: Routledge, 2000).
10 All studies of MENA order post-2011 cited in this chapter, bar MENARA's,
    fall under this generalisation. In reviewing their findings, I deduced their con-
    ceptualisations of 'order' from the term's usage in their text.
11 Rózsa, 'Geo-Strategic Consequences', 16, 29.
12 Ibid. 7.
13 Ibid. 7, 19.
14 Lynch, 'The New Arab Order', 120.
15 Ibid. 120.
16 Ibid. 124.
17 Ibid. 116–18.
18 Ibid. 116–17.
19 Ibid., 116–17, 126. Other examples of IR-realist accounts of regional order
    post-2011 include Aras and Yorulmazlar, 'Mideast Geopolitics'; Amour, 'Israel,
    the Arab Spring'.
20 On the distinction between normative, descriptive, and intentional/functional
    conceptions of order, see Hedley Bull, *The Anarchical Society: A Study of Order
    in World Politics* (London: Macmillan, 1977), xii–xiiv, 3–4.
21 Lynch, 'The New Arab Order', 116, 119.

22 Ibid. 121, 125.
23 Ibid. 116.
24 The constructivist gauntlet thrown down by Malmvig was picked up by Beck and Richter, 'Fluctuating Regional (Dis-)Order'; Heydemann and Chace-Donahue, 'Sovereignty versus Sectarianism', 19; Zartman, 'States, Boundaries'; Elizabeth Monier, 'The Arabness of Middle East Regionalism: The Arab Spring and Competition for Discursive Hegemony between Egypt, Iran and Turkey', *Contemporary Politics* 20, no. 4 (2014): 421–34. For a historical sociology approach that favours ideology over identity as key analytical category, see Stein, 'Ideological Codependency'. In contrast with Malmvig, Heydemann and Chace-Donahue see 'continuity rather than change in the structure of the regional order' post-2011 insofar as the conflicts that 'roil the [Levant and the] greater Arab east' have not caused 'significant changes in the internal borders of current states' nor replaced sovereignty for sectarianism as the region's hegemonic norm. Heydemann and Chace-Donahue, 'Sovereignty versus Sectarianism', 19.
25 Helle Malmvig, 'Power, Identity and Securitization in Middle East: Regional Order after the Arab Uprisings', *Mediterranean Politics* 19, no. 1 (2014): 145.
26 Ibid. 146.
27 Which Hinnebusch dubs 'complex realism', see Raymond Hinnebusch, *The International Politics of the Middle East* (Manchester: Manchester University Press, 2015), 1.
28 Hinnebusch, 'The Arab Uprising', 110–11.
29 Ibid., 111–12, 118; Hinnebusch, *The International Politics of the Middle East*, 9, 18.
30 The Iran-led Resistance Axis included Syria, Lebanese Hezbollah and Palestinian Hamas, and for a time drew support from Turkey and Qatar. It confronted the Moderate Bloc of Egypt, Jordan, Saudi Arabia and the remaining GCC states. The brutality of the Assad regime against Syrian citizens drove Hamas to break away from the Axis by late 2011. Hinnebusch, 'The Arab Uprising', 113–14, 116, 120.
31 Hinnebusch, 'The Arab Uprising', 114–15, 122.
32 Ibid. 110, 118.
33 Ibid. 111, 118, 122.; Hinnebusch, *The International Politics of the Middle East*, 276. Throughout the text, Hinnebusch often uses the terms identity, ideology, and discourse interchangeably. The explanation, perhaps, is that he conceives of them all essentially as ideational factors that give rise to norms that can 'constrain and shape the pursuit of state interests.' Hinnebusch, 'The Arab Uprising', 110.
34 Hinnebusch, 'The Arab Uprising', 117–18, 122.
35 Ibid. 110.

36 Ibid. 111, 114, 117–18.
37 Ibid. 117. In Hinnebusch's analysis, order slides along a scale between two ideal-types: 'Hobbesian' in which violence in the interstate power struggle is entirely unrestricted, or restricted merely by a balanced distribution of power among states, and 'Lockean' in which states' resort to violence is restricted by a more elaborate range of solutions, such as trans-state identity-based norms, collective institutions, complex economic interdependence, concert and/or contractual international regimes. Hinnebusch, 'The Arab Uprising', 111, 117, 118; Hinnebusch, *The International Politics of the Middle East*, 10, 20. To an extent, this approach builds on Alexander Wendt, *Social Theory of International Politics* (Cambridge: Cambridge University Press, 1999), 246–312.
38 'Order' is a key object of analysis across Hinnebusch's work, yet he does not put forward a definition of the concept at the outset, and furthermore uses it in several different ways across and within his texts (for example, juxtaposed with fragmentation of the state system, in Hinnebusch, *The International Politics of the Middle East*, 7; juxtaposed with conflict, war, lack of peace, or insecurity, in Hinnebusch, *The International Politics of the Middle East*, 10, 16, 20, 175, 222, 292; interchanged with anarchy, in Hinnebusch, 'The Arab Uprising', Chapter 10; or describing the systemic power structure, in Hinnebusch, 'The Arab Uprising', 120; in reference to domestic political order or public order, in Hinnebusch, 'The Arab Uprising', 119; Hinnebusch, *The International Politics of the Middle East*, 274; and finally 'normative order' as the framework of negotiated transnational norms that limit interstate violence, in Hinnebusch, *The International Politics of the Middle East*, 73; Hinnebusch, 'The Arab Uprising', 110, 111.) Therefore, my understanding of Hinnebusch's concept of order is deduced from his most frequent reference to it, as for example in Hinnebusch, 'The Arab Uprising', 111; Hinnebusch, *The International Politics of the Middle East*, 10, 16–19.
39 Hinnebusch, 'The Arab Uprising', 110–11.
40 Hinnebusch interchangeably uses 'Middle East' and 'MENA', defining the latter as 'constituted around an Arab core, with a shared identity but fragmented into multiple territorial states; the core is flanked by a periphery of non-Arab states – Turkey, Iran and Israel – which are an integral part of the region's conflicts and its balance of power'. Hinnebusch, *The International Politics of the Middle East*, 1. The region's core is distinguished as constituting an 'overarching Arab polity . . . [made up] of semi-permeable autonomous units' rather than a system of self-contained, bordered nation states. In fact for this reason the Arab core is perceived as a globally 'unique' type of state system. Hinnebusch, *The International Politics of the Middle East*, 69, 72, 75.

41 Hinnebusch, *The International Politics of the Middle East*, 1.

42 Ibid. 275.

43 Hinnebusch, 'The Arab Uprising', 122–3, 277; Hinnebusch, *The International Politics of the Middle East*, 277. It could be argued that Hinnebusch takes it for granted that Israel is precluded from launching a hegemonic bid because it so obviously lacks the soft-power resources essential for leadership, yet elsewhere he does consider an earlier Israeli bid for regional hegemony (that was counterbalanced by the Syrian–Iranian alliance). Hinnebusch, *The International Politics of the Middle East*, 309; Raymond Hinnebusch, 'Historical Context of State Formation in the Middle East: Structure and Agency', in Raymond Hinnebusch and Jasmine Gani, eds, *The Routledge Handbook to the Middle East and North African State and States System* (Abingdon and New York: Routledge, 2019), 33.

44 Beyond studies reviewed above, the point applies also to Aras and Yorulmazlar, 'Mideast Geopolitics'; Zartman, 'States, Boundaries'; Monier, 'The Arabness of Middle East Regionalism'; Jordi Quero and Eduard Soler i Lecha, 'Regional Order and Regional Powers in the Middle East and North Africa', in Immaculada Szmolka, ed., *Political Change in the Middle East and North Africa: After the Arab Spring* (Edinburgh: Edinburgh University Press, 2017), 276. Makdisi goes so far as describing Israel as a regional hegemon (presumably in terms of its power position, rather than leadership position), but otherwise refers to it mostly in passive terms: as threatened by the Arabs, protected by the Americans, partnered with by the Saudis. In the final analysis, Israel is not mentioned among the local powers that scrambled to shape the post-2011 regional order. Karim Makdisi, 'Intervention and the Arab Uprisings: From Transformation to Maintenance of Regional Order', in Rasmus Boserup et al., eds, *New Conflict Dynamics. Between Regional Autonomy and Intervention in the Middle East and North Africa* (Copenhagen: Danish Institute for International Studies, 2017), 102–5.

45 Benedetta Berti, 'Israel and the Arab Spring: Understanding Attitudes and Responses to the "New Middle East"', in Lorenzo Vidino, ed., *The West and the Muslim Brotherhood after the Arab Spring* (Al Mesbar Studies & Research Center in collaboration with The Foreign Policy Research Institute 2013), 130–47; Martin Beck, '"Watching and Waiting" and "Much Ado about Nothing"? Making Sense of the Israeli Response to the Arab Uprisings', *Palgrave Communications* 2, no. 1 (2016): 160–79; Dünya Başol, 'Arab Spring and Israeli Security: The New Threats', *Alternative Politics* 3, no. 3 (2011): 509–46; Efraim Inbar, 'The Strategic Implications for Israel', in Efraim Inbar, ed., *The Arab Spring, Democracy and Security: Domestic and International Ramifications*

(London: Routledge, 2013), 145–65; Tami Amanda Jacoby, 'The Season's Pendulum: Arab Spring Politics and Israeli Security', in Elizabeth Monier, ed., *Regional Insecurity after the Arab Uprisings: Narratives of Security and Threat* (Basingstoke: Palgrave Macmillan, 2015), 168–86; Clive Jones and Beverley Milton-Edwards, 'Missing the "Devils" We Knew? Israel and Political Islam amid the Arab Awakening', *International Affairs* 89, no. 2 (2013): 399–415; Ilan Peleg, 'Israel and the Arab Spring: The Victory of Anxiety', in Mark Haas and David Lesch, eds, *The Arab Spring: Change and Resistance in the Middle East* (Boulder: Westview Press, 2013), 174–94; Shmuel Sandler, 'The Arab Spring, Democracy and Security', in Efraim Inbar, ed., *The Arab Spring, Democracy and Security: Domestic and International Ramifications* (London: Routledge, 2013), 128–44; Avi Shlaim, 'Israel, Palestine, and the Arab Uprisings', in Fawaz Gerges, ed., *The New Middle East: Protest and Revolution in the Arab World* (Cambridge: Cambridge University Press, 2013), 380–401.

46   Amour, 'Israel, the Arab Spring'; Asher Susser, 'Israel's Place in a Changing Regional Order (1948–2013)', *Israel Studies* 19, no. 2 (2014): 218–38.

47   Amichai Magen, 'Comparative Assessment of Israel's Foreign Policy Response to the "Arab Spring"', *Journal of European Integration* 37, no. 1 (2015): 114–15. Magen explores Israel's reaction in unilateral terms, placing it in a comparative framework that assesses it against the reactions of 'other *external* actors, especially the US, EU and Turkey' (my emphasis).

48   Hedley Norman Bull and Adam Watson, eds, *The Expansion of International Society* (New York: Oxford University Press, 1984), 1.

49   Bull, *The Anarchical Society*, 13, 14; Bull and Watson, *The Expansion of International Society*, 1–2, 117, 120.

50   Coexistence encapsulates 'three basic values of all social life': the triumvirate of security against violation of body, promises and property. Bull, *The Anarchical Society*, 5, 7. Bull does not proceed to spell out how it is possible to discern this 'recognition' or 'consciousness' of common interests in coexistence among states. Nor does he indicate whether states' 'consciousness' is of subjective or intersubjective nature. Throughout the text Bull interchanges the term 'consciousness' with states' 'recognition', 'sense', 'conception' or 'acceptance' of, or consensus over common or shared interests in maintaining coexistence; Bull, *The Anarchical Society*, 14, 15, 42–3, 70, 249–50.; Bull and Watson, *The Expansion of International Society*, 1.

51   Bull, *The Anarchical Society*, 15, 249, 315; Bull and Watson, *The Expansion of International Society*, 120.

52   In Bull's precise formulation, international order is 'a pattern of activity that sustains the elementary or primary goals of the society of states, or international

society'. Bull, *The Anarchical Society*, 8; 'By international order is meant a pattern or disposition of international activity that sustains those goals of the society of states that are elementary, primary or universal.' Bull, *The Anarchical Society*, 16.

53 Bull, *The Anarchical Society*, xii, 60.

54 Ibid. 42–3.

55 Bull identifies coexistence as the elementary or primary shared goal of states, whose fulfilment perpetuates society itself while enabling the realisation of any further – advanced, secondary, special – goals held individually or commonly by society's members. Optimum order, he write, obtains when the pattern of social activity sustains secondary goals beyond coexistence, such as peace, cooperation, justice, human dignity or universal welfare. Bull, *The Anarchical Society*, 4–5, 86–7, 89, 96–7, 253, 302.

56 Bull, *The Anarchical Society*, 3, 249–50. In the Oxford English Dictionary, the word contrived is defined as 'deliberately created rather than arising naturally or spontaneously'. 'Definition of Contrived', Oxford University Press, Lexico.com. Available at <https://www.lexico.com/definition/contrived> (last accessed 19 October 2020).

57 Bull, *The Anarchical Society*, 249–50.

58 'Foreword to the Fourth Edition by Andrew Hurrell', in Hedley Bull et al., *The Anarchical Society: A Study of Order in World Politics*, 4th edn (Basingstoke: Palgrave Macmillan, 2012 (1977), xvi. See also Bull et al., *The Anarchical Society*, 15–16. For the alternative position within the English School that sees shared culture as prerequisite for international society, see Barry Buzan, 'Culture and International Society', *International Affairs* 86, no. 1 (2010): 1–25.

59 Like Bull, Hinnebusch sees order as potential and functional: a particular pattern of interstate activity whose emergence constitutes a system's interdependent units as a society of states. However, whereas Bull defines order as any pattern of interstate activity contrived to sustain coexistence, Hinnebusch sees order in activity patterns that work more specifically to restrain interstate violence. Hinnebusch, *The International Politics of the Middle East*, 17–18, 72; Raymond Hinnebusch, 'War in the Middle East', in Raymond Hinnebusch and Jasmine Gani, eds, *The Routledge Handbook to the Middle East and North African State and States System* (Abingdon and New York: Routledge, 2019), 358, ft 4; Raymond Hinnebusch, 'Order and Change in the Middle East: A Neo-Gramscian Twist on the International Society Approach', in Barry Buzan and Ana Gonzalez-Pelaez, eds, *International Society and the Middle East: English School Theory at the Regional Level* (Basingstoke: Palgrave Macmillan, 2009), 201. Other studies of MENA order that explicitly reference Bull, or

employ the English School concepts via Buzan, include Soler i Lecha et al., 'Re-conceptualizing Orders', 38; Louise Fawcett, 'Iran and the Regionalization of (In)security', *International Politics* 52, no. 5 (2015): 647; Raslan Ibrahim, 'Primary and Secondary Institutions in Regional International Society: Sovereignty and the League of Arab States', in Cornelia Navari and Tonny Bremms Knudsen, eds, *International Organization in the Anarchical Society* (Palgrave Macmillan, 2019); Bassam Tibi, 'The Middle East Torn Between Rival Choices: Islamism, International Security and Democratic Peace', in Elizabeth Monier, ed., *Regional Insecurity after the Arab Uprisings: Narratives of Security and Threat* (Basingstoke: Palgrave Macmillan, 2015), 207; Amour, 'Israel, the Arab Spring', 296.

60 Hinnebusch, 'Order and Change', 201–3.

61 Ibid. 224.

62 Hinnebusch, 'The Arab Uprising', 110–11; Hinnebusch, *The International Politics of the Middle East*, 5–6; Hinnebusch, 'Order and Change', 222.

63 Hinnebusch, 'The Arab Uprising', 111; Hinnebusch, *The International Politics of the Middle East*, 6.

64 Ibid. 111.

65 Ibid. 111. Alternatively referred to as 'cold wars' or 'discourse wars' by Hinnebusch, 'The Arab Uprising', 110–14.

66 Malmvig, 'Power, Identity and Securitization', 145.

67 Rózsa, 'Geo-Strategic Consequences', 7.

68 Whereas Hinnebusch asserts that in the MENA, 'The most typical balancing dynamic has been "soft balancing"', Beck argues that the region is character-ised by 'hard-power rather than soft-power use', Martin Beck, 'The Concept of Regional Power as Applied to the Middle East', in Henner Fürtig, ed., *Regional Powers in the Middle East: New Constellations after the Arab Revolts* (New York: Palgrave Macmillan, 2014), 5; Hinnebusch, 'The Arab Uprising', 111.

69 Hinnebusch, 'The Arab Uprising', 111.

70 Aaron Klieman, 'The Israel–Jordan Tacit Security Regime', in Efraim Inbar, ed., *Regional Security Regimes: Israel and its Neighbors* (Albany: State University of New York Press, 1995), 130.

71 Clive Jones and Yoel Guzansky, 'Israel's Relations with the Gulf States: Toward the Emergence of a Tacit Security Regime?' *Contemporary Security Policy* 38, no. 3 (2017): 398–419; Efraim Inbar and Shmuel Sandler, 'The Changing Israeli Strategic Equation: Toward a Security Regime', *Review of International Studies* 21, no. 1 (1995): 41–59; Yaacov Bar-Siman-Tov, 'Security Regimes: Mediating Between War and Peace in the Arab–Israeli Conflict', in Efraim Inbar, ed.,

Regional Security Regimes: Israel and its Neighbors (Albany: State University of New York Press, 1995), 33–55; Efraim Inbar, ed., *Regional Security Regimes: Israel and its Neighbors* (Albany: State University of New York Press, 1995).

72 Noa Schonmann, 'Fortitude at Stake: The Accidental Crisis in American–Israeli Relations, August 1958', *Israel Affairs* 23, no. 4 (2017): 626–49.

73 Louise Fawcett, ed., *International Relations of the Middle East*, third edn (Oxford: Oxford University Press, 2013), 187; Louise Fawcett, 'States and Sovereignty in the Middle East: Myths and Realities', *International Affairs* 93, no. 4 (2017): 793.

74 Fawcett does not use the term 'secondary' institutions, but all her examples (League of Arab States, Organization of Islamic Conference, Baghdad Pact, Gulf Cooperation Council, and so on) comfortably fall under this category. Buzan introduced the distinction between primary institutions, which are constitutive of international society and 'evolved rather than designed, constitutive rather than instrumental' (for example, sovereignty, power-balancing) and secondary institutions that are instrumentally designed and take organisational form (for example, the WTO, Amnesty). He added that 'secondary institutions do not define international societies, but they do matter, not least as expressions of, and possibly benchmarks for, primary institutions.' Barry Buzan and Ana Gonzalez-Pelaez, eds, *International Society and the Middle East: English School Theory at the Regional Level* (Basingstoke: Palgrave Macmillan, 2009), 27, 44.

75 Louise Fawcett, 'Regional Leadership? Understanding Power and Transformation in the Middle East', in Nadine Godehardt and Dirk Nabers, eds, *Regional Powers and Regional Orders* (London: Routledge, 2011), 161; Fawcett, 'States and Sovereignty', 792–3.

76 Heller echoes Fawcett's point when he argues that Israel does not have the power to shape the regional order, and at best can block undesirable developments and avoid being overrun. Like Fawcett, Heller bases his conclusion on Israel's exclusion from secondary institutions, but his examples are primarily from non-security fields: 'In none of the arrangements or institutions normally associated with global or even regional order does Israel's voice carry much weight . . . And it does not even belong to the plethora of Middle East governmental or private associations that address – even if they do not effectively regulate – cultural, educational, public security, and scientific affairs.' Mark Heller, 'Israel: Extra-regional Foundations of a Regional Power Manqué', in Nadine Godehardt and Dirk Nabers, eds, *Regional Powers and Regional Orders* (London: Routledge, 2011), 237–8.

77 Simon W. Murden, 'The Secondary Institutions of the Middle Eastern Regional Interstate Society', in Barry Buzan and Ana Gonzalez-Pelaez, eds,

International Society and the Middle East: English School Theory at the Regional Level (Basingstoke: Palgrave Macmillan, 2009), 117; Fawcett, 'Regionalizing Security', 40. A more recent strand of literature that reasserts this point in the post-2011 context includes: Sally Khalifa Isaac, 'A Resurgence in Arab Regional Institutions? The Cases of the Arab League and the Gulf Cooperation Council Post-2011', in Elizabeth Monier, ed., *Regional Insecurity after the Arab Uprisings: Narratives of Security and Threat* (Basingstoke: Palgrave Macmillan, 2015), 158; Mervat Rishmawi, 'The League of Arab States in the Wake of the "Arab Spring"' Delivering Democracy (5th CIHRS' Annual Report on the Human Rights Situation in the Arab World), Cairo Institute for Human Rights Studies (2013); Ibrahim, 'Primary and Secondary', 311; Avraham Sela, 'The Vicissitudes of the Arab States System: From Its Emergence to the Arab Spring', *India Quarterly* 73, no. 2 (2017): 165; Martin Beck, 'The End of Regional Middle Eastern Exceptionalism? The Arab League and the Gulf Cooperation Council after the Arab Uprisings', *Democracy and Security* 11, no. 2 (2015): 200.

78 Heller proffers only one, historically rather minor example to substantiate this claim: extension of Israeli military support to minorities in conflict with states hostile to Israel (for example, Iraq's Kurds, Lebanon's Maronites, even South Sudanese factions during the civil war). Mark Heller, 'Israel as a Regional Power: Prospects and Problems', in Henner Fürtig, ed., *Regional Powers in the Middle East: New Constellations after the Arab Revolts* (New York: Palgrave Macmillan, 2014), 170.

79 Heller, 'Israel as a Regional Power'; Robert Kappel, 'Israel: The Partial Regional Power in the Middle East', in Henner Fürtig, ed., *Regional Powers in the Middle East: New Constellations after the Arab Revolts* (New York: Palgrave Macmillan, 2014), 145–61; Fawcett, 'States and Sovereignty', 792–3; Beck, 'The Concept of Regional Power', 18.

80 Hinnebusch, 'The Arab Uprising', 114. Beck defines 'regional powers' as '(state) actors whose power is, to a high degree, based on leadership in their world area'. See Martin Beck, 'Israel: Regional Politics in a Highly Fragmented Region', in Daniel Flemes, ed., *Regional Leadership in the Global System: Ideas, Interests and Strategies of Regional Powers* (London: Routledge, 2010), 127–48; Beck, 'The Concept of Regional Power'. While Beck combines the two terms into one, Heller distinguishes 'regional power' ('an actor – state or even non-state actor – that is able to advance regional or at least sub regional order to suit its own purposes') from 'regional leadership' ('the ability to shape the perceptions and influence the positions of others in order to promote a regional order or regime'). Heller, 'Israel: Extra-regional', 237.

81 Heller, 'Israel as a Regional Power', 171; Heller, 'Israel: Extra-regional', 237.

82 Hinnebusch, 'The Arab Uprising', 123; Heller, 'Israel: Extra-regional', 237.

83 Fawcett, 'Regional Leadership', 164, 162.

84 Heller, 'Israel as a Regional Power', 170; Shlaim, 'Israel, Palestine', 400; Magen, 'Comparative Assessment', 117–18. The former was articulated by Israel former prime minister Ehud Barak (Aluf Benn, 'Israel is Blind to the Arab Revolutions', *The Guardian*, 23 March 2011); the latter by Israeli prime minister Benjamin Netanyahu (Gilad Morag, '4th of July: Israel celebrate US Independence Day', [Hebrew] *Ynet*, 4 July 2013. Available at <https://www.ynet.co.il/articles/0,73 40,L-4401030,00.htm> (last accessed 2 November 2020).

85 Avi Shlaim, 'Israeli Interference in Internal Arab Politics: The Case of Lebanon', in Giacomo Luciani and Ghassan Salame, eds, *The Politics of Arab Integration* (London: Croom Helm, 1988), 232–3.

86 Inbar, 'The Strategic Implications', 149–50; Heller, 'Israel as a Regional Power', 170.

87 Howard Becker, *Outsiders: Studies in the Sociology of Deviance* (New York: Free Press, 2018); Robert K. Merton, 'Insiders and Outsiders: A Chapter in the Sociology of Knowledge', *American Journal of Sociology* 78, no. 1 (1972): 21–2. The term 'outsider' has been applied to Israel by scholars who used it in this non-member, external actor, sense. See Heller, 'Israel as a Regional Power', 169; Rózsa, 'Geo-Strategic Consequences', 19; Bruce Maddy-Weitzman, *The Crystallization of the Arab State System, 1945–1954* (Syracuse: Syracuse University Press, 1993), 176.

88 Heller, 'Israel: Extra-regional', 238; Kappel, 'Israel', 145; Inbar, 'The Strategic Implications', 149–50.

89 Ian Black, 'Just Below the Surface: Israel, the Arab Gulf States and the Limits of Cooperation', LSE Middle East Report, The London School of Economics and Political Science (2019), 5.

90 Jones and Guzansky, 'Israel's Relations', 403; Uzi Rabi and Chelsi Mueller, 'The Gulf Arab States and Israel since 1967: From 'No Negotiation' to Tacit Cooperation', *British Journal of Middle Eastern Studies* 44, no. 4 (October 2017): 576. Available at <https://doi.org/10.1080/13530194.2017.1360013> (last accessed 16 October 2022).

91 Asher Orkaby, 'The 1964 Israeli Airlift to Yemen and the Expansion of Weapons Diplomacy', *Diplomacy & Statecraft* 26, no. 4 (October 2015): 659–77. Available at <https://doi.org/10.1080/09592296.2015.1096691> (last accessed 16 October 2022). For debate over the extent of Saudi knowledge of the Israeli use of their airspace, and mention of other possible episodes of tacit coordination, see Elie Podeh, 'Saudi Arabia and Israel: From Secret to

Public Engagement, 1948–2018', *The Middle East Journal* 72, no. 4 (2018): 567–8.

92 Podeh, 'Saudi Arabia and Israel', 572–3.

93 Podeh, 'Saudi Arabia and Israel', 573; Jones and Guzansky, 'Israel's Relations', 404; Rabi and Mueller, 'The Gulf Arab States and Israel', 583.

94 Podeh, 'Saudi Arabia and Israel', 573.

95 Ultimately the process culminated in the signing of a peace treaty with Jordan in 1994, and the Interim Accords with the PLO in 1993 and 1995. Elie Podeh, *Chances for Peace: Missed Opportunities in the Arab–Israeli Conflict* (Austin: University of Texas Press, 2015), 263, 290; Elie Podeh, 'Israel and the Arab Peace Initiative, 2002–2014: A Plausible Missed Opportunity', *Middle East Journal* 68, no. 4 (2014): 586.

96 Black, 'Just Below the Surface', 6; Rabi and Mueller, 'The Gulf Arab States and Israel', 577–85; Jones and Guzansky, 'Israel's Relations', 404–5.

97 Podeh, 'Saudi Arabia and Israel', 576.

98 Black, 'Just Below the Surface', 6–7; Podeh, 'Saudi Arabia and Israel', 576; Barak Ravid, 'WikiLeaks Blows Cover Off Israel's Covert Gulf States Ties', *Haaretz*, 29 November 2010.

99 Black, 'Just Below the Surface', 17.

100 Black, 'Just Below the Surface', 12. For list of news reports see Podeh, 'Saudi Arabia and Israel', 577. In an interview to Podeh, Olmert added that 'there were [even] more extraordinary things' going on than Dagan's 2010 visit to Saudi Arabia.

101 Ravid, 'WikiLeaks Blows Cover Off Israel's Covert Gulf States Ties'.

102 Sigurd Neubauer, 'Israel: A Strategic Partner for the UAE?' *Gulf State Analytics*, 9 November 2017; Black, 'Just Below the Surface', 12–14.

103 Podeh, 'Saudi Arabia and Israel', 577.

104 Jones and Guzansky, 'Israel's Relations', 398–9.

105 Black, 'Just Below the Surface', 10–20; Podeh, 'Saudi Arabia and Israel', 563.

106 Black, 'Just Below the Surface', 13–22.

107 Ibid. 22.

108 Amos Harel, 'Israeli Military Chief Gives Unprecedented Interview to Saudi Media: "Ready to Share Intel on Iran"', *Haaretz*, 17 November 2017; Podeh, 'Saudi Arabia and Israel', 563.

109 Black, 'Just Below the Surface', 24; Podeh, 'Saudi Arabia and Israel', 579.

110 Podeh, 'Saudi Arabia and Israel', 563.

111 Black, 'Just Below the Surface', 8, 12.

112 Patrick Wintour, 'US Backtracks on Iran-focused Conference in Poland after Objections', *The Guardian*, 23 January 2019.

113 Podeh, 'Saudi Arabia and Israel', 584. I use Podeh's words here, but while he traces this shift back to the 1990 Gulf War, I see it emerging only in 2006.

114 Inbar, 'The Strategic Implications', 154; Malmvig, 'Power, Identity and Securitization', 146; Hinnebusch, 'The Arab Uprising', 115; Del Sarto et al., *Interregnum*, 4, 43–5; Andrea Dessì and Lorenzo Kamel, 'The Gaza Equation: The Regional Dimension of a Local Conflict', MENARA Working Papers (September 2018), 10; Black, 'Just Below the Surface', 14–15. Few scholars see merit in the argument that the question remained as salient after 2011, among them Karim Makdisi et al., 'Regional Order from the Outside in: External Intervention, Regional Actors, Conflicts and Agenda in the MENA Region', MENARA Concept Papers 5 (November 2017), 10; Shlaim, 'Israel, Palestine'.

115 Rabi and Mueller, 'The Gulf Arab states and Israel', 583.

116 Condoleezza Rice, *No Higher Honor: A Memoir of My Years in Washington* (New York: Crown Publishers, 2011), 550; Black, 'Just Below the Surface', 16.

117 Hinnebusch, 'The Arab Uprising', 114–15, 122.

4

IRAN'S SYRIA POLICY AND ITS REGIONAL DIMENSIONS

Nader Entessar

Introduction: An Overview

The aim of this chapter is to analyse Iran's Syria policy within the broad context of Tehran's regional policies and regional security concerns. Although the origins of the current Syrian conflict are complex, heterogenous and beyond the scope of this chapter, what is important to note is that the new 'Middle East cold war' between Iran and Saudi Arabia has added a new layer to the evolving Syrian conflict. In addition, as Christopher Phillips has noted, several other players have exacerbated the tragedy in Syria by intervening to advance their own regional goals.[1] In April 2017, the Trump administration's unilateral airstrike against Syria over its alleged use of chemical weapons against civilians suggested the possibility of a creeping US military intervention and a self-admitted plan to 'destabilize Syria'.[2] Thus, instead of a remapping of the Syrian conflict in the direction of a peaceful political transition and the sustained restoration of peace, the continuation of the Syrian conflict until recently seemed to have become a distinct possibility for the foreseeable future. However, the gradual steps taken since 2020 by some Arab countries towards a rapprochement with Damascus may signal a thaw in the Syrian imbroglio.

There is already a growing body of literature tracing the current conflict in Syria to the cycle of violence that followed the spread of the 'Arab Spring' in early 2011. The ensuing war in Syria emerged as a crisis not only for Damascus but also for Tehran and the 'Axis of Resistance' that included Iran, Syria and Lebanon's Hezbollah, as well as the Palestinian group Hamas.[3] This regional alliance, solidified by a hitherto confidential military pact between Iran and Syria in 2006, self-articulated in terms of hostility to Israel, opposition to US hegemony in the Middle East and antagonism towards pro-Western Arab status quo powers, most notably Saudi Arabia and Egypt under Mubarak. Inevitably, the evolution of the Iran nuclear crisis with its distinct security dimension had definite repercussions for this alliance. That is, from Iran's perspective, this alliance served the country as a deterrent against the threat of military strike by Israel and/or the US on its nuclear facilities. Future historians will be able to determine if Israel's decision not to strike Iran was due to the Israeli concern about Iran's ability to retaliate effectively through its allies in Gaza, southern Lebanon and Syria. At the moment, however, we lack sufficient data to provide a definitive answer to this question, although one can reasonably assume that Israel considered the Iranian ability to retaliate through its allies in the region as credible. From Iran's vantage point, this capability underpinned Tehran's strategy of 'extended deterrence' premised on both 'asymmetrical warfare' and the extension of the theatre of conflict, in the event of a unilateral strike on Iran's nuclear facilities, throughout the region.[4] For Iran's regional allies, on the other hand, this meant that they would be targets in a conflict or regional crisis if Iran's adversaries sought to weaken Iran's regional resolve by undermining its deterrent capability that relied extensively on the Axis of Resistance. The Arab League's March 2016 decision to label Hezbollah a terrorist organisation was definitely a step in this direction.[5] Indeed, overall this is a key factor that distinguishes the current Syria crisis from the prior 'struggle for Syria' in the late 1940s to mid-1960s, masterfully depicted in Patrick Seale's classic study that focuses on the interplay between internal turmoil and the struggle for regional hegemony.[6] Unlike the previous crisis, the present one was less about leadership in the Arab 'sub-system' and the exigencies of the Arab–Israeli conflict and more about an associated crisis that at once raised the multiple issues of democracy, the rise of radical Islamism, Sunni–Shi'ite sectarianism,[7] Kurdish autonomy,[8] foreign meddling and intervention, Iranian–Saudi power politics, Qatar's regional rise and the fallout from the Iran nuclear crisis.

Simultaneously, the present Syrian crisis has created a new opportunity (as well as pitfalls) for Russia to extend its influence in the Middle East and thus reverse decades of retreat from the region. Moscow has managed to pursue this objective by moving closer to Iran and its Axis of Resistance and by forming a partnership, albeit a fluid one, with the Axis of Resistance.[9] One intended consequence of this partnership of convenience was to change the fortunes of war in favour of the Syrian government, which was able to regain control of Aleppo, Palmyra and a number of other urban centres held by the opposition, with direct help from Iran and Hezbollah forces on the ground and Russian air support. These victories marked a turning point in the conflict, representing a dead end for the rebels, who had little or no chance of reversing the tides against them short of direct US military intervention.[10] The unintended consequence was the potential danger of a US–Russia rivalry inside Syria that imperiled regional and world peace.

Although Moscow's interests in Syria do not always coincide with those of Tehran, there has been a steady move towards the reconciliation of Iranian and Russian interests in Syria since the victory of Ebrahim Raisi in Iran's presidential election of 2021. On 20 January 2022, during his official visit to Moscow, President Raisi gave a major speech to the State Duma of the Russian Federation in which he outlined the framework for the expansion of Iranian–Russian relations in all fields. Raisi specifically praised the 'successful model of Iran–Russia cooperation' in Syria and pledged to strengthen this relationship as a model for strengthening regional security.[11] Whether Moscow views its expanding relations with Tehran as 'strategic' may be debatable. However, Russia will most likely continue to view Iran as an important pillar of its geostrategic presence in the Middle East, especially in Syria.

During the 2011–14 period, the Iran nuclear crisis and the Syrian crisis went hand in hand, the latter exacerbated by the influx of money and arms from Gulf Cooperation Council (GCC) states to the Syrian rebels, and the Arab League's related decision to expel Syria in November 2011 and impose an economic and political blockade on Damascus, effectively slamming shut all diplomatic doors.[12] In March 2013, the Arab League invited the Saudi-backed Syrian opposition leader, Moaz al-Khatib, to take the Syrian seat at its Doha summit, signalling another indication of the eroding influence of the Axis of Resistance. This was augmented by Hamas's decision to abandon the Axis of Resistance after two years of bloodshed in Syria and to court the anti-Damascus governments in Qatar and Egypt under the short-lived Muslim Brotherhood president Mohamed Morsi. This led Tehran, which had aided Hamas in Gaza for years, to significantly reduce its financial support for the movement.[13]

This was followed by a rapprochement between Hamas and the Palestinian Authority controlling the West Bank, brokered by Egypt, derived in part from a growing sentiment in the Arab world that the days of the pro-Iran Baathist regime in Syria were numbered and it was only a matter of time before Assad's government in Damascus would be replaced by a Sunni-led alternative. Coinciding with the intense nuclear negotiations, the Syrian conflict was, indirectly at least, tantamount to Western leverage vis-à-vis Iran that also banked on Iran's new concerns about the break-up of Iraq and the announcement by the Islamic State (ISIS) of a trans-border Islamic caliphate in July 2014, followed by spectacular military achievements, which were attributable to the group's foreign backing, internal discipline, reliance on extreme violence and ruthless extermination of enemies, and sophisticated manipulation of the internet and social media.[14] It has been observed that 'in its assault on Mosul in June 2014, ISIS was careful to join forces with local Baathist and tribal groups, recruiting from among the city's own youth as well.'[15] The group's success was partly attributable to a dreadful strategic error by US president Barack Obama, who initially branded ISIS's takeover of Mosul as 'an internal Iraqi problem' and failed to provide any credible US military assistance to repel ISIS's assault on Iraq's third largest city.[16] ISIS fighters overran much of the province of Nineveh, the cities of Fallujah and Tikrit, and several towns around Kirkuk, as well as taking over Iraq's largest oil refinery in Baiji, some 130 miles north of Baghdad.

Similarly, in Syria, ISIS fought against not only the Syrian government, but also the Kurds and other rebel groups, including al-Nusra, which declared war on ISIS as it seized territory, equipment and provisions from them. ISIS also infused itself among the tribal networks in peripheral areas and sought to mobilise the local population by providing social services, thanks in large measure to its successful oil smuggling following its seizure of Syria's largest oil fields at al-Omar and the Shaer gas field near Homs. The Obama administration's decision not to target the ISIS oil convoys through the porous Turkish borders was a contributing factor to ISIS's staying power.[17]

Together, the twin military setbacks in Iraq and Syria, transpiring at a time of robust international sanctions on Iran limiting its ability to protect its regional alliance from multiple shocks, played a crucial role in accelerating Iran's desire to end the nuclear crisis as soon as possible in order to salvage its regional standing. Simultaneously, the developments in Iraq and Syria were met by a steady increase in Iran's military presence in both countries, thus reflecting the flip side of the twin crises as essentially crises of opportunity for Iran to extend its spheres of influence, but only insofar as Tehran was able to help the Iraqi and Syrian governments reverse their military misfortunes and gain the upper hand against their armed adversaries, above all ISIS and other Sunni jihadists harbouring hatred of Shi'ites.

Iran's anti-ISIS strategy was perceived domestically in defensive terms, with civilian and military officials constantly reminding the nation that if Iran failed to fight ISIS beyond its territories it would soon have to fight it inside Iran.[18] In Iraq, this meant a tactical alliance between Iran and the pro-Iran Shi'ite forces and the US-led coalition against ISIS. However, in Syria the outcome was vastly different and meant new, and unprecedented strategic cooperation with the Russian military, which began to flex its muscle in Syria in September 2015, only two months after the signing of the Iran nuclear agreement, or the Joint Comprehensive Plan of Action (JCPOA). The resulting Iran–Russia strategic cooperation in Syria, whereby Russian air power and growing Iranian land power converged in Syrian theatres of conflict on behalf of the embattled government of Bashar al-Assad, was uniquely responsible for turning the tide of conflict in favour of the government, which was able to reclaim control of vast swathes of Syrian territory, including the commercial hub of Aleppo, from the hands of the opposition. This was a major blow to the anti-Iran Arab bloc that had insisted on the departure of Bashar al-Assad and was counting on the continuation of the Iran nuclear crisis to cripple Iran's ability to rescue its Syrian ally.

Another blow to this bloc was Turkey's changing regional policy, which had initially aligned itself with Saudi Arabia on Syria, following the Turkish miscalculation regarding the imminent collapse of the Assad government, hoping for an 'Ankara moment' in the Middle East that never arrived.[19] In the aftermath of a failed military coup in January 2016, the Turkish government led by President Recep Tayyip Erdoğan recalculated its foreign policy agenda and, increasingly, sided with Russia and Iran in an active search for a viable peace in Syria, resulting in several rounds of peace talks in Astana, Kazakhstan. While these and the related efforts proceeded, a cloud of uncertainty still hovered over Syria's future. It was abundantly clear, however, that the attempts to defeat the Axis of Resistance in Syria had failed and there would be no remaking of Syria that would put this important Arab country in the orbit of pro-West status quo powers. In addition to Turkey, even Egypt was reconsidering its anti-Syrian position and moving closer to Iran and Syria, just as new tensions between Egypt and Saudi Arabia were emerging.

Thus, within the span of the Rouhani administration's first four years in office, Iran had managed to recuperate a good deal of its regional strategic losses, albeit with some attrition of influence in Syria due to the influx of Russian power and diplomacy whose aims did not always correspond with the interests and prerogatives of the Axis of Resistance. While it was too early to draw firm conclusions about the new geopolitical landscape in the Middle East, it was clear that there were exorbitant costs to the winning side that affected the net assessment of the Syrian conflict, and that the Israeli-led interpretation that Syria was now an 'extension of Iran' due to the influx of Iranian forces was an exaggeration; such Israeli assessments turned the Syrian government into an epiphenomenon, ignored Russia's role and influence and assumed a singular Iranian approach towards Syria. In fact, there were concerns within Iran about the scope of the country's influence in a post-conflict Syria, in light of the prominent role of Russia and, to a lesser extent, Turkey, which followed its own 'sphere of influence' agenda in the war-torn country. The fact that Iranian forces were now in closer proximity to Israel as a result of the Syrian conflict was also a complicating factor for Iran's foreign policy that, for decades, had essentially viewed Israel as a hostile, albeit 'out of area', power. Iran's more direct involvement in the stalemated Arab–Israeli conflict was thus portended by the Syrian conflict which, as stated above, had its origins in the Iran nuclear crisis. The termination of this crisis, on the other hand, reflecting a new momentary thaw in Iran–West relations, boosted Iran's regional diplomacy and, in particular, enabled the Rouhani administration and its foreign policy team to expand their role in shaping Iran's Syria policy.[20]

A new Syria policy was thus formulated by Tehran that focused on a diplomatic, rather than purely military, resolution of the conflict, highlighted by the Iranian foreign minister Mohammad Javad Zarif's extensive tour of the region after the conclusion of the nuclear talks, showcasing a four-point plan that called for an immediate ceasefire, followed by constitutional reforms to safeguard Syrian minorities, free and internationally supervised elections, and the formation of a national unity government based on the new constitutional institutions. Also, in 2013 Iran fully supported the US–Russia agreement on the elimination of Syria's chemical weapons.[21] In turn, such efforts by Tehran enabled Iran's inclusion in the so-called Geneva talks on Syria, which had transpired in the early rounds without Iran's participation; the UN, under pressure from Saudi Arabia and Western governments, had withdrawn the invitation to Iran to take part in the first round of the Geneva talks.

Such opposition gradually melted away as the Iran nuclear talks showed signs of progress, prompting US secretary of state John Kerry to publicly state in January 2014 that Iran could play a constructive role in finding a resolution to Syria's civil war. In addition to Kerry, other Western diplomats involved in the nuclear negotiations, such as the French foreign minister Laurent Fabius and the British foreign secretary William Hague, also advocated Iran's inclusion in the Geneva peace process once the nuclear talks proved productive. Within Iran, on the other hand, these new developments triggered new discussions and debates about the end-goal of Iran's new conflict-management role in Syria. Was there an alternative to Bashar al-Assad? What was the best way to prevent the 'Balkanisation' of Syria, and was a return to the status quo ante possible? Was Syria destined to experience more foreign meddling in the future, in light of the US's toying with a 'safe zone' option in Syria that would likely entail increased US military presence in the country? Could Syria evolve from a failed state to a reinvigorated new state with healthy relations with Turkey, which was concerned with the growing power of the Syrian Kurdish groups in its vicinity? Was it possible to turn the hitherto centralised (unitary) political system in Syria into a federalist system which could sustain itself over the long run? And finally, did Iran have to make any concessions, for example, on the geopolitical front, in order to advance the anti-ISIS and counterterrorism objective in Syria and Iraq? The last issue owed its complexity to a certain Iranian ambivalence regarding the US's intentions in Syria, stemming from the belief of some Iranian officials that Washington was propping up Islamist extremists in Syria in order to weaken both the Syrian government and the Iran-led Axis of Resistance. Certain disclosures of US documents by Wikileaks seemed to corroborate this fear, reflecting a basic chasm between the public counterterrorism stance of the US government and its private view that saw the 'potential threat to the (Syrian) regime from the increasing presence of transiting Islamist extremists' as an 'opportunity'.[22]

With the US and Turkey pushing for a 'safe zone' in Syria, Iranian suspicion grew that perhaps US intentions were less about fighting terrorism and more about carving out a sphere of influence inside Syria on a long-term basis.[23] In early 2015, such suspicions were fuelled by, among other things, the decision of the al-Qaida affiliate, the Nusra Front, to quit its frontline positions against ISIS in northern Syria, thus making 'a US–Turkish agreement on establishing a safe zone in northern Syria more likely'.[24] There were logistical nightmares associated with a 'safe zone' in Syria, including the estimated tens of thousands of US ground forces needed to enforce it, not to mention the potential danger of US conflict with the Syrian government and its Iranian and Russian allies. A 'safe zone' would inevitably require a 'no-fly zone' that, in turn, would require 'as many as 70,000 American servicemen to dismantle Syria's sophisticated anti-aircraft system, and then impose a 24-hour watch over the country', as noted by US General Martin Dempsey in 2013.[25] Clearly, for the 'overstretched' US military, which grappled with a host of other global issues and threats, such as North Korea and disputes in the South China Sea, the prospect of a major military re-entry in the Middle East after the phased troop reductions in Iraq and Afghanistan was a cause for concern, dictating caution in order to avoid past mistakes that had cost US taxpayers trillions of dollars and thousands of American lives. Now led by the new US president Donald Trump, who had voiced criticism of US military adventures abroad and who seemed inclined to forge a counterterrorism partnership with Russia and various regional states, Washington had to craft a new Middle East policy that prioritised crisis management above all else. In turn, this had raised hopes in Iran that the US and Iran could find some common denominators in Syria and elsewhere in the turbulent Middle East, warranting selective cooperation. For this to transpire, however, an important prerequisite was for the US to re-examine its Iran policy and to consider refining and nuancing its traditional 'containment' approach that constantly prioritised deterrence over any positive cooperation.

The Evolution of the Iran–Syria Alliance

Traced by various scholars to the tumults of the Iran–Iraq war (1980–8) and the upheavals in Lebanon that saw the emergence of the Shi'ite group Hezbollah in 1982, the alliance between post-revolutionary Iran and Syria has been an enduring aspect of Middle East politics for over four decades. Despite differences in their forms of government, one being republican-theocratic and the other secular, the two countries have been able to maintain, and manage, their alliance as a result of a host of geopolitical, ideological and religious factors binding them together. Led by the Alawite minority, which constitutes approximately 12 per cent of the Syrian population, Damascus since 1970 has essentially moved within the Shi'ite 'orbit', in light of the fundamental principles and tenets of Alawism, which have also evolved in the modern era closer to Iran's brand of Twelver Shi'ism. According to Sabrina Mervin, 'This doctrinal overture started in the early twentieth century, developed in the 1950s and continued under the presidency of Hafez al-Assad.'[26] Emerging scholarship on Syria demonstrates that contemporary Syrian history is often treated in 'essentialist' terms and reduced to a single overarching theme of religion (and sects). In his thoughtful narrative on the Alawites, for example, Stefan Winter refers to them as a 'branch of Imami Shiism', traced to the establishment of the Shi'a Hamdanid dynasty in Aleppo in 947. Winter's *A History of 'Alawis* [Alawites] is a reminder that for centuries the Alawites were a persecuted minority. The fourteenth-century Sunni scholar Ibn Taymiyya called for their extermination, and the Alawites survived for centuries mainly through their mountain refuge in north-western Syria, before emerging from isolation during the French mandate period (1923–46), rising through the bureaucratic and military institutions of the postcolonial state and finally assuming political power through the Baathist coup of 1970.[27] The most prominent opponent to Assad's rule was the Muslim Brotherhood, which was brutally suppressed in Hama in 1982.[28] Despite unbridled historical hatred of the Alawites by some Sunnis, there was no effective organised opposition in Syria until the Arab Spring's outbreak in 2011. Some of the (exiled) opposition groups that were groomed by Saudi Arabia and, to a lesser extent, Qatar jockeyed over influence and control once the militarisation phase of opposition to Assad's regime began in 2011–12.[29] The spillover effects of conflicts in Lebanon, Iraq and the Kurdish regions of Turkey for Syria, coupled with the huge influx of foreign jihadist fighters into the country, created two overlapping conflicts in the country. One conflict pitted the Syrian government against a diverse Syrian opposition and the other conflict involved fighting between government forces and various Salafi–Jihadist groups such as ISIS, which were able to seize sizable territories in both Iraq and Syria in 2014 and, increasingly, also fought other rebel groups competing with them.[30] Together, these groups turned Syria into a major theatre of operation for their 'global jihad', attracting tens of thousands of foreign fighters.[31]

During the eight-year war with Iraq, Iran was able to count on Syria as a critical ally against a common foe (Saddam Hussein), who competed with the Assad government for Baathist Arab leadership. Concomitant with the rise of pro-Iran Shi'ites in Lebanon, Syria was able to obtain material support from Iran given its central location as a transit point between Iran and Lebanon.[32] In much of the literature on Syria–Iran relations, the functional utility of this alliance for both sides is often emphasised and the 'strategic depth', particularly for Iran, in making Syria 'the first line of defense', is singled out as a primary motivating factor behind the Tehran–Damascus alliance.[33] From the prism of 'alignment theory', this fits the description of 'omnialignment', denoting alliances that use a combined (domestic and foreign) strategy to deal with security challenges that feed off one another.[34]

The issue of 'strategic depth' indeed forms a core assumption of Iranian and Syrian thinking about this alliance, although it is fair to say that it primarily serves Iran's foreign 'power projection' beyond its borders. Alawite-controlled Syria's close identification with Iran, on the other hand, would make it a prime candidate by the Sunni jihadists and their Gulf patron states, who took advantage of the government's vulnerabilities to cause Syria's fragmentation as a prelude to the reassertion of Sunni rule in Damascus, with the preceding Libya campaign – that overthrew the dictator Moammar Qaddafi in October 2011 – as a 'force multiplier' in the Syrian civil war. However, Libya's quick descent into chaos and the disagreements at the UN on replicating NATO's role in Syria, which unlike Qaddafi enjoyed external support from Iran and Russia, meant that Bashar al-Assad would not be fated to the same end as Qaddafi.[35] Iran alone spent undetermined billions to prop up the Assad government, in addition to a gradual increase in the scope of its direct military involvement in the Syrian war, which was initially kept out of the public spotlight.[36] Iran's military support came both directly, by dispatching more and more military advisers, volunteers (mobilised from inside Iran as well as from Iraq, Afghanistan, Pakistan, and elsewhere), soldiers numbering in the thousands, and, indirectly, through a major influx of Hezbollah fighters to Syria. No accurate figures are available, and according to one estimate about 7,000–10,000 Iranian soldiers and up to 10,000 Hezbollah militiamen have taken part in the Syrian conflict, including 1,000–2,000 killed in action, several Iranian military advisers among them.[37] Officially, one stated rationale for Iran's growing involvement in the Syrian conflict was to extend a helping hand in protecting the various Shi'ite sacred sites, such as the shrine of Sayeda Zeinab, the Prophet's granddaughter, or the shrine of Hujr bin Adi al-Kindi, a companion of the Prophet, which Sunni rebels desecrated in April 2013.[38]

Yet, despite all of Iran's and Hezbollah's combined effort and sacrifice, initially the tide of war in Syria continued to turn menacingly against their ally in Damascus, thus warranting Iran's appeal to Russia for direct military intervention to salvage Assad's government. This appeal, reportedly made through a personal presentation to Russia's President Putin by the head of Iran's Quds Force, General Qassem Soleimani in July 2015, resonated with Russia, which was equally concerned about the loss of its strategic assets in the Mediterranean.[39] Moscow's fateful decision to commence an air campaign beginning in September 2015 and, subsequently, to utilise Iran's airbase in Hamadan for the Syria operations, heralded a new page in the Iranian–Syrian alliance, now bolstered by the Russian army. One way to describe this development is by reference to theories of alliance-bandwagoning, which shed light on the empirical reality of a Russia–Syria–Iran–Hezbollah 'united front' in the Syrian war. By early 2017, it was becoming clear that the Axis of Resistance, increasingly projected as a 'clear winner' in the Western media,[40] itself was experiencing some evolutionary changes as well.

A New Axis of Resistance in the Making

From the volcanic dust of the Syrian crisis, signs of a new Axis of Resistance were emerging, with long-term consequences. First, a closer military partnership with Russia, reflected in the sale of the S-300 missile defence system to Iran and the installation of S-300 and S-400 systems in Syria, added real muscle to the Axis of Resistance by bolstering its military and deterrent capability. Second, the Syrian war shifted the geopolitical tectonics in the Middle East and, in turn, raised new questions, opportunities, risks and challenges for the Axis of Resistance, particularly regarding its purpose and mission. One of the significant ramifications of the Axis' strategic partnership with Russia was that Russia inevitably weighed heavily on the future decisions of the Axis, which were not always easy to deal with since Russia was primarily concerned with the NATO threat, and Moscow's Middle East policies are subsets of its global policies. Whether or not this would constrain the Axis of Resistance in the future depended on a myriad of factors including the future of Russia–NATO relations and the evolution of interstate relations in the Gulf and beyond. What was clear, however, was that the Axis of Resistance could enjoy greater future stability and viability by following the prescriptions of 'smart diplomacy' and making the necessary adjustments in tune with the evolving context of its existence. One such adjustment was in the realm of self-representation, hitherto limited to a negative discourse of opposition, which had to be revised along a more positive discourse that emphasised nation-building, state-building, and adherence to international norms and principles. This was largely achieved by Hezbollah partaking in a new (coalition) government of national unity inside Lebanon that included forces backed by both Iran and Saudi Arabia, marking a definite evolution of Lebanese politics.

Another adjustment was in the area of cooperative security, requiring the use of a new language of security that was inclusive and promoted linkage with the Arab camp led by Saudi Arabia, and contested the idea of 'zero-sum security' in the region as the antidote to the present polarisations and the divisive discourses of a new 'Middle East cold war', which tended to cloud areas of shared interests between the opposing camps, such as with respect to fighting extremism.[41] A key challenge was how to restore peace in Syria.

Determined to find a durable political solution for the bloody conflict in Syria, Iran was seriously contemplating a new approach that was future oriented and realistic, instead of clinging to the traditional view that can be summed up in one sentence: there is no alternative to Bashar al-Assad. But after a catastrophic six-year conflict exacting so many lives, including scores of Iranians and Shi'ite Lebanese, Tehran was finally warming to a post-Assad political transition, provided that it did not spell doom for its old alliance with Damascus (and any strategic loss). Needless to say, this was a highly sensitive national security issue for Iran and its regional alliance system at a crucial time when the Saudi-led bloc was on the offensive and seeking to limit or neutralise Iran's regional power projections. This is why any changes in Iran's public stance on Syria, such as President Rouhani's call in a press conference in April 2017 for 'certain reforms in Syria', were bound to unnerve some Iranian policy centres focused on Syria.[42] Such statements were meant to showcase Iran's new flexibility, coinciding with a draft Russian-proposed new constitution for Damascus that emphasised political pluralism and envisaged a federalist system for the war-ravaged country.

Rouhani's key ally was the retired Rear Admiral Ali Shamkhani, the head of Iran's Supreme National Security Council, who shouldered the responsibility of coordinating Iran's Syria policy with Russia. Shamkhani was considered a pragmatic-centrist politician who supported the Iran nuclear deal and occasionally sent reassuring signals in backing the administration's foreign policies. Of course, much depended on the US, which had prioritised fighting ISIS in both Syria and Iraq. Washington's policy was seriously questioned by, among others, some fifty-one former US diplomats in a 'dissent letter' to the White House that called for US air strikes on the Syrian regime, ostensibly to extract more concessions from Damascus.[43] If the US had followed this approach, the situation would have turned considerably more volatile, further escalating US–Russia tensions. The 'dissent letter' did not bother to discuss the possible unintended consequences of a serious escalation of the conflict as a result of US military attacks against the Syrian military, which would have only benefitted radical jihadists on the US's terrorism list. The problem with the US's insistence that 'Assad must go' was that it did not properly prognosticate 'the day after'; that is, whether or not a Libyan-style chaos would follow once the authoritarian head of Syria was removed. All paper agreements could fall to the side, further sliding Syria into chaos, if the necessary guarantees for a durable political solution were not somehow interwoven with a post-Assad scenario. With or without Assad, however, the long list of Syria's endemic problems – such as the Kurds' quest for autonomy, the infiltration of terrorist groups and religious sectarianism – remained, which was why it was necessary to avoid (Assad-obsessive) political reductionism and focus instead on the hugely complex political and societal processes. This explains why Iran has been so intent on finding a political solution to the Syrian conflict.

The Astana Rounds and the Troika Peace Diplomacy

By late 2016 and early 2017, with the balance of forces tipped in favour of the Syrian government, and Turkey plagued by waves of war refugees and conflict-spillover that heightened security concerns to unprecedented levels, the stage was set for the troika of Russia, Turkey and Iran to collaborate by initiating a new peace process in Astana, Kazakhstan, that paralleled the deadlocked Geneva talks.[44] The Kazakhstan Foreign Ministry played host and sent invitations to representatives of the UN, US and Jordan, whose government acted as interlocutors with the Syrian opposition and ensured the latter's participation in the first meeting in late December 2016. The US ambassador to Kazakhstan participated as an observer. Among the rebel groups in the delegations were Jaish al-Sham, Failaq al-Sham, Fastaqim, the Sultan Murad Division, Jabhat Shamiyya and Suqoor al-Sham. Yahya al-Aridi, an opposition spokesperson, told the press at Astana that the opposition demanded an unobstructed delivery of aid, the release of opposition prisoners in Syrian government custody, and the departure of all foreign fighters from Syria, including those from Iran and Lebanon. This sentiment was shared by Turkey, which in essence negotiated on behalf of the opposition and whose foreign minister Melvut Cavusoglu insisted that Hezbollah must return to Lebanon.

A huge difference between Astana and Geneva was a shift in the attitude of the opposition towards the Syrian government. This was articulated by the editor-in-chief of Syria's *Watan* newspaper, Waddah Abd Rabbo, who noticed that in the previous, failed, Geneva round of negotiations, the opposition was always fixated on discussing 'dictator Assad', whereas in Astana, the opposition was ready to negotiate a peace process.[45] According to Naser al-Hariri, an opposition delegate at the first Astana meeting, 'In Geneva, there was no plan, no nothing. Here in Astana, you feel things are planned, you feel the influential parties are trying to reach a specific objective.'[46] That objective was, first and foremost, brokering a nationwide Syrian ceasefire, one that would be both more comprehensive and sustainable than the two previous 'partial' ceasefire attempts in February and September 2016; the last one, organised by the US and Russia, had collapsed after only one week due mainly to a US–British airstrike aimed at ISIS that instead killed dozens of Syrian government soldiers, perhaps attributable to disagreements between the Pentagon and the US Department of State.[47]

The ceasefire breakthrough in Astana was announced on 28 December 2016 in a joint statement by Russia, Turkey and Iran, who agreed to monitor and enforce the ceasefire deal, aimed at minimising violence, building confidence, ensuring humanitarian access, and the protection and free movement of civilians. The agreement did not cover ISIS, al-Nusra Front, and other terrorist groups, and the troika urged the Syrian opposition to cut ties with them. Afterwards, there were complaints of ceasefire violations by both sides and clashes continued. In February, there was a fresh rebel offensive in Daraa, followed by a rebel surprise attack near Damascus in March, but these did not result in the complete collapse of the ceasefire. At the third Astana round in mid-March 2017, both sides remained committed to the ceasefire agreement in place from the second Astana round in January. A potentially important development was Russia's call for a joint working committee to work on a new Syrian constitution.[48] The debates about the new constitution revolved around the central question of the structure and format of the government: should it maintain its present highly centralised form or move towards a more decentralised system, based on equal citizenship of Arab, Kurdish, Assyrian, Turkmen and other groups in Syria?

At this stage of the Syrian conflict, the pendulum had swung in favour of some form of Kurdish autonomy and, despite resistance by Turkey, it was perhaps inevitable that the Syrian Kurds would emerge from the bloody conflict stronger and with a new level of regional autonomy in north-east Syria. The exact nature of the territory to be held by Syrian Kurds in the aftermath of the conflict had yet to be determined and, certainly, it depended on the future evolution of the conflict on the ground and the ability of the Kurds to negotiate successfully with the Syrian government. Another key issue was the changing make-up of the Sunni and Shi'ite regions in the course of the six-year-old conflict, causing catastrophic population displacement. In order to address the grievances of its Sunni majority, the Syrian government, in addition to a new inclusionary approach, needed to mollify sectarian tensions by granting local autonomy to the Sunni-dominated towns and villages; otherwise, it was almost certain that such tensions would continue. Certain administrative changes that would accommodate themselves to a new distribution of power aimed at appeasing Syrian Sunnis seemed necessary, although it is fair to say that the flip side of such initiatives was to institutionalise a confessional system not unlike Lebanon. Therefore, a delicate balance was needed between the state's prerogative for national survival, territorial integrity and independence on the one hand and, on the other, local and regional autonomy and redistribution of power at the national and sub-national levels, taking into consideration the significant changes in the war-induced demographic structure of different regions.

By spring 2017, the Astana peace process had been established as a 'subset' of the Geneva process, where the US, Europe and the Arab world weighed in and the two processes became quite complementary.[49] A fourth round in Astana was due in May 2017, pending the outcome of an 'expert' meeting of the sponsoring states in Tehran. Both the Astana and Geneva processes faced identical problems, such as how to achieve a durable peace when ISIS and other terror groups continued to wage war, how to maintain a ceasefire which did not cover the terrorist-held territories, and how to create a manageable political transition that did not reduce the power of the central authority. The advantage of even a partial and fragile ceasefire, for example, under the guise of a 'de-escalation' zone(s), which Iran supported, was that it could be telescoped to confidence and trust-building between the warring parties, if micro-supervised successfully by the monitoring parties, and thus lay the basis for a more durable peace.

Conclusion

Iran's involvement in Syria is a function of fluid variables that highlight Iran's security and threat perception, complex and evolving regional politics, and great power interests. The July 2020 signing of the Iran–Syria security agreement which calls for Tehran's cooperation with Damascus to strengthen Syria's air defence system is a reflection of Iran's broader regional security complex.[50] Economically, participation in the Syrian conflict has come at great cost to Iran. The post-COVID-19 realities and the ever-increasing US sanctions on Iran have created socio-economic challenges for Tehran. Also, notwithstanding overlapping goals between Iran and Russia, these two countries have pursued separate goals.[51] Although Iran has spent significant political and strategic capital in Syria, it has not yet gained any economic benefits from its Syrian policy. As noted by Hamidreza Azizi, a regional studies professor at Shahid Beheshti University in Tehran, Iran intends to play a major role in Syria's reconstruction. There is a considerable difference between what Iran expects to accomplish after the Syrian conflict winds down and Tehran's approach to reconstruction in the aftermath of wars in Lebanon and Iraq. In Azizi's words, in post-Saddam Iraq and post-2006 Lebanon, Iran

> contributed largely non-refundable aid aimed primarily at securing Tehran's political interests, i.e. supporting pro-Islamic Republic groups and factions. However, nowadays, when Iranian officials talk about Iran's role in post-war Syria, they insist not only that Tehran will not allocate unconditional financial resources to Damascus, but that Iran expects to be compensated for its expenditures aimed at bolstering the Assad government.[52]

In addition to signing a number of memorandums of understanding and banking agreements with Damascus, the Islamic Republic is now encouraging Iran's private sector to become the vanguard of Iranian economic activities in Syrian reconstruction efforts. In short, in order to understand Iran's Syria policy and its broader facets, one needs to look at a wide spectrum of issues that shape the contours of the Islamic Republic's long-term strategic interests and its perception of its legitimate role as a major player in the region.

Notes

1 For a detailed study of the role of international actors in the Syrian crisis, see Christopher Phillips, *The Battle for Syria: International Rivalry in the New Middle East* (New Haven, Yale University Press, 2016).

2 David Edwards, 'The Goal is to Destabilize Syria: Sean Spicer Baffles Reporters with Trump's Middle East Policy', *The Raw Story*, 10 April 2017. Available at <https://www.rawstory.com/2017/04/the-goal-is-to-destabilize-syria-sean-sp icer-baffles-reporters-with-trumps-middle-east-policy/> (last accessed 9 October 2022).

3 Rola El Husseini, 'Hezbollah and the Axis of Refusal: Hamas, Iran and Syria', *Third World Quarterly* 31, no. 5 (2010): 803–15. See also Nadia von Maltzahn,

The Syria–Iran Axis: Cultural Diplomacy and International Relations in the Middle East (London: I. B. Tauris, 2013).

4 For more on this see, Kaveh Afrasiabi, 'How Iran Will Fight Back', *World Security Network*, 18 December 2004. Available at <https://www.worldsecuritynetwork.com/Iran/Afrasiabi-Kaveh/How-Iran-will-fight-back> (last accessed 9 October 2022).

5 'Arab League Labels Hezbollah a "Terrorist" Group', *Al Jazeera*, 11 March 2016. Available at <https://www.aljazeera.com/news/2016/3/12/arab-league-labels-hezbollah-a-terrorist-group> (last accessed 9 October 2022).

6 Patrick Seale, *The Struggle for Syria: A Study in Post-war Arab Politics, 1945–1958*, new edition (New Haven, CT: Yale University Press, 1987); Curtis Ryan, 'The New Arab Cold War and the Struggle for Syria', *Middle East Report* 262 (Spring 2012). Available at <https://merip.org/2012/03/the-new-arab-cold-war-and-the-struggle-for-syria/> (last accessed 9 October 2022).

7 Christopher Phillips, 'Sectarianism and Conflict in Syria', *Third World Quarterly* 36, no. 2 (2015): 357–76. See also Daniel Byman, 'Sectarianism Afflicts the New Middle East', *Survival* 56, no. 1 (2014): 79–100, and Paulo Gabriel Hilu Pinto, 'The Shattered Nation: The Sectarianization of the Syrian Conflict', in Nader Hashemi and Danny Postel, eds, *Sectarianization: Mapping the New Politics of the Middle East* (New York: Oxford University Press, 2017), 123–42.

8 For background information on Syria's Kurds, see Harriet Allsopp, *The Kurds of Syria: Political Parties and Identities in the Middle East* (London: I. B. Tauris, 2014). Allsopp has noted that the power vacuum in the Kurdish regions of Syria provided the Kurdish autonomy groups an opportunity to expand their influence and to 'apply a form of bottom-up management', 208. See also Michael M. Gunter, *Out of Nowhere: The Kurds of Syria in Peace and War* (London: Hurst, 2014).

9 For background information on Russia–Syria relations, see Roy Allison, 'Russia and Syria: Explaining Alignment with a Regime in Crisis', *International Affairs* 89, no. 4 (July 2013): 795–823.

10 Aron Lund, 'Turning Point in Aleppo', Carnegie Middle East Center, *Diwan*, 1 December 2016. Available at <https://carnegie-mec.org/diwan/66314> (last accessed 9 October 2022).

11 'Iran–Russia Coop. in Syria Strengthened Regional Security', *Mehr News Agency*, 20 January 2022. Available at <https://en.mehrnews.com/news/183093/Iran-Russia-coop-in-Syria-strengthened-regional-security> (last accessed 9 October 2022); and 'New Chapter in Strategic Cooperation with Russia', *Kayhan*, 20 January 2022, 1, 7.

12 Karen DeYoung and Liz Sly, 'Syrian Rebels Get Influx of Arms with Gulf

Neighbours' Money, US Cooperation', *Washington Post*, 15 May 2012. Available at <https://www.washingtonpost.com/world/national-security/syrian-rebels-get-influx-of-arms-with-gulf-neighbors-money-us-coordination/2012/05/15/gIQAds2TSU_story.html> (last accessed 9 October 2022). For a concise critical analysis of the role of the Western media in underestimating and/or under-reporting the role of extremists in the Syrian opposition, see Max Abrahms, 'Syria's Extremist Opposition: How Western Media Have Whitewashed the Rebels' Record', *Foreign Affairs*, 30 October 2017. Available at <https://www.foreignaffairs.com/articles/middle-east/2017-10-30/syrias-extremist-opposition> (last accessed 9 October 2022).

13   It is worth noting that some Arab states have now taken steps to break the thaw in their relations with Damascus and bring back Syria to the Arab fold. For example, in October 2021, King Abdullah II of Jordan spoke with Assad in the first such call since 2012. This was followed by the reopening of the main Jordan–Syria border crossing. In November 2021, the UAE foreign minister Sheikh Abdullah bin Zayed al-Nahyan visited Bashar al-Assad in Damascus, signalling a move towards Syria's readmission to the Arab League. For details, see Radwan Ziadeh, 'Rehabilitation of the Assad Regime', Arab Center Washington DC, *Policy Analysis*, 15 December 2021. Available at <https://arabcenterdc.org/resource/rehabilitation-of-the-assad-regime/> (last accessed 9 October 2022).

14   Patrick Cockburn, *The Rise of Islamic State: ISIS and the New Sunni Revolution* (New York: Verso Books, 2015).

15   Abdel Bari Atwan, *The Islamic State: The Digital Caliphate* (Berkeley, CA: University of California Press, 2015), 56.

16   'Obama: Up to Iraq to Solve Its Problems', *NBC-2*, 13 June 2014.

17   Fazel Hawramy, Shalaw Mohammed and Luke Harding, 'Inside Islamic State's Oil Empire: How Captured Oil Fields Fuel ISIS Hegemony', *The Guardian*, 19 November 2014. Available at <https://www.theguardian.com/world/2014/nov/19/-sp-islamic-state-oil-empire-iraq-isis> (last accessed 9 October 2022). See also Rudy Panko, 'Report: US Pilots in Syria Ordered to Ignore ISIS Oil Convoys', *Russia Insider*, 14 December 2015. Available at <https://russia-insider.com/en/report-us-pilots-syria-ordered-ignore-isis-oil-convoys/ri11832> (last accessed 9 October 2022). It has been suggested that the US's fateful decision to initially tolerate ISIS's oil transactions stemmed from the pressure of a number of hawkish members of the US Congress, in concert with the Turkish, Israeli and Saudi intelligence, to provide a 'political shield' for ISIS's oil smuggling. See Gordon Duff, 'How John McCain Crippled Obama's War on ISIS', *New Eastern Outlook*, 14 December 2015. Available at <https://journal-neo.org/2015/12/14/how-john-mccain-crippled-obama-s-war-on-isis/> (last accessed 9 October 2022).

18 Dina Esfandiary and Ariane Tabatabai, 'Iran's ISIS Policy', *International Affairs* 91, no. 1 (January 2015): 1–15.

19 André Bank and Roy Karadag, 'The "Ankara Moment": The Politics of Turkey's Regional Power in the Middle East, 2007–11', *Third World Quarterly* 34, no. 2 (2013): 287–304. Also, see Idris Demir, ed., *Turkey's Foreign Policy Towards the Middle East: Under the Shadow of the Arab Spring* (Newcastle-upon-Tyne: Cambridge Scholars Publishing, 2017); Burak Bekdil, 'Turkey's Double Game with ISIS', *Middle East Quarterly* 22, no. 3 (Summer 2015): 1–8; and Kaveh L. Afrasiabi, 'The Limits of Turkey's Double Game', *Iranian Diplomacy*, 22 February 2017. Available at <http://www.irdiplomacy.ir/en/news/1967324/the-limits-of-turkey-rsquo-s-double-game> (last accessed 9 October 2022).

20 In July 2015, the US secretary of state John Kerry stated that the Iranian foreign minister Zarif specifically told him that 'If we get this [JCPOA] finished, I am now empowered to work with and talk to you about regional issues.' See Jeffrey Goldberg, 'John Kerry on the Risk of Congress "Screwing" the Ayatollah', *The Atlantic*, 5 August 2015. Available at <https://www.theatlantic.com/international/archive/2015/08/john-kerry-interview-iran-nuclear-deal/400457/> (last accessed 9 October 2022).

21 In September 2013, Foreign Minister Zarif stated: 'We certainly wanted the issue of chemical weapons addressed . . . We had a lot of diplomatic contacts . . . We were in Moscow when the agreement was reached at the level of deputy foreign minister . . . To that extent we were a party, but obviously this was a Russian–American agreement and we helped along as we could.' Quoted in Andrew Parasiliti, 'Iran's Foreign Minister Offers Help with Syrian Chemical Weapons', *Al-Monitor*, 30 September 2013. Available at <https://www.al-monitor.com/originals/2013/09/foreign-minister-zarif-seeks-iranian-role-in-syria-talks.html> (last accessed 9 October 2022). Four years later, at the Munich Security conference, Zarif complained that 'The use of chemical weapons can never be condoned . . . Unfortunately, the terrorist organizations Nusra and Daesh (Islamic State) still possess chemical weapons.' Quoted in 'Iran's Zarif Says Use of Chemical Weapons in Syria Cannot be Condoned', *Reuters*, 19 February 2017. Available at <https://www.reuters.com/article/us-mideast-crisis-syria-iran-idUSKBN15Y080> (last accessed 9 October 2022).

22 For more on this issue, see Janani Ganesan, 'Decoding the Current War in Syria: The Wikileaks Files', *Versobooks.com*, 31 August 2015. Available at <https://www.versobooks.com/blogs/2219-decoding-the-current-war-in-syria-the-wikileaks-files> (last accessed 9 October 2022). According to Ganesan, these Wikileaks releases show that the US targeted the Syrian government for 'regime change' as of 2006. This coincided with the rise of Iran's Ahmadinejad and his

singular pursuit of Iran's civilian nuclear programme deemed 'proliferation-prone' by US and other Western powers. A relevant work is by David Keen, *Useful Enemies: When Waging Wars Is More Important Than Winning Them* (New Haven, CT: Yale University Press, 2014). Keen, however, overlooks the functional utility of Islamists by world powers, for example, the US's support for the Afghan Mujahedin against the occupying Soviet forces during the 1980s.

23 In early 2017, the US forces stationed in Syria were assisting the Syrian Democratic Forces (SDF) to re-take the ISIS-occupied Raqqa. The secular SDF's primary Kurdish element is the People's Protection Units (YPG), and ally of the US and of Turkey's nemesis, the People's Workers Party (the PKK) and, thus, by extension, an enemy of America's NATO ally, Turkey. See, Shoshana Bryen, 'A Slippery Slope in Iraq and Syria', *The Washington Times*, 21 March 2017. Available at <https://www.washingtontimes.com/news/2017/mar/21/iraq-and-syria-security-could-get-worse/> (last accessed 9 October 2022).

24 Ashish Kumar Sen, 'Al-Qaeda Affiliate Gets Out of the Way in Syria', Atlantic Council, *New Atlanticist*, 12 August 2015. Available at <https://www.atlanticcouncil.org/blogs/new-atlanticist/al-qaeda-affiliate-gets-out-of-the-way-in-syria/> (last accessed 9 October 2022). A former US diplomat has noted: 'The emergence of al-Nusra, arguably the most effective opposition force in the (Syrian) war, undermined the Obama administration narrative that al-Qaeda was on a path to strategic defeat, although it too dropped its affiliation with al-Qaeda in July 2016 as it attempted to re-position itself within the Syrian opposition hierarchy.' P. J. Crowley, *Red Line: American Foreign Policy in a Time of Fractured Politics and Failing States* (Lanham, MD: Roman & Littlefield, 2017), 158.

25 Quoted in Mark Mazzetti, Robert F. Worth and Michael R. Gordon, 'Obama's Uncertain Path Amid Syria Bloodshed', *New York Times*, 22 October 2013. Available at <https://www.nytimes.com/2013/10/23/world/middleeast/obamas-uncertain-path-amid-syria-bloodshed.html?referrer=&_r=3> (last accessed 9 October 2022).

26 Sabrina Mervin, 'Introduction', in Sabrina Mervin, ed., *The Shi'a Worlds and Iran* (London: Saqi Books, 2010), 10.

27 Stefan Winter, *A History of the 'Alawis: From Medieval Aleppo to the Turkish Republic* (Princeton: Princeton University Press, 2016).

28 Eberhard Kienle, ed., *Contemporary Syria: Liberalization Between Cold War and Cold Peace* (London: I. B. Tauris, 1994).

29 Samer N. Abboud, *Syria: Hot Spots in Global Politics*, second edn (Cambridge: Polity, 2018).

30 For a good study of the views of ISIS and other Jihadist groups operating in Syria and Iraq, see Shiraz Maher, *Salafi-Jihadism: The History of an Idea* (New York: Oxford University Press, 2016).

31 According to a US intelligence report in 2016, more than 44,000 fighters from more than 100 countries had gone to Syria. See 'Over 40,000 Foreign Militants from 100 Countries Fighting in Syria – US State Department', *Russia Today*, 3 June 2016. Available at https://www.rt.com/usa/345269-40000-foreign-terro rists-syria/> (last accessed 9 November 2022).

32 Raymond Hinnebusch, 'Syria: Defying the Hegemon', in Rick Fawn and Raymond Hinnebusch, eds, *The Iraq War: Causes and Consequences* (Boulder, CO: Lynne Rienner Publishers, 2006), 129–47.

33 Representative work is Jubin Goodarzi, 'Iran: Syria as the First Line of Defense', in Julien Barnes-Dacey and Daniel Levy, eds, *The Regional Struggle for Syria* (London: European Council on Foreign Relations, 2013), 25–31. Also, Paul Danahar, *The New Middle East: The World After the Arab Spring* (London: Bloomsbury, 2013).

34 For more on 'omnialignment', see Richard J. Harknett and Jeffrey A. VanDenBerg, 'Alignment Theory and Interrelated Threats: Jordan and the Persian Gulf Crisis', *Security Studies* 6, no. 3 (Spring 1997): 112–53.

35 Elizabeth A. Kennedy, 'Syrians Inspired by Gaddafi's Death', *The Independent*, 21 October 2011. Available at <https://www.independent.co.uk/news/world /middle-east/syrians-inspired-by-gaddafi-s-death-2374026.html> (last accessed 9 October 2022); and Ed Husain, 'Why Assad Need Not Fear Ghaddafi's Fate', *Financial Times*, 23 August 2011. Available at <https://www.ft.com/content /73d4c680-ccb7-11e0-b923-00144feabdc0> (last accessed 9 October 2022).

36 After 2011, Iran increased its financial 'loans' to Syria. See Eli Lake, 'Iran Spends Billions to Prop Up Assad', *Bloomberg Opinion*, 9 June 2015. Available at <https://www.bloomberg.com/opinion/articles/2015-06-09/iran-spends-billio ns-to-prop-up-assad> (last accessed 9 October 2022).

37 Sam Dagher and Asa Fitch, 'Iran Expands Role in Syria in Conjunction with Russia's Airstrikes', *The Wall Street Journal*, 2 October 2015. Available at <https://www.wsj.com/articles/iran-expands-role-in-syria-in-conjunction-with-russias-airstrikes-1443811030> (last accessed 9 October 2022). Also, see Dominic Evans and Miriam Karouny, 'Iranian Guards Commander Killed in Syria', *Reuters*, 14 February 2013. Available at <https://www.reuters.com/arti cle/us-syria-crisis-iran/iranian-guards-commander-killed-in-syria-idUSBRE91D 0EY20130214> (last accessed 9 October 2022).

38 Thomas Erdbrink and Hania Mourtada, 'Iran Warns Syrian Rebels After Report of Shrine Desecration', *New York Times*, 6 May 2013. Available at <https://www

.nytimes.com/2013/05/07/world/middleeast/iran-warns-syrian-rebels-after-report-of-shrine-desecration.html> (last accessed 9 October 2022).

39 Bozorgmehr Sharafedin, 'Report and Denial that Iranian Commander Met Putin in Moscow', *Reuters*, 16 December 2015. Available at <https://www.reuters.com/article/us-mideast-crisis-iran-russia/report-and-denial-that-iranian-commander-met-putin-in-moscow-idUSKBN0TZ1NW20151216> (last accessed 9 October 2022); and Laila Bassam and Tom Perry, 'How Iranian General Plotted Out Syrian Assault in Moscow', *Reuters*, 6 October 2015. Available at <https://www.reuters.com/article/us-mideast-crisis-syria-soleimani-insigh/how-iranian-general-plotted-out-syrian-assault-in-moscow-idUSKCN0S02BV20151006> (last accessed 9 October 2022).

40 Maria Abi-Habib, 'Syria's Civil War Produces a Clear Winner: Hezbollah', *The Wall Street Journal*, 3 April 2017. Available at <https://www.wsj.com/articles/syrias-civil-war-produces-a-clear-winner-hezbollah-1491173790> (last accessed 9 October). Such declarations of winners and losers in an ongoing conflict were somewhat premature and underestimated the degree to which the war could potentially drag on and witness changes in the fortunes of the declared winners over time. For background analysis of Hezbollah's growing involvement in Syria, see Marisa Sullivan, 'Hezbollah in Syria', Institute for the Study of War, *Middle East Security Report*, no. 19, April 2014. Available at <https://www.understandingwar.org/sites/default/files/Hezbollah_Sullivan_FINAL.pdf> (last accessed 9 October 2022).

41 F. Gregory Gause III, 'Beyond Sectarianism: The New Middle East Cold War', Brookings Doha Center Analysis Paper, July 2014. Available at <https://www.brookings.edu/wp-content/uploads/2016/06/English-PDF-1.pdf> (last accessed 9 October 2022). For a succinct analysis of Iran's decision calculus see Kayhan Barzegar and Abdolrasool Divsallar, 'Political Rationality in Iranian Foreign Policy', *The Washington Quarterly* 40, no. 1 (spring 2017): 39–53.

42 'Some Reforms Necessary in Syria – Pres. Rouhani', *Mehr News Agency*, 10 April 2017. Available at <https://en.mehrnews.com/news/124698/Some-reforms-necessary-in-Syria-Pres-Rouhani> (last accessed 9 October 2022).

43 Mark Landler, '51 U.S. Diplomats Urge Strikes Against Assad in Syria', *New York Times*, 16 June 2016. Available at <https://www.nytimes.com/2016/06/17/world/middleeast/syria-assad-obama-airstrikes-diplomats-memo.html> (last accessed 9 October 2022).

44 Mohammad Khajouei, 'Iran, Russia, Turkey Triangle: Strategic Coalition or Tactical Alliance?' *Iran Review*, 23 August 2016. Available at <http://www.iranreview.org/content/Documents/Iran-Russia-Turkey-Triangle-Strategic-Coalition-or-Tactical-Alliance-.htm> (last accessed 9 October 2022).

45 Erika Solomon, 'West Sidelined to the Bar in Russia-led Syria Talks', *Financial Times*, 25 January 2017. Available at <https://www.ft.com/content/1569031e -e2fe-11e6-8405-9e5580d6e5fb> (last accessed 9 October 2022).

46 Mehmet Ersoy, 'Astana Peace Talks: West Losing Its Influence in Middle East', *Global Research*, 28 January 2017. Available at <https://www.globalresearch .ca/astana-peace-talks-west-losing-its-influence-in-middle-east/5571471> (last accessed 9 October 2022).

47 Magnus Lundgren, 'Mediation in Syria: Initiatives, Strategies, and Obstacles, 2011–2016', *Contemporary Security Policy* 37, no. 2 (2016): 273–88.

48 The Russian-proposed changes in the Syrian constitution called for decentralised authorities as well as elements of federalism like 'association areas' and strengthening the parliament at the expense of the presidency. This was opposed by the Arab Syrian opposition. See Henry Meyer, 'Syrian Opposition Rejects Russian Draft of New Constitution', *Bloomberg*, 25 January 2017. Available at <https://www .bloomberg.com/news/articles/2017-01-25/syria-opposition-rejects-russian-dra ft-of-new-constitution> (last accessed 9 October 2022).

49 'New Round of Syria Talks Kick off in Geneva on Back of Astana Progress', *Russia Today*, 23 February 2017. Available at <https://www.rt.com/news/3783 60-geneva-talks-un-syria/> (last accessed 9 November 2022).

50 'Iran, Syria Sign Military, Security Agreement', *Fars News Agency*, 8 July 2020. Available at <https://www.farsnews.ir/en/news/13990418000862/> (last accessed 9 October 2022).

51 Sinan Hatahet, 'Russia and Iran: Economic Influence in Syria', Chatham House Research Paper, May 2020, 1–19.

52 Hamidreza Azizi, 'Iran Seeks Economic Benefits from Syria', Atlantic Council, *IranSource*, 22 February 2019. Available at <https://www .atlanticcouncil.org/blogs/iransource/iran-seeks-economic-benefits-from-syria/> (last accessed 9 October 2022); and Seyyed Mehdi Talebi, 'Dimensions of Iran's Trade and Economic Map in Syria', *Farhikhtegan*, 24 June 2020. Available at <https://farhikhtegandaily.com/images/newspaper/2020/06/1785/7_1785 .pdf> (last accessed 9 October 2022). Also, see *Tasnim News Agency*, 14 October 2018. Available at <https://www.tasnimnews.com/fa/news/1397/07/22/18 52300/> (last accessed 9 October 2022).

5

TURKEY AND THE SYRIAN CRISIS

Gencer Özcan and Soli Özel

Introduction

The uprisings in Syria started out like all the other revolts that convulsed the Arab world in 2011: the protesters demanded better governance, freedom and dignity. Yet the events unfolded in a dramatically different way in Syria than in other countries. The special characteristics of Syria as a political entity and the nature of its regime and alliances played a part in the specific and tragic trajectory of the uprising. Turkey's response to the crisis was a function of both its objective condition as Syria's northern neighbour with a border of some 600 miles and the ideological proclivities of its governing party's leadership. Contrary to earlier expectations by nearly all Western actors and certainly Turkey's rulers, it became obvious fairly early that the crisis would last longer than anticipated. In fact, the uprising morphed into a struggle for regional supremacy and later mutated into a crisis of international magnitude. The ruling Justice and Development Party (AKP) leadership anticipated that the Muslim Brotherhood, its ideological kin in Arab countries, would seize power in all the rebellious countries in a short span of time and therefore saw a window of opportunity for the same in the Syrian crisis.

However, it did not take long before the crisis became a liability rather than an asset for the AKP leadership's strategies to hold on to power. Ankara's early conviction that it could master the evolution of events in its southern neighbour proved to be naïve and overly optimistic. Rather, the ramifications of the crisis soon overwhelmed Ankara. As early as 2012, the AKP leadership had to face the magnitude of the spillover effects of the unfolding civil war. The Syrian government's decision in July 2012 to pull out from the eastern parts of the country was the first fallout from the crisis. Dubbed the 'Rojava Revolution', the formation of three Kurdish cantons by the Partiya Yekîtiya Demokrat/Democratic Union Party (PYD) in early 2013 continuously complicated Turkey's stance in Syria. After all, the PYD was the Syrian affiliate of the Partiya Karkerên Kurdistanê (PKK) in northern Syria that had been at war with the Turkish state since 1984 and was recognised as a terrorist organisation by Turkey's allies. For the Turkish government, the formation of a Kurdish political entity just south of the border, let alone one that was created by Turkey's nemesis the PKK or its affiliate in Syria, was unacceptable.

The meteoric rise of the Islamic State (IS) in 2014 added yet another complication to the situation Turkey was facing. The expansion of IS rule produced new power configurations in areas it occupied in large parts of Syria and Iraq. The successes of IS compelled otherwise contending parties to put their differences aside and improvise ad hoc alliances. In September 2014, when Turkey chose not to intervene as IS besieged the Kurdish town of Kobani, the Obama administration extended military support to Kurdish forces to defend the town. The successful resistance in Kobani marked the beginning of a modus operandi between the PYD and the US in the fight against IS. As neither the US nor its allies were willing to put boots on the ground in the fight, Washington increased its level of cooperation with the PYD through an intensive train-and-equip programme. Its continuing success earned the PYD more sympathy and legitimacy in the power corridors of Europe while rendering Turkey's allies indifferent to Ankara's complaints that the PYD was the Syrian offspring of the PKK.

The steady acceleration in the influx of refugees into Turkey was yet another negative externality from the war. The AKP government initially encouraged this and presented it to the public as both a neighbourly/humanitarian and implicitly religious duty but now had to cope with a massive humanitarian and logistical issue. The number of Syrian refugees reached unprecedented levels, resulting in Turkey hosting more refugees than any other country in the world, which caused manifold problems for Ankara. Efforts to keep the refugees in camps proved futile since their numbers exponentially increased, leading to social and political tensions across the country. Refugees trying to reach European countries exacerbated problems between Turkey and the EU. Furthermore, the spillover effect precipitated by the refugees' efforts to reach

Europe combined with the rise of IS changed the major powers' position vis
à vis Syria. European countries softened their stance and became more lenient towards the Syrian government. The rise of IS foreshadowed what might
happen to Syria should the Assad regime disappear. After the Russian military campaign was launched in late 2015, the prevailing power configuration
changed once again, making Moscow the pivotal country involved in the crisis.
The events following the Russian intervention eventually forced Ankara to
discontinue its previous policy towards Syria and to go as far as aligning its
policies with Moscow and Tehran, effectively giving up on its goal of getting rid of the Assad regime and establishing a Sunni/Muslim Brotherhood-
dominated government.

Since the beginning of the war, and particularly as Ankara's goals shifted,
numerous scholarly publications dealing with the way Turkey was involved
in the Syrian crisis, and how the crisis affected Turkish policy choices, have
appeared. This literature by and large relied on realist and neo-realist perspectives in explaining Ankara's changing priorities. As such, it primarily focused
on how Turkey made a volte-face with the Syrian regime when the first uprisings broke out in March 2011.[1] In general, this literature dealt with the dynamics that led to Turkey's abandonment of the 'Zero Problem with Neighbours'
policy.[2] When the crisis spilled over and dragged other powers into the conflict, another body of literature on how Turkey's policy towards Syria marred
its relations with third countries emerged.[3] Other consequences of the crisis,
such as the formation of Kurdish cantons[4] and the rise of the Islamic State[5]
produced a separate body of literature. However, scholarly interest in Turkey's
involvement in the crisis that the refugee problem galvanised was unprecedented. As the first group of refugees reached European cities, the issue immediately prompted a sudden surge of studies on migration from Syria and the
way the AKP administration handled the issue.[6] The cross-border operations
the Turkish Armed Forces (TAF) began to conduct in 2016 added yet another
layer of literature on Turkey's handling of the gangrenous conflict.[7] Many
of these studies accurately focused on critical questions about the effective-
ness of the TAF and the extent to which the operations changed the course
of events on the ground. Although all these studies pertinently address various aspects of Turkey's engagement in Syria, the way the AKP administration
instrumentalised the TAF's cross-border operations in Syria for its domestic
purposes was overlooked. Therefore, the present chapter argues that beyond
the contingencies that they were meant to address, cross-border operations

provided indispensable externalities for the AKP administration. They were the catalysts in the consolidation of the new presidential regime that the AKP, or more exactly its leader President Recep Tayyip Erdoğan, managed to get approved in a highly charged referendum.

Second Image Reversed: Foreign Policy Shapes Domestic Politics

As the crisis in Syria unfolded and turned into one that was of international magnitude, Turkey itself underwent one of the most substantial political transformations of the republican period. The metamorphosis of the political system began in earnest after the elections of 12 June 2011, which the AKP won by a landslide. Confident that its position in parliament was securely consolidated, the AKP leadership sought to enact a number of constitutional amendments. Their search for partners in pushing an ambitious domestic political agenda forward proceeded as rebellion engulfed Syria. Very early on, Turkey declared that the goal of its foreign policy towards Syria was regime change. Although the dynamics that instigated the Syrian crisis and the AKP's desire to introduce a presidential system in Turkey were independent of each other, both processes were intertwined in various ways. Whereas in the initial stages of the crisis, Turkey's policies in Syria were in line with the strategies that the AKP leadership pursued to maintain its power, in the later stages those policies became a liability as the ramifications of the crisis overwhelmed opportunities. During critical stages of this profound domestic transformation, AKP governments had to deal with the unexpected fallout of the Syrian crisis. These complications forced the AKP leadership to change its political strategies and to forge new domestic alliances. In turn, domestic expediencies forced themselves on the AKP's decisions concerning Syria. Therefore, in order to understand Turkey's policies in Syria accurately, it is necessary to look both at the AKP's choices in the field and the challenges its leadership faced at home. A comprehensive picture of Turkey's policy choices, therefore, takes into account the intensive interplay between power strategies the AKP leadership deployed to maintain its dominant position in domestic politics and the regional dynamics set in motion by the Arab uprisings, which both helped and hindered those strategies.

We identify three discernible phases in Turkey's policies during the course of the Syrian crisis, each characterised by a different constellation of forces that dominated the course of events on the ground. For each phase, there were different challenges that the AKP leadership had to meet and various power strategies it improvised. The first phase consisted of efforts by different actors to deploy or activate their proxies on the ground. The war by proxy and the regime's counter-strategies led to a stalemate, which lasted until the rise of IS at the beginning of 2014. The rise of IS changed the power configuration on the ground and set new dynamics in motion. In the two years between early 2014 and late 2015, the theatre of war was dominated by events pertaining to IS activities on the ground. The period that followed was defined by the massive Russian military campaign unleashed in late 2015 and its consequences. The Russian campaign decimated most of the armed groups supported by Turkey, forced those groups to evacuate Aleppo, and thereby reinstituted the government's control over all major Syrian cities. The Russian campaign eventually forced Turkey to abandon its policy of regime change and to align its position with Russia and Iran, the two major powers that supported and sustained the Syrian government since the uprising's outbreak.

The Proxy War Phase

When the uprisings reached Syria, it appeared unlikely that the AKP government would terminate its close cooperation with Damascus and become the leading sponsor of the anti-Assad opposition.[8] Good neighbourly relations with Syria had been considered the best example of what the AKP governments dubbed their 'Zero Problem with Neighbours' policy. Even in February 2011, while uprisings were already shaking Arab autocracies across the Middle East, the prime ministers of both countries, Recep Tayyip Erdoğan and Muhammad Naji al-Otari, attended a ceremony laying the foundation stone for a new 'Friendship Dam' on the River Orontes.[9] In praising the friendship between the two countries, Erdoğan appeared to have paid little attention to the prospects of Arab uprisings spilling over to Syria within a few months. Photographs depicting Erdoğan and Assad cordially hugging each other ornamented propaganda booklets that the AKP prepared for the 12 June 2011 general elections. Soon after this celebration, however, and anticipating that the course of events would follow a trajectory similar to Tunisia and Egypt, the AKP government abandoned its motto 'Common history, common destiny and common future with Syria', in August 2011. Having already failed in convincing the regime to include Muslim Brotherhood members in its cabinet and in the wake of the Hama massacre, the AKP government began to pursue an audacious policy of regime change in its neighbour. Turkey, alongside the US, Britain and France, at first led a diplomatic offensive, attempting to isolate the

Syrian government and to impose successive non-elected exile groups as the 'legitimate representatives' of the Syrian people.[10] Later, Turkey became one of the countries that funded, trained and supplied arms to proxies comprised of Salafi and Muslim Brotherhood-affiliated groups.[11] The Syrian Arab Army managed to remain in control of most of the country by the end of 2011. Yet the armed groups, as a result of more strategic weapons such as anti-tank missiles that they received from abroad, succeeded in seizing larger areas of the country in early 2012. In response to rebel advances, the Syrian Arab Army reprioritised its strategy of counterinsurgency and abandoned northern and eastern Syria in mid-2012.

Until the latter part of 2012 the AKP leadership appeared certain that the Syrian regime would fall quickly. Pro-government dailies published countless headlines highlighting the atrocities committed by the Syrian army and proclaimed that the days of the regime were numbered. On 24 August 2012, professing that the fall of the Syrian regime was just a matter of time, Foreign Minister Ahmet Davutoğlu stated that 'a regime that is alienated from its people will not stay alive.'[12] On 5 September 2012, Erdoğan confidently declared that

> God willing, we shall soon go to Damascus, embrace our brothers with love. That day is also getting closer. We shall recite Fatiha [the opening sura of the Quran] before the tomb of Salahaddin Ayyubi and pray in the Umayyad Mosque.[13]

The uprising in Tunisia began three months after the 12 September 2010 referendum for constitutional amendments in Turkey. These amendments were meant to be the first stage of the transformation to a presidential system that the AKP desired. The first elections held after the referendum took place on 12 June 2011, when protests had already began to engulf Syria. There were two themes that the AKP's campaign propaganda highlighted. First, in order to get the support of larger segments of society, most noticeably the Kurds, the AKP emphasised a need for 'advanced democracy' to overcome Turkey's 'democracy deficit' and called for a 'new democratic constitution written by civilians for the first time in the republican period'.[14] The song composed for the elections was 'Biz Hepimiz Türkiye'yiz' (We are all Turkey). Secondly, propaganda activities increasingly emphasised Erdoğan's qualities as a global leader. One of the campaign's leading slogans was 'Leader Turkey'. AKP spokespeople did not conceal that regime change in Syria could create opportunities for their party to realise its 'aspirations to make Turkey great again'. Although the election results did not produce an overwhelming parliamentary majority for the AKP, the party's leadership doubled its efforts to replace the country's parliamentary system with a presidential one. Within this political context, a development similar to what happened in Egypt, that is, the formation of a Muslim Brotherhood regime in Syria, would have constituted another foreign policy victory for the AKP leadership. Erdoğan's declarations in late June 2012 illustrate the extent of the ambitious expectations that prevailed among the AKP's top brass:

> The great states are envied. If you do not have a claim of being greater, of being stronger, you just shut your eyes to everyone and everything, but you get stuck where you were . . . We have great targets. We, God willing, endeavour to make Turkey one of the ten most powerful countries of the world by 2023.[15]

After the elections, the Syrian crisis continued to be another element that the AKP leadership instrumentalised for its overall political strategy. Putting the AKP leadership on the side of democracies, the AKP deliberately employed a rhetoric through which opposition parties were constantly accused of supporting or collaborating with the Syrian regime. Instead of using an inclusive rhetoric to build a nationwide consensus, AKP propaganda reiterated that 'the main opposition party [Cumhuriyet Halk Partisi] RPP was acting as the Baath Party of Turkey or the accomplice of the Syrian regime.' In September 2011 the AKP's then spokesperson Hüseyin Çelik professed 'a genetic linkage between the RPP and Baath parties in Arab countries'. In order to deride the RPP's leader Kemal Kılıçdaroğlu, he went so far as to claim that the confessional identity of Kılıçdaroğlu, a Turkish Alevi, could have been influential in the formulation of RPP's policy towards the predominantly Alawite Syrian regime.[16]

However, events in Syria did not follow the trajectory that the AKP leadership had hoped for. The first fallout was the Syrian government's decision to leave control of the country's northern provinces to the PYD. In fact, signs that the Syrian regime would rekindle its intimate connections with the PKK from the 1980s and the 1990s had already become visible as early as April 2011 when the regime allowed PKK militias to enter Syria from their base in the Qandil mountains of Iraq. Saleh Muslim, the co-chair of the PYD, was among those who were allowed to return to Syria. Releasing some of the PKK operatives from prison in May was another move that indicated what Damascus had in mind. It was also reported that the PKK dispatched hundreds of armed fighters to form the PYD's military wing, the Yekîneyên Parastina Gel/People's Protection Forces (YPG). Amid accusations of 'silencing' other Kurdish figures and of monopolising the Kurdish political sphere, the PYD established itself as the hegemonic organisation among Syrian Kurds. Later, in early 2013, the PYD declared that it had established three cantons in the provinces along Turkey's border. Paradoxically, these developments coincided with the peace process that the AKP government initiated with the PKK at the end of 2012. Although uncomfortable with the formation of these cantons, the AKP government kept communication channels open with the PYD. Perceived as an embryonic state, however, the consolidation of the cantonal administrations controlled by the PYD in Syria became a source of irritation for Ankara.[17]

In the meantime, Turkey's support for radical groups generated serious tensions in relations with countries that cooperated with Ankara in Syria. As the crisis prolonged, the AKP government opted to collaborate with groups such as Jabhat al-Nusra and other al-Qaida affiliates. Media reports raised allegations of extensive assistance to such groups, which ranged from arms transfers to logistics, and the provision of medical services. Turkey's support for Jabhat al-Nusra became even more controversial after it was revealed that members of the organisation were involved in the deadly raid on the US embassy in Benghazi in September 2012.

After that raid, the US suspended its support for Jabhat al-Nusra-affiliated groups and demanded that Turkey also terminate its support for the groups. Divergence between the US and Turkey became even more conspicuous when the Obama administration decided to designate al-Nusra, the Syrian branch of al-Qaida, as a terrorist organisation in December 2012. Feridun Sinirlioğlu, the undersecretary of the Turkish Foreign Ministry, was reported to have said that the designation was a 'hasty' decision.[18] In light of the changing US attitude towards al-Nusra, Turkey's support for Salafi groups came under increasing criticism. Despite Turkey's declaration that it put al-Nusra on its list of terrorist organisations, allegations that the AKP government maintained support for the organisation continued.[19] In September 2013 further claims were raised that al-Nusra continued to transfer its fighters through Turkey and that it also began to recruit from within the country.[20]

From early 2013 onwards the AKP government faced growing criticism from Western allies for its lenient discourse on the Salafi/Takfiri groups. The stormy summit meetings between Erdoğan and Obama on 16 May 2013 high-lighted the fact that the divergence between the two allies was getting wider. Although in a different form and in an indirect way, another blow came when the US suspended its decision to punish Damascus for its use of chemical weapons in Ghouta, in south-western Syria, on 21 August 2013. The US decision not to strike revealed the fact that Washington was no longer on the same page as Ankara about regime change in Damascus. Prior to this incident, Turkey's massive political investment in Egypt was written off as well. President Morsi's ouster in a coup in July 2013 brought the AKP leadership's great expectations to lead a Muslim Brotherhood bloc in the Arab world to a sudden halt. Its policy of supporting the Brotherhood across the region was unravelling when the most shining example of Turkey's alliances in the Middle East disappeared as a result of an Emirati and Saudi-backed military coup.[21] Last but not least, Turkey's relations with its Western allies deteriorated further in late May 2013 when the Gezi Park protests broke out and rocked the entire country for two weeks. The way in which the AKP government put down these protests shattered Turkey's image as a model of democracy in the Middle East.

Turkey's policy towards Syria was also severely complicated by several challenges from within. These challenges initially had nothing to do with the crisis in Syria. Yet they were rapidly associated with it and amplified the ramifications of the crisis. In early 2012, the Gülenist movement, the AKP's ally in undercutting the political influence of the military and in the subversion of the Kemalist judiciary, openly challenged Prime Minister Erdoğan. A Gülenist-affiliated public prosecutor called on the chief of intelligence Hakan Fidan, one of Erdoğan's most trusted lieutenants, for a deposition, clearly intending to arrest Fidan ostensibly for his participation in secret negotiations with the PKK in Oslo. Indeed, it was subsequently revealed that the transcripts of the Oslo negotiations between Turkish intelligence and PKK operatives in Europe, at which Fidan was present, were leaked by the Gülenist apparatus that secretly recorded them. The struggle became an open fight in December 2013 when the Gülenists in the security apparatus and the judiciary, armed with well-documented corruption charges, aimed to apprehend family members of a number of ministers. It did not take long for the fight to spill over to Syria. The Gülenists mobilised their clandestine networks within the security establishment to undermine the government's efforts to support opposition forces in Syria. The struggle became visible when members of the gendarmerie and the intelligence service bickered over trucks carrying ammunition for the armed groups in Syria. These challenges confounded various agencies in Turkey's security establishment at a time when they were supposed to act in harmony. In the following phase, these challenges would increasingly eclipse the complications of the Syrian crisis and become the AKP leadership's major preoccupation.

The IS Phase

The forceful appearance of the Islamic State (IS) on the Syrian scene and its rapid expansion into eastern parts of Syria changed the entire context of the crisis and created a new power configuration on the ground. In July 2014, IS solidified its hold on the eastern banks of the Euphrates in Syria and then extended its control over the city of Mosul. As IS fighters overran large territories at the expense of the Syrian military and other armed groups, the group emerged as a major fighting force and a vicious political foe. The new circumstances compelled the US and European countries to revise their position vis-à-vis Salafi jihadist groups fighting against the Syrian government. This brought Turkey's relations with those groups into the spotlight and drove another wedge between Turkey and its Western allies. It was true that the success of a Sunni movement that fought both the Syrian regime and the Kurds led Ankara to initially see a window of opportunity in the expansion of IS's control in Syria and Iraq. By the same token, Turkish authorities reportedly felt confident that the IS forces that captured the city of Mosul would not attack the Turkish consulate there or harm its personnel. The AKP government was, therefore, taken aback when IS forces raided the consulate and took forty-nine people hostage. The hostage crisis paralysed Turkey as the AKP government refrained from taking an active role in the international coalition led by the US to fight IS.[22] On 7 August 2014, Foreign Minister Ahmet Davutoğlu went so far as to describe IS as an organisation 'born out of previous discontent and anger'.[23]

When IS laid siege to the PYD/YPG-controlled town of Kobani on 13 September 2014, it triggered a chain reaction that created more complications for Turkey. While the PYD forces stubbornly defended downtown Kobani, Turkey preferred to remain indifferent. Although he called IS a terrorist organisation, President Erdoğan told a group of Syrian refugees on 7 October 2014 that 'Kobani's fall was just a matter of time', wishfully alluding that the resistance was doomed.[24] On 16 October 2014, Prime Minister Ahmet Davutoğlu resolutely declared that 'even for purposes of humanitarian aid, Turkey will not open a corridor' and 'not meddle with the Kobani issue'.[25] However, Turkey's intransigence did not deter its allies, most notably the US. Washington forged an ad hoc alliance with the YPG as a 'capable and effective local militia' for the ground war against IS.[26] Turning a deaf ear to Turkey's complaints that the organisation was the extension of the PKK in Syria, in October 2014 the US increased its support for the resistance in Kobani. Eventually, in the face of strong pressure from its allies, the AKP government stepped back.[27] 'Within hours of Erdoğan announcing that Turkey wouldn't help the PYD terrorists,' as Patrick Cockburn noted, 'permission was being given for Iraqi Kurds to reinforce the PYD fighters at Kobani.'[28] Although Kurdistan Regional Government (KRG) reinforcements were allowed to go through Turkey, the impression lingered that the AKP government did not support Kurdish forces at a time when help (against IS) was needed most. As a consequence of its successful campaigns, the PYD gained recognition as the only significant force on the ground capable of fighting IS. Cast as the Stalingrad of Kurds, the resistance that the PYD forces put up in Kobani prompted worldwide sympathy. As a token of its increasing legitimacy, the co-chairpersons of the PYD were given official receptions in European capitals.[29]

The rise of IS changed the power configuration in the Syrian theatre of war, set new priorities for regional powers, and led to the transformation of Western perceptions of the warring parties in Syria. Washington's priority shifted from regime change in Syria to the containment and destruction of IS. With the IS-organised bombings in European capitals, the crisis was further internationalised, leading to the formation of a multinational coalition for the implementation of President Obama's plan to 'degrade and ultimately destroy' IS. The immediate consequences of changing US policy were twofold. First, Russia and Iran supported the US-sponsored coalition and joined the international effort to fight IS as silent players. Second, the YPG turned out to be the most effective ground force the US could have recruited. It was obvious that both consequences complicated Ankara's relations with Washington in several ways. Turkey's support for some Salafi groups in Syria came under the spotlight once again and the AKP government was increasingly exposed to criticism that its relations were perfidious.

The other complication that the rise of IS caused was far more troublesome for Turkey. The advancement of IS empowered Syrian Kurds in a number of significant ways. Led by the PKK's affiliate, they were catapulted into a position of primacy in dealing with the IS offensive that advanced into the areas where Kurdish cantons were established. Some began to call this period the 'age of the Kurds'. For Turkey, the Kurdish issue gained prominence in its policy towards Syria and gradually eclipsed its regime change policy. The success in resisting IS legitimised the PYD/YPG, and the US and European countries pretended not to see the organic links between the YPG and the PKK. They chose to consider the former as an entirely new native Syrian Kurdish organisation. By the latter part of 2014, the AKP government's position in the Middle East was already in a cul-de-sac. Ankara's alienation was highlighted when Turkey's bid to join the UN Security Council was frustrated by a campaign orchestrated by the UAE and Saudi Arabia.

The year 2015 was the last year Turkey tried to find allies for its regime change policy. Seeing the death of Saudi's King Abdullah on 23 January 2015 as a window of opportunity, the AKP leadership tried to mend fences with the House of Saud.[30] President Erdoğan announced a day of national mourning and attended the funeral of the late king, with whom he had remained at loggerheads over the Egyptian coup and the Palestinian issue. Erdoğan's expectations materialised as the new King Salman set aside these differences and agreed to boost aid to the armed groups fighting the Syrian Army.[31] The deal struck on 1 March 2015 sponsored a new umbrella organisation, Jaysh al-Fatah, the 'Army of Conquest', led by Ahrar al-Sham and al-Qaida affiliate Jabhat al-Nusra.[32] As a token of this rapprochement, Turkey expressed its support for the Saudi-led mission in Yemen.[33] The outcomes of the deal became obvious before long when Jaysh al-Fatah swiftly seized most of Idlib province.[34] Jaysh al-Fatah's steady advance towards the areas in the vicinity of Lataqiyya eventually prompted the Russian decision to launch a large-scale aerial campaign commencing in late September 2015. The direct Russian intervention in the Syrian civil war provoked a fateful chain of events that ultimately led Turkey to abandon its policy of regime change.

During the period that IS rose to the top of the international agenda, AKP governments faced serious challenges from within as well. The Gülenist organisation stepped up its efforts to weaken the government, undermining the latter's efforts in dealing with the Syrian crisis. This included leaking classified information on covert operations in Syria and intercepting trucks carrying material for the armed groups. The AKP's election strategies for the 30 March 2014 local elections were informed by the challenges that the Gülenists posed. Some of the slogans used for the elections, such as 'Struggle for Independence', reflected the extent to which the AKP leadership was concerned about the

Gülenist attack. It is also worth noting that Erdoğan launched his campaign with a meeting in Sivas, where one of the critical congresses that prepared the ground for the War of Liberation in the wake of World War I was held.[35]

The failure of the peace process with the PKK was another matter the AKP government had to address. The peace plan, dubbed the 'Solution Process', was an effort to gain Kurdish support for the AKP leadership's aspirations for a presidential system. However, while the PKK decided to translate the legitimacy it gained in Syria into political status in Turkey, Erdoğan already realised that the peace process would not necessarily produce Kurdish support for his efforts to transform Turkey's political system. Thus, in the wake of the 7 June 2015 general election, when the AKP lost its parliamentary majority, its leadership decided to change its alliance strategy, abandoned the already much weakened 'Solution Process' altogether and began to mend fences with the Nationalist Action Party (MHP).[36] The volte-face gained momentum when the PKK resumed violent offensives against the security forces. Out of a miscalculation that what it achieved against the IS in Syria would be repeated in towns across south-eastern Turkey, the PKK launched its ill-advised 'War of the Trenches' in December 2015. The tension continued throughout 2016, reaching its climax on 15 July, when some Gülenist officers organised a putsch. After the botched putsch attempt, the AKP leadership changed its power strategy and formed a tighter alliance with the MHP that propped up the government to survive the crisis. Under emergency rule, the AKP succeeded in getting its constitutional amendments for the presidential system ratified in a referendum held on 16 April 2017. As Turkey's political system transformed, Ankara's stance towards Syria also went through a substantial change as a result of the Russian intervention.

Russia Reigns

Marking the beginning of the last phase of the crisis, the Russian military intervention launched on 30 September 2015 set new dynamics in motion, changing the power configuration on the ground once again. The Obama administration's deliberate reluctance to become involved further amplified the impact that the Russian intervention had on the course of events. Moreover, failing to address the ramifications of the refugee crisis, European leaders acquiesced to Russia's intervention. Turkey complained about the Russian move since the intervention concentrated on the strategic province of Idlib, located between Aleppo and Turkey's borders, where Turkey's lines of

supply to opposition groups ran. The Russian aerial campaign aimed to neutralise armed resistance groups situated along the Turkish border. Therefore,
the intervention upended Turkey's position in northern Syria. Turkey could
no longer use its de facto air cover to assist the groups it had supported since
early 2015. The preponderance of Russian aerial operations brought to a halt
Jaysh al-Fatah's advance in Idlib and obliterated the armed resistance. Ankara's
ill-advised decision to take down a Russian Su-24 in November 2015 gave further momentum to the deterioration of Turkey's and its allies' military position as Moscow intensified its efforts in northern Aleppo to decimate groups
supported by Ankara. Within eight weeks, Russia's aerial campaign decisively
changed the military equation on the ground at the expense of armed groups
of opposition supported by Turkey and Saudi Arabia.

Deepening the crisis between the two countries, the Su-24 incident highlighted Turkey's isolation as Ankara's expectation of NATO support after the
incident went unfulfilled. Despite Turkey's calls for solidarity, its NATO allies
made clear that the alliance would not run the risk of escalation with Russia.
The increasing Russian pressure left the AKP leadership with no option but
to step back. The crisis officially ended after President Erdoğan extended his
apologies (to the Russian president) in a letter in late June 2016. It is also
worth noting that this rapprochement came only a fortnight before the 15 July
putsch, when Gülenist cadres within the Turkish Armed Forces attempted
to overthrow the AKP government. Whereas the Russian president was one
of the first leaders to extend his support to Erdoğan almost immediately after
tanks took to the streets of Istanbul and Ankara, thereby gaining the gratitude
of the Turkish public, the US was blamed for being behind the putsch. The
Turco-Russian rapprochement gained further momentum after the two leaders met on 9 August 2016 at a summit in Saint Petersburg. In the wake of the
summit, the convergence of interests of the two leaders over Syria became
palpable.

The new modus vivendi enabled Turkey to pursue its other goals.
The YPG's seizure on 12 August 2016 of the strategic city of Manbij (the
last stronghold of IS on the northern edge of Syria) alarmed Ankara, as that
organisation had moved a step closer to realising its aim of linking Kobani and
Afrin cantons, building a continuous belt stretching from Iraq to Turkey.
It is understood that Turkey's reluctance to cooperate with the US forces to
repel IS from the Manbij Pocket led Washington to turn a deaf ear to Ankara's
claims and go ahead with the YPG.[37] In line with previous declarations that the

YPG's presence on the west banks of the Euphrates would not be tolerated, Turkey launched its first cross-border operation in Syria on 24 August 2016, dubbed 'Operation Euphrates Shield'. The operation's aim was twofold: to remove IS from the border and to stymie the formation of a contiguous belt of cantons controlled by the YPG that stretched from Kobani to Afrin, the Kurdish enclave in north-west Syria close to the Turkish border.[38] Operation Euphrates Shield also threatened the YPG's foothold in Manbij, located on the west bank of the Euphrates.

The operation underscored the entente between Turkey and Russia. Beyond allowing Turkey the use of Syrian airspace over the operation zone, the Russians extended intelligence support to Turkish forces during the operation, as, incidentally did the US, since one aim of the operation was to terminate the IS presence in the area.[39] However, Turkey's desire to control the town of al-Bab, thirty kilometres north-east of Aleppo, and larger areas in northern Aleppo, was frustrated by the Russian aerial operation launched in mid-November 2016.[40] The objectives of Operation Euphrates Shield clearly indicated that Turkey's priorities had to a significant extent differed from what they had previously been when the Army of Conquest was steadily advancing towards Lataqiyya in the summer of 2015. By late 2016, one unexpected consequence of the Syrian crisis, namely the creation of a US-supported Kurdish political entity governed by the PKK affiliate in Syria, was of much greater concern for Ankara. In line with this change, Ankara increasingly aligned its policies with Moscow. Turkey suspended its support for armed opposition groups around Aleppo and mediated between these groups and Russia. The battle of Aleppo ended in December 2016. Turkey and Russia coordinated the evacuation of al-Nusra fighters from the city.[41] Together with the loss of Aleppo, the Moscow Declaration of 20 December 2016 marked the end of Turkey's regime change policy in Syria.

The operation problematised Turkey's relations with the US, however. As Turkey intensified its struggle with the YPG, the US Central Command (CENTCOM) had already designated the group as 'the most successful anti-IS ground force in Syria'.[42] The US troop deployment to Manbij to deter Turkey from seizing the town and the subsequent unfulfilled agreement guaranteeing the YPG's pull-out from the area on the western banks of the Euphrates, led to a further deterioration in relations between Washington and Ankara. Tensions reached a climax when, in April 2017, Turkish air strikes on YPG targets in north-eastern Syria prompted Washington's condemnation and led to the positioning of US troops along the Turkey–Syria border to discourage further Turkish incursions.[43]

In late January 2018, after securing Russian consent, Turkey launched yet another incursion, 'Operation Olive Branch', to seize the PKK-controlled province of Afrin in northern Syria. The YPG chose not to resist and the TAF seized control of the town with ease. The operation proved that 'without direct U.S. assistance, the YPG failed to hold its ground even in rural areas, where it had been preparing a defence against a potential Turkish incursion for years.'[44] After the operation, Ankara reiterated its warnings that if Manbij was not evacuated by the YPG, Turkish troops would attack it to push the YPG fighters out. In June 2018, Ankara's pressure eventually compelled the US to sign an agreement called the Manbij Road Map, which stipulated that the two countries would take necessary steps to dismantle the local system of governance run by the Syrian Democratic Forces.[45] However, the roadmap failed to dovetail divergent interests of the two countries and became another source of frustration that Ankara kept complaining about. When the US State Department put a bounty on three key PKK leaders in November 2018,[46] President Erdoğan's spokesperson Ibrahim Kalın qualified the announcement as deceptive for its attempt to distinguish the YPG from the PKK.[47]

Divergence between the perspectives of Turkey and the US coincided with convergence between the policies that Turkey and Russia pursued. Yet another concrete outcome of the Turco-Russian modus vivendi was the agreement on de-escalation zones reached in Sochi, Russia on 17 September 2018. With the Sochi Agreement, Turkey acquiesced to assist Russia in establishing a series of de-escalation zones; the largest one was in Idlib province, close to Turkey's borders, through which the lifelines of the armed opposition had ran since early 2015. The de-escalation zones enabled the Syrian Army to freeze offensive campaigns on certain fronts so that it could amass resources to fight in areas that were more convenient. As Aaron Stein suggests, the de-escalation zone in Idlib was functioning as 'an insurgent sink, where populations from insurgent-held territory are bused and relocated after a campaign of mass punishment forces capitulation'.[48]

This became blatantly obvious when the US army established observation posts between Tel Abyad and Ras al-Ayn, in northern Syria, in response to the Turkish Army massing troops in the area in December 2018. After a long delay, the third incursion inside Syria dubbed 'Operation Peace Spring' began on 9 October 2019. The operation's aim was twofold: to create a safe zone for refugees along the southern side of the border, and to terminate the YPG's presence there. However, the operation had to be 'suspended' following Russian and American initiatives. While the US put pressure on the YPG to pull its forces from the area between Tel Abyad and Ras al-Ayn, President Putin convinced Erdoğan not to go further towards Kobani and Haseke. Although the operation's long-term consequences in terms of the way it came to an end remain to be seen, several conclusions can be drawn. One is that the operation changed the power configuration in northern Syria in several ways. It ended YPG aspirations to form a belt running from Qamishli in the east to Manbij on the west bank of the Euphrates. The belt seems to have punched through two pockets around Tel Abyad and Ras al-Ayn. This was also a blow to the YPG's expectations that the US would back its hegemony in northern Syria in return for the sacrifices it had made during the war against IS. The second point is that in the wake of the operation, negotiations between the Syrian government and the YPG had already begun. Although news that the two have agreed on engaging in long-term cooperation needs confirmation, the operation raised the likelihood of a compromise between the YPG and the Syrian government. It is paradoxical that Turkey's operation produced circumstances that are beneficial to the Syrian government. In other words, Operation Peace Spring, like the previous operations, brought about the sort of changes that the Syrian government had aspired to achieve.

The mass movement of military-aged males and their families to Turkish-controlled or influenced areas in Syria is now a key element of the Russian strategy to de-escalate the conflict and force the active pockets of the insurgency to capitulate to regime control. Turkey, in essence, enabled the Russian effort to restore the Assad regime's control throughout Syria. In return, Turkey won from Russia the freedom to operate against Turkey's Kurdish enemies and, eventually, to create a degree of stability in the north. The current stability in northern Syria allows Ankara to reverse the flow of refugee travel and ensure that refugees leave Turkey for Syria (and not vice versa).[49]

As of 2020, Idlib, the last rebel stronghold seemed to be the centre of gravity of the crisis. Both Syria and Turkey have diametrically opposed agendas as regards the north-western province. For the regime, the province is of critical importance for its strategic location straddling Lataqiyya and Aleppo. The armed groups still control major motorways connecting Aleppo and other major cities, including Damascus. On Turkey's part, the province is seen as a huge camp where hundreds of thousands of internally displaced Syrians, looking to reaching Turkey, took refuge. Having already received more than four million refugees, Turkey is determined to prevent further refugee flows by using all means at its disposal. While Ankara deployed large numbers of troops there, the Syrian Arab Army has also been increasingly massing troops around the provincial capital and advancing towards the north since the end of 2019. However, as the crisis exhausted all resources that both sides could utilise, the current power configuration does not favour any party to gain the upper hand and break the impasse. However, while intensive troop deployments by the Turkish Armed Forces and Syrian Arab Army in the province indicate the parties' commitment to their aims, it is also true that both sides are reluctant to be the first one to challenge the status quo. The aerial bombardment carried out by the Russian Air Force against a Turkish convoy on 28 February 2020, which caused the loss of thirty-four Turkish soldiers stationed in Idlib, and Turkey's heavy-handed retaliation, did not change the ongoing stand-off. Moreover, the haste with which Turkey and Russia signed a new agreement on 5 March 2020 to de-escalate the situation highlighted the extent of the delicate relations between the two countries. However, given Turkey's determination to retain Idlib as a safe zone for refugees, and Syria's exhaustion under international sanctions, one can speculate that the stalemate will not change in the foreseeable future.

Conclusion

Turkey's Syria policy failed due to a number of grave miscalculations. The policy was primarily based on the assumption that the Assad regime was weak and could easily be brought down relatively quickly by the uprising. However, the crisis highlighted that the regime's domestic support was not confined to the Alawite minority, and it could mobilise larger segments of society when threatened. Furthermore, the regime was able to sustain the support it received from Iran, Russia and Hezbollah. As permanent members of the Security Council, Russia and China effectively blocked UN resolutions calling for sanctions against the regime. Another miscalculation on the part of the AKP leadership was the belief that Turkey had the capacity to steer the course of events in Syria. When events began to follow a different path, Ankara had to cope with the wide-ranging ramifications for Turkey of the violence that engulfed its neighbour. Turkey's ambitious policies made the AKP governments' stance towards Syria more vulnerable to the cross-currents of regional politics. In fact, the more aggressively Turkey dealt with the Syrian crisis, the greater impact the course of events in Syria had on Turkey's domestic politics. The events proved what one observer foresaw during the Arab uprisings' initial phase: 'Building regional influence of the type to which Turkey aspires is a process that takes place gradually and incrementally over decades and not as an immediate result of the hyperactivity of Davutoğlu's diplomacy.'[50] Or, as the late Zbigniew Brzezinski would say, the Arab uprisings led Turkey to pursue policies that reflected the 'imprudent self-delusion' usually generated by ideological proclivities.[51]

Turkey's strategy of relying on war by proxy failed. Ankara's efforts to unite different opposition groups and turn them into an effective fighting force proved futile. Rather than joining forces, the groups fighting at the behest of Saudi Arabia, Turkey and Qatar became further divided. The political vacuum created by the withdrawal of the Syrian Army from northern Syria in July 2012, the growing magnitude of the refugee influx and the meteoric rise of the Islamic State in 2014, caused problems that Turkey was unable to overcome. The IS phenomenon set new dynamics in motion and heralded a new phase in the Syrian crisis. It took the crisis beyond Syria's borders.

While all major actors overhauled their policies to address the threat that IS posed, Turkey overconfidently insisted on its regime change policy and as a result received the ire of allies for aiding and abetting violent jihadi groups. The last-ditch effort by the AKP leadership to change the course of events in Syria was its modus vivendi with the Russians. The effort enabled armed groups Turkey supported to take control of the strategically important Idlib province, yet also provoked a heavy-handed Russian response, beginning on 30 October 2015. In return for the control of Idlib province, the Saudi–Turkish modus vivendi paved the way for a new phase in the crisis, at the end of which Turkey found itself on the other side of the conflict. In the last phase of the crisis, after exhausting its military and diplomatic capacities and estranged from its allies, notably the US, Turkey came to terms with the new realities on the ground and began to align its policies with Russia and Iran.

Turkey's policies in Syria ran into a cul-de-sac in mid-2013. The political crises that AKP governments had to cope with further multiplied. The Gezi protests that erupted in late May 2013 presaged what would occur in the following months. The coup in Egypt in July 2013 that ousted the Muslim Brotherhood government which Ankara had cultivated deep relations with was a blow to the AKP's hitherto successful regional policies and the leadership role that Erdoğan aspired to. The Egyptian coup also rekindled the latent power struggle between Ankara and the Gulf monarchies, complicating Turkey's policies in other parts of the Middle East, including Syria.

The latter part of 2013 also witnessed a power struggle within Turkey's security establishment in which segments of the military and police acting at the behest of the Gülenist Order intensified their efforts to undermine the AKP government. Beyond the severe political complications at home, the Gülenist Order challenged the government's policies by exposing its covert operations in Syria. By the end of 2013, Syria had already become a battleground between the Gülenists and the government. The perennial domestic political crises since the end of 2013, and a long series of elections and referenda that piled one upon the other since 2014, made Turkey's politics more susceptible to the outcomes of the Syrian crisis. Furthermore, in the wake of the 7 June 2015 elections, the AKP leadership had to make enormous efforts to overcome a series of crises which reached their climax in the 15 July 2016 putsch. In short, the developments in 2013, starting with the tempestuous dinner at the White House when Erdoğan visited President Obama, the Gezi uprising, the failure of Obama to punish the Assad regime after the latter used chemical weapons, and finally the attacks by the Gülen movement, assumed by the government to be close to and even controlled by agencies in the US, raised the level of suspicion of Washington's intentions. When the allies failed to react properly in solidarity with their democratically elected ally on the night of the coup attempt, the lure of Russia as a reliable partner became almost irresistible.

As this chapter has argued, the way the civil war in Syria unfolded exacerbated crises in Turkey and thus complicated the power strategies that the AKP had been pursuing at home and abroad. Turkey's policy of regime change in Syria became both irrelevant and counterproductive when the Assad regime did not fall quickly, the struggle became protracted, and the uprising developed along a different trajectory than those in Tunisia, Egypt and Libya. In the initial phase of the crisis, Turkey seemed to have considerable influence over the way events unfolded on the ground. However, the manner in which the crisis evolved did not create circumstances that were conducive for the AKP leadership to achieve the type of change it aspired to in Damascus. While the earlier phases of the crisis created a wide array of possibilities that the AKP leadership took advantage of, the later phases of the crisis circumscribed Turkey's room for manoeuvre in regional affairs.

Turkey's predicament brings to mind a Turkish expression: 'Dimyat'a pirince giderken evdeki bulgurdan olmak' (literal translation: 'Losing the crack wheat at home, trying to get rice at Dimyat'). This corresponds to 'The camel that went seeking horns lost his ears'. Not only were Turkey's great, and arguably greatly exaggerated and unrealistic, hopes as an aspiring regional hegemon thwarted by forces that proved to be formidable on the ground, but one by one Ankara also lost elements of its claim to be an 'order-setting' regional power. Yet, it must also be noted that currently Turkey has nearly 20,000 troops in four different parts of Syria: al-Bab/Jerablus, Afrin, Idlib and the north-east. It is a power to be reckoned with. The declared security threat of a contiguous Kurdish cantonal zone governed by the PKK affiliate has been dealt a mortal blow. In conjunction with a military presence in the north of Iraq, Turkey created a security zone to the south of its border on the soil of both its neighbours. It still has to contend with Syrian, American and Russian military presence, particularly in Idlib and the north-east of Syria, where the Syrian army has been deployed after eight years of absence. In Idlib a delicate equilibrium still exists. The threat of a major assault by the Syrian army and its Iranian and Hezbollah allies against Jihadi groups, concentrated in the area that is adjacent to the Turkish border, continues. In such an eventuality, another major refugee wave will force itself on Turkey's borders, a calamity that the country no longer has the capacity to absorb as in earlier periods.

Notes

1   Raymond Hinnebusch, 'Back to Enmity: Turkey–Syria Relations since the Syrian Uprising', *Orient Journal of German Orient Institute* 56, no. 1 (2015): 14–22; Gencer Özcan, 'If the Crisis is What We Make of It: Turkey and the Uprisings in Syria', in Fuat Aksu and Helin Sarı Ertem, eds, *Analyzing Foreign Policy Crises in Turkey: Conceptual, Theoretical and Practical Discussions* (Cambridge: Cambridge Publishing House, 2017), 178–98; Özlem Tür and M. Kumral, 'Paradoxes in Turkey's Syria Policy: Analyzing the Critical Episode of Agenda Building', *New Perspectives on Turkey* 55 (2016): 107–32; Şener Aktürk, 'Türkiye'nin Rusya ile İlişkilerinin Yükselişi ve Gerilemesi, 1992–2015, Neorealist bir Değerlendirme', in Gencer Özcan et al., eds, *Kuşku ile Komşuluk, Türkiye ve Rusya İlişkilerinde Değişen Dinamikler* (Istanbul: İletişim, 2017), 129–45.

2   Birgül Demirtaş, 'Turkish Syrian Relations: From Friend "Esad" to Enemy "Esed"', *Middle East Policy* 20, no. 1 (2013): 111–20; C. Akça Ataç, 'Pax Ottomanica No More! The "Peace" Discourse in Turkish Foreign Policy in the Post-Davutoğlu Era and the Prolonged Syrian Crisis', *Digest of Middle East Studies* 28, no. 1 (2019): 48–69.

3   Gencer Özcan, 'Rusya'nın Suriye Bunalımına Müdahalesi ve Türkiye', in

Gencer Özcan et al., eds, *Kuşku ile Komşuluk, Türkiye ve Rusya İlişkilerinde Değişen Dinamikler* (Istanbul: İletişim, 2017): 269–98; Çiğdem Nas, 'The EU's Approach to the Syrian Crisis: Turkey as a Partner?' *Uluslararası İlişkiler* 16, no. 62 (2019): 45–64; Burcu Sarı Karademir, 'A Dance of Entanglement: US–Turkish Relations in the Context of the Syrian Conflict', *Uluslararası İlişkiler* 16, no. 62 (2019): 27–43; İnan Rüma and Mitat Çelikpala, 'Russian and Turkish Foreign Policy Activism in the Syrian Theatre', *Uluslararası İlişkiler Dergisi* 16, no. 62 (2019): 65–84.

4 Fehim Taştekin, *Rojava: Kürtlerin Zamanı* (Istanbul: İletişim, 2016).

5 Fehim Taştekin, *Karanlık Çöktüğünde – IŞİD: Din Adına Şiddetin Dünü ve Bugünü* (Istanbul: Doğan Kitap, 2016); A. Salih Bıçakçı, 'Sway on a Tightrope: The Development of a Mutualistic Relationship between Turkey and DAESH', *Uluslararası İlişkiler* 16, no. 62 (2019): 101–33; Haldun Yalçınkaya, 'Foreign Fighters of ISIS and Their Threat: The Experience of Turkey (2014–2016)', *Uluslararası İlişkiler* 14, no. 53 (2017): 23–43.

6 Lisa Haferlach and Dilek Kurban, 'Lessons Learnt from the EU–Turkey Refugee Agreement in Guiding EU Migration Partnerships with Origin and Transit Countries', *Global Policy* 8, no. 4 (2017): 85–93; Özgehan Şenyuva and Çiğdem Üstün, 'A Deal to End "the" Deal: Why the Refugee Agreement is a Threat to Turkey–EU Relations', The German Marshall Fund of the United States, no. 132, 5 July 2016. Available at <https://www.gmfus.org/news/deal-end-%E2%80%9Cthe%E2%80%9D-deal-why-refugee-agreement-threat-turkey-eu-relations> (last accessed 18 February 2018); Çağla Lüleci-Sula and İsmail Erkam Sula, 'Migration Management in Turkey: Discourse and Practice', *Uluslararası İlişkiler* 18, no. 72 (2021): 1–17; Ela Gökalp Aras and Zeynep Sahin Mencutek, 'The International Migration and Foreign Policy Nexus: The Case of Syrian Refugee Crisis in Turkey', *Migration Letters* 12, no. 3 (2015): 193–208.

7 Sıtkı Egeli, 'Dost-Düşman-Dost Döngüsü ve Türkiye-Rusya Askeri Rekabetinin Dönüşümü', in Gencer Özcan et al., eds, *Kuşku ile Komşuluk, Türkiye ve Rusya İlişkilerinde Değişen Dinamikler* (Istanbul: İletişim, 2017), 166, 178.

8 Özcan, 'If the Crisis is What We Make of It', 178–98.

9 Ümit Çetin, '45 milyon Liralık Temel Atıldı Asi Barajı 'Dostluk'la Dolacak', *Hürriyet*, 7 February 2011.

10 L. Barkan, 'Syrian Opposition Forms Political Coalition, Joint Military Council Following Foreign Pressure', Middle East Media Research Institute (MEMRI), Inquiry & Analysis Series Report, no. 919, 14 January 2013, 4. Available at <http://www.memri.org/report/en/print6931.html> (last accessed 20 October 2022).

11 Christopher Phillips, *The Battle for Syria: International Rivalry in the New Middle East* (New Haven: Yale University Press, 2018), 36.

12 'Davutoğlu Esad'a Ömür Biçti', *Hürriyet Planet*, 25 August 2012. Available at <http://www.hurriyet.com.tr/planet/21300142.asp> (last accessed 19 October 2015).

13 Sinan Tartanoğlu, 'Erdoğan Suriye için Politika Değişikliği Sinyali Verdi: Esed Yine Esad mı Oluyor?' *Cumhuriyet*, 25 September 2015.

14 'AK Parti 2011 Genel Seçimleri Seçim Beyannamesi', İstanbul, AK Parti Tanıtım ve Medya Başkanlığı, 2011, 19–33.

15 'Erdoğan: Baas mı CHP mi?' *Cumhuriyet*, 29 June 2012.

16 'CHP Türkiye'nin Baas Partisidir', *Habertürk*, 8 September 2011. The same rhetoric remained in use: 'CHP-HDP Esad' ın Türkiye Temsilcisi', *Sabah*, 11 May 2015.

17 Deniz Zeyrek, 'Kürt Kartını Düşünme!' *Radikal*, 26 October 2011.

18 Semih Idiz, 'Why is Jabhat al-Nusra No Longer Useful to Turkey?' *Al Monitor*, 10 June 2014. Available at <https://www.al-monitor.com/pulse/originals/2014/06/idiz-turkey-syria-opposition-nusra-terrorist-unsc-erdogan.html> (last accessed 10 October 2019).

19 Tolga Tanış, 'Suriye'ye Silahın Belgesi', *Hürriyet*, 15 December 2013.

20 İdris Emen, 'Adıyaman-Suriye Cihat Hattı', *Radikal*, 29 September 2013.

21 See Chapter 8 in this volume, Samer Shehata, 'The Regional Dimensions of Egypt's "Failed Democratic Transition"'.

22 'Cook: 'ABD'nin YPG'yle Çalışma Kararını Türkiye Verdi'', *Voice of America*, 27 May 2017. Available at <https://www.amerikaninsesi.com/a/cook-abd-nin-ypg-yle-calisma-kararini-bir-sekilde-turkiye-vermis-oldu/3873540.html?utm_source=dlvr.it&utm_medium=twitter> (last accessed 20 October 2022).

23 'Davutoğlu, IŞİD İçin 'Öfkeli Çocuklar' Dedi mi? Cumhuriyet.com.tr Sordu, İşte Anket Sonucu . . .', *Cumhuriyet.com.tr*, 27 December 2016. Available at <http://www.cumhuriyet.com.tr/haber/siyaset/651414/davutoglu-isid-icin-ofkeli-cocuklar-dedi-mi-cumhuriyetcomtr-sordu-iste-anket-sonucu.html> (last accessed 10 October 2019).

24 'Erdoğan: Kobani Düştü Düşecek!' *Habertürk*, 7 October 2014. Available at <https://www.haberturk.com/gundem/haber/997321-erdogan-kobani-dustu-dusecek#> (last accessed 29 January 2019).

25 'Davutoğlu: Türkiye Kobani'ye Köprü Açmayacak', *Türkiye*, 16 October 2104.

26 Aaron Stein, 'What's the Matter in Manbij? How An Obscure Syrian Town Could Determine the Future of the U.S.–Turkish Alliance and What to Do About It', *War on the Rocks*, 21 May 2018. Available at <https://waronthero

cks.com/2018/05/whats-the-matter-in-manbij-how-an-obscure-syrian-town-co
uld-determine-the-future-of-the-u-s-turkish-alliance-and-what-to-do-about-it/>
(last accessed 30 October 2019).

27 'Obama, Erdoğan'ı Aradı, Kobani'ye Koridor Açıldı', *Cumhuriyet*, 21 October
2104.

28 Patrick Cockburn, 'Whose Side Is Turkey On?' *London Review of Books* 36,
no. 21 (2014): 8.

29 Fehim Taştekin, 'Hollande–PYD Meeting Challenges Erdogan', *Al Monitor*,
12 February 2015. Available at <https://www.al-monitor.com/pulse/originals
/2015/02/turkey-france-kurdish-guerillas-elysee.html> (last accessed 30 October
2019).

30 Ayşe Şahin, 'Erdoğan's Visit to Riyadh Strengthens Relations, Alliance on
Regional Issues', *Daily Sabah*, 2 March 2015.

31 'İşte Esad'ı Devirme Planı', *Cumhuriyet*, 13 April 2015. Available at <http://
www.cumhuriyet.com.tr/haber/dunya/253491/iste_Esad_i_devirme_plani.html>
(last accessed 30 October 2019).

32 Hassan Hassan, 'Syria's Revitalized Rebels Make Big Gains in Assad's Heartland',
Foreign Policy, 28 April 2015.

33 Aaron Stein, 'Turkey's Yemen Dilemma: Why Ankara Joined the Saudi Campaign
Against the Houthis', *Foreign Policy*, 7 April 2015.

34 Robin Yassin-Kassab and Leila Al-Shami, *Burning Country: Syrians in Revolution
and War* (London: Pluto Press, 2016), 143; Mahmut Hamsici, 'Suriye: İslamcı
Grupların Hedefinde Akdeniz mi Var?', *BBC Türkçe*, 28 April 2015. Available
at <http://www.bbc.com/turkce/haberler/2015/04/150427_suriye_idlib_ana
liz_mahmut_hamsici> (last accessed 20 October 2022); Mahmut Hamsici,
'Türkiye, S. Arabistan ve Katar'ın 'Suriye İttifakı' Ne Anlama Geliyor?', *BBC
Türkçe*, 6 May 2015.

35 'Erdoğan: İstiklal Mücadelesi Sürecindeyiz', *A Haber*, 25 December 2013.
Available at <http:// www.ahaber.com.tr/gundem/2013/12/25/erdogan-istiklal
-mucadelesi-surecindeyiz> (last accessed 30 October 2019).

36 Cuma Çiçek and Vahap Coşkun, *Dolmabahçe'den Günümüze Çözüm Süreci:
Başarısızlığı Anlamak ve Yeni Bir Yol Bulmak* (Ankara: Barış Vakfı, 2016), 7.

37 'Ignoring Turkey, U.S. Backs Kurds in Drive against ISIS in Syria', *The
Washington Post*, 1 June 2016.

38 Jim Zanotti and Clayton Thomas, 'Background and U.S. Relations in Brief',
Congressional Research Services, 19 September 2017, 2. Available at <https://
www.refworld.org/pdfid/59c3800f3d.pdf> (last accessed 20 October 2022).

39 'Dostum Putin'in Desteği Önemli', *Sabah*, 26 October 2016; 'Izvestiya: Rusya
Fırat Kalkanına İstihbarat Sağlıyor', *Hürriyet*, 28 October 2016; 'Komutanlar
Anlaştı Hava Sahası Açıldı', *Aydınlık*, 13 November 2016.

40 Semih Idiz, 'Do We Know the Full Truth About the Euphrates Shield?' *Turkish Daily News*, 6 December 2016.

41 Ahmet Takan, 'Rusya ile 2'nci Krizin Eşiğinden Nasıl Dönüldü?' *Yeni Çağ*, 15 December 2016.

42 Liz Sly, 'U.S. Military Aid Is Fuelling Big Ambitions for Syria's Leftist Kurdish Militia', *Washington Post*, 7 January 2017.

43 Zanotti and Thomas, 'Background and U.S. Relations in Brief', 2.

44 Burak Kadercan, 'Between a Rock and Dynamite: American Options in the Face of the Turkish–YPG Crisis', *War on Rocks*, 6 April 2018. Available at <https:// warontherocks.com/2018/04/between-a-rock-and-dynamite-american-options -in-the-face-of-the-turkish-ypg-crisis/> (last accessed 30 October 2019).

45 Aaron Stein, 'The Roadmap to Nowhere: Manbij, Turkey, and America's Dilemma in Syria', *War on the Rocks*, 29 June 2018. Available at <https://waront herocks.com/2018/06/the-roadmap-to-nowhere-manbij-turkey-and-americas-di lemma-in-syria/> (last accessed 10 October 2019).

46 'US State Department Offers Reward for Information on Key PKK Leaders', *Turkish Daily News*, 6 November 2018; Richard Spencer, 'US Courts Erdogan with a $12m Bounty on PKK Guerrillas', *The Sunday Times*, 7 November 2018.

47 'Who are the PKK Leaders with the US Bounties on Their Heads?' *TRT World*, 8 November 2018. Available at <https://www.trtworld.com/mea/who-are-the- pkk-leaders-with-the-us-bounties-on-their-heads-21499> (last accessed 10 Oct- ober 2019).

48 Stein, 'Prisoners of Idlib'.

49 Stein, 'Prisoners of Idlib'.

50 Svante E. Cornell, 'What Drives Turkish Foreign Policy? Changes in Turkey', *The Middle East Quarterly* 19, no. 1 (2012): 13–24.

51 Zbigniew Brzezinski, *Strategic Vision: America and the Crisis of Global Power* (New York: Basic Books, 2012), 150.

6

IMPLICATIONS OF THE QATAR CRISIS FOR 'POST-GCC' REGIONAL POLITICS

Kristian Coates Ulrichsen

The stand-off that began in June 2017 between Saudi Arabia, Bahrain and the UAE, supported by Egypt, on the one hand, and Qatar, on the other, developed into the most serious rupture in Gulf politics since Kuwait was invaded and occupied by Iraqi forces in 1990. While the 'Qatar crisis' did not escalate into military conflict, as some, including the emir of Kuwait, initially feared, and ultimately was resolved at a 'reconciliation' summit that took place at the Saudi heritage site of Al-Ula in January 2021, its impact reverberated across the political, economic, institutional and social fabric of Gulf societies. The rancour and mutual recrimination that became a fixture of the crisis inflicted just as much damage on ties of trust and the formerly close-knit extended familial links that extend across borders as the more tangible political and economic measures imposed on Qatar in 2017 by the 'Anti-Terror Quartet'. The blockade of Qatar also hit heavily on raw nerves and points of weakness within the Gulf Cooperation Council (GCC) that left the six-member organisation struggling to regain its relevance amid the rise of a more assertive set of leaders focused more heavily on national rather than regional priorities.

This chapter examines the range of implications – immediate and longer term, tangible as well as intangible – for the conduct of regional politics among the Arab Gulf states. It begins from the assumption that while the 'rise' of the Gulf states as a regional centre of gravity began in the 2000s and therefore predated the Arab Spring, it was the shock of the 2011 uprisings that heralded the transition of three GCC countries – Qatar, Saudi Arabia and the UAE – into assertive and even interventionist regional actors. The impact of this shift in regional posture was magnified significantly by the rivalry that developed in and after 2011 as the perceived Qatari willingness to embrace political transitions that included Islamist groups in North Africa (and Syria) spurred the UAE, led by Abu Dhabi and, to a lesser extent, Saudi Arabia to back counter-groups.

There are five sections to this chapter. It begins by charting how the Gulf states became prominent in regional and international affairs during the decade preceding the Arab Spring, through a combination of the assumption of positions of leadership by a more assertive newer generation of decision-makers in Qatar and the UAE as well as the sustained boom in oil prices and government revenues after 2003. The second section examines how the Arab Spring and its aftermath shattered any lingering notions of a common threat perception among Arab Gulf states that had provided at least a baseline consensus since the GCC was established in 1981. Qatari assertiveness in throwing its geopolitical weight behind the uprisings in North Africa and Syria in 2011 triggered the UAE and Saudi Arabia to do the same, but in support of different groups, and not only magnified some of the splits that emerged in regional states undergoing post-2011 political transitions, but also placed Doha and Abu Dhabi/Riyadh in each other's sights as perceived threats to their own interests of national security and regional stability.

In section three, the focus shifts to analysis of how the GCC crises of recent years – both the 2014 and the 2017 iterations of the dispute with Qatar – have hit consequentially on weak points within the GCC in ways that magnify raw nerves that have run through Gulf politics since the regional order came into being with the independence of Kuwait in 1961, and Bahrain, Qatar and the UAE in 1971. These include the core–periphery imbalance within the GCC and the long-standing concern among the five smaller Gulf states at the prospect that Saudi Arabia (assisted, on this occasion, by the UAE) could 'throw its weight around' and try to bind its neighbours into a geopolitical straitjacket. Another element that caused concern, especially in Kuwait and Oman, was the manifestation of the first signs of Saudi and Emirati pressure against Qatar within weeks of the young new emir Tamim bin Hamad's accession to power in June 2013. With Kuwait and Oman both having aging leaders and facing transitions of their own, which, in Oman's case took place in January 2020 and in Kuwait's in September 2020, the sight of two conventionally more powerful states subjecting a smaller neighbour to what looked like a regional power play resonated in Kuwait City and Muscat.

The chapter draws to a close with two sections that consider the implications of the Qatar crisis for the future of Gulf politics against the backdrop of a shifting regional order. Section four explores the durability of the new 'axis' that connects Saudi Arabia and the UAE based around the two crown princes, Mohammed bin Zayed Al Nayhan in Abu Dhabi and Mohammed bin Salman Al Saud in Riyadh. The Saudi–Emirati alignment was formalised in the Saudi Emirati Coordination Council that began to meet regularly in 2018 and has redefined Gulf politics around an exclusionary rather than inclusionary angle. However, cracks have appeared over seemingly divergent Saudi and Emirati support for political outcomes in Yemen that has created fractures in the relationship between Abu Dhabi and Riyadh. This leads into the final section of the chapter which asks whether and how the GCC might recohere, especially in light of the 'reconciliation' of January 2021 under a new secretary general, Nayef al-Hajraf from Kuwait, who took office in February 2020 just as the COVID-19 pandemic was intensifying.

I

The roots of the Gulf states' breakout as prominent actors in regional and, increasingly, international affairs predated, by at least a decade, the Arab Spring, but acquired greater momentum and urgency with the onset of the region-wide political protests of 2011. Beginning in the 1990s and accelerating in the 2000s, the centre of economic and, to an extent, political gravity in the Arab world moved towards the Gulf states as Dubai, Doha and Abu Dhabi evolved into hubs for regional commerce and investment. Their substantial energy resources and the capital accumulation during the post-2003 oil price boom propelled Qatar, the UAE and Saudi Arabia into positions of greater prominence in a regional order which itself was in a state of flux as 'traditional' centres of influence, such as Egypt, Syria and Iraq, became less influential.[1]

In three of the major regional protagonists – Abu Dhabi and Dubai (in the UAE) as well as Qatar – the growth of regional ambitions was also bound up with the emergence in positions of leadership of a new and younger generation of decision-makers in the 1990s and early 2000s. This occurred first in Qatar, when the crown prince, Sheikh Hamad bin Khalifa Al Thani, gradually assumed control of day-to-day policymaking in a process that began in 1989 and climaxed with the overthrow of his father, Emir Khalifa bin Hamad Al Thani, in 1995. As emir, Sheikh Hamad bin Khalifa became one of the two architects of Qatar's international rise, together with Sheikh Hamad bin Jassim

Al Thani, who became foreign minister in 1992, as they focused on developing Qatar's massive reserves of natural gas and the associated liquefied natural gas (LNG) export infrastructure.[2]

In the UAE, the process of generational change unfolded first in Dubai, where Mohammed bin Rashid Al Maktoum became the figurehead in Dubai's breakneck economic growth as crown prince in the mid-1990s, well before he succeeded his brother, Sheikh Maktoum bin Rashid Al Maktoum, as ruler in 2006.[3] In Abu Dhabi, Sheikh Mohammed bin Zayed first rose to prominence in the 1990s as the armed forces chief of staff and, after being entrusted by his father, the UAE's founding president, Sheikh Zayed bin Sultan Al Nahyan, to spearhead the UAE's response to the 9/11 attacks in the US (in which two Emirati citizens were involved and much of the logistical and financial support flowed through the UAE), was named deputy crown prince of Abu Dhabi in 2003 before becoming crown prince a year later when his brother, Sheikh Khalifa bin Zayed Al Nahyan, succeeded Sheikh Zayed as president of the UAE and ruler of Abu Dhabi.[4] Already by September 2004, a US diplomatic cable noted the close ties between Mohammed bin Rashid in Dubai and Mohammed bin Zayed in Abu Dhabi, and observed that 'the two have the ability to see the bigger picture and have compatible visions for the country's development.'[5]

The rise of the 'two Hamads' in Qatar (which became a potent source of Saudi–Emirati grievance in the 2014 and 2017 disputes), and 'MBR' in Dubai and 'MBZ' in Abu Dhabi, brought to prominence a younger set of decision-makers whose assertiveness was quite different in practice from the more pragmatic and consensual generation of 'state-builders' they succeeded. A similar dynamic took place a decade later in Saudi Arabia with the startling rise of Mohammed bin Salman after he became the head of his father's royal court in 2013, minister of defence and deputy crown prince in 2015, and crown prince in 2017. While in the Saudi case the king remained one of the 'old guard', and Mohammed bin Zayed remained only the crown prince of Abu Dhabi rather than its ruler, the consolidation of power and concentration of decision-making authority in this coterie of younger royals, including Sheikh Tamim in Qatar after 2013, was a significant departure from the 'collective deliberation within ruling houses' that they replaced.[6]

Even as this generational transition unfolded, policymakers in Riyadh, Abu Dhabi and Doha also developed more assertive approaches to international governance in the decade prior to the Arab Spring, and especially in the aftermath of the 2007–8 global financial crisis, which largely bypassed the GCC, with the notable exception of Dubai and the partial exception of Kuwait. Saudi Arabia, for example, received international praise for its role in stabilising world oil markets in late 2008 and early 2009. In the autumn of 2008, GCC-based sovereign wealth funds accounted for up to one-third of the financing that flowed to struggling European financial institutions hit hard by the credit crunch.[7] Comments made in November 2008 by Saudi Arabia's minister of finance, Ibrahim al-Assaf, and the UAE's central bank governor, Nasser al-Suwaidi, left little doubt that they expected a greater say in debates over the reshaping of global institutions in return for the provision of financial assistance.[8] Abu Dhabi and Qatar also began to carve out specialist niches in specific fields, such as renewable energy research and diplomacy mediation respectively, in part through careful leveraging of financial reserves and investment policy.[9]

II

The political upheaval in the Middle East and North Africa that started in Tunisia in December 2010 thus came at a moment of self-confidence in GCC states flush with years of oil-fuelled budget surpluses and, in Qatar's case, by the stunning award of the 2022 FIFA World Cup just two weeks beforehand. And yet, the Arab Spring cracked open the fault lines within the GCC that had operated largely below the surface in the 1990s and the 2000s, with the exception of a Saudi–Qatar dispute that had seen the Saudis withdraw their ambassador from Doha from 2002 to 2007 over anger at Al Jazeera coverage of the kingdom. As Doha and Abu Dhabi adopted diametrically opposed positions to the regional upheaval and the role that Islamist movements should (or should not) play in political transitions, and as Saudi Arabia moved decisively into the Emirati camp after years of strained relations with the UAE, a regional polarisation occurred as Qatar's initial adventurism prompted the Emiratis and Saudis to follow suit albeit in different directions.

Although it is beyond the scope of this chapter to examine in detail the Qatari, Saudi and Emirati responses to the turbulent aftermath of the regional uprisings in North Africa and Syria, it is relevant to note that support did not flow in the same direction but followed trajectories that widened existing political or religious fissures in host societies already experiencing rapid upheaval. This was especially apparent in Libya, where the UAE and Qatar backed different groups of militias on the ground even as they both participated in the

NATO-led 'no fly zone' in the air.[10] Whereas Qatari support was associated with Islamist groups in and around Benghazi in eastern Libya, the UAE threw its support behind 'nationalist' (anti-Islamist) and tribally oriented militias in the north-west of the country.[11] The seeds of the discord that would divide post-Qaddafi Libya between 'Islamist' and 'nationalist' (anti-Islamist) militias, with hundreds of other smaller groups complicating this broader split, were laid from the beginning and magnified by the difference in approach between Qatari and Emirati backers of local Libyan militias.[12]

Somewhat similar dynamics were also observable in Syria in 2012 as the Qataris and Saudis channelled assistance to different bands of anti-Assad rebels that undermined attempts to create a broadly unified opposition coalition.[13] However, it was events in Egypt which developed into a microcosm of the zero-sum approach that pitted Qatar against the UAE, led by Abu Dhabi and supported after 2013 by Saudi Arabia, and which laid the seeds for the diplomatic ruptures in 2014 and 2017. The rift that developed was anchored both in actions as well as in perceptions that increasingly governed how protagonists in Riyadh and Abu Dhabi viewed their counterparts in Doha and vice versa. After the fall of President Hosni Mubarak in February 2011, Saudi Arabia and the UAE provided political and economic support to the Supreme Council of the Armed Forces (SCAF) after it assumed temporary control in Egypt. Once Mohamed Morsi won the June 2012 presidential election, Qatar provided his Muslim Brotherhood government with more than US$7 billion in financial assistance and loans which were intended to kick-start the ailing Egyptian economy, as well as cargoes of LNG to keep the power sector functioning.[14]

Virtually as soon as Morsi was ousted on 3 July 2013, after a series of massive protests that leaked recordings later appeared to suggest may have been financed, in part, from UAE sources, the Qatari aid to Egypt was replaced by larger sums of Saudi and Emirati assistance.[15] Within days of the military takeover, Saudi Arabia and the UAE pledged US$5 billion and US$3 billion respectively that comprised central bank deposits, grants, cash, energy products and interest-free loans.[16] This was the prelude to a continuing pipeline of Saudi and Emirati financial support to the military-led government of General, later President, al-Sisi, whose investment minister, Ashraf Salman, told a business conference in Dubai in March 2015 that Egypt had received US$23 billion in aid during the first eighteen months after the coup.[17] This took place as initial concerns in Abu Dhabi and, to a lesser extent, Riyadh that the Muslim Brotherhood appeared to be the real 'winner' from the Arab Spring coalesced into anger that Qatar had, at the very least, seemed to have been comfortable with such a direction of change in regional politics.[18]

The oppositional policies of Qatar and Abu Dhabi (as the driving political force within the UAE) to the regional upheaval in and after 2011 illustrates the folly of any attempt to view the GCC states through a monolithic lens in their responses to the Arab Spring. On the surface, Qatar and Abu Dhabi are outwardly similar as energy-rich emirates grown wealthy on enormous reserves of gas, in the case of Qatar, and oil, in Abu Dhabi's case, although the Al Thani and Al Nahyan ruling families have had a history of fractious relations that extend back for decades.[19] During the 2000s, the governments of Qatar and the UAE had nevertheless made several attempts to foster close bilateral links which attracted the ire of Saudi Arabia and showed the fluidity of intra-regional ties. After 2011, however, as David Roberts has observed, the two states' policy responses to the Arab Spring diverged beyond the point of no return, as Qatar increasingly picked winners associated with Islamist move-ments while Abu Dhabi spearheaded a security-centric approach that included a harsh crackdown on Islamists both at home and across the region.[20]

Two points of contention, one that predated 2011 and another that became apparent in the aftermath of the Arab Spring, contributed to the breakdown of the baseline commonality in Gulf states' threat perceptions. They shared enough in common vis-à-vis external threats to have kept the GCC together for thirty years, even if they did not always agree on how to respond to them. The longer-term flashpoint, which came to a head in 2011, was the differing perceptions of Islamism and of political Islam, with Qatari leaders showing themselves to be relaxed about the possibility that Islamist groups might win elections and come to power in regional states, whereas the leadership in Abu Dhabi, and especially Mohammed bin Zayed, adopted a zero-tolerance approach based on a perception that Islamist groups posed an existential threat to national and regional security.[21] This linked into the second flashpoint after 2011, which was the perception that Qatar was sup-porting anti-system movements in contrast to the preference in Abu Dhabi and Riyadh for outcomes that maintained an authoritarian status quo.

III

The crises within the GCC that pitted Qatar against three of its fellow member states in 2014, when Saudi Arabia, Bahrain and the UAE withdrew their ambassadors from Doha for nine months, citing Qatar's post-Arab Spring policies as posing a threat to regional stability and security, and again in 2017, when the same three states plus Egypt came together in an attempt to isolate Qatar politically and economically, have hit several of the GCC's weak points hard and touched on latent problems that were never fully resolved in the bloc's nearly-forty-year history. As an organisation composed of one very large state and five states of varying smallness, the GCC had from the beginning an imbalance in conventional power that left all the smaller members wary at various points to the prospect of Saudi Arabia throwing its weight around or the GCC becoming even more Saudi-centric. Saudi Arabia is seven times larger in size than the next biggest GCC member, Oman, which itself is larger than the four other members – Bahrain, Kuwait, Qatar and the UAE – put together, and the GCC has based its secretariat in Riyadh since its formation in 1981.[22]

Core–periphery tensions have been manifest on several occasions in GCC history. In 1982, Kuwaiti officials opposed an early GCC plan for a unified security pact over a clause that would have allowed forces from any other GCC state (which in practice for Kuwait meant Saudi Arabia) to pursue wanted suspects up to twenty kilometres inside its territory, and maintained their opposition to a later 1994 iteration of the pact.[23] Unease at potential Saudi dominance in the GCC burst into the open in May 2009 when the UAE dramatically withdrew from the long-planned monetary union just weeks after the site of the GCC Central Bank was awarded to Riyadh rather than to a furious Abu Dhabi.[24] Four years later, Omani opposition to Saudi proposals to form a closer, integrative Gulf Union were expressed in uncharacteristically blunt and direct terms by the minister responsible for foreign affairs, Yusuf bin Alawi, as he stated: 'We are against a union. We will not prevent a union, but if it happens, we will not be part of it.'[25]

Despite these periods of tension, however, the inherent pragmatism within the GCC prior to the sharpening of the zero-sum approach to regional politics after 2011 was encapsulated by Yusuf bin Alawi, when he stated that

> the GCC was meant to be a collective decision-making body, but not every member agrees with all its decisions . . . Therefore, within the GCC, an understanding has emerged that those decisions that may lead to internal divisions and discords can be discussed and decided outside of the GCC framework.[26]

The result was an inbuilt flexibility in the GCC that was tested after 2011 by Saudi-led attempts under King Abdullah first to broaden and later the above-described attempt to deepen the GCC into a Gulf Union, which was opposed, forcefully and in unusually public terms, by Oman in 2013.[27]

Such flexibility also enabled the GCC to survive as one of the most durable examples of regional organisation in an Arab political landscape that had witnessed the rise and fall of numerous unions and councils since the 1950s. It also acknowledged the fact that there was no clean or simple division within the GCC on any of the major fissures in regional politics, which instead cut different ways that depended on the issue. The Muslim Brotherhood, for example, was active in Gulf politics in Kuwait and Bahrain (albeit associated with the political opposition in Kuwait and government loyalists in Bahrain) even as Qatar came under growing pressure from Abu Dhabi and Riyadh over its perceived support for the organisation in Syria and in North Africa.[28] Oman and Kuwait, in addition to Qatar, maintained pragmatic working relationships with Iran, as did Dubai within the UAE, whose ruler, Sheikh Mohammed bin Rashid Al Maktoum, welcomed the dialogue that led to the Joint Comprehensive Plan of Action in 2015.[29]

The sight of Saudi Arabia and the UAE throwing their weight around in 2014 and especially in 2017 and attempting to impose what might be labelled a 'geopolitical straitjacket' on the other members of the GCC – especially pertaining to their conduct of regional and foreign affairs – therefore hit hard on the weak points within Gulf politics that for decades had been left unaddressed precisely because of their sensitivity. The flexibility inherent within the GCC for member states to pursue their own national projects and their guardianship of sovereignty in sensitive areas meant the GCC had always functioned best as a technocratic organisation rather than a 'one-size-fits-all' bloc.[30] For this reason, the list of thirteen 'conditions' presented by the 'quartet' of Saudi Arabia, Bahrain, Egypt and the UAE to Qatar in June 2017 caused concern in other regional capitals, not least because of its attempt to dictate to Qatar what foreign policy relationships – whether with Iran, Turkey or Islamist movements – it would have to curtail.[31]

The inclusion of the demand that Qatar 'curb diplomatic ties with Iran and close its diplomatic missions there' resonated with officials in Kuwait and Oman, whose leaderships had not only maintained pragmatic working relationships with Iran but also had been at the forefront of an initiative to try and dial down Iran–GCC tensions in January 2017, just months before the June 2017 blockade of Qatar was launched. This initiative, which began when the emir of Kuwait sent a letter to President Rouhani of Iran calling for dialogue, culminated in Rouhani visiting Kuwait City and Muscat in February 2017 and Emir Sabah travelling to Muscat to confer with Sultan Qaboos on possible steps forward.[32] The fact that the Saudis and Emiratis placed the demand that Qatar cut ties with Iran as the very top of their list just four months later had a chilling effect and spawned concerns in Kuwait and Oman that they too might one day become targets.[33] So, too, did the fact that the initial Saudi and Emirati pressure on Qatar began within weeks of Emir Tamim's accession to power in 2013, which sparked concerns in Kuwait City and (especially) Muscat that the same could happen when Kuwait and Oman underwent their own leadership transitions.[34]

IV

While the GCC was not without its problems and, as described above, its structural weaknesses, which failed, after all, to prevent three of its members from turning on a fourth twice in three years, it was at least an inclusive sub-regional project that was pragmatic enough, for most of its history, to accommodate members' differences on specific issues. The annual GCC summit which took place in Kuwait City on 5 December 2017 – six months to the day since the blockade of Qatar was launched – became emblematic of the shift towards a newer and far more exclusionary turn in Gulf politics. While the fact that the summit took place was itself a breakthrough, and a success for Kuwaiti diplomatic efforts, the meeting broke down in acrimony after little more than an opening session, and was upstaged by a simultaneous announcement from Abu Dhabi that a Saudi–Emirati Coordination Council, formed initially in 2016, had suddenly been activated. The emphasis on the bilateral council with the UAE (which was followed by a Saudi–Kuwaiti Coordination Council in July 2018 and a Saudi–Bahraini Coordination Council in July 2019) covered a full spectrum of military, political, and economic and development affairs.[35]

Co-chaired by the crown princes of Saudi Arabia and Abu Dhabi, Mohammed bin Salman and Mohammed bin Zayed, the Saudi–Emirati Coordination Council met for the first time in Jeddah in June 2018 and came to symbolise the exclusionary new axis in Gulf politics.[36] The fact that military coordination was placed first in the list of fields for Saudi–Emirati coordination in the December 2017 press release was testament to the already close security relationship between the two countries, albeit one placed under growing strain by the war in Yemen. A symbol of the Riyadh–Abu Dhabi alignment, the Saudi–Emirati Coordination Council built on the close personal relationship that existed between the two crown princes despite the generational difference in age between Mohammed bin Zayed (born in 1961) and Mohammed bin Salman (born in 1985). The two men collaborated closely in the decision to intervene militarily in Yemen in March 2015 and Mohammed bin Zayed actively promoted Mohammed bin Salman to the Obama administration in Washington DC, while they worked closely together before and during the Gulf crisis in 2017.[37]

In January 2019, the first meeting of the Executive Committee of the Saudi–Emirati Coordination Council in Abu Dhabi exhibited the scope and scale of the planned integration of activities across multiple sectors of policymaking to put the so-called 'Strategy of Resolve' into practice. The initiatives included a cross-border cryptocurrency and a common market for civil aviation as part of forty-four joint strategic objectives, which also encompassed cooperation on security supply chains and joint manufacturing of light weapons and ammunition, as well as coordination in foreign military assistance.[38] The measures indicated how the Saudi–Emirati Coordination Council had shifted beyond the initial May 2016 emphasis on the promotion of 'religious, historical, social and cultural ties' to acquire a hard political and military dimension. Should all the projects materialise over the planned five-year timespan, they would pose a significant challenge to GCC-wide attempts to develop closer coordination among all six member states rather than on a bilateral 'hub and spoke' basis that seems to be the purpose of the Saudi–Emirati, but also perhaps the Saudi–Kuwaiti and Saudi–Bahraini councils as well. And yet, a spate of disagreements between Saudi and Emirati officials in 2020 and 2021, including spats at OPEC+ summits in November 2020 and July 2021 over production quotas, the announcement of new Saudi tariffs that seemed designed to target goods made in regional free zones, predominantly in the UAE, and suggestions by the Saudi leadership that foreign firms wishing to do business with public agencies would have to base their regional headquarters in the kingdom from 2024, all called into question the coordination of policies between Saudi Arabia and the UAE, to say nothing of the other four GCC states.[39]

It remains to be seen whether the Saudi–Emirati alignment, which, in practice, appears to be with Abu Dhabi more so than with the UAE as a whole, endures the strains that have been placed upon it by the backing of different groups with seemingly competing visions in Yemen. Saudi and Emirati military and political objectives in Yemen were not congruent and diverged over time. The clashes in summer 2019 between the Southern Transition Council

(STC), associated with UAE interests in southern Yemen, and the Saudi-based Yemeni government-in-exile of President Abdrabbuh Mansur Hadi, as well as the failure to implement the Riyadh Agreement signed between the Hadi government and the STC in November 2019, provided a portent of tension if the conflict in Yemen eventually gives way to a comprehensive political settlement.[40] Neither the Emirati decision to redeploy its forces from Yemen in mid-2019 nor the decision of the Abu Dhabi-based STC leadership to declare STC self-rule in April 2020 appeared to have been cleared with the Saudis beforehand.[41] Nor is it clear if the proximity between Abu Dhabi and Riyadh has the support of all the other six emirates in the UAE, especially Dubai, which has suffered economically and commercially from the blockade of Qatar and whose ruler, Sheikh Mohammed bin Rashid Al Maktoum, has been bypassed in the Saudi–Emirati Coordination Council, despite also being the prime minister and vice president of the UAE.[42]

V

The GCC has endured as a bloc, and it has continued to function on a technocratic level even as its annual leaders' summits between 2017 and 2019 were hit by the reluctance of the leaders of the states involved in the Qatar rift to meet in person even within the GCC rubric. The appointment in February 2020 of a new secretary general, Nayef al-Hajraf, triggered hopes that, under the leadership of a secretary general from one of the 'balancing' states (Kuwait) that had refused to take sides in 2017, the GCC might become more involved in the search for a resolution of the crisis. And yet, it took the electoral defeat of Donald Trump in November 2020, and the prospect of a Biden administration entering office on 20 January 2021, to generate meaningful movement on efforts to end the Gulf rift.[43] Trump's looming departure from office, and the fact of a Democrat president who had campaigned on a promise to make Saudi Arabia 'a pariah state' (which was later watered down in office) meant that the Saudi leadership had an interest in drawing a line under the Trump years, and did so at a carefully choreographed GCC summit on 5 January 2021, during which Mohammed bin Salman greeted and embraced Qatar's emir as he arrived at Al-Ula, in a move designed to portray the crown prince as a regional statesman far removed from the negative image he had cultivated during the Trump years.[44]

It is also the case that the GCC continued throughout the post-2017 rift to convene its regular sector-specific ministerial meetings in an indicator of how a 'GCC 2.0' might function, by focusing on technocratic aspects of common regional interest and stripping away the political dimension as far as possible. The survival of the GCC was aided by fortuitous timing in that its rotating chairmanship was held by Kuwait (in 2017–18) and by Oman (in 2018–19) during the opening two years of the crisis. This enabled many of the ministerial meetings to take place in the relatively 'safe spaces' of Kuwait City and Muscat between 2017 and 2019 and allowed the work of technocratic committees to go on, largely unaffected by the broader political storm. Examples included GCC ministerial meetings in Kuwait of the financial and economic committee in May and November 2018, of housing affairs and health in October 2018, and ministers and chiefs of commerce in November 2018, and GCC ministerial committee meetings in Muscat on youth affairs and sports in April 2018, and the annual gatherings of the GCC Trade Cooperation Committee and Industrial Cooperation Committee in May 2019.[45]

Somewhat similar 'workarounds' occurred in the military and security sphere. US officials expressed concern in autumn 2017 that the blockade of Qatar might impact regional security, defence and counterterrorism cooperation, and threatened to withdraw from joint exercises if Qatar were excluded.[46] Officials in blockading states responded by assuring US counterparts that cooperation on counterterrorism and regional security would remain unaffected by the political and economic measures against Qatar, and a Qatari contingent duly participated in the Joint Gulf Shield exercise in Saudi Arabia in March and April 2018.[47] All six GCC states' chiefs of staff later met in Kuwait in September 2018 together with the US Central Command (CENTCOM) commander, General Joseph Votel, and were included in White House attempts to establish a Middle East Strategic Alliance (MESA), often referred to erroneously as an 'Arab NATO', together with Jordan and Egypt. Egypt's abrupt withdrawal from MESA in April 2019 illustrated how difficulties in aligning US partners cut across regional geopolitical tensions, as Egypt was closely aligned with Saudi Arabia and the UAE and one of the quartet of states against Qatar.[48]

However, neither the reassertion of a common external threat – the attacks on maritime and energy targets in and around Saudi Arabia and the UAE which culminated in the cruise missile and drone strikes on Saudi oil facilities in September 2019 – nor the sudden 'black swan' emergence of a common challenge (COVID-19) was able to make inroads into the Qatar rift which had begun instead to take on aspects of permanence. The attacks – unattributable but broadly understood by most analysts to be linked to Iran or Iranian-backed groups – on shipping off the coast of the UAE and in the Gulf of Oman in May and June 2019, and on the Saudi oil processing facility at Abqaiq and the oilfield at Khurais in September, had a sobering impact on the leadership in Riyadh and Abu Dhabi because the Trump administration chose not to do anything in response – unlike after the Iranian shooting down of a US drone over the Gulf in June 2019, when the US launched a cyberattack that targeted Iran's electronic warfare capabilities, or after the death of a US contractor in Iraq in December 2019, which sparked a tit-for-tat escalation which culminated in the US killing of General Qassem Soleimani in January 2020.[49]

The lack of a visible US response to the attacks on shipping or to the assault on the nerve centre of the Saudi economy made the Saudis and Emiratis reassess the nature of the US security guarantee they had until then (largely) taken for granted.[50] President Trump denied he had offered the Saudis any pledge of protection after the Aramco attacks and added pointedly:'That was an attack on Saudi Arabia, and that wasn't an attack on us.'[51] The notion that a US government might draw a distinction between its own interests and those of its regional partners was arguably a 'wake-up' moment for Riyadh and Abu Dhabi just as Trump's initial decision to take sides (on Twitter) and back the Saudis and Emiratis against Qatar in June 2017 was for Doha: that US support could no longer be taken absolutely for granted. In response, the Emirati leadership began to reach out to Iranian counterparts in a bid to de-escalate regional tension while the Saudis opened discrete backchannels to Iran through Pakistan and Iraq.[52]

The aftermath of the Abqaiq attack in September 2019 raised hopes of a partial reconciliation, or at least a thaw in Saudi–Qatari tension. The Qatari chief of staff attended a meeting of GCC chiefs of staff in Riyadh which reaffirmed the collective security principle that an attack against a member state was an attack against all.[53] Qatari and Saudi officials also began a dialogue which appeared to be making progress in October and November 2019 before it cooled in December and was suspended, soon after Mohammed bin Salman spent four days in Abu Dhabi with Mohammed bin Zayed for the Formula One Grand Prix and the biannual meeting of the Saudi–Emirati Coordination Council.[54] By early 2020, tensions had again risen between Riyadh and Doha, with the Qatari minister of health reportedly being denied permission to enter

Saudi Arabia to attend a meeting of GCC health ministers in the early stages of the COVID-19 crisis.[55]

COVID-19 also failed to yield a breakthrough in the GCC rift even as the opening months of the pandemic revealed how the virus represented a common challenge to all regional states – including Iran – and one that did not respect political or geopolitical boundaries. While all parties to the Gulf crisis faced similar public health and budgetary pressures arising from COVID-19 and the disruption to world energy markets, they continued to engage in tit-for-tat point-scoring over the blockade, with Bahrain, for example, accusing the Qatari authorities of attempting to meddle in their affairs after Qatar Airways flew a group of Bahraini citizens stranded in Iran to Doha for onward passage to Bahrain.[56] Prominent social media influencers in Saudi Arabia and the UAE also voiced conspiracy theories that suggested that Qatar was behind COVID-19 in an attempt to disrupt 2020, the year of Saudi Arabia's presidency of the G20 and Dubai's hosting of the World Expo.[57]

The fact that Mohammed bin Zayed was willing to speak to Syria's president, Bashar al-Assad, on 27 March 2020 to express 'humanitarian solidarity during trying times', but remained unwilling to engage with the Qatari leadership, illustrated the degree to which the GCC rift remained 'stuck', even with the dramatically changed regional and global environment of the pandemic.[58] Later, in July 2020, UAE officials reportedly undermined another attempt by US officials to broker a resolution to one aspect of the Gulf crisis that would have reopened Saudi airspace to Qatar-bound traffic and ensured that aircraft carrying US civilian and military officials flying into and out of Doha would no longer have to overfly Iranian airspace.[59]

The fact that it took the prospect of a change of leadership in Washington DC to bring the Gulf crisis to an end, at least in a formal sense of reaching an agreement to 'move on', is symbolic for a rift that began in 2017 with more than half an eye on Washington. That the crisis that began in the opening months of the Trump presidency came to an end in the final fortnight of that presidency is in large part a reflection that the return to a far more conventional style of politics signalled the end to any lingering hopes that the attempted power play of 2017 could still yield results. With Trump continuing to loom large over Republican politics and the Biden presidency sagging in opinion polls, especially after the chaotic withdrawal from Afghanistan in August 2021, it may only become clear in the longer term whether the Gulf crisis that marred almost the entirety of the Trump administration was fully resolved by his departure from the White House, or if it was merely placed 'on hold' only to flare up again in another 'unconventional' administration.

Whether the agreement signed at Al-Ula to lift the blockade of Qatar – which, like the Riyadh Agreement of 2014 was kept secret – actually addresses any of the underlying points of tension between Qatar and its neighbours, also remains to be seen, just as it only became apparent in 2017 that the 2014 Riyadh Agreement had failed to prevent a further outbreak of regional tension.[60] However, the fact that subsequent meetings involving Emirati and Qatari, and Egyptian and Qatari delegations, occurred in Kuwait suggested not only that there is a follow-up process to address points of concern, which was missing in 2014, and that Kuwait will continue to play a mediatory role after the death in September 2020 of Emir Sabah, the man who did more than most to prevent the crisis from escalating in June 2017.[61] The gradual resumption of high-level visits in 2021, including four separate trips by Emir Tamim to Saudi Arabia, a visit by the UAE national security advisor, Sheikh Tahnoon bin Zayed Al Nahyan, to Doha in August 2021, and a regional tour by Mohammed bin Salman to every other Gulf capital, including Doha, in December 2021, suggested at least that direct dialogue had been re-established, albeit seemingly on a series of bilateral bases, rather than working through the GCC as an institution.[62] Whether the newfound sense of vulnerability in Gulf capitals following the 2019 attacks, and the perception that the US is disengaging from the region is enough to draw the GCC states together once more, perhaps vis-à-vis Iran, is able to paper over the deep cracks exposed by the Gulf crisis will determine if the GCC is fit for purpose as it enters its fifth decade in existence.

Notes

1   Kristian Coates Ulrichsen, *The Gulf States in International Political Economy* (Basingstoke: Palgrave Macmillan, 2015), 1.

2   Allen Fromherz, *Qatar: A Modern History* (London: I. B. Tauris, 2012), 84–5.

3   Jim Krane, *Dubai: The Story of the World's Fastest City* (London: Atlantic Books, 2009), 34.

4   'With MBZ's Promotion, Sheikha Fatima's Sons Take Center Stage', *Gulf States Newsletter*, vol. 27, issue 724, 12 December 2003, 1.

5   US Diplomatic Cable 04ABUDHABI3410_a, 'UAE Succession Update: The Post-Zayed Scenario', 28 September 2004. Available online at the Public Library

of US Diplomacy, <https://wikileaks.org/plusd/cables/04ABUDHABI3410
_a.html> (last accessed 20 October 2022).

6 Kristin Smith Diwan, 'The New Rules of Monarchy in the Gulf', *Lawfare*, 3 September 2017.

7 Richard Youngs, 'Impasse in Euro-Gulf Relations', Foundation for International Relations and Foreign Dialogue (FRIDE) Working Paper 80, April 2009, 1.

8 'Saudi Arabia Not Mulling More Cash for IMF: Minister', *Reuters*, 16 November 2008; 'Gulf Central Bankers Wary of Oil, Property Declines', *Gulf Times*, 22 November 2008.

9 Christopher M. Davidson, *Abu Dhabi: Oil and Beyond* (London, Hurst & Co., 2009), 76; A. H. Gulbrandsen, 'Bridging the Gulf: Qatari Business Diplomacy and Conflict Mediation' (MA Thesis, Georgetown University, 2010), 75.

10 Jean-Marc Rickli, 'The Political Rationale and Implications of the United Arab Emirates' Military Involvement in Libya', in Dag Henriksen and Ann Karin Larsen, eds, *Political Rationale and International Consequences of the War in Libya* (Oxford: Oxford University Press, 2016), 146–8.

11 Mary Fitzgerald, 'Libya's New Power Brokers?' *Foreign Policy*, 27 August 2014.

12 Ibid.

13 Rania Abouzeid, 'Syria's Secular and Islamist Rebels: Who are the Saudis and Qataris Arming?' *Time*, 18 September 2012.

14 'Difficult Geopolitical Context', *Gulf States Newsletter*, vol. 36, issue 926, 21 June 2012, 3; 'Morsi's Fall Prompts "Re-Set" in Gulf Ties with Egypt', *Oxford Analytica*, 9 July 2013.

15 David Kirkpatrick, 'Recordings Suggest Emirates and Egyptian Military Pushed Ousting of Morsi', *New York Times*, 1 March 2015.

16 Patrick Werr, 'UAE Offers Egypt $3 Billion Support, Saudis $5 Billion', *Reuters*, 9 July 2013.

17 Tom Arnold, 'Egypt Got $23 Billion in Aid from Gulf in 18 Months – Minister', *Reuters*, 2 March 2015.

18 Courtney Freer, 'From Co-Optation to Crackdown: Gulf States' Reactions to the Rise of the Muslim Brotherhood during the Arab Spring', in Marc Lynch, ed., *The Qatar Crisis*, POMEPS Briefings 31, October 2017, 68.

19 Simon Smith, *Britain's Revival and Fall in the Gulf: Kuwait, Bahrain, Qatar and the Trucial States, 1950–1971* (Abingdon: Routledge, 2004), 231.

20 David B. Roberts, 'Qatar and the UAE: Exploring Divergent Responses to the Arab Spring', *Middle East Journal*, 71, no. 4 (2017): 548–9.

21 Robert Worth, 'Mohammed bin Zayed's Dark Vision of the Middle East's Future', *New York Times*, 9 January 2020.

22 Rory Miller, *Desert Kingdoms to Global Powers: The Rise of the Arab Gulf* (New Haven, CT: Yale University Press, 2016), 8.

23 Joseph Kechichian, 'The Gulf Security Pact: Another GCC Dilemma', *Al Jazeera*, 24 February 2014.

24 Soren Billing and Tom Arnold, 'GCC Monetary Union "Dead" after UAE Pullout – Analysts', *ArabianBusiness.com*, 20 May 2009.

25 'GCC Unity Questioned as Summit Begins', *Gulf States Newsletter*, vol. 37, issue 960, 12 December 2013, 7.

26 Cited in Mehran Kamrava, *Troubled Waters: Insecurity in the Persian Gulf* (New York: Cornell University Press, 2018), 81–2.

27 'Oman Goes Blunt "Against" a Gulf Union', *Al Arabiya*, 7 December 2013.

28 Courtney Freer, *Rentier Islamism: The Influence of the Muslim Brotherhood in Gulf Monarchies* (New York: Oxford University Press, 2018), 157.

29 Simeon Kerr, 'Dubai Keen to Capitalize on Iran Opening', *Financial Times*, 21 January 2014.

30 Christian Koch, 'GCC Confronted by Dichotomy', Gulf Research Center online blog, 22 December 2012.

31 Author interviews with Omani and Kuwaiti diplomats, Washington DC, August 2017, November 2018 and August 2019. A list of the thirteen demands presented on 23 June 2017 is available at <https://gulfnews.com/world/gulf/qatar/what-are-the-13-demands-given-to-qatar-1.2048118> (last accessed 20 October 2022).

32 'Rouhani Visits Oman and Kuwait', Economist Intelligence Unit, 16 February 2017.

33 Author interviews with Omani and Kuwaiti diplomats, Washington DC, August 2017, November 2018 and August 2019.

34 In the event, the Omani transition from Sultan Qaboos bin Said to Sultan Haitham bin Tariq in January 2020 proceeded smoothly, but the impact of COVID-19 means that Oman remains vulnerable to pressure from its neighbours should it ever need economic assistance, which could come with strings and conditions attached.

35 Kristin Smith Diwan, 'The GCC is Becoming More – and Less – than the Sum of its Parts', Arab Gulf States Institute in Washington, 13 August 13, 2019.

36 Kristian Coates Ulrichsen, 'The Exclusionary Turn in GCC Politics', Arab Center Washington, 21 August 2019.

37 Author interviews with two senior Obama administration officials, Washington DC and Houston, August and November 2018.

38 'Saudi–Emirati Coordination Council Announces 7 Joint Initiatives', *Gulf News*, 19 January 2019.

39 David Gardner, 'Saudi–UAE Competition Threatens to Upend the GCC', *Financial Times*, 7 July 2021.

40 Declan Walsh and Saeed Al-Batati, 'Ally Attacks Ally in Yemen's War Within a War', *New York Times*, 29 August 2019; Andrew England and Simeon Kerr, 'UAE Attacks on Yemen Reveal Fractures in Saudi-led Coalition', *Financial Times*, 29 August 2019.

41 Fatima Abo Alasrar, 'Yemen's Competition for Saudi Patronage Heats Up as the STC Declares Self-Rule', Middle East Institute blog, 29 April 2020.

42 'Saudi–Emirati Coordination Council: All You Need to Know', *The National*, 7 June 2018.

43 Barak Ravid, 'Kushner to Visit Saudi Arabia and Qatar Seeking Deal to End Crisis', *Axios*, 29 November 2020.

44 Kristian Coates Ulrichsen, 'Has the GCC Crisis been Resolved?' *Al Jazeera*, 6 January 2021.

45 Information compiled by the author from press releases available on the GCC website and local media reports in GCC member states.

46 Maria Abi-Habib and Gordon Lubold, 'U.S. Suspends Military Exercises with Gulf Allies over Qatar Spat', *Wall Street Journal*, 6 October 2017.

47 'Qatari Forces Participate in Gulf Shield Drill in Saudi Arabia', *Al Jazeera*, 18 April 2018.

48 Joyce Karam, 'With Egypt's Withdrawal, Hopes for Mesa Alliance are Diminished but Not Dead', *The National*, 15 April 2019.

49 Kristian Coates Ulrichsen, 'Rebalancing Regional Security in the Persian Gulf', Rice University's Baker Institute for Public Policy Working Paper, February 2020, 9–11.

50 David Kirkpatrick and Ben Hubbard, 'Attack on Saudi Oil Facilities Tests U.S. Guarantee to Defend Gulf', *New York Times*, 19 September 2019.

51 Steve Holland and Rania El Gamal, 'Trump Says He Does Not Want War After Attack on Saudi Oil Facilities', *Reuters*, 16 September 2019.

52 Liz Sly, 'The UAE's Ambitions Backfire as It Finds Itself on the Front Line of U.S.–Iran Tensions', *Washington Post*, 11 August 2019; Farnaz Fassihi and Ben Hubbard, 'Saudi Arabia and Iran Make Quiet Openings to Head Off War', *New York Times*, 4 October 2019.

53 Sylvia Westall, 'Qatar Condemns Saudi Aramco Attacks, Calls for Collective Security', *Reuters*, 16 September 2019.

54 'Qatar Says Talks to End GCC Crisis Were Suspended in January', *Al Jazeera*, 15 February 2020.

55 'Saudi Arabia Refuses Entry to Qatar Health Minister for Key GCC Coronavirus Meeting', *The New Arab*, 20 February 2020.

56 'Bahrain Blasts Qatar over Stranded Nationals', *The New Arab*, 1 April 2020.
57 Ismaeel Naar, 'Twitter User Ridiculed for Insinuating Coronavirus is a "Qatari Plot"', *Al Arabiya English*, 4 March 2020.
58 Tawfiq Nasrallah, 'COVID-19: Mohammed bin Zayed Expresses Solidarity with Syrian People', *Gulf News*, 27 March 2020.
59 Eric Shawn, 'UAE Said to Be Holding Up Gulf Deal That Could End Qatar Blockade and Protect US Interests in Middle East', *Fox News*, 9 July 2020.
60 Dania Thafer and Patrick Theros, 'What the Al-Ula GCC Summit Has (and Has Not) Accomplished', Gulf International Forum, 11 January 2021.
61 'UAE, Qatari Delegations Meet in Kuwait to Follow up on Al-Ula Declaration', *Arab News*, 22 February 2021; 'Egyptian, Qatari Delegations Meet in Kuwait to Agree on Cooperation Mechanism Following Al-Ula Summit', *Egypt Today*, 24 February 2021.
62 'Senior UAE Official Meets Qatar's Emir in Rare Visit: State Media', *Al Jazeera*, 26 August 2021; Kristian Coates Ulrichsen, 'Mohammed bin Salman's Regional Rebranding Campaign', Arab Center Washington, 16 December 2021.

7

SOVEREIGNTY FOR SECURITY:
THE PARADOX OF URGENCY AND
INTERVENTION IN YEMEN

Waleed Mahdi

Introduction

The war in Yemen that began in 2015 challenges any analysis that reduces the conflict to a mere clash between two distinct sectarian, tribal, partisan, regional, or even global forces. Such a binary unravels through a constant shifting of multilayered local alliances formed in concert with, sometimes as a response to, foreign interventions. Key to Yemen's transformation from a peaceful revolutionary call for regime change in 2011 into violence is the violation of the country's sovereignty. This is not to suggest the existence of neat binaries between domestic and foreign agendas, but to emphasise, as this chapter will demonstrate, how violation of sovereignty has been integral to Yemen's sociopolitical reality.

The 2011 revolutionary demands were soon compromised by a transitional plan to transfer power in the form of the National Dialogue Conference (2012–14). The outcome of the concerted efforts to secure a peaceful transition was a new constitution and a proposal for a Yemeni federal governance system of six semi-autonomous regions. But the failure to fulfil this outcome was in part predictable since the proposed resolutions were manufactured in response to top-down foreign dictates that imposed what was considered a proper political process for Yemen. This process was developed through a Gulf Cooperation Council (GCC) initiative that compromised 'justice for peace',[1] and which was monitored by what came to be known as the Group of Ten Ambassadors (aka Friends of Yemen), representing the Kingdom of

Saudi Arabia, the United Arab Emirates, Oman, Kuwait, Bahrain, the United States, the United Kingdom, France, Russia and China.[2] Even though women and youth voices were incorporated into the conference, the GCC initiative sustained, if not empowered, 'traditional rival elites' who had already dominated Yemen's political scene for three decades.[3] This developed in a context of suspicion from revolutionaries who have wrestled with mounting pressures from state and political parties over who ought to represent them from the early days of the revolution.[4]

It is important to draw a distinction between the idea and the reality of the conference. The conference itself, Sheila Carapico argues, was a 'Yemeni initiative drawing on indigenous precedents and activism' for 'a new, negotiated social contract between regions, parties and stakeholders in a pluralistic and decentralized polity'.[5] The conference, however, was brokered through a GCC initiative that Carapico describes as a 'Western-backed effort by wealthy, misogynistic and distinctly anti-democratic gerontocracies to tame popular energies, partly by co-opting key elites into a process of managed political change and security restructuring'.[6] The imbalance in the vision for a 'new Yemen' was, in a sense, a result of a contradictory reality in which youth aspirations and elitist ambitions clashed and yielded to foreign interventions and inorganic dictates of state-building.

Perhaps the most crucial factor for such regional and international interventions was a sense of urgency to intervene in Yemeni politics and save the country from violence and chaos. The intervention compromised Yemeni sovereignty for the promise of local, regional and even global security. This compromise was predicated on the presumption that security was contingent on a perception of peace beholden to the fragile nature of state power. The prospect of a deeply fractured state through military division, sectarian unrest, tribal conflict, regional disunity and partisan polarisation seemed too chaotic and destabilising. And so diplomatic interventions were justified in the name of rescuing the 'failing state' of Yemen from becoming a 'failed state', concepts loaded with definitional inadequacies and Eurocentric assumptions about development and security.[7]

This chapter critiques the paradox of urgency and intervention in Yemen, which has compromised the country's sovereignty for security and, ironically, has contributed to conditions that have disrupted both. The chapter locates this paradox at the crossroads of a post-9/11 US-led 'war-on-terror' campaign in Yemen and post-2011 competing narratives surrounding Yemenis' future at the interplay of domestic needs and foreign plans. While 9/11 provided the context for developing a US security fetish around Yemen, I argue that the post-2011 Arab Spring context has further elucidated this security fetish as part of a regional struggle to shape a new Middle East order, spearheaded by Saudi Arabia, Iran, Turkey, Qatar and the UAE, among others. The purpose of this chapter is not to offer a comprehensive account of all direct and indirect foreign interventions in Yemen but to reveal what I call the paradox of sovereignty for security in Yemen, traced primarily through US diplomatic and militarised interventions along with its regional allies, particularly Saudi Arabia and the UAE. This is not to dismiss the devastating nature of foreign intervention of countries like Iran, but to ensure focus on the meanings and implications of the chapter's case for the sovereignty for security paradox. The outcome of this paradox in both post-9/11 and post-Arab Spring Yemen, I stress, is a society whose struggle to attain a sense of sovereignty has been constantly checked by a morally justified discourse of intervention that further disrupts the country and entrenches Yemenis into violence and chaos.

Droning Sovereignty

The US's use of drones increased from 50 in 2000 to 7,500 by 2010.[8] Key to this transformation was the increasing threat of al-Qaida operatives and the Obama administration's adoption of targeted killing as an efficient 'war-on-terror' tool. While Yemen was not officially declared a war zone in the first decade of the twenty-first century, drone strikes emerged as a viable tool in engaging the rising threat of the Yemen-based al-Qaida in the Arabian Peninsula (AQAP). On 12 October 2000, less than a year before 9/11, al-Qaida attacked the USS Cole, a navy destroyer, in the Yemeni harbour of Aden. On Christmas day in 2009, Umar Farouk Abdulmutallab, a Nigerian al-Qaida operative trained in Yemen, was arrested before carrying out his mission to blow up an airliner approaching Detroit using explosives hidden in his underwear. Considering al-Qaida's increasing threat in the years separating these two incidents, the US found its violations of Yemen's sovereignty justifiable, often legitimised through Yemeni government concessions. What started as a limited drone strike on a vehicle of six al-Qaida suspects on 3 November 2002 evolved into a systematic drone strike campaign in 2009, when President Barack Obama embraced the lethal option as part of his administration's 'kill-don't-capture' doctrine.[9]

Scholars and activists critiqued the Obama administration's deployment of lethal drone technology in Yemen for institutionalising what appeared to be an inherently flawed system of hard power.[10] Perhaps the most immediate frustrations related to the secretive nature of this deployment and the administration's denials of its existence. The administration conceded to rising pressure from media and civil rights organisations and disclosed its targeted killing programme only in June of 2012.[11] Then, this programme was presented as part of a US package of humanitarian support for Yemen and its stability. It was rhetorically promoted as a necessary course of action to save Yemenis and Americans from the AQAP's threats. The alternative, President Obama cautioned, would be 'far more civilian casualties – not just in our cities at home and our facilities abroad, but also in the very places like Sana'a and Kabul and Mogadishu where terrorists seek a foothold'.[12] But the rising toll of civilian casualities in Yemen, including women and children, was an early telling sign of defectiveness in intelligence gathering, strike precision, understanding of militancy and knowledge of Yemen's multilayered structure. The deaths of at least forty-five civilians, including fifteen women and twenty-two children in the al-Ma'ajalah Massacre (17 December 2009) as well as the deaths of twelve men and injury of fifteen others in the Rada'a wedding procession (12 December 2013) were traumatising to many in Yemen.[13]

One may argue that the US did not technically violate Yemen's sovereignty since the drone programme was sanctioned by President Ali Abdullah Saleh – whose rule spanned the period 1978 to 2012 – and was further supported by President Abdrabbuh Mansur Hadi, who presided over the country from 2012 until he was driven out of the capital in 2014 (but was recognised by major international powers until his relinquish of office in 2022). This argument, however, falls short because it locates sovereignty in presidents who lack public and/or parliamentary support to permit US drone and missile strikes in Yemen. In fact, it was not until 2010 that a leaked US secret cable outlined President Saleh's complicity in covering up the US drone programme. According to US ambassador Stephen Seche's diplomatic cable, President Saleh confirmed to him, 'We'll continue saying the bombs are ours, not yours.'[14] That President Saleh lied to his own people about the identity of the drone operators implies a sense of complicity by attempting to assure the weary Yemeni public about the sovereignty of their state. Accounts of Yemeni forms for peaceful and even violent responses to this violation demonstrate the level of rejection and anger directed at, what appears to be, a governmental betrayal of the sanctity of Yemeni lives.[15] In 2013, anti-drone murals decorated Sana'a streets.[16] In the same year, a non-binding vote from the Yemeni parliament demanded an ending of drone strikes to preserve Yemeni airspace, protect civilian lives and maintain the country's sovereignty.[17]

Linking the authority of Yemeni presidents to Yemen's sovereignty is also problematic, especially when recognising the power dynamics between those representing Yemen and the US. Whether mobilised by fear of political fallout considering the Bush administration's 'you are with us or against us' mantra, opportunism to maximize US financial support, realism about the Yemeni government's inability to exercise full control of Yemen's security, desire to consolidate his centralised power in a multipolar domestic polity, or a mixture of all of these factors, President Saleh accepted US$400 million dollars of aid in exchange for cooperating with the US, which meant accepting training support from the US of Yemeni military personnel, contributing to the creation of a 'counterterrorism camp' in Yemen, and sanctioning the US targeted killing programme.[18] That President Hadi embraced the drone programme as an effective tool in the war against AQAP – and was further backed by his foreign minister Abu Bakr al-Qirbi who described the strikes as both a 'necessary evil' and a 'very limited affair' – should be properly contextualised as statements made by a transitional government exacerbated by intervening foreign powers and weakened by their inability to solidify public support for their role in ending the 2011 peaceful revolutionary momentum.[19]

Perhaps the power dynamics that have defined the relationship between Yemeni presidents Saleh and Hadi with both the US government and the Yemeni people can best be understood through, what Ashraf Ghani and Clare Lockhart call, the 'sovereignty gap'. This gap appears at the disjuncture between 'the *de jure* assumption that all states are "sovereign" regardless of their performance in practice' and 'the de facto reality that many are malfunctioning or collapsed states, incapable of providing their citizens with even the most basic services, and where the reciprocal set of rights and obligations are not a reality'.[20] Under President Saleh, the state was 'incapable of providing welfare, protection, or education to the population', and Yemenis incessantly complained about 'the absence of "security" (*amān*) and "stability" (*istiqrār*), the inability of the state to guarantee safe passage from one region to another, to put a stop to extralegal justice, and to disarm the citizenry'.[21] The situation became even more desperate under President Hadi's rule.

Considering this sovereignty gap, the two elected Yemeni presidents officiated the US invasive deployment of targeted killing technology in Yemen – thereby exempting the US from criticism of violating the country's sovereignty – while these leaders lacked the legitimate authority to do so as questionably elected autocrats whose governments could not fulfil the basic needs of their society. Put differently, Presidents Saleh and Hadi operated within a sovereignty gap that enabled them to offer concessions to the US to violate Yemen's skies while themselves lacking the legitimacy to do so in the name of their own people. This peculiar situation was made possible primarily because of the post-9/11 US-drawn links between stability and security. What is also problematic, I suggest, is the very conception of sovereignty in an international system that only recognises states rather than peoples as the ultimate embodiment of autonomy.

Furthermore, Presidents Saleh and Hadi were never in a position of power to deny, or even strictly regulate, the US's access to Yemeni skies and the targeting of Yemeni lives. Apart from the 2002 strike when President Saleh reportedly provided the final approval, the re-launching of the drone programme since 2009 was pursued with less rigour in seeking authorisation from Yemeni authorities as the ultimate permission was reserved for either the CIA or the US president, depending on the target level. Victoria Clark reads this change as a culmination of Washington's frustrations with President Saleh's counterterrorism efforts, especially his government's lack of strict confinement policies of terrorism suspects and a relaxed rehabilitation programme for those imprisoned.[22] The presence of US ambassadors outside diplomatic circles and in Yemeni tribal spheres of influence reflected the US's growing mistrust of President Saleh. Ambassador Edmund Hull, for instance, was welcomed in Marib governorate in 2004 to lay the foundation stone of a Yemeni Civilisation Museum funded by a US$3 million 'gift from the American people' alongside a US$5.7 million medical equipment gift for a new hospital, and a US$40,000 donation to farmers to improve their irrigation methods.[23] By Ambassador Gerald Feierstein's time (2010–13), there was growing public sentiment that perceived the US embassy as a front for homeland security rather than a site for diplomacy. And 2011 did not, by any means, produce revolutionary conditions strong enough to challenge the US's increasing violations of Yemeni sovereignty. If anything, the US narrative of intervention for security solidified as the number of drone strikes increased from eleven strikes in 2011 to ninety strikes by mid-2017, and concerns for civilian casualties receded.[24] In fact, it was this history of US violations of Yemen's sovereignty that constituted a precedent for the post-2011 paradox of sovereignty for security, effectively devastating Yemen's chances of transitioning coherently into an autonomous state.

From Revolution to Crisis

The date 11 February 2011 is that which many Yemenis commemorate as the moment when their revolutionary momentum transcended their demand for the political transformation of the country's thirty-three-year-old autocratic regime and evolved into larger-than-life experiences defined by how they perceived themselves, mobilised each other, narrated their agency, and organised not only their political sentiments but also their artistic creativity and creative sensibility.[25] Hundreds of slogans were raised across the various public squares of change – most prominently in Sana'a, Taiz and Aden – that reflected a society in motion, interconnected with other Arab revolutionary spheres like Tunisia and Egypt, and ready to reconcile past grievances with contemporary realities and future aspirations. The revolutionary moment was euphoric, but it also embedded consciousness of the complicated realities of the time and the multilayered counter-revolutionary forces, including efforts by regional and international powers to reduce the revolution to a political crisis.

Efforts to label Yemen's revolution a 'crisis' in the name of security were immediate. In less than two months, the US ambassador to Yemen described the revolutionary scene as 'a political crisis' and expressed concern for the country's 'security and stability'.[26] Meanwhile, the GCC held a meeting in Riyadh for the purpose of ending what GCC secretary general Rashid al-Zayani described then as Yemen's 'crisis'.[27] Not long thereafter, the GCC initiative gained international recognition as the only legible political framework to safeguard Yemen's transition and maintain security at the cost of stifling all forms of grassroots protests. It's quite ironic how such foreign intervention in the name of security developed in response to a Yemeni revolutionary context, which Ross Porter considers as 'a security event' itself 'punctuating a life of state-induced insecurity'.[28]

Foreign interference in Yemen's political transition may not have been presented in Yemeni official media at the time as a violation of Yemen's sovereignty since the country's political elites themselves provided a sense of legitimacy in their welcoming of such external pressures. At the grassroots level, however, the narrative surrounding foreign interference was different.

Protestors, for instance, rejected how the GCC initiative offered President Saleh a safe exit out of the presidency through immunity and safeguarded his presence in the country's political power structure through a power-sharing agreement that granted his party fifty percent of the government's cabinet. The slogan, *la ḍamāna la ḥaṣāna, yethakam Saleh wa a'wāna* (no assurance, no immunity, Saleh and his circle should be prosecuted) was a popular response from the streets that saw the GCC initiative as an immediate threat to the protestors' aspirations for grassroots-led regime change. Other slogans raised at the time included *ya khalīji la tobāder, Ali Saleh ba yughāder* (Gulf members: do not offer initiatives, Saleh will leave), *Nuwāb ayn al al-amāna? Ṣawitu ḍid al-ḥaṣāna* (oh, parliament members: where is your integrity, vote against the immunity), and *la ḥaṣāna, maṭlabna al-muḥākama*) no immunity, our demand is prosecution). The Homeland Group for Popular Youth Revolution (aka *Takatul waṭan lil-thawrah ashababiyya asha'biyya*) even raised a public banner, which critiqued in simple terms the impact of foreign interference on Yemenis. The banner read, *niẓām Saleh yaqtulna bi ḍamānatikum* (Saleh's regime is killing us with your assurance). The statement is typed in red with marks of what appears to be the dripping blood of the regime's victims. The top of the banner features flags of key power players involved in diluting the revolutionary momentum at the time in the following order: the US, UAE, Qatar, Saudi Arabia, Bahrain, Kuwait, Oman and the EU.

The GCC initiative also required the election of then Vice President Hadi as president, the only candidate that was allowed on the ballot. This election sought to legitimise Hadi's ascendance to power but eventually came to symbolise the demise of the Yemeni revolution and the subsequent years of violence and disorder in the country. Protestors, at least those who were not committed to major political parties at the time, rejected the process as undemocratic and counterrevolutionary. The raised slogans captured the heated nature of this rejection: *la ḥaṣāna la intikhāb, yasqut Ali wal-aḥzāb* (no immunity, no election, down with Ali and political parties), *thawra, thawra, la intikhāb, ḍid al-fāsid wal-kadhāb* (revolution, revolution, no election, we are against the corrupt and the liar), *intikhābakum baṭil, la ḥaṣāna lil-qātil* (your election is void, no immunity for the killer), *ashabāb ma hu rāji', lil-intikhāb muqaṭi'* (the youth are not turning back and will boycott the election), *thawra taṣn' waṭan, la tuḥshar fi ṣanduq* (a revolution creates a homeland and cannot be confined to a ballot box), and *al-musharaka fi intikhabāt 21 fibrāyer khiyyana li-dimā' ashhuhadā'* (participating in the 21 February elections is a betrayal to the martyrs' blood). This rejection echoed a line from the national anthem stipulating *lan tara aldoniyya 'la arḍi waṣiyya* (the world will not see a trustee over my land).

The rejection of foreign interference in 2011 was not limited to Yemen's capital, Sanaʿa. On 20 June Houthis (aka Ansarullah) raised slogans in Saʿada governorate that equated *isqāṭ anizām* (toppling the regime) with *isqāṭ al-wiṣaya al-amrikyya* (bringing down the American trusteeship) and described the US as *'dowat ashhuʿūb wa muthīrat al-ḥurūb* (enemy of the peoples and warmongering). On 29 June, hundreds of women marched the streets of Ibb governorate and chanted: *sajjil ana yamaniyya, la wiṣaya ajnabiyya, amrikyya or ūrubiyya, khalījiyya or suʿdiyya* (write down that I am a female Yemeni: no foreign trusteeship, American or European, Gulf or Saudi) and *qasaman bi-llah al-jabbār ma nihiya illa aḥrar* (by God Almighty, we will only live free).[29] And on 20 December, the largest and longest march in Yemen's modern history took place from Taiz governorate, the birthplace of the 2011 Yemeni revolution, to Sanaʿa, a nearly 300-kilometre-long journey in which hundreds of peaceful protestors walked on foot for five days to complete. Dubbed *Masīrat al-Ḥayāh* (March of Life), its primary motivation was rejecting the GCC initiative and its supposed safeguarding of the country's transition. Protestors captured the imagination of villagers and city dwellers whenever they passed, further inspiring them to join the march. The march, then, constituted a manifestation of the grassroots rejection of external interference in the Yemeni political transition at the time.[30]

Overall, the desire to retain control of their country's future was key to the Yemeni revolutionaries' demands, even though they were eventually silenced through a compromised transitional process that was steered by powerful regional and international actors involved in Yemen's internal affairs. This is not to suggest that Yemeni revolutionaries rejected entirely such foreign dictates, but to emphasise how their eventual acceptance of the GCC initiative was essentially a concession informed by calculations of risk and decades of manipulation of disorder rather than innate support for foreign intervention. Kamilia Al-Eriani illustrates this dynamic:

> Although many Yemenis were suspicious of national elites as well as the GCCI, the *fragile* and *chaotic* 'reality' of their state forced them to calculate the risks and act rationally to *save* Yemen. Worries/hopes cultivated over the years due to a culture of security imposed on Yemen from without and

nurtured within acted as a regime of power. This disciplining power, generated over the state security, permitted Yemenis to cultivate and embody hope
mobilized by international and regional powers to retain the waning power
of the Yemeni state. By voting for the GCCI, they reproduced the domination of US–GCC states over Yemen.[31]

The GCC initiative's premise of managing a crisis rather than honouring
the revolutionaries' aspirations for a 'new Yemen' reinforced such foreign
domination of the country, further feeding frustration with President Hadi's
transitional government and fuelling the rise of armed militias with narratives advocating sovereignty, leading among which was one promoted by
the Houthis. With a sensational slogan, *Allāhu akbar; al-mawt li-'Amrīkā;
al-mawt li-'Isrā'īl; al-la'nah 'alā 'l-Yahūd; an-naṣr lil-'Islām* (God is great;
Death to America; Death to Israel; Curse to the Jews; Victory to Islam),
Houthis advanced rhetoric that demanded respect for the country's sovereignty from the US–Saudi security axis, but not without a twist of irony in
their susceptibility to Iranian influence. On 20 May and 8 June 2012, for
instance, Houthis raised slogans that rejected violations of Yemeni sovereignty, including: *rafḍ attadakhul al-amrīki* (rejection of American interference), *la lil-tadakhul al-amrīki fi asho'ūn al-yamaniyya* (no to American
interference in Yemeni affairs), and *asiyada al-waṭaniyya lan takūn qiṭ'a
tanhashaha ḥukumat anifāq* (national sovereignty will not be a piece of meat
for the government of hypocrisy to swallow). But it was not until President
Hadi decided to lift government subsidies on fuel prices in response to reform
pressures from the International Monetary Fund (IMF) that Houthis decided
to advance their militia and assume control of Sana'a on 21 September
2014, effectively toppling the GCC's internationally recognised transitional
framework and Hadi's presidency. Isa Blumi reads the IMF's reform pressures on President Hadi at the time as another sign of foreign disruption of
Yemen:

> There is much to say about how global financial interests expected the
> country's anointed leaders to adopt an entirely exploitative system of eco-
> nomic liberalization that included a renewed rush to privatize the country's
> resources after 2012. Ostensibly, the kind of neoliberal project that would
> assure South Arabia's full integration into a 'globalized' regime required a
> new set of coercive tools that induced Yemen's destruction.[32]

Therefore, Yemen's transition from a revolution in 2011 into 'a crisis' in 2014 was primarily an outcome of constant foreign interference in the country. And the link between the UN Security Council's regular description of Yemen as a 'failed state' in 2014 – particularly in the post-Houthi militia's take-over of the capital Sana'a, the collapse of UN-recognised political institutions, and the departure of many diplomatic missions – and the Saudi-led narrative of benign military intervention to restore the legitimacy of exiled President Hadi through the 2015 coalition dubbed *'sifat al-ḥazm* (Operation Decisive Storm), created another cycle of interference that proved ever more destructive.

The 'Failed State' Conundrum

Long before March 2015, when Saudi Arabia utilised the UN's 2014 designation of Yemen as a 'failed state' to advance its narrative of benign military intervention and restore the legitimacy of exiled President Hadi,[33] the US had already utilised such constructs as 'fragile state' or 'failing state' in a post-9/11 'war on terror' narrative that conceived state failure in Yemen as a threat to US national security. Historically, such constructs emerged as post-Cold War signifiers of international law and order that enabled Western powers to police and control the global South. And Yemen was frequently described as a weak state, a failing state, or on the brink of becoming a failed state during the 1990s and 2000s.[34] However, it was not until the emergence of the 'war on terror' narrative in the post-9/11 context that Yemenis experienced more directly US violations of their sovereignty in the name of security.

The US National Security Strategy (2002) clearly articulated how the US was threatened 'less by conquering states' than 'by failing ones'.[35] The Commission on Weak States and US National Security (2004) argued that

> weak and failed governments generate instability, which harms their citizens, drags down their neighbors, and ultimately threatens US interests in building an effective international system, providing the foundation for continued prosperity, and, not least, protecting Americans from external threats to our security.[36]

The same year, the United States' Office of the Coordinator for Reconstruction and Stabilization and the subsequent year the 'National Intelligence Strategy of the United States' (2005) further foregrounded weak and failed states as threats to international and US security.[37] In 2006, the National Security Council echoed the same message.[38] Despite evidence that suggested the connection between state failure and terrorism was 'an exaggerated one' (David Chandler, 2006) and 'mythic' (Aidan Hehir, 2009),[39] this connection justified the US government's use of drones in direct violation of the sovereignty of Yemen's skies.

That Saudi Arabia utilised the 'failed state' concept in mobilising international support for its military intervention in Yemen since 2015 underscores the practical importance of the term in circumventing Yemeni sovereignty and legitimising foreign intervention in the name of security and state-building. It also points to the term's theoretical limitations in its lack of recognition of localised governance models and its disruptive role in exacerbating conditions of stability so essential to both security and state-building. The result is a paradox of urgency and intervention that builds on a narrative of rescuing Yemen from disorder but, in fact, further entrenches the country into chaos. To argue that violations of Yemeni sovereignty in the name of security are a direct result of the 'failed state' designation is, therefore, hardly a convincing argument. The designation rather offers convenience, as Maria-Louise Clausen contends, for foreign political actors such as Saudi Arabia and the US – as this chapter demonstrates – since it corresponds to an existing international system of norms that legitimises intervention in 'failed states' like Yemen without respect to the issue of sovereignty. This convenience underscores a structural problem in the existing international system since it primarily upholds governing mechanisms that are meant to protect Western powers and their allies. After all, the 'failed state' construct is not a mere 'label' but 'an ideology' that coordinates the interests of various states through a conflated correlation of intervention and state-building with security and development.[40]

What is unsettling about the Yemeni case is how key power players such as the US, Saudi Arabia and the UAE promoted Yemen's stability and security in their interference but pursued their own national security priorities at the cost of Yemen's stability and security. Consider the US's role in the Saudi-led militarised coalition in Yemen since 2015. Even though the US has not formally joined the coalition as a member, its involvement has been mobilised by a post-9/11 'war on terror' sovereignty for security narrative – manifested primarily through the drone programme – which itself provided a necessary platform for the Saudi rational for militarised intervention, that is, justifying militarised violence, once again in the name of rescuing Yemenis from themselves. US support for the Saudi mission was far more than rhetorical. US weapons sales of US$110 billion to Saudi Arabia in 2017 eclipsed the US$8.4

billion sales of weapons to Riyadh between 2001 and 2016.[41] In addition to arms sales, the US supported the Saudi-led militarised disruption of Yemen through intelligence sharing of targeted sites. The support also included mid-air refuelling of the coalition's aircraft. Between March 2015 and February 2017 alone, the US contributed no fewer than 7,564 refuelling missions that amounted to fifty-four million pounds of transferred fuel.[42] 'Given that many of the bombing sorties could not happen without this action,' observes Helen Lackner, 'the US Air Force must be considered an active participant in the air strikes, most likely including strikes which have killed civilians and destroyed civilian facilities.'[43] Parallel to this support, the US independently pursued its drone campaign in the country, further creating conditions of disorder.

Riyadh's use of the 'failed state' designation as a political convenience is further underscored by its history of violations of Yemen's sovereignty, which dates to 1934, only two years after the kingdom's establishment. These violations ranged in terms of political influence in Yemen, patronage of the country's non-state actors, and an unstated policy to ensure that 'Yemen was both weak enough and strong enough not to be a threat to the Saudi regime.'[44] By the 2000s, three issues became prominent for Saudi policymakers, that is, an increase in both 'illegal immigration and smuggling of weapons, explosives, and narcotics' alongside the 1,200-kilometre-long Saudi–Yemeni border, 'the merger in early January 2009 of the Yemeni and Saudi Al Qaida branches into AQAP', and the emergence of Houthis since 2004.[45] Such threat perceptions eventually guided Saudi efforts to thwart the 2011 Yemeni revolutionary momentum and to maintain status-quo politics through violent means after 2015.

Meanwhile, the role of the UAE in Yemen, which was especially disruptive across Yemen's south, was the result of a different threat perception than those motivating the US and Saudi Arabia (read, fear of the Muslim Brotherhood). The Emirati contribution to the militarised campaign in Yemen since 2015 capitalised significantly on the similar 'failed state' rationale, which expected Yemenis to suspend their demands for sovereignty in exchange for a hollow promise of stability and security, but in fact, advanced a different agenda. The Emirati investment in building militias – such as the 'Elite Forces' in Hadramaut and Shabwa governorates and the 'Security Belt' in Abyan, Aden and Lahej governorates – sought to create new actors that were not affiliated with Islah, the Yemeni political party most closely inspired by the Muslim Brotherhood. This not only translated into antagonising a vital political ally in the Saudi military coalition in Yemen but often led to supporting extremist militants, such as members of Abu al-Abbas Brigade in Taiz, whose leader was on the US terrorist list but still earned UAE financial and logistical support.[46]

Even though foreign interference in Yemen such as that spearheaded by the US, Saudi Arabia and the UAE was mediated as a noble effort to urgently respond to the deteriorating situation in the country, it effectively contributed to Yemen's contemporary scene of chaos and disorder. Saving the 'failed state' of Yemen was merely a signifier for intervention that seemed more of a geopolitical response to the threat perceptions of foreign powers than it was an effort to safeguard the country's transition to peace and order.

Conclusion

The narrative of urgency and intervention in Yemen since the turn of the twenty-first century has been paradoxical in that it has proven self-contradictory. The competing interests of foreign powers, although supposedly unified in their support for Yemen's stability, are more defined by the differing national priorities of intervening powers than serious concerns for the well-being of Yemeni geopolitics. While the 'failed state' theory provides important insight into Yemen's conditions that have generated anxiety for and legitimised the intervention of foreign powers, it fails to account for the process of normalising such disruptions.

Therefore, using the 'failed state' theory to explain such interventions in Yemen is both limited and limiting. Not only does it dismiss Yemen's resilient tribal system in sociopolitical governance, but it also fails to recognise the capability of local actors to develop an organic governing model, especially during the 2011 revolutionary moment. Foreign intervention in Yemen has led to empowering status quo politics (2000–10), co-opting the youth revolution (2011–14) and supporting the Saudi-led military coalition (2015–present), while militarily sustaining a targeted killing campaign throughout these years, all in the name of security, a fleeting concept that infantilised Yemenis and failed to recognise their ability to develop their own mechanisms for lasting peace. In this context, Yemen's biggest challenge during the 2011 revolution was not the possibility of becoming a failed state, as promoted at the time, but the immediate foreign interference and violation of the country's sovereignty in the name of saving it from becoming a failed state, since those violations themselves created conditions for the country's insecurity.

This chapter does not dismiss the complexity of the Yemeni scene and the multitude of factors that contribute to the country's contemporary war-within-war context. Rather, it demands a serious pause to assess the damaging effects of foreign adventurism in Yemen. The rapid disintegration of the 2011 revolutionary momentum in Yemen into a top-down concerted attempt to recycle elites into power – at the cost of safeguarding the political transition towards pluralism – and the Saudi-led military campaign in the country since 2015 have accompanied a wave of disruptive violence and disorder rooted in Yemenis' search for sovereignty and self-determination. Not only did the GCC initiative constitute a counter-revolutionary measure in co-opting the revolutionaries' aspirations for a new Yemen in the name of saving Yemenis from an imminent civil war, but it also ironically fostered a destabilising environment that rendered the current reality of violence a foregone conclusion. The active involvement of the GCC in the Yemeni scene starting with a roadmap initiative to peaceful transition through national dialogue and ending with a full-scale military intervention was riddled with regional anxieties, shifting alliances and divergent politics among GCC member states themselves.

This chapter's focus on the US, Saudi Arabia and the UAE is not to disregard the damaging effects of the interventions of other foreign powers like Qatar, Iran, Turkey, Russia, China and other European states, which have further added layers to contemporary articulations of violence in Yemen, albeit in varying degrees of directness and intensity. Still, these three countries have been at the forefront in destabilising revolutionary and transition conditions in Yemen in the name of security, only to advance their own national security agendas. Overall, I should stress that the presence of tolerance in today's Yemen, or its lack thereof, is informed by the fragile nature of the country's autonomy from foreign disruption of its institutions, primarily articulated through its contemporary military division, sectarian unrest, tribal conflict, regional disunity and partisan polarisation – all while Yemen emerges as a constantly disruptive site to any attempt to develop solid, regional meta-narratives around its identity politics.

Notes

1 Ibrahim Fraihat, *Unfinished Revolutions: Yemen, Libya, and Tunisia after the Arab Spring* (New Haven, CT: Yale University Press, 2016), 51.
2 Qatar was initially part of the coalition but withdrew in protest.

3   Helen Lackner, ed., *Why Yemen Matters: A Society in Transition* (London: Saqi, 2014), 1.

4   See Ross Porter, 'Freedom, Power and the Crisis of Politics in Revolutionary Yemen', *Middle East Critique* 26, no. 3 (2017): 265–81.

5   Sheila Carapico, 'Yemen between Revolution and Counter-terrorism', in Helen Lackner, ed., *Why Yemen Matters: A Society in Transition* (London: Saqi, 2014), 29–49, 47.

6   Carapico, 'Yemen between Revolution and Counter-terrorism', 47.

7   See David Chandler, *Empire in Denial: The Politics of State-building* (London: Pluto, 2006); Susan L. Woodward, *The Ideology of Failed States: Why Intervention Fails* (Cambridge: Cambridge University Press, 2017).

8   Medea Benjamin, *Drone Warfare: Killing by Remote Control* (London: Verso, 2013).

9   'CIA "Killed al-Qaeda Suspects" in Yemen', *BBC News*, 5 November 2002. Available at <http://news.bbc.co.uk/2/hi/2402479.stm> (last accessed 21 October 2022); Benjamin, *Drone Warfare*.

10 Amrit Singh, 'Death by Drone: Civilian Harm Caused by US Targeted Killings in Yemen', Open Society Justice Initiative and Mwatana Organization for Human Rights, 2015; Benjamin, *Drone Warfare*; Daniel Martin Varisco, 'Drone Strikes in the War on Terror: The Case of Post-Arab-Spring Yemen', Gulf Studies Center, 1 December 2015; Jeremy Scahill, *Dirty Wars: The World is a Battlefield* (New York: Nation Books, 2013).

11 Adam Entous, 'US Acknowledges Its Drone Strikes', *Wall Street Journal*, 15 June 2012. Available at <https://www.wsj.com/articles/SB10001424052702303410404577468981916011456> (last accessed 21 October 2022).

12 'Obama's Speech on Drone Policy', *New York Times*, 23 May 2013. Available at <https://www.nytimes.com/2013/05/24/us/politics/transcript-of-obamas-speech-on-drone-policy.html> (last accessed 21 October 2022).

13 'A Wedding that Became a Funeral: US Drone Attack on Marriage Procession in Yemen', Human Rights Watch, 19 February 2014. Available at <https://www.hrw.org/report/2014/02/19/wedding-became-funeral/us-drone-attack-marriage-procession-yemen> (last accessed 21 October 2022).

14 Pam Benson, 'U.S. Role in Yemen Covered up by Its President, WikiLeaks File Reveals', *CNN*, 29 November 2010. Available at <http://www.cnn.com/2010/US/11/28/wikileaks.yemen/index.html> (last accessed 21 October 2022).

15 See Waleed F. Mahdi, 'Echoes of a Scream: US Drones and Articulations of the Houthi Sarkha Slogan in Yemen', in Eid Mohamed and Ayman El Desouky, eds, *Cultural Production and Social Movements After the Arab Spring: Nationalism, Politics and Transnational Identity* (London: I. B. Tauris, 2021), 205–21.

16 In the '12 Hours' street art campaign, youth street artists created their own murals around a mutually agreed-upon theme at the top of each hour. Critiquing drones was one of such critical themes for the artists. Available at <https://muradsubay.com/campaigns/12-hours> (last accessed 21 October 2022).

17 As reported by the Yemeni state news agency SABA; see, 'Yemeni Parliament in Non-Binding Vote against Drone Attacks', *Reuters*, 15 December 2013. Available at <https://www.reuters.com/article/us-yemen-drones/yemeni-parliament-in-non-binding-vote-against-drone-attacks-idUSBRE9BE0EN20131215> (last accessed 21 October 2022).

18 Jeremy Scahill, 'The Dangerous US Game in Yemen', *The Nation*, 18 April 2011. Available at <http://www.thenation.com/article/159578/dangerous-us-game-yemen?page=0,1> (last accessed 21 October 2022).

19 Scott Shane, 'Yemen's Leader, President Hadi, Praises US Drone Strikes', *New York Times*, 29 September 2012. Available at <https://www.nytimes.com/2012/09/29/world/middleeast/yemens-leader-president-hadi-praises-us-drone-strikes.html> (last accessed 21 October 2022); 'Yemeni Parliament in Non-binding Vote against Drone Attacks'.

20 Ashraf Ghani and Clare Lockhart, *Fixing Failed States: A Framework for Rebuilding a Fractured World* (Oxford: Oxford University Press, 2009), 21.

21 Lisa Wedeen, *Peripheral Visions: Publics, Power, and Performance in Yemen* (Chicago: University of Chicago Press, 2008), 1.

22 Victoria Clark, *Yemen: Dancing on the Heads of Snakes* (New Haven, CT: Yale University Press, 2010), 194–204.

23 'U.S. Ambassador and Tunisia RPCV Edmund Hull Lays the Foundation Stone to the Yemen Civilization Museum in Marib', Peace Corps Online, 22 July 2004. Available at <http://peacecorpsonline.org/messages/messages/467/2022573.html> (last accessed 21 October 2022).

24 See Helen Lackner, *Yemen in Crisis: Autocracy, Neo-Liberalism and the Disintegration of a State* (London: Saqi Books, 2017), 58.

25 See for example Ross Porter, 'Tricking Time, Overthrowing a Regime: Reining in the Future in the Yemeni Youth Revolution', *The Cambridge Journal of Anthropology* 34, no. 1 (Spring 2016): 58–71.

26 Gerald Feierstein, 'Lecture on the Role of the US as an Active Power in the International Community and Its Relations with Yemen' (delivered at the US Embassy in Yemen, 3 April 2011); as quoted in Kamilia Al-Eriani, 'Mourning the Death of a State to Enliven it: Notes on the "Weak" Yemeni State', *International Journal of Cultural Studies* 23, no. 2 (2020): 227–44.

27 Saudi Embassy's monthly newsletter (March 2011); as quoted in Al-Eriani, 'Mourning the Death of a State to Enliven it'.

28 Ross Porter, 'Security against the State in Revolutionary Yemen', *Cultural Anthropology* 35, no. 2 (2020): 204–10, 209.

29 'Yemeni Women's Urgent Message to the International Community', *YouTube*, 29 June 2011. Available at <https://www.youtube.com/watch?v=L-YeS6a uDBI> (last accessed 21 October 2022).

30 See Olfat al-Dobai, 'Masīrat al-ḥayāh: al-ḍaou al-qadim min Taiz bi 'oyūn tha'irah' (The March to Life: The Light Coming from Taiz with Revolutionary Eyes), The Council of the Popular Revolutionary Leadership, 2012.

31 Kamilia Al-Eriani, 'Mourning the Death of a State to Enliven it', 234–5.

32 Isa Blumi, *Destroying Yemen: What Chaos in Arabia Tells Us about the World* (Oakland: University of California Press, 2018), 22–3.

33 Maria-Louise Clausen, 'Justifying Military Intervention: Yemen as a Failed State', *Third World Quarterly* 40, no. 3, 2019): 488–502.

34 Christopher Boucek and Marina Ottaway, eds, *Yemen on the Brink* (Washington DC: Carnegie Endowment for International Peace), 2010.

35 'The National Security Strategy', The National Security Council, September 2002. Available at <https://georgewbush-whitehouse.archives.gov/nsc/nss /2002/> (last accessed 21 October 2022).

36 Jeremy M. Weinstein, John Edward Porter and Stuart E. Eizenstat, 'On the Brink: Weak States and US National Security', The Commission on Weak States and US National Security, 8 June 2004, 6–7.

37 'Signing of a Presidential Directive to Improve Management of U.S. Efforts for Reconstruction and Stabilization', Office of the Coordinator for Reconstruction and Stabilization, special briefing, 14 December 2005. Available at <https://20 01-2009.state.gov/r/pa/prs/ps/2005/58085.htm> (last accessed 21 October 2022); 'The National Intelligence Strategy of the United States of America: Transformation through Integration and Innovation', October, 2005. Available at <https://www.dni.gov/files/documents/CHCO/nis.pdf> (last accessed 21 October 2022).

38 'National Strategy for Combatting Terrorism', The National Security Council, September 2006. Available at <https://georgewbush-whitehouse.archives.gov /nsc/nsct/2006/> (last accessed 21 October 2022).

39 Chandler, *Empire in Denial*, 189–90; Aidan Hehir, 'The Myth of the Failed State and the War on Terror: A Challenge to the Conventional Wisdom', in David Chandler, ed., *Statebuilding and Intervention: Policies, Practices and Paradigms* (London: Routledge, 2009), 72–98, 73.

40 Woodward, *The Ideology of Failed States*, 3.

41 Lackner, *Yemen in Crisis*, 58.

42 Ibid. 57.

43 Ibid. 57.

44 Ibid. 71.

45 Marieke Brandt, *Tribes and Politics in Yemen: A History of the Houthi Conflict* (Oxford: Oxford University Press, 2017), 90.

46 Sudarsan Raghavan, 'The U.S. Put a Yemeni Warlord on a Terrorist List. One of Its Close Allies Is Still Arming Him', *Washington Post*, 29 December 2018. Available at <https://www.washingtonpost.com/world/middle_east/the-us-put-a-yemeni-warlord-on-a-terrorist-list-one-of-its-close-allies-is-still-arming-him/2018/12/28/f3c4fb5b-f366-4570-b27b-75a3ed0f0f52_story.html> (last accessed 21 October 2022).

8

THE REGIONAL DIMENSIONS OF EGYPT'S 'FAILED DEMOCRATIC TRANSITION'

Samer S. Shehata*

Introduction

W hat role, if any, did regional factors play in Egypt's 'failed democratisation' and the reconsolidation of authoritarianism under Abdel Fattah al-Sisi? Most accounts of Egypt's failed democratisation focus on Mohamed Morsi and the Muslim Brotherhood's shortcomings, political polarisation between Islamists and 'liberals', or the Egyptian military and the 'deep state'. Each of these narratives is largely correct.[1]

Mohamed Morsi and the Muslim Brotherhood demonstrated a staggering degree of incompetence during their short time in power. Many accuse them of far worse: reneging on campaign promises, intimidating critics, secret deals with the military, violence against opponents, and attempting to monopolise power and take over the Egyptian state.

This led to Morsi's downfall, according to this narrative. At the end of only one year in power, Morsi and the Muslim Brotherhood had demonstrated both their inexperience and their true intentions and, in the process, alienated the vast majority of Egyptians – so much so that millions took to the streets on 30 June 2013 to demand Morsi's ouster, more than at any time during the 2011 uprising against Hosni Mubarak.

Another narrative focuses on political polarisation. Unlike Tunisia, Egypt's Islamist and 'secular' forces failed to reach a critical consensus about a new constitution, the role of religion in politics and the basic rules of the political game in post-Mubarak Egypt. Unwilling to compromise, tensions

193

between Islamists and 'liberals' increased to the point of intense hostility and deep mistrust. All sides became locked in what was perceived to be an existential struggle over the character of the Egyptian state and the identity of the nation. Heightened political tensions revealed the Muslim Brotherhood to be much less liberal than it claimed, while Egypt's 'liberals' turned out to be far less committed to democracy when they lost elections.[2]

A third explanation attributes the failure of democratisation to the military and the 'deep state'. Democracy, this argument posits, posed a threat to the country's previously unaccountable generals. Democratic politics entails civilian oversight of the armed forces and requires officers to take orders from elected officials. It also entails greater scrutiny of military budgets. Egypt's generals had become thoroughly accustomed to operating within an 'officers' republic', one in which they enjoyed tremendous power and controlled vast economic resources. Democracy threatened their power and economic empire.

The 2011 uprising and the Muslim Brotherhood's ascendancy also threatened Egypt's 'deep state'. Multiple intelligence services, high ranking interior and defence ministry officials, judges, powerful media figures and other elites entrenched within the state had no interest in losing their power and privilege. This network worked assiduously from the moment of Mubarak's ouster to thwart political change and subvert democratisation. According to this narrative, although Mubarak was removed from office on 11 February 2011, the Mubarak regime (read, the 'deep state') was largely left intact. What occurred in 2011, therefore, was not a genuine 'revolution' – a radical transformation of political and economic structures – but a more limited uprising. Although the uprising led to the removal of the head of state, it left the regime largely intact.

Each of these narratives captures an important dimension of Egypt's political trajectory after 2011. Each narrative focuses on a different aspect of political events and processes which ultimately culminated in the 2013 coup and the country's 'failed democratic transition'. These accounts are also not mutually exclusive. In fact, they are more accurate when taken together. Even together, however, they remain seriously incomplete.

This chapter argues that any explanation of Egypt's 'failed democratic transition' that does not integrate the role of regional actors is both historically inaccurate and empirically incomplete. Powerful regional states worked to block political change in Egypt from the first days of the 2011 uprising. Saudi Arabia, the UAE and Israel mobilised to prevent Mubarak's overthrow, following which these states worked continuously to influence the trajectory of Egyptian politics in a manner that would further their interests and block democratisation by supporting local actors, regulating aid and investment flows, through propaganda and disinformation, and by attempting to influence the policies of the US and other powerful states and institutions towards Egypt in the post-Mubarak period.

The 2011 Arab uprisings, and Egypt's 25 January 'revolution' in particular, were correctly perceived by Saudi Arabia, the UAE and Israel, as well as most Arab Gulf states, as profoundly threatening. The mobilisation of millions of ordinary, politically disenfranchised Arabs demanding 'the fall of the regime' constituted a direct challenge to the region's autocrats. Demands for accountable government, the rule of law and political participation were antithetical to the authoritarian regional order and increased the threat perception of these regimes as well as Israel. Arab rulers, and particularly Gulf ruling families, experienced the uprisings as existential threats. In response, they mobilised immediately to counter this threat. They did this independently and by supporting Egyptian actors who shared similar goals.

This analysis also points to larger theoretical issues about the character of authoritarianism in the Middle East and beyond. Rather than understanding authoritarianism as a regime type or political structure that takes place within national borders, as is most often the case, I understand authoritarianism as a transnational phenomenon. Authoritarianism is not simply an attribute of individual regimes, discreetly confined inside state borders. As I demonstrate below, in order to understand Egypt's 'failed democratic transition', one must simultaneously examine what are traditionally understood as 'domestic', 'regional' and 'international' factors and their transnational linkages. 'Domestic' and 'regional' politics in Egypt, especially since 2011, have been inextricably intertwined, so much so that at times they become difficult, if not impossible, to separate.

Rather than rejecting the narratives presented above, this chapter argues that regional factors also played an important role in facilitating the failure of democratisation in Egypt. Thus, any account of Egypt's 'failed democratisation' that does not highlight and integrate the role of regional factors is both incomplete and inaccurate.[3]

Saudi Arabia, the UAE and Israel's Response to the 2011 Uprising

Even before the 2013 coup against Morsi, powerful regional actors desperately tried to prevent political change from taking place in Egypt. They did this by directly supporting Mubarak during the eighteen-day uprising and by aggressively lobbying the US, European powers and other countries to continue supporting the beleaguered autocrat, despite growing protests and calls for his resignation.

From the first days of the 25 January 'revolution', Saudi Arabia, the UAE and Israel mobilised to prevent Mubarak's removal. They did this through public statements and favourable media coverage of Mubarak; by constantly and aggressively lobbying the US and other countries to continue supporting the octogenarian president; and by trying to limit external, and particularly American, pressure on him to resign.

Saudi Arabia's King Abdullah called Mubarak from the US, where the ailing monarch was recovering from surgery, on 28 January 2011, the fourth day of the uprising, to express his support for the Egyptian president, even before Mubarak's first statement about the protests. The king also issued a rare public statement criticising the demonstrations in Egypt for imperiling the country's 'stability and security', and as the work of foreign meddling.[4] The statement went further, declaring that 'the Kingdom of Saudi Arabia and its people and government declare its stand *with all its resources* with the government of Egypt and its people.'[5]

The Israelis were also alarmed at the challenge to Mubarak, 'with top officials closeted in round-the-clock strategy sessions' as soon as the seriousness of the protests became apparent.[6] In a press conference with visiting German chancellor Angela Merkel on 30 January 2011, Benjamin Netanyahu said his government was 'anxiously monitoring' the situation in Egypt and that he was following the events with 'vigilance and worry'.[7] Sensitive to how Israeli statements about Egyptian domestic politics would be perceived, Netanyahu ordered his ministers 'to make no comment' on events in Cairo 'to avoid inflaming an already explosive situation'.[8] At the same time, the Israeli Foreign Ministry urgently instructed 'Israeli ambassadors in a dozen key capitals', including the US, Canada, China, Russia and several European countries, 'to impress on host governments that Egypt's stability is paramount'[9] and to get this message out as soon as possible.[10]

The UAE was also deeply concerned about unfolding developments in Cairo. On 6 February 2011, Abu Dhabi's Crown Prince Mohamed bin Zayed issued a statement similar to the Saudi declaration, describing the protests as 'foreign attempts to interfere in the internal affairs of Egypt'.[11] Bin Zayed spoke with US president Barack Obama the following day and the Emirati foreign minister was quickly dispatched to Cairo to meet Mubarak, in a show of diplomatic support for the embattled autocrat.[12]

Israeli, Saudi and Emirati officials were also frequently on the phone with their White House counterparts throughout the eighteen-day uprising, often voicing their displeasure at US pressure on Mubarak.[13] The State Department was also receiving 'daily calls from Israel, Saudi Arabia and others who feared an Egypt without Mr Mubarak would destabilize the entire region'.[14]

On 28 January 2011, the 'Friday of Rage', after the largest demonstrations to date in Cairo and with Mubarak's ruling party headquarters in flames, a journalist asked the White House press secretary about US aid to Egypt in a press conference dominated by questions about the country. When Press Secretary Robert Gibbs responded that the US 'will be reviewing our assistance posture based on events now and in the coming days', the prospect of the US cutting more than a billion dollars of annual aid to Egypt because of the protests was raised publicly.[15] When pressed further, Gibbs confirmed that Obama had been involved in such discussions and that all aid, including military assistance, was under consideration.

The very next day Obama had a 'tense' phone conversation with the Saudi king in which Abdullah reportedly warned Obama not to humiliate Mubarak and threatened to replace any aid cut by the US to Egypt.[16] The prospect of US aid being cut to Egypt also deeply alarmed Israel.[17]

It would be difficult to exaggerate the amount or urgency of lobbying by high-level Saudi, Emirati and Israeli officials towards their US counterparts during this period.[18] This included frequent calls to Secretary of State Hillary Clinton, Defense Secretary Robert Gates, and lower-level administration officials. Ehud Barak, Israel's defence minister, for example, spoke with Gates about Egypt on 29 January 2011, the fifth day of the protests.[19] He then requested to meet Gates while visiting the US on 8 February 2011.[20] The message coming from Arab and Israeli officials was the same: 'Forcing Mubarak out risks instability.'[21]

As the demonstrations continued, the Obama administration's position toward the situation evolved. On the first day of demonstrations, Hillary Clinton declared that the Egyptian government was 'stable' and looking for ways to deal with the 'legitimate needs of the Egyptian people'.[22] As protests continued the following day, Clinton implored both demonstrators and the police to 'exercise restraint', equating peaceful protesters with the repressive apparatus of the Mubarak regime.[23] As it became increasingly clear that

Mubarak's hold on power was in jeopardy the administration's position shifted.

Following the 'Friday of Rage' and Mubarak's first speech during the uprising that evening, and after the police had withdrawn from the streets, Obama phoned Mubarak. He urged the Egyptian president to 'take concrete steps' to deliver on his promises of reform and democracy.[24] From this point onwards, despite disagreements among senior White House officials, the Obama administration's position on Egypt shifted to one of calling for change without explicitly calling on Mubarak to resign.[25]

A few days later, after Mubarak's second speech during the uprising, Obama delivered prepared remarks about Egypt from the White House. He praised Egyptians for their passion and dignity and Egypt's military for its professionalism. He claimed that the US had stood for 'a set of core principles' during the crisis: opposing violence, human rights and democracy, and 'the need for change'. Obama said he conveyed to Mubarak his 'belief that an orderly transition must . . . begin now'.[26] When Press Secretary Gibbs was asked the following day about what the administration meant by a transition beginning 'now', Gibbs retorted, 'Now means yesterday.'[27] More and more senior American officials began speaking of the need for an 'orderly transition' to begin immediately.

As it became increasingly clear that Mubarak would be unable to end the crisis and with the Egyptian military now deployed on the streets and US officials speaking about the need for change, both Israel and the UAE also appear to have accepted the idea of an 'orderly transition', as long as it did not entail handing power over to the Egyptian people. Of course, for the US an 'orderly transition' did not also mean democracy. The emphasis by American officials was more on an 'orderly transition' that a 'democratic' one.

US calls for 'an orderly transition' were more about safeguarding American interests than fulfilling the aspirations of the Egyptian people. This became apparent a few days later when Clinton spoke about the need to support Mubarak's newly appointed vice president. Addressing the Munich Security Conference on 5 February 2011, with millions of Egyptians still on the streets demanding 'the fall of the regime', Clinton warned of the dangers of 'forces . . . that will try to derail or overtake the [transition] process to pursue their own specific agenda', a likely reference to Islamist groups and the experience of the 1979 Iranian Revolution.[28] It was for this reason, Clinton declared, that it is 'important to support the transition process announced by the Egyptian government, actually headed by now Vice President Omar Suleiman . . .'[29] An 'orderly transition' for Clinton and other US officials meant support for Mubarak's long-time confidant and newly appointed vice president, not democracy.

It is entirely unsurprising that Clinton would lend her support to Suleiman. After all, he was the CIA's man in Cairo.[30] His appointment as vice president days earlier was intended as a concession to protesters, one that was immediately rejected. The veteran head of General Intelligence had long-standing ties to the US and Israel. He was Mubarak's point man on the Palestinian–Israeli conflict, which put him in frequent contact with both Israel and the Palestinians. Suleiman also worked closely with his American counterparts on joint intelligence and counterterrorism operations, including the CIA's illegal rendition programme. There are also reports of his involvement in the torture of detainees at the request of the US.[31]

Suleiman was also trusted and well liked by the Israelis according to a State Department cable that reported Israeli Defence Ministry officials being 'full of praise for Soliman'.[32] It was for these reasons that his appointment was greeted positively by Israel.[33] Israel's security calculus and strategic outlook is premised on peace with Egypt and many Israelis considered Mubarak essential for maintaining peace.[34]

Peace with Egypt not only meant the absence of war, it also allowed Israel to act militarily in Gaza, the West Bank, Lebanon and elsewhere without fear of Egyptian military involvement. Israel was also able to reduce its military expenditures and make cuts to the size of its army, as a result of the peace treaty.[35] Peace also brought cheap Egyptian natural gas to Israel and Cairo's support negotiating with the Palestinians, reducing smuggling from Gaza, and 'squeezing Hamas'.[36] The prospect of an Egypt without Mubarak was deeply troubling for Israeli officials and one they actively tried to prevent.

Saudi Influence in Egyptian Politics under the SCAF: February 2011 to July 2012

Although Israel, the UAE and Saudi Arabia were unable to prevent Mubarak's ouster, the Egyptian uprising did not result in the worst possible outcome from the perspective of Tel Aviv, Abu Dhabi or Riyadh (this would come sixteen months later when Mohamed Morsi was elected president). When Mubarak was forced from power on 11 February 2011, the Egyptian military, in the form of the Supreme Council of the Armed Forces (SCAF), delegated itself responsibility for the country's 'transition'.

The official reaction from Saudi Arabia and the UAE was immediately positive and welcomed the military's new role in the country's administration. The UAE confirmed 'its confidence in the ability of the Supreme Council of the Armed Forces in running the country's affairs' during what it described as 'delicate circumstances', while Saudi Arabia praised the military's role in 'the return of peace and stability'.[37] Such declarations were indicative of the good relations between the Gulf monarchies and the Egyptian military and the hope by Gulf leaders that Egypt's generals would restore 'stability' and pursue policies friendly to their interests.

Tensions rose almost immediately after Mubarak's removal, however. It was no secret to many Egyptians that the Gulf states, apart from Qatar, had opposed the 'revolution'. In addition to the strategic reasons for supporting Mubarak, the Egyptian president had also developed close personal friendships with many of the Gulf's ruling families after nearly three decades in power. And in the months immediately following his ouster, as many Egyptians demanded that Mubarak be held accountable for killing protesters and other crimes during his three-decade reign, news reports circulated that Saudi Arabia, the UAE and Kuwait were pressuring the Egyptian government not to put the deposed president on trial. These reports claimed that the Saudi government threatened to expel millions of Egyptian workers and halt Saudi investment if Mubarak were put on trial. So widespread were the reports that the SCAF, Egypt's prime minister, and the Saudi ambassador to Cairo each issued statements denying them.[38]

Tensions flared again in August 2011 when more than 4,000 Egyptians were stranded in Jeddah after performing *umrah*, the lesser pilgrimage. The pilgrims were forced to wait in the airport for several days, in poor conditions and without food, for flights back to Egypt. Many claimed they were deliberately mistreated and humiliated by Saudi staff, and some complained of being physically abused while being stuck at the airport. According to *Al-Masry Al-Youm*, 'Some of the pilgrims attributed the poor treatment by the Saudi officials to the kingdom's hostility toward the Egyptian revolution and to the Mubarak trial, and not to technical problems, as the Saudi authorities claimed.'[39]

A number of pilgrims staged a sit-in on the Saudi airliner that brought them home, refusing to disembark until they received an apology and compensation. Many filed police reports against Saudi Arabian Airlines, Jeddah Airport and the Egyptian consulate in Saudi Arabia after returning to Egypt. Protests also took place outside the Saudi embassy in Cairo decrying the mistreatment the pilgrims experienced. The Saudi ambassador in Cairo denied any connection between the 'Egyptian pilgrims' crisis' and the Mubarak trial.[40]

Tensions continued and came to a head in April 2012 when a young Egyptian human rights lawyer was arrested as he entered Saudi Arabia with his wife to perform *umrah*. Ahmed al-Gizawy had previously filed a lawsuit in Egypt against the Saudi king and government, on behalf of Egyptians in the kingdom, alleging their mistreatment and torture.[41] He had called for the release of Egyptian prisoners and for their compensation as a result of human rights abuses. Initial reports of al-Gizawy's arrest claimed he had been charged with 'insulting the king'.[42] Saudi authorities denied this, accusing him of smuggling prescription drugs into the kingdom and sentencing him to a year in prison and public flogging.[43]

Egyptians were outraged by the case, which reflected wider concerns about the treatment of Egyptians in Saudi Arabia and other oil-rich Gulf states.[44] Like other foreign workers, Egyptians in the Gulf had few protections and sometimes suffered abuse. Reflecting the spirit of renewed pride and nationalism following the 'revolution', many Egyptians demanded their government stand up for its citizens working abroad. The al-Gizawy case was widely covered in the press, causing a 'whirlwind of protest and anger'.[45] Prominent personalities called on the government to demand the young lawyer's release, with one Egyptian prosecutor declaring that if al-Gizawy was flogged, 'we will flog their [Saudi] ambassador in Cairo.'[46]

Protests erupted outside the Saudi consulates in Alexandria and Suez and the embassy in Cairo. People also demonstrated in front of the Foreign Affairs Ministry demanding that Egyptian officials defend the imprisoned lawyer. Protesters in front of the Saudi embassy called for al-Gizawy's release, denounced the treatment of Egyptian prisoners in the kingdom and hurled insults at the Saudi monarchy. The protests were boisterous, which led to the security forces being deployed. Soon afterwards Saudi Arabia closed its embassy and consulates and recalled its ambassador, citing the 'unjustified demonstrations', 'hostile slogans' and threats to embassy staff.[47]

Egyptian officials immediately mobilised to resolve the crisis. Field Marshall Tantawi, head of the SCAF and the country's de facto ruler, called the Saudi king that evening to try to 'heal the rift', while the Foreign Ministry released a statement criticising the protester's 'irresponsible actions'.[48] Egypt's foreign minister said that communications with the Saudi government were taking place 'at all levels' to 'contain the crisis', while the cabinet proclaimed Egypt's '"love and respect" for Saudi Arabia'.[49]

In an effort to mend relations, a 113-person delegation of parliamentarians and prominent personalities led by the speaker of the parliament, Mohamed Saad el-Katatni, travelled to Riyadh less than a week later. The group included the speaker of the Shura Council, leaders of political parties and representatives of al-Azhar and the Coptic Church. The delegation met the Saudi king, the crown prince, the foreign and defence ministers, and the Saudi ambassador to Egypt. The Egyptians emphasised the deep ties between both countries and called for the return of the kingdom's ambassador.[50]

Two days later, on 5 May 2011, the Saudi ambassador returned to Cairo.[51] The following day, Egypt's head of intelligence travelled to Riyadh to meet the Saudi foreign minister and deliver a letter from Tantawi to the king.[52]

Saudi Support for Egypt's Salafis

Saudi attempts to influence Egyptian domestic politics did not end after Mubarak's ouster. One of the most significant channels of Saudi influence was Egypt's Salafis.[53] Long before 2011, Saudi Arabia had contributed to the wildly successful spread of Salafism in Egypt through years of financial support for Salafi charities and educational activities and Saudi-financed television stations based in Cairo.

There is substantial evidence that Saudi Arabia redoubled its support for Egypt's Salafis after Mubarak's ouster as a strategy to further its interests in Egypt and the wider region. By doing so, Riyadh was further cultivating an existing ally within the Egyptian political scene while simultaneously blunting the growing power of the Muslim Brotherhood.

Egypt's Muslim Brotherhood represented a threat to Saudi Arabia (and the UAE). The Muslim Brotherhood embodied a different model of political Islam from the one supposedly practised in the kingdom. It was ostensibly committed to electoral democracy and representative government and was critical of American and Israeli hegemony.

There were other major differences between the popular Islamist movement and the Saudi regime's political outlook. Unlike Riyadh, the Muslim Brotherhood was not inherently anti-Iran, nor was it as vehemently anti-Shiʿa as Egypt's Salafis.[54] And like other political forces in Egypt following the 'revolution', the Muslim Brotherhood called for a more independent foreign policy that restored Egypt's leadership role in the Arab world.

Egypt's Salafis, by contrast, were deeply suspicious of Iran and inherently hostile to Shi'a Islam. They saw Saudi Arabia as a natural ally and defended the kingdom against domestic critics. For example, soon after the protests following al-Gizawi's arrest, Egyptian Salafis denounced the demonstrations. At least two prominent Salafi groups issued apologies to the Saudi authorities for the anti-Saudi protest.[55]

Less than a year later, in April 2013, as relations between Egypt and Iran appeared to thaw following Morsi's visit to Tehran and Ahmadinejad's visit to Cairo, and limited flights between both capitals brought a handful of Iranian tourists to the cash-strapped country, Egyptian Salafis denounced the development and warned of a 'Shi'a invasion'.[56] Dozens of Salafis protested in front of the senior Iranian diplomat's residence in Cairo, demanding that Egypt sever relations with Iran and denouncing the Muslim Brotherhood. Protests were also held in front of the Muslim Brotherhood's headquarters. Egypt's most prominent Salafi organisation, the Salafi Call, and its recently established political party, also launched a campaign against the Egyptian–Iranian rapprochement, holding seminars 'to educate citizens about the "danger of Shias"', according to Yasser Borhami, a key figure in both organisations.[57]

It was for these reasons that Saudi Arabia poured millions of dollars into Egypt in support of Salafi groups after Mubarak's ouster. The Saudis understood that Egypt's Salafis shared much of their worldview and that a powerful Salafi political presence in Egypt would limit the rising influence of the Muslim Brotherhood.

Although accurate figures about the amount of Gulf money that entered the country in support of the Salafis after the 'revolution' are impossible to verify, it is widely believed that the sums were staggering. The deterioration of the security situation after Mubarak's ouster contributed to the relative ease with which unregulated money, and arms, flowed into the country.

My interviews, in addition to government investigations and think tank reports, also suggest the scale of foreign funding was enormous. A report commissioned by Egypt's Justice Ministry in November 2011 found that the country's second largest Salafi group, Gam'eyat Ansar al-Sunna al-Muhammadiyya, received 296 million pounds (approximately US$50 million at the time) from Kuwait and Qatar in the nine months following Mubarak's ouster.[58] The group's leaders and the Kuwaiti ambassador in Cairo denied this, although the ambassador acknowledged that Kuwaiti charities had long provided aid to Egypt.[59]

The Nour Party was also widely believed to have received significant funding from Saudi Arabia. The party was established in June 2011 by the Salafi Call to compete in the first legislative elections after the 'revolution'. The Salafi Call had no previous experience in formal politics and established the party only four months after Mubarak's ouster.

Allegations of massive Saudi support circulated even before the party's founding. By May 2011, several protests had taken place outside the Saudi embassy in Cairo against alleged Saudi funding of Salafi groups.[60] The issue received increasing attention in the summer of 2011 and during the run up to the parliamentary elections. A major protest in Tahrir Square on 31 July 2011, intended as an expression of national unity, quickly turned into a demonstration of Salafi power. Salafis far outnumbered others, raising Saudi flags as well as black and Egyptian flags adorned with Quranic verses, while chanting for an Islamic state and the sharia. Tahrir Square, which had been a symbol of Egypt's revolutionary youth, was transformed into a site of Salafi power. The protest was quickly dubbed 'Kandahar Friday'.

The 2011 parliamentary elections drew even greater attention to the issue of Salafi funding. Stephane Lacroix noted that 'those who followed the Nour Party's campaign were surprised at the considerable resources the party seemed to have at its disposal.' Indeed, the party appeared to have seemingly unlimited campaign funds. It established numerous offices around the country and, with its Salafi allies, fielded candidates in all of the country's electoral districts. In Alexandria alone, the party produced half a million copies of one of its 'well designed [campaign] posters'.[61] It distributed several tons of meat during the Eid al-Adha holiday, which fell immediately before the elections, and ran television commercials before election day.

Der Spiegel reported that the Nour Party received 'over USD 100 million in campaign funds' from Saudi Arabia.[62] An Egyptian government report suggested that 'al-Nour party had benefitted from 50 million US dollars coming from Saudi Arabia and Kuwait in order to finance its activities' and party leaders boasted that if elected, 'they would receive more money from pan-Islamic charities to implement their promises and finance social programs in poor neighbourhoods.'[63] Although the party denied receiving Saudi money,[64] it did not reveal the sources of its funding.[65] So widespread were allegations of Saudi funding that the Saudi ambassador felt obliged to deny the kingdom was bankrolling Egypt's Salafis on multiple occasions, including in a meeting with the Egyptian Coptic Pope in August 2011.[66]

The Nour Party's unexpectedly strong performance was the biggest surprise of the 2011 elections and confirmed to many that it benefitted from significant financing from abroad. Nour's 'Islamic Bloc' alliance, formed with two smaller Salafi parties, received nearly 28 per cent of the vote. The results were shocking for a party that was barely six months old and without previous electoral experience. Only the Muslim Brotherhood's Democratic Alliance, a coalition between the Muslim Brotherhood's Freedom and Justice Party and several smaller parties, received more votes (37.5 per cent), leaving Nour and its allies with the second largest parliamentary bloc.

Tarek al-Zomor, the head of the Salafi Building and Development Party (BDP), part of Nour's electoral coalition in 2011, confirmed to me that massive amounts of Saudi money 'poured into the country' (*dakh al-amwal*), sometimes in 'suitcases full of cash', to support the party's campaign efforts.[67] Al-Zomor emphasised that Saudi funding was not new but had increased exponentially after 2011. He said Riyadh's fear of the Muslim Brotherhood was the reason for this. 'Saudi Arabia did not want to see an Islamic democracy succeed because it would serve as a competitor or an alternative model of Islam and politics than the Saudi political system.'

Al-Zomor also claimed that Abdel Rahim Ali, the editor and chief of Al Bawaba news and a prominent anti-Islamist journalist with connections to the UAE, approached him in 2012 to persuade him and the BDP to back Ahmed Shafiq and not Morsi in the presidential elections.[68] Ali promised that the BDP would be rewarded with thirty seats in the next elections, about fifteen more than they had won in the 2011 elections, if they agreed. According to al-Zomor, Ali made clear the offer was from the Emirates. Other 'liberal' party leaders I interviewed recounted similar stories about Emirati offers of financial support during this period.[69]

Mohamed Morsi's One-year Presidency: July 2012 to July 2013

The worst-case scenario for the counter-revolutionary Gulf states materialised in July 2012, more than a year after Mubarak's ouster, when the Muslim Brotherhood candidate Mohamed Morsi was elected president. A senior American diplomat told me that 'the Emiratis were frantic after Morsi's victory and . . . did not hide their reaction.'[70] Dexter Filkins similarly described Morsi's election as 'a nightmare' for Saudi Arabia and the UAE, and quotes an unnamed senior American diplomat as stating: 'When Morsi got elected, the Saudis and the Emiratis went into overdrive.'[71] Other American officials told him that Mohamed bin Zayed and Bandar bin Sultan, the director of Saudi intelligence, 'began plotting with others in their governments to remove Morsi from power'.

According to Filkins, bin Zayed and bin Sultan reached out to Abdel Fattah al-Sisi, then defence minister, shortly after Morsi's election, and promised him 'twenty billion dollars in economic aid if Morsi were deposed'.[72] Although this claim cannot be verified, it accords with subsequent events.[73] Immediately after Morsi's ouster in July 2013, Saudi Arabia, the UAE and Kuwait offered Egypt US$12 billion of aid. Over the next eighteen months, the three countries poured US$23 billion of aid into the country, according to Egypt's investment minister, Ashraf Salman.[74] Saudi Arabia and the UAE subsequently committed additional billions in the form of aid, loans, investment and fuel. I examine the financial support these states provided in greater detail below.

Whether or not US$20 billion of aid was promised to Egypt's generals to depose Morsi, it is clear that Saudi and Emirati economic support all but dried up after Morsi's election. In other words, not only did Saudi Arabia, the UAE and Kuwait open the floodgates of financial assistance to Egypt at unprecedented levels after the coup, they starved Egypt of economic aid and financial investment during Morsi's time in office.

This was confirmed to me in an interview with Abdel Hafez al-Sawy, an economist who served on the Freedom and Justice Party's Economic Committee. Al-Sawy recalled Morsi's first overseas trip, only eleven days after being sworn into office, as evidence of his government's openness and desire for Gulf investment. Al-Sawy claimed that Morsi travelled to Riyadh to reassure the Saudis that he was not interested in 'exporting' revolution and posed no threat to the kingdom. He also hoped to secure US$8.5 billion worth of Saudi investment.[75]

> We welcomed any new foreign investment in Egypt, especially if it was from the Gulf countries. With the January 2011 revolution, however, there was a decrease in investment from both Saudi Arabia and the Emirates. After Morsi was elected, it stopped almost completely.[76]

Al-Sawy described meetings he attended with Saudi businessmen during Morsi's presidency. A number of industrial and agricultural projects on the

North Sea coast and in Sinai were discussed. The businessmen were enthusiastic about investing in the projects, according to al-Sawy, but after several meetings they told their Egyptian hosts, 'We are just waiting for the [Saudi] government to give us the green light to invest in Egypt.' Al-Sawy chuckled recalling the encounter before adding, 'Of course, they did not get the green light.'[77]

Although both Saudi Arabia and the UAE pledged several billion dollars of aid to Egypt after the 'revolution', significantly smaller amounts were actually delivered. According to Yasmine Farouk,

> In May 2011, Saudi Arabia had pledged a $4 billion loan to Egypt, including a $1 billion deposit at the Central Bank of Egypt (CBE). There was also a confirmation of a supplementary $2.7 billion aid package upon the Saudi ambassador's return in May 2012 [following the al-Gizawy affair, discussed above]. Yet, in August 2012, Saudi Arabia had pumped only $1.7 billion into Egypt's economy. Similarly, the UAE pledged $3 billion in financial aid to Egypt in October 2011. Until July 2013, the UAE was still deciding on 'the mechanism' of delivery. As for Kuwait, in January 2012 it pledged a $100 million loan to be delivered by January to finance large-scale projects. No proof was made public that such a transfer took place.[78]

The period after Mubarak's ouster was one of acute economic uncertainty and deteriorating economic conditions. Foreign currency reserves plummeted from US$36 billion before the uprising to around US$13 billion by March 2013, 'barely enough to cover three months' imports'.[79] Foreign direct investment was not forthcoming because of political instability, while tourism, a major source of foreign revenue and a significant employer, declined precipitously. Although leaders in Riyadh, Abu Dhabi and Kuwait City promised Egypt economic support after the 'revolution', the amounts that were actually delivered were significantly less than what was promised. This contrasts markedly to the period after Morsi's ouster, when Egypt received unprecedented amounts of aid and investment from these countries.

While Saudi Arabia and the UAE experienced the Arab uprisings and the ascendance of Islamist parties in terms of increased threat perception, Qatar viewed these developments as an opportunity to extend its influence vis-à-vis regional rivals, the UAE and Saudi Arabia. The tiny Gulf nation with super-sized ambitions promoted the uprisings through Al Jazeera, which in the eyes of many became a cheerleader for the 'revolutions'. Qatar also employed its wealth to promote its foreign policy agenda. Thus, unlike Saudi Arabia, the UAE and Kuwait, Qatar's interest in providing aid and investment to Egypt increased after Mubarak's ouster, skyrocketed with Morsi's election, and declined with his removal.[80]

Doha deposited US$500 million in direct budget support in Egypt's Central Bank in August 2012, after Morsi's election, and committed an addition US$1.5 billion by December.[81] Then, in May 2013, 'when the country's international reserves had reached a dangerously low level and it had become clear Cairo would not secure a much-postponed loan from the International Monetary Fund', Qatar deposited an additional US$3 billion in Egypt's Central Bank, less than three months before Morsi's ouster.[82] Overall, during Morsi's one year in power, the tiny gas-rich nation gave Egypt US$7.5 billion in loans and grants.[83] Following the coup, in September 2013, after receiving huge amounts of aid from rivals Saudi Arabia and the UAE, Egypt returned US$2 billion dollars of Qatari deposits from its Central Bank, reflecting worsening ties between the two countries.

The Campaign against Morsi and the Muslim Brotherhood

Writing only a few days before massive anti-Morsi demonstrations and Morsi's subsequent ouster, Mohamad Elmasry presciently analysed 'an effective propaganda campaign' intended to demonise the Islamist president and discredit the Muslim Brotherhood in the eyes of Egyptians.[84] Led by an array of Mubarak loyalists and 'liberal' and 'secular' opposition forces, the efforts included a series of recurring rumours and allegations against Morsi and the Muslim Brotherhood.

In addition to these efforts (or more likely, in coordination with them), was a wider media and disinformation campaign orchestrated by the UAE and Saudi Arabia against Morsi and the Muslim Brotherhood. Saudi and Emirati media outlets such as Al Arabiya and Sky News Arabia, and 'other Emirati linked Egyptian media' ran a 'constant, incessant, and effective' campaign, according to Ben Rhodes, deputy national security adviser to Obama, 'to denigrate any nonmilitary Egyptian government, denigrate our ambassador, and denigrate our policy'.[85] What struck Rhodes as 'extraordinary' was that US allies, Saudi Arabia and the UAE, would plan and finance a media effort, including attacks against US policy and an American ambassador, to 'overturn the democratically elected government' of another US ally.

The Saudi and Emirati campaign against Morsi and the Muslim Brotherhood was not limited to the media, however. One Egyptian diplomat told me that European officials reported that Turki Al Faisal, the former head of Saudi intelligence and former Saudi ambassador to the UK and US, toured European capitals before the coup to lobby against the Morsi government. Without informing the Egyptians, Al Faisal argued to European leaders that the Muslim Brotherhood was dangerous and that it was not in their interests to support the Morsi government.[86]

Such accounts mirror published reports about Emirati lobbying efforts in Washington. David Kirkpatrick described Yousef Al Otaiba, the UAE's powerful ambassador to the US, as 'the most energetic opponent in Washington of Morsi and the Muslim Brotherhood'.[87] Kirkpatrick recounts how Al Otaiba constantly lobbied Rhodes and other American officials against Morsi and the Islamist movement: 'Otaiba argued to Rhodes that the Brotherhood was inherently antidemocratic'; 'Its pan-Islamic ideology left no room for nation-states or borders'; 'It posed an existential threat to the UAE and every other American ally in the region'; and 'Its rejection should be the bedrock of Washington's policy toward Egypt.'[88]

Three months after the coup, Turki Al Faisal spoke about Saudi strategic thinking towards Egypt at a conference in Washington DC.

> Egypt holds a special place in Saudi security interests ... King Abdullah held the closest of relations with President Mubarak for over 30 years. Abandoning him or any close ally during a revolutionary uprising *was not* and *will never be* a policy option for the Kingdom, which must uphold and defend its values.[89]

He then described Morsi's government as 'unable and incompetent to govern a country such as Egypt' before repeating the false claim that the protests against Morsi were 'the largest-ever demonstrations, anywhere'.[90] Al Faisal boasted that 'King Abdullah was the first leader to congratulate the Egyptian leadership [after Morsi's ouster] and has led the regional push to support this action', before further criticising Washington's position: 'Saudi Arabia unconditionally authorized $5 billion in grants, loans and deposits to Egypt's emerging government, which stands in stark comparison to the conditional loans that the United States and Europe have promised and keep threatening to freeze.'[91]

The most spectacular evidence of Gulf involvement in the coup, if true, are a series of secretly recorded conversations between Egypt's top generals that were released in March 2015. The leaked recordings were first broadcast by a Muslim Brotherhood-affiliated satellite television station (Mekameleen) operating from Turkey. The recordings were analysed by a British forensic speech and acoustic laboratory that found 'no indications' they were fabricated.[92]

The extensive recordings include telephone calls and meetings between high-ranking generals, including al-Sisi, discussing topics ranging from the Tamarod movement, which organised the signature campaign against Morsi and the 30 June anti-Morsi protests; Gulf financial support; Morsi's imprisonment; and other topics. One of the recordings includes a conversation between General Abbas Kamel, the head of al-Sisi's office when al-Sisi was defence minister, and General Sedky Sobhy, military chief of staff. (Kamel later became head of the president's office when al-Sisi became president and then head of General Intelligence in 2018, while Sobhy rose to defence minister in 2014 after al-Sisi resigned the post to run for president.)[93] The generals can be heard discussing money provided by the UAE for the Tamarod movement and clearly suggest that both the UAE and the military financed the supposedly independent, civil society, anti-Morsi, youth movement. The wide-ranging recordings include the recognisable voices of well-known generals, including al-Sisi himself.[94]

Other evidence also indicates that the Egyptian military worked secretly to undermine Morsi. The *Wall Street Journal* reported that regular and clandestine meetings took place between senior generals and representatives of a number of Egypt's leading opposition figures and political parties to discuss Morsi's potential removal.[95] According to multiple interviews with individuals who attended the meetings, 'Senior aides to Mr ElBaredei, former presidential candidate and Arab League chief Mr Moussa, and another presidential candidate, Hamdeen Sabahy . . .' were told that if enough people protested against Morsi, the military would be prepared to remove him. Some of the meetings took place in the Navy Officer's Club in Cairo and became more frequent as the 30 June protests neared.

The UAE, Saudi Arabia and Israel also lobbied senior US officials to abandon Morsi, particularly as tensions increased between the opposition and the Morsi government in May and June 2013. According to Kirkpatrick, the US defence secretary Hagel 'recalled that he had been besieged by complaints about Morsi from the defense ministers in Israel, Saudi Arabia, and the United Arab Emirates – especially from Mohammed bin Zayed'. Hagel recounted how before the coup the Israelis were also backing al-Sisi. 'The Israelis', he said, 'were letting us know very clearly that al-Sisi was the only guy protecting everything here, and they were concerned.'[96]

The 2013 Coup and the Rabʻa Massacre

Saudi Arabia, the UAE and Kuwait wasted no time in endorsing the coup and praising the Egyptian military. All three countries issued statements immediately after Morsi's ouster. The Saudi statement was issued the evening of 3 July in the name of King Abdullah. The king congratulated Adly Mansour, the head of the Supreme Constitutional Court who was named interim president, praised the Egyptian military and singled out al-Sisi for managing to 'save Egypt at this critical juncture from a dark tunnel'.[97] The Saudi monarch wished Egypt 'stability and security' and, unsurprisingly, made no mention of democracy.[98]

The UAE also welcomed Morsi's removal on the day of the coup with the country's foreign minister praising the Egyptian military and declaring that he had followed the events in Egypt with 'much consideration and satisfaction'.[99] The following day the UAE's president, vice president and Mohamed bin Zayed all sent congratulatory cables to Egypt's interim president and praised developments in the country.[100]

Kuwait was similarly quick to welcome Morsi's removal. The Kuwaiti emir sent a congratulatory cable to Mansour praising 'the positive historic role of the Egyptian armed forces, headed by Gen Abdel Fatah al-Sisi'. He expressed his desire to bolster cooperation with Cairo, and other high-ranking Kuwaiti officials sent similar messages, including the crown prince and the prime minister. Kuwait's deputy prime minister and foreign minister also issued statements expressing solidarity with Egyptians 'for realizing legitimate demands for security and stability and progress', while also praising the role of the Egyptian military.[101]

Also remarkable was the speed with which the counter-revolutionary Gulf states committed huge amounts of aid to support Egypt's generals. Saudi Arabia pledged US$5 billion only five days after Morsi was deposed. The UAE pledged US$3 billion and Kuwait followed with US$4 billion two days later.[102]

While the three Gulf states were writing large cheques, Israel was lobbying the US not to suspend aid to Cairo. The Obama administration's initial reaction to Morsi's ouster, as well as that of the EU, individual European states and the African Union, contrasted sharply with that of Saudi Arabia, the UAE and Kuwait. Obama declared on 3 July that the US was 'deeply concerned by the decision of the Egyptian Armed Forces to remove President Morsy and suspend the Egyptian constitution'. He called for a quick return to a 'democratically elected civilian government', warned against arresting Morsi and his supporters, and stated that he had asked US officials 'to review the implications [of events in Egypt] under U.S. law for our assistance to the Government of Egypt', implying the possibility of suspending aid to the country.[103] He stopped short of characterising Morsi's ouster as a coup, however, as doing so would have required suspending aid under US law. Some American officials, including Senator John McCain, did describe Morsi's ouster in such terms and called for US aid to be suspended.[104]

The possible suspension of American military and economic assistance to Egypt immediately prompted Israel and the American Israel Public Affairs Committee (AIPAC) to feverishly lobby the US to continue supporting Egypt's generals.[105] 'According to a senior US official quoted by *Haaretz*, Israel's top political echelon had engaged in "marathon phone calls" with Washington' in the days after the coup, 'warning that any suspension of aid could impact on Israel's security'.[106] Netanyahu called Secretatry of State John Kerry, the defence minister Moshe Yaalon spoke with Chuck Hagel, and Israel's national security adviser lobbied Obama's national security chief Susan Rice, urging them not to suspend aid to Cairo.[107]

Renewed calls for US sanctions on Egypt were raised again the following month, after massive state violence was used to end pro-Morsi protests. Shortly after Morsi's ouster, the Muslim Brotherhood organised two large sit-ins that lasted more than a month and included thousands of men, women and children camped out in two urban squares in Cairo. According to the government, negotiations over ending the protests had stalled. Frustrated by the continuing sit-ins, which symbolised internal political division and support for the deposed president among some, and with complaints that the sit-ins disrupted life and increased traffic, and with allegations of violence and terrorism by Morsi supporters, the government violently dispersed the gatherings on the morning of 14 August 2013.[108]

The violence employed against protesters was massive, prompting Human Rights Watch (HRW) to describe it as 'serious violations of international human rights law' that 'likely amounted to crimes against humanity'.[109] HRW determined the government had used 'indiscriminate and deliberate use of lethal force' which resulted in 'at least 817 and likely more than 1,000' people killed in the larger sit-in at Rab'a al-Adawiyya Square, and an additional eighty-seven killed at the second protest at al-Nahda Square. The government claimed the police only used force in response to violence by Morsi supporters, including gunfire, and that eight police officers were killed in the confrontations.[110]

Obama interrupted his seaside holiday the following day to deliver critical remarks about the violence. While he acknowledged the importance of the US–Egyptian relationship, Obama harshly criticised Egypt's interim government. 'The United States strongly condemns the steps that have been taken by Egypt's interim government and security forces. We deplore violence against civilians.'[111] 'The Egyptian people deserve better', Obama declared, calling on the government to 'respect the universal rights of the people', including the right to protest peacefully. In response to the violence against pro-Morsi protesters, Obama cancelled Operation Bright Star, the bi-annual, joint military exercises scheduled for the following month. He also asked his 'national security team to assess the implications of the actions taken by the interim government and further steps that we may take as necessary with respect to the US–Egyptian relationship', again, holding out the possibility of further sanctions against Egypt's new rulers.[112]

The Saudi reaction to the Rab'a massacre could not have contrasted more sharply. In fact, it was, in part, a reaction to US and Western criticism of Egypt's interim government. One day after Obama's remarks, King Abdullah made a rare televised statement about the events in Egypt:

> The Kingdom of Saudi Arabia, its people and government, stood and stands today with its brothers in Egypt against terrorism . . . I call on the honest men of Egypt and the Arab and Muslim nations . . . to stand as one man and with one heart in the face of attempts to destabilize a country that is at the forefront of Arab and Muslim history.[113]

Abdullah characterised the Muslim Brotherhood as terrorists, implied there were foreign attempts to destabilise Egypt, and justified the Egyptian government's actions.

'Within hours of the king's speech' the Saudi foreign minister, Saud Al Faisal, flew to Paris to lobby, pressure and cajole the French to refrain from sanctioning Egypt's generals for the violence. When he returned to Riyadh a few days later, Al Faisal declared that Saudi Arabia would be willing to make up any reduction in aid to Egypt from the US or Europe, 'effectively neutralizing the West's main leverage over Cairo'.[114]

In an interview with Nabil Fahmy, a career Egyptian diplomat who was appointed foreign minister shortly after Morsi's ouster, Fahmy recounted Al Faisal's trip to France in support of Egypt. Fahmy told me that Al Faisal did this 'on his own' and without informing or coordinating with the Egyptians.

> Saud basically told the Western Europeans: 'You take on the Egyptians, you take on us. This is not going to be an argument with the Egyptians.' Literally, he went and did this with the French president . . . that's the point he made to them. And he made the same point to the British . . . he was tremendously blunt . . . And [King] Abdullah made a statement saying, 'OK . . . we are with these guys.'[115]

The forceful and unified Saudi, Emirati and Kuwaiti position on Egypt reduced the ability of the US and European governments to influence Egypt's generals, either to restore Morsi, push for democracy, limit repression, negotiate the shape of a new government, or to contest the legitimacy of the new regime going forward.[116]

Egypt's generals also received support from Israel and AIPAC for a second time, following the Rab'a massacre.[117] Israeli efforts to 'intensify its diplomatic campaign' came after France, Britain and Australia called for a closed door UN Security Council meeting to discuss the violence in Egypt and as EU foreign ministers scheduled a meeting to discuss suspending aid to Cairo.[118] Israel's ambassadors were mobilised in 'Washington, London, Paris, Berlin, Brussels, and other capitals' and directed to lobby governments to continue supporting the Egyptian military, despite the violence against civilians.[119] Netanyahu also spoke directly with US officials, including Kerry, Martin Dempsey (chairman of the Joint Chiefs of Staff) and two dozen US congressmen who happened to be visiting Israel at the time. Other Israeli officials, including the defence minister, spoke to their US counterparts to press Israel's position on Egypt.[120]

Al-Sisi and the Reconsolidation of Authoritarianism in Egypt

In addition to US$12 billion of aid delivered immediately after Morsi's ouster, Gulf largesse continued to support the emerging post-Morsi authoritarian order. Eighteen months after the coup, Egypt's investment minister stated that the total value of aid received from the three Gulf states had reached US$23 billion.[121] Although it is difficult to accurately determine the total amount of Gulf support Egypt has received since 2013, the amounts have been both unprecedented and staggering and have been critical in reconsolidating an authoritarian order.

Saudi Arabia, Kuwait and the UAE pledged an additional US$12 billion of financial aid, investment and central bank deposits at the Sharm El Sheikh investment conference in March 2015.[122] Oman pledged US$500 million in aid and investment at the high-profile event attended by heads of state, investors and business people.[123] Billions of additional Saudi and Emirati private sector investment deals were signed in the energy, real estate, retail and transportation sectors at the conference, in addition to memorandums of understanding (MOUs) for future projects. According to Egypt's investment minister, US$38.2 billion worth of investments were finalised at the event, a figure that included both Gulf and non-Gulf investments, with MOUs for possible future deals worth billions more.[124]

One year later, in April 2016, when King Salman visited Cairo, additional economic agreements were signed worth billions more.[125] This included a US$23 billion deal with Aramco to provide Egypt with 700,000 barrels of petroleum products per month for five years, payable at 2 per cent interest over fifteen years.[126] Salman also announced the establishment of a 60 billion riyal (US$16 billion) Saudi–Egyptian investment fund, an agreement for a Sinai economic free zone, a US$2.2 billion electricity plant, US$3.3 billion in investments in the Suez Canal industrial zone, and other smaller projects.[127] Along with these announcements, however, came news that Saudi Arabia would take possession of two Red Sea islands, Tiran and Sanafir.[128]

In November 2019, Mohamed bin Zayed announced the establishment of a US$20 billion 'joint strategic investment platform' between the UAE and Egypt. The crown prince made the announcement while al-Sisi was visiting the Emirates accompanied by Egypt's head of general intelligence and foreign minister. Investments in the platform are to be channelled through the Abu Dhabi Development Holding Company and a newly established Egyptian sovereign wealth fund. When making the announcement, bin Zayed declared that 'Egypt's security is as important as the UAE's security', and that 'confronting the challenges and risks facing the Arab region requires intensifying the ongoing consultations between our countries and joint Arab action.' 'Egypt', he proclaimed, 'is one of the cornerstones of Arab security.'[129]

The tremendous official support from the Gulf states also created a Gulf-friendly business environment that encouraged Saudi and Emirati private businesses, including smaller firms, to invest in Egypt. By 2018, the Egyptian minister of trade said that Saudi investments made up 11 per cent of foreign investment in the country, with more than 5,000 Saudi companies operating an estimated US$27 billion worth of investments.[130]

Similarly, the increase in Emirati foreign direct investment since Morsi's ouster has been described as 'striking'.[131] Much of this has been in commercial and residential real estate, including some of the largest and best-known shopping malls, luxury housing developments, grocery store chains and entertainment: 'FDI from the UAE averaged about $1 billion per year between 2014/15 and 2017/18.'[132]

As stated previously, it is difficult to accurately determine the amount of Gulf economic assistance and investment Egypt received since Morsi's ouster. A 2019 article in the Kuwaiti daily *Al Qabas* reported that 'sources in the Egyptian Central Bank estimated the amount of aid that Cairo received from the Gulf states, since the January 25, 2011 revolution to be approximately 92 billion dollars.'[133] This mind-boggling figure would include aid and investment from Qatar, Bahrain and Oman, as well as other Gulf support (primarily Saudi) received before Morsi's presidency. The article does note that there are 'no accurate statistics about the details of the aid Egypt received' and that there are 'inconsistencies . . . in the announced government statistics'. However, even if one were to deduct the substantial Qatari aid during the Morsi period (at least US$7 billion), and Saudi support before Morsi's ouster (perhaps US$1–2 billion), the Sisi regime would still have received an eye-popping US$80 billion of economic assistance and investment from the Gulf (primarily from Saudi Arabia, the UAE and Kuwait) in the span of six years.[134]

Such figures are not only enormous, but they also dwarf the amount of aid received from the US and European countries. To put this in perspective, the US has provided Egypt with approximately US$80 billion in military and economic aid, not including private sector investment, over the span of more than seventy years, since 1948. The majority of this has come since the Egyptian–Israeli Peace Agreement in 1979, over a forty-year period, with Egypt receiving US$70 billion in US military and economic assistance since 1980.

The aid and investment Egypt received from the three counter-revolutionary Gulf states in the six short years between 2013 and 2019, demonstrates in stark numerical terms that these states have played an even larger role in bankrolling Egyptian authoritarianism than the US. Although Jason Brownlee is correct that the US has engaged in 'democracy prevention' in Egypt, the counter-revolutionary Gulf states – much closer to Egypt, with much more at stake, and part of a Middle East regional authoritarian complex – have invested even more heavily in 'democracy prevention' and, since 2013, have been critical to the reconsolidation of a transnational Egyptian authoritarianism under Abdel Fattah al-Sisi.[135] To further highlight this point, Saudi Arabia and the UAE pledged an additional US\$17 billion in investments and central bank deposits to the Sisi regime in 2022, in the midst of the country's economic difficulties as a result of sharp spikes in global oil and food prices caused, in part, by the Russian invasion of Ukraine.[136]

Conclusion

The argument advanced in this chapter is not simply that the regional environment in the Middle East was unconducive to democratisation in Egypt following the 2011 Arab uprisings. Rather, it is that powerful regional actors – Saudi Arabia, the UAE and Israel – actively undermined Egypt's democratic transition. Stated differently, these countries succeeded in helping facilitate the country's 'failed' democratisation. They did this because of their increased threat perception as a result of the Arab uprisings. Saudi Arabia, UAE and Kuwait subsequently played a critical role in reconsolidating a new transnational authoritarian order in Egypt under Abdel Fattah al-Sisi.

The Arab uprisings were profoundly threatening for autocrats across the region, perhaps none more so than the Egyptian 'revolution'. The mobilisation of millions of disenfranchised Arab citizens protesting against repression, corruption and social injustice, and demanding 'the fall of the regime', was correctly perceived by rulers in Riyadh and Abu Dhabi as a direct threat to their own regimes. The uprisings entailed the possibility of democracy and Islamist political forces taking root not only in Egypt, Tunisia and other countries experiencing protests, but throughout the region. For Israel, the prospect of a democratic Egypt or an Islamist-led government in Cairo was also alarming and fundamentally threatened Israel's national and regional security calculus.

For Saudi Arabia and the UAE, the threat was not about 'national security' but about regime security. In response, Riyadh and Abu Dhabi actively worked to influence political developments in Cairo (and elsewhere) to reduce such threats. They did this through direct and indirect influence and through multiple methods and channels. During the eighteen-day uprising against Mubarak, for example, Riyadh and Abu Dhabi provided direct diplomatic support to Egypt's embattled autocrat. Both countries denounced the protests as the work of foreign agents and, along with Israel, attempted to influence

US policy towards the unfolding events. All three countries intensely lobbied the Obama administration to back Mubarak and refrain from supporting the protesters. The Saudis even offered to replace any American aid, if it were cut to Mubarak, in the midst of the uprising.

Similarly, in the run-up to Egypt's first democratic legislative elections, Saudi Arabia generously financed Egypt's Salafis with millions of dollars in cash in order to limit the growing power of the Muslim Brotherhood. My interviews also suggest that the UAE offered support to 'liberal' and Salafi parties and candidates in the 2011 legislative and 2012 presidential elections with the same purpose.

After Morsi was elected, Saudi and Emirati investment in Egypt slowed considerably while economic aid virtually ended. And while Riyadh and Abu Dhabi turned off economic and financial support to Cairo, both governments, along with Israel, lobbied the US and European powers against the Morsi government.

There is also significant evidence from multiple sources, including US officials, that the UAE, and possibly Saudi Arabia, coordinated with Egypt's generals to remove Morsi from power. The Emirates bankrolled the 'grass-roots' Tamarod movement with the aim of galvanising public opinion against Morsi and the Muslim Brotherhood in the spring of 2013. Of course, Morsi and the Muslim Brotherhood were already quickly losing popularity as a result of their own actions. Tamarod's activities, however, were critical in mobilising millions to take to the streets on 30 June 2013 in the largest protests in the country's history.

It is important to state explicitly that I am not arguing that powerful regional actors simply willed the failure of Egypt's 'democratic transition'. Saudi, Emirati and Israeli efforts would likely have amounted to little if it were not for the alignment of goals and interests between powerful Egyptian and regional actors. It was precisely these overlapping interests and transnational linkages that helped facilitate a mutually desired outcome. Moreover, as stated in the introduction, the domestic political drama encompassing Mohamed Morsi's failures, political polarisation between Islamists and 'liberals', and the military and 'the deep state' was the necessary context that enabled regional actors to operate effectively.

Nor am I arguing that large segments of Egyptian society had not already turned against Morsi by early 2013. Morsi was neither an effective nor competent leader. Nor was he sufficiently committed to inclusive politics or equal rights for all Egyptians. In fact, Morsi and the Muslim Brotherhood were their own worst enemies. Morsi's leadership style, language and actions were enough to turn millions against him and the Islamist movement from which he hailed.

My argument has focused on the powerful regional actors who have worked actively, assiduously and effectively to influence the trajectory of Egyptian politics, independently and through cooperation with al-Sisi, the Egyptian military and other actors with the goal of removing Morsi and aborting Egypt's democratic experiment (with the support of millions of Egyptians, although not necessarily the majority). They did this for understandable and self-interested reasons. Thus, it would be empirically incomplete and historically inaccurate to exclude the role of regional actors or transnational factors in any account of Egypt's 'failed democratic transition'.

Notes

* I would like to thank Timothy Kaldas, Ahmed Abdelaziz, and Ahmed Mohsen for helpful suggestions on earlier drafts of this chapter. I would also like to thank those individuals who agreed to be interviewed for this research, including Mr Abdel Hafez al-Sawy, Dr Amr Darrag, Ambassador Nabil Fahmy, Dr Ayman Nour, Mr Tarek al-Zomor, and a number of others who wished to remain anonymous. Of course, any errors are my own.

1 Some of the most astute observers of Egyptian politics neglect regional and international factors when discussing Egypt's 'failed democratisation'. Some of this is likely because Saudi and Emirati influence on Egyptian politics was less visible before 2013 and because 'domestic' factors are often assumed to be separate and more important than regional or international ones. Nathan Brown, for example, writing shortly after Morsi's ouster, discusses all three arguments presented above but makes no mention of regional or international factors. Similarly, Tarek Masoud analyses the same arguments in a 2014 article before proposing another – that 'Egypt lacked the social infrastructure necessary to sustain democratic competition', thus resulting in a 'stillborn democracy'. Both accounts are excellent but make no mention of regional or international factors. This neglect has mostly continued, unfortunately. For example, in a 2020 survey of fourteen Egyptian politics experts about why democratisation failed, only two mentioned regional or international issues. See Nathan Brown, 'Egypt's Failed Transition', *Journal of Democracy* 24, no. 4 (2013): 45–58; Tarek Masoud, 'Egyptian Democracy: Smothered in the Cradle, or Stillborn?' *The Brown Journal of World Affairs* 20, no. 2 (Spring/Summer 2014): 3–17; Amy Hawthorne and Andrew Miller, 'Why Did Egyptian Democratization Fail:

Fourteen Experts Respond', *POMED*, January 2020. Available at <https://po
med.org/wp-content/uploads/2020/01/200128b_EgyptDemocracy.pdf> (last
accessed 23 October 2022).

Imad Harb's insightful 2018 analysis is an exception. See his 'Regional
States and Egypt's Democratic Transition', Arab Center, Washington DC,
25 October 2018. Available at <https://arabcenterdc.org/resource/regional-
states-and-egypts-democratic-transition/> (last accessed 23 October 2022).
My approach extends and deepens the focus on the regional and international
by demonstrating their connection with the domestic, thus highlighting the
transnational dimensions of Egypt's 'failed democratisation' and its current
authoritarianism. My analysis also involves primary research, including interviews with principals and close observers in Cairo, Istanbul, London and
Washington DC, and the use of Egyptian and foreign primary and secondary
sources.

2 I place 'secular' and 'liberal' in quotations when describing Egypt's political
forces because many of these individuals and groups are not fully committed to
secular and liberal principles, especially when it comes to the rights of Islamists
to participate in the political process. As such, they can perhaps be more accurately described as 'anti-Islamist'. See Samer Shehata, 'In Egypt, Democrats vs.
Liberals', *New York Times*, 2 July 2013. Available at <https://www.nytimes
.com/2013/07/03/opinion/in-egypt-democrats-vs-liberals.html> (last accessed
23 October 2022).

3 Rather than a 'failed democratic transition', we can alternatively think of the
trajectory of Egyptian politics after 2011 as the success of the counter-revolution
and the strength of a regional authoritarian complex.

4 'Saudi King Expresses Support for Mubarak', *Reuters*, 29 January 2011.
Available at <https://www.reuters.com/article/egypt-saudi-idAFLDE70S08V
20110129> (last accessed 23 October 2022).

5 'In Quotes: Reaction to Egypt Protests', *BBC*, 30 January 2011. Available at
<https://www.bbc.com/news/world-middle-east-12316019> (last accessed
23 October 2022) (my emphasis).

6 Ethan Bronner, 'Israel Shaken as Turbulence Rocks an Ally', *New York Times*,
30 January 2011. Available at <https://www.nytimes.com/2011/01/31/world
/middleeast/31israel.html> (last accessed 23 October 2022).

7 'Israel "Fears" Post-Mubarak Era', *Al Jazeera*, 31 January 2011. Available at
<https://www.aljazeera.com/news/middleeast/2011/01/201113177145613
.html> (last accessed 23 October 2022).

8 Douglas Hamilton, 'Israel Shocked by Obama's "Betrayal" of Mubarak',
Reuters, 31 January 2011. Available at <https://www.reuters.com/article/us-

egypt-israel-usa/israel-shocked-by-obamas-betrayal-of-mubarak-idUSTRE70U
53720110131> (last accessed 23 October 2022).

9   Ibid.
10   Barak Ravid, 'Israel Urges World to Curb Criticism of Egypt's Mubarak',
     Haaretz, 31 January 2011. Available at <https://www.haaretz.com/2011-01-31
     /ty-article/israel-urges-world-to-curb-criticism-of-egypts-mubarak/0000017f
     -f55c-d887-a7ff-fdfc248d0000> (last accessed 23 October 2022).
11   Kareem Shaheen, 'Sheikh Abdullah Meets Mubarak in Cairo', *The National*,
     9 February 2011. Available at <https://www.thenationalnews.com/uae/sheikh
     -abdullah-meets-mubarak-in-cairo-1.417157> (last accessed 23 October 2022).
12   'UAE President Sends Letter to Hosni Mubarak', *Kuwait News Agency*,
     8 February 2011. Available at <https://www.kuna.net.kw/ArticleDetails.aspx
     ?id=2143560&language=en> (last accessed 23 October 2022).
13   Helene Cooper, Mark Landler and David E. Sanger, 'In U.S. Signals to Egypt,
     Obama Straddled a Rift', *New York Times*, 12 February 2011. Available at
     <https://www.nytimes.com/2011/02/13/world/middleeast/13diplomacy.
     html?scp=7&sq=saudi%20egypt&st=cse> (last accessed 23 October 2022).
14   Ibid.
15   Press Briefing by Press Secretary Robert Gibbs, 28 January 2011. Available at
     <https://obamawhitehouse.archives.gov/the-press-office/2011/01/28/press-
     briefing-press-secretary-robert-gibbs-1282011> (last accessed 23 October 2022).
16   'Saudis Told Obama Not to Humiliate Mubarak', *The Times*, 10 February
     2011. Available at <https://www.thetimes.co.uk/article/saudis-told-obama
     -not-to-humiliate-mubarak-k8zfmbkh2rk> (last accessed 23 October 2022).
17   Mark Landler, 'Clinton Calls for "Orderly Transition" in Egypt', *New York
     Times*, 30 January 2011.
18   Mark Landler and Helene Cooper, 'Allies Press U.S. to Go Slow on Egypt',
     New York Times, 8 February 2011. Available at <https://www.nytimes.com/20
     11/02/09/world/middleeast/09diplomacy.html?_r=1&ref=saudiarabia> (last
     accessed 23 October 2022).
19   'Israel "Fears" Post-Mubarak Era', *Al Jazeera*, 31 January 2011. Available at
     <https://www.aljazeera.com/news/middleeast/2011/01/201113177145613
     .html> (last accessed 23 October 2022).
20   'Report: Saudis Warned Obama Not to "Humiliate" Mubarak', *Fox News*,
     10 February 2011. Available at <https://www.foxnews.com/politics/report
     -saudis-warned-obama-not-to-humiliate-mubarak> (last accessed 23 October
     2022).
21   Mark Landler and Helene Cooper, 'Allies Press U.S. to Go Slow on Egypt'.
22   'Remarks with Spanish Foreign Minister Trinidad Jimenez after Their Meeting',

US Department of State, 25 January 2011. Available at <https://2009-2017.st
ate.gov/secretary/20092013clinton/rm/2011/01/155280.htm> (last accessed
23 October 2022).

23 Available at <https://2009-2017.state.gov/secretary/20092013clinton/rm/20
11/01/155388.htm> (last accessed 23 October 2022).

24 'Remarks by the President on the Situation in Egypt', 28 January 2011. Available
at <https://obamawhitehouse.archives.gov/photos-and-video/video/2011/01
/28/president-obama-situation-egypt#transcript> (last accessed 23 October
2022). Obama also called on Egypt's security forces to refrain from violence
against peaceful protesters.

25 For example, Vice President Joe Biden refused to describe Mubarak as a 'dictator' in an interview with the *PBS NewsHour* and the Obama administration's
special envoy to Egypt, Frank Wisner, said that Mubarak 'must stay in office
to steer . . . changes through', after returning from meeting Mubarak in Cairo.
See 'Exclusive/Biden: Mubarak Is Not a Dictator, But People Have a Right to
Protest', *PBS NewsHour*, 27 January 2011. Available at <https://www.pbs.org
/newshour/show/exclusive-biden-mubarak-is-not-a-dictator-but-people-have
-a-right-to-protest> (last accessed 23 October 2022). See Jill Dougherty, 'U.S.
Pressure for Mubarak transition', *CNN*, 5 February 2011. Available at <https://
edition.cnn.com/2011/POLITICS/02/05/egypt.us/index.html> (last accessed
23 October 2022).

26 Obama said he conveyed to Mubarak his 'belief that an orderly transition must
be meaningful . . . peaceful and it must begin now'. 'Remarks by the President
on the Situation in Egypt, 1 February 2011'. Available at <https://obamawhi
tehouse.archives.gov/the-press-office/2011/02/01/remarks-president-situation
-egypt> (last accessed 23 October 2022).

27 'Press Briefing by Press Secretary Robert Gibbs, 2/2/2011'. Available at
<https://obamawhitehouse.archives.gov/the-press-office/2011/02/02/press-br
iefing-press-secretary-robert-gibbs-222011> (last accessed 23 October 2022).

28 Frank Wisner also spoke of the possibility of 'radicals' taking advantage of the
situation in Egypt during his remarks to the Munich Security Conference.
'Administration Drop Kicks Ambassador for Remarks on Mubarak, but Echoes
Sentiment', *Fox News*, 7 February 2011. Available at <https://obamawhiteh
ouse.archives.gov/the-press-office/2011/02/02/press-briefing-press-secretary
-robert-gibbs-222011> (last accessed 23 October 2022).

29 'U.S Department of State, Question and Answer Session at the Munich
Conference, Remarks by Hillary Rodham Clinton, February 5, 2011'. Available
at <https://2009-2017.state.gov/secretary/20092013clinton/rm/2011/02/156
045.htm> (last accessed 23 October 2022).

30 Jane Mayer, 'Who is Omar Suleiman?' *The New Yorker*, 29 January 2011.

Available at <https://www.newyorker.com/news/news-desk/who-is-omar-sule iman> (last accessed 23 October 2022).

31 Lisa Hajjar, 'Omar Suleiman, the CIA's man in Cairo and Egypt's Torturer-in Chief', *Jadaliyya*, 30 January 2011. Available at <https://www.jadaliyya.com /Details/23636/Omar-Suleiman,-the-CIA%60s-Man-in-Cairo-and-Egypt%60s -Torturer-in-Chief> (last accessed 23 October 2022).

32 'Defense Minister Barak's Discussions in Egypt focus on Shalit, Tahdiya, Anti-smuggling, and Iran', *Wikileaks*, 29 August 2008. Available at <https://wiki leaks.org/plusd/cables/08TELAVIV1984_a.html> (last accessed 23 October 2022).

33 Karl Vick, 'As Egypt's Crisis Grows, So Do anxieties in Israel', *Time*, 30 January 2011. Available at <http://content.time.com/time/world/article/0,8599,2045 166,00.html> (last accessed 23 October 2022). See also Ethan Bronner, 'Israel Shaken as Turbulence Rocks an Ally', *New York Times,* 30 January 2011. Available at <https://www.nytimes.com/2011/01/31/world/middleeast/31is rael.html> (last accessed 23 October 2022).

34 Ethan Bronner, 'Israel Shaken as Turbulence Rocks an Ally'. During the uprising, a former Israeli ambassador to Cairo, Eli Shaked, wrote in an Israeli newspaper that 'the only people in Egypt who are committed to peace are the people in Mubarak's inner circle, and if the next president is not one of them, we are going to be in trouble.'

35 Ibid.

36 Ethan Bronner, 'Quiet Worries as Israel Watches an Ally Depart', *New York Times*, 11 February 2011. Available at <https://www.nytimes.com/2011/02 /12/world/middleeast/12israel.html> (last accessed 23 October 2022).

37 'Abraz Ahdath al-'Am 2011: al-Idafa al-Hadayya Ashar' [Most notable events in 2011: the eleventh addendum], *Saudi Press Agency*, 12 February 2011. Available at <https://www.spa.gov.sa/957125?lang=ar&newsid=957125> (last accessed 23 October 2022); and 'United Arab Emirates: Confident the Egyptian Army Can Run the Country', *BNO News*, 11 February 2011.

38 'Al-Sa'wdiyya tinfi mumarasat dughut 'la al-Majlis al a'la lil Quwat al-Musalaha al-Misriyya' [Saudi Arabia denies exerting pressure on the Egyptian Armed Forces', *Al Itihad*, 25 March 2011. Available at <https://www.alittihad.ae/ article/28395/2011/-المسلحة-للقوات-الأعلى-المجلس-على-ط-ضغو-ممارسة-تنفي-السعودية المصرية> (last accessed 23 October 2022). See Mohamed Al Hinawi, 'Al-A'la lil Qawat al-Musalaha tinfi wujud dughut Su'wdiyya wa Imaratiyya 'ala Misr', *Al-Youm Al-Sab'*, 26 April 2011. Available at <https://www.youm7.com/story/2011/4/26/ 398771/-مصر-على-اتية-إمار-و-سعودية-ط-ضغو-جود-و-ينفى-المسلحة-للقوات-الأعلى> (last accessed 23 October 2022). See also Gamal Essam El-Din, 'Gulf Arab States Don't Want Mubarak Tried – *AhramOnline* Asks Why', *AhramOnline*, 30 April 2011.

Available at <http://english.ahram.org.eg/NewsPrint/11106.aspx> (last accessed 23 October 2022).

39 'Mu'tamarun uharirun mahadir did al-Sa'wdiyya . . . wa al-A'iduwn: al-Mamlaka tu'qibna 'al al-thawra' [Pilgrims file complaints against Saudi [Airlines] . . . and the returnees: the kingdom punishes us because of the revolution], *Al-Masry Al-Youm*, 1 September 2011. Available at <https://today.almasryalyoum.com/article2.aspx?ArticleID=309233> (last accessed 23 October 2022).

40 'Itahamat lil hukuma 'bil taqa'us' 'an rud 'al-ihanat al-Sa'wdiyya' lil mu'tamarun' [Accusations of government 'failure' to respond to 'Saudi insults' to the pilgrims], *Al-Masry Al-Youm*, 2 September 2011. Available at <https://www.almasryalyoum.com/news/details/1811863> (last accessed 23 October 2022).

41 AFP Jeddah, 'Tajeel Muhakamat al-Muhami Ahmed al-Gizawi fi al-Sa'wdiyya' [Delay in the trial of lawyer Ahmed al-Gizawi in Saudi Arabia], *Al Youm Al Sab'*, 26 December 2012. Available at <https://www.youm7.com/story/2012/12/26 /تأجيل-محاكمة-المحامى-أحمد-الجيزاوى-فى-السعودية/889138> (last accessed 23 October 2022); 'Saudi Recalls Ambassador from Egypt, Closes Embassy in Response to Protests', *Ahram Online*, 28 April 2012. Available at <http://english.ahram.org.eg/News/40359.aspx> (last accessed 23 October 2022).

42 Sami Abd Al Radi, 'Ahmed al-Gizawi . . . wa 'Fasil min al-'ak' [Ahmed al-Gizawi . . . and 'a segment of the mess'], *Al-Masry Al-Youm*, 29 April 2012. Available at <https://www.almasryalyoum.com/news/details/219617> (last accessed 23 October 2022).

43 Kareem Fahim, 'Saudis Close Embassy in Egypt', *New York Times*, 28 April 2012. Available at <https://www.nytimes.com/2012/04/29/world/middleeast /saudi-arabia-recalls-envoy-to-egypt.html> (last accessed 23 October 2022).

44 'EOHR Calls SCAF to Handle the Detention Case of Ahmed al-Gizawy', Egyptian Organization for Human Rights, 23 April 2012. Available at <http:// en.eohr.org/2012/04/23/eohr-calls-scaf-to-handle-the-detention-case-of-ah med-al-gizawy/#more-1087> (last accessed summer 2019).

45 Sami Abd Al Radi, 'Ahmed al-Gizawi . . . wa 'Fasil min al-'ak' [Ahmed al-Gizawi . . . and 'a segment of the mess'], *Al-Masry Al-Youm*, 29 April 2012. Available at <https://www.almasryalyoum.com/news/details/219617> (last accessed 23 October 2022).

46 Ibid.

47 'Update: Saudi Ambassador to Leave Egypt for a Consultation with Saudi Officials', *Egypt Independent*, 28 April 2012. Available at <https://ww.egyptindependent.com/saudi-arabia-recalls-ambassador-egypt-closes-embassy-cairo-news-1/> (last accessed 23 October 2022).

48 'Saudi Recalls Cairo Envoy in Blow to Egypt Ties', *Reuters*, 28 April 2012.

Available at <https://www.reuters.com/article/us-saudi-egypt/saudi-recalls-cairo-envoy-in-blow-to-egypt-ties-idUSBRE83R09220120428> (last accessed 23 October 2022).

49 'Wazeer al-Kharijayya: Itisalat 'al-kul al-mustawiyyat ma' al-Riyaad lihtiwa' al-Azma' [The foreign minister: communication at all levels with Riyadh to contain the crisis], *Al-Masry Al-Youm*, 30 April 2012. Available at <https://www.almasryalyoum.com/news/details/175648> (last accessed 23 October 2022).

50 'Istiqbal Rasmy lil Wafd al-Sha'bi al-Masry bi'l Sa'wdiyya' [Official reception for the Egyptian Popular Delegation in Saudi Arabia], *Al Wafd*, 4 May 2012. Available at <https://alwafd.news/-ملفات-محلية/205819-استقبال-رسمى-للوفد-الشعبى-المصرى-بالسعودية> (last accessed 23 October 2022).

51 'Tantawi Meets with Saudi Ambassador to Cairo', *Egypt Independent*, 7 May 2012. Available at <https://ww.egyptindependent.com/tantawi-meets-saudi-ambassador-cairo-nehal-news-1-hold/> (last accessed 23 October 2022).

52 'Mowafi, Al Faisal Discuss Country – Saudi Relations', Egypt State Information Service, 7 May 2012.

53 Salafism has traditionally been apolitical, focusing on religious practice, eschewing formal politics and subscribing to the principle of obedience to a Muslim ruler. Salafism provided pious Egyptians with a non-political message quite distinct from the politically engaged ideology of the Muslim Brotherhood.

54 My claim is that Egyptian Salafis were inherently and more virulently anti-Shi'a than the Muslim Brotherhood, not that the Muslim Brotherhood did not, at times, contribute to anti-Shi'a sentiment. For example, at a rally on 15 June 2013 in support of Syria which Morsi attended, several Sunni clerics called for jihad against the Assad regime, labelling its supporters 'infidels'. Morsi also spoke at the rally, urging international intervention, calling for Hezbollah to withdraw from the country, and announcing that Egypt was cutting diplomatic relations with Damascus. Eight days later four Egyptian Shi'a were killed by a mob led by Salafi sheikhs in a village on the outskirts of Cairo. In a report about the incident, Human Rights Watch noted that the Muslim Brotherhood 'condoned and at times participated in anti-Shi'a hate speech' that produced the conditions that led to such violence. See, 'Egypt: Lynching of Shia Follows Months of Hate Speech', Human Rights Watch, 27 June 2013. Available at <https://www.hrw.org/news/2013/06/27/egypt-lynching-shia-follows-months-hate-speech> (last accessed 23 October 2022).

55 'Salafis Apologize to Saudi Arabia for the Demonstrations and Protests in Front of Its Embassy', *Al-Masry Al-Youm*, 1 May 2012. Available at <https://www.almasryalyoum.com/news/details/175885> (last accessed 23 October 2022).

56 Ahmed Aboulenein, 'Salafi Protest Shi'a "invasion"', *Daily News Egypt*, 5 April 2013. Available at <https://www.dailynewssegypt.com/2013/04/05/salafis-pr otest-shia-invasion/> (last accessed 23 October 2022).

57 'Salafis to Lobby against Rapprochement with Iran', *Egypt Independent*, 3 April 2013. Available at <https://egyptindependent.com/salafis-lobby-against-rappr ochement-iran/> (last accessed 23 October 2022).

58 Sabri Hassanein, 'The Salafis Deny Receiving 296 Million Pounds and a Report Reveals Funding of NGOs', *Elaph*, 18 November 2011. Available at <https:// elaph.com/Web/news/2011/11/696557.html> (last accessed 23 October 2022).

59 Habib Toumi, 'Kuwait Denies Funding Egyptian Salafi Group', *Gulf News*, 3 January 2012. Available at <https://gulfnews.com/world/gulf/kuwait/kuwa it-denies-funding-egyptian-salafi-group-1.960635> (last accessed 23 October 2022).

60 Osama El-Mahdy, 'Protest before Saudi Embassy against Financing Salafis', *Egypt Independent*, 17 May 2011. Available at <https://www.egyptindepen dent.com/protest-saudi-embassy-against-financing-salafis/> (last accessed 23 October 2022)

61 Stephane Lacroix, 'Sheikhs and Politicians: Inside the New Egyptian Salafism', Brookings Doha Center, Policy Briefing, 11 June 2012, 3.

62 'Hybrid Threats: The Spread of Salafism in Egypt', NATO Strategic Communications Centre of Excellence, n.d. Available at <https://www.stratco mcoe.org/hybrid-threats-spread-salafism-egypt> (last accessed 6 June 2019; no longer available).

63 'Salafist/Wahhabite Financial Support to Educational, Social and Religious Institutions', Directorate-General for External Policies, European Parliament, 2013, 8. Available at <https://www.europarl.europa.eu/RegData/etudes/etud es/join/2013/457136/EXPO-AFET_ET(2013)457136_EN.pdf> (last accessed 23 October 2022).

64 Mohamed Kamal, 'Al Nour: "Lam Nitluk Tamweel min al-Sa'wdiyya wa nesta'd lil Intikhibat bi jidayya"' [Nour Party: 'We have not received funding from Saudi Arabia and we are preparing for the elections seriously'], *Al-Youm Al-Sab'*, 14 November 2011. Available at <https://web.archive.org/web/20111 229074615/http://www.youm7.com/News.asp?NewsID=492676&SecID=2 96&IssueID=93> (last accessed 23 October 2022).

65 'Al-Nour Party', *AhramOnline*, 4 December 2011. Available at <https://engl ish.ahram.org.eg/NewsContent/33/104/26693/Elections-/Political-Parties/Al Nour-Party.aspx> (last accessed 23 October 2022).

66 Randa Abul Azm, 'Saudi Envoy to Egypt Denies Kingdom Offered Salafis

Billions', *Al Arabiya*, 1 August 2011. Available at <https://english.alarabiya.net/articles/2011/08/01/160331> (last accessed 23 October 2022).

67 Interview with Tarek al-Zomor, Istanbul, Turkey, 15 April 2019.

68 Ali's name came up in several interviews with Islamist and non-Islamist figures as someone in the payroll of the UAE. In addition to *Al Bawaba*, Ali hosted the controversial 'Black Box' television programme which infamously aired secretly recorded private telephone conversations between prominent political personalities in an attempt to discredit them. The channel is owned by businessman Tarek Nour, who served as the general coordinator of al-Sisi's presidential campaign in 2014. Ali's programme was taken off air in 2014.

69 Interview, Cairo, Egypt, December 2018.

70 Interview, Washington DC, 19 July 2019.

71 Dexter Filkins, 'A Saudi Prince's Quest to Remake the Middle East', *The New Yorker*, 2 April 2018. Available at <https://www.newyorker.com/magazine/2018/04/09/a-saudi-princes-quest-to-remake-the-middle-east> (last accessed 23 October 2022).

72 According to multiple sources, including several individuals I interviewed, UAE and Saudi officials lobbied vigorously against the Morsi government and in support of the coup in Washington DC and European capitals.

73 Anonymous Saudi activist Mujtahid bin Hareth bin Hammam, with over two million Twitter followers, claimed in late July 2013 that King Abdullah gave the Egyptian military US$1 billion dollars to stage the coup. 'The Saudi king is using his political and financial powers to convince the West to refrain from adopting a strong stance toward the crisis in Egypt, Mujtahid charged.' See 'Saudi Activist Says Money Given to Egyptian General to Oust Morsi', *UPI*, 30 July 2013. Available at <https://www.upi.com/Top_News/World-News/2013/07/30/Saudi-activist-says-money-given-to-Egyptian-general-to-oust-Morsi/53881375183115/?spt=hts&or=2&ur3=1> (last accessed 23 October 2022).

74 'Egypt Got $23 Billion in Aid from Gulf in 18 Months – Minister', *Reuters*, 2 March 2015. Available at <https://uk.reuters.com/article/uk-egypt-investment-gulf/egypt-got-23-billion-in-aid-from-gulf-in-18-months-minister-idUKKBN0LY0UT20150302> (last accessed summer 2019).

75 'Egypt's Morsi Discusses $8.5bn in Saudi Investments', *Ahram Online*, 11 September 2012. Available at <https://english.ahram.org.eg/NewsAFCON/2017/52537.aspx> (last accessed 23 October 2022).

76 Interview, Istanbul, Turkey, 15 April 2019.

77 Interview, Istanbul, Turkey, 15 April 2019.

78 Yasmine Farouk, 'More than Money: Post-Mubarak Egypt, Saudi Arabia, and

the Gulf', Gulf Research Center, April 2014, 10–11. Farouk notes that in 2011, the minister of finance Hazem al-Beblawi, criticised the Gulf states, except Qatar, for 'delaying the financial packages they had promised to Egypt and criticized their reluctance to support Egypt in the negotiations with international and regional donors', (8). Available at <https://www.files.ethz.ch/isn/179860/Egypt_Money_new_29-4-14_2576.pdf> (last accessed 23 October 2022).

79 'Going to the Dogs; Egypt's Economy', *Economist*, vol. 406, issue 8829, 30 March 2013, 45–6. See 'Egypt Defiant as Arab Spring Drains Foreign Reserves', *Global Capital*, 8 June 2011. Available at<https://www.globalcapital.com/special-report-archive?issueid=yw0c4l30csqp&article=yvxkv8b42rl3> (last accessed summer 2019).

80 Doha invested heavily in Morsi's Egypt in the hope of supplanting Riyadh's relationship with Cairo, solidifying a new strategic alliance, and boosting the standing of Islamist movements across the region.

81 Marwa Awad, 'Qatar Says to Invest $18 Billion in Egypt', *Reuters*, 6 September 2012. Available at <https://www.reuters.com/article/us-egypt-qatar-investment-idUSBRE8850YK20120906> (last accessed 23 October 2022). Qatar also announced it would invest up to US$18 billion in tourism and industrial projects in Egypt over five years, although nothing close to these figures materialised during Morsi's one year in office.

82 Heba Saleh, 'Egypt Returns $2bn to Qatar in Sign of Worsening Bilateral Ties', *Financial Times*, 19 September 2013.

83 'Egypt Returns $2bn to Qatar after Talks to Securitise It Fail', *AhramOnline*, 19 September 2013. Available at <https://english.ahram.org.eg/NewsContent/3/12/82019/Business/Economy/Egypt-returns--bn-to-Qatar-after-talks-to-securiti.aspx> (last accessed 23 October 2022).

84 Mohamad Elmasry, 'Unpacking Anti-Muslim Brotherhood Discourse', *Jadaliyya*, 28 June 2013. Available at <https://www.jadaliyya.com/Details/28855> (last accessed 23 October 2022).

85 David D. Kirkpatrick, *Into the Hands of the Soldiers: Freedom and Chaos in Egypt and the Middle East* (New York: Viking, 2018), 208. Rhodes was closely involved in formulating US policy towards Egypt at the time. Kirkpatrick's excellent account is based on unrivalled access to key American officials who formulated US policy towards Egypt between 2011 and 2013.

86 Interview, Anonymous, 2019.

87 David D. Kirkpatrick, *Into the Hands of the Soldiers*, 207–8.

88 This account accords with what I was told by a senior US State Department official I interviewed in Washington DC in 2019.

89 Turki Al Faisal bin Abdul Aziz Al Saud, 'Saudi Arabia's Foreign Policy', *Middle*

East Policy 20, no. 4 (Winter 2013). Available at <https://www.mepc.org/saudi
-arabias-foreign-policy> (last accessed 23 October 2022) (my emphasis).

90 Although the 30 June protests were significantly larger than any of the protests
against Mubarak in 2011, the claims that they included '33 million' Egyptians
or were the largest protests in history, have been thoroughly debunked. The bil-
lionaire Naguib Sawiris, Egypt's richest man, seems to be one of the sources for
such claims. The claims function, in part, to justify Morsi's ouster by asserting
that more people protested against Morsi on 30 June 2013 than the number of
people who voted for him in the 2012 presidential election. Sawiris claimed in
a tweet on 30 June 2013 that the BBC had reported: 'The number of people
protesting today is the largest number in a political event in the history of man-
kind. Keep impressing .. Egypt.' There is no evidence that the BBC made such a
claim. Available at <https://twitter.com/NaguibSawiris/status/351449907774
754817> (last accessed 23 October 2022). Gigi Ibrahim, famous from the 2011
uprising, similarly tweeted on 30 June 2013, somewhat more cautiously, that 'I
think this might be the largest protest in terms of numbers in history and definitely in Egypt ever.' Available at <https://twitter.com/Gsquare86/status/351
433925807177728> (last accessed 23 October 2022). For academic debunking
of such claims based on spatial analysis, see Noah Shachtman, 'How Many
people are in Tahrir Square? Here's How to Tell' (updated), *Wired*, 1 February
2011. Available at <https://www.wired.com/2011/02/how-many-people
-are-in-tahrir-square-heres-how-to-tell/> (last accessed 23 October 2022); and
Neil Ketchley, 'How Egypt's Generals Used Street Protests to Stage a Coup',
Washington Post, 3 July 2017.

91 Turki Al Faisal bin Abdul Aziz Al Saud, 'Saudi Arabia's Foreign Policy', *Middle
East Policy* 20, no. 4 (Winter 2013). Available at <https://www.mepc.org/saudi
-arabias-foreign-policy> (last accessed 23 October 2022).

92 David D. Kirkpatrick, 'Recordings Suggest Emirates and Egyptian Military
Pushed Ousting of Morsi', *New York Times*, 1 March 2015. Available at
<https://www.nytimes.com/2015/03/02/world/middleeast/recordings-sug
gest-emirates-and-egyptian-military-pushed-ousting-of-morsi.html> (last accessed 23 October 2022).

93 'Nabtha 'an mudiri jihaz al-Mukhabarat al-Masry al-Sabiq wa al-Haly' [A profile of the previous and current Egyptian Intelligence Service directors], *BBC*,
18 January 2018. Available at <https://www.bbc.com/arabic/in-depth-4273
5396> (last accessed 23 October 2022).

94 Naguib Sawiris also claimed after the coup that he had funded Tamarod. See Ben
Hubbard and David D. Kirkpatrick, 'Sudden Improvements in Egypt Suggest
a Campaign to Undermine Morsi', *New York Times*, 10 July 2013. Available

at <https://www.nytimes.com/2013/07/11/world/middleeast/improvements-in-egypt-suggest-a-campaign-that-undermined-morsi.html> (last accessed 23 October 2022).

95   Charles Levinson and Matt Bradley, 'In Egypt, the "Deep State" Rises Again', *Wall Street Journal*, 19 July 2013.

96   David D. Kirkpatrick, *Into the Hands of the Soldiers*, 226–7.

97   'Custodian of the Two Holy Mosques Congratulates Chancellor Adli Mansour, President of the Arab Republic of Egypt on Assuming Office at this Critical Point of Egypt's History', *Saudi Press Agency*, 3 July 2013. Available at <https://www.spa.gov.sa/viewstory.php?newsid=1126337> (last accessed 23 October 2022).

98   'Saudi King Calls on Arabs to Stand with Egypt', *Reuters*, 16 August 2013. Available at <https://www.reuters.com/article/us-egypt-protests-saudi/saudi-king-calls-on-arabs-to-stand-with-egypt-idUSBRE97F0NF20130816> (last accessed 23 October 2022).

99   'Gulf Arabs Welcome Ouster of Egypt's President', *Reuters*, 3 July 2013. Available at <https://uk.reuters.com/article/uk-egypt-protests-gcc/gulf-arabs-welcome-ouster-of-egypts-president-idUKBRE9621EL20130703> (last accessed summer 2019). See also, Nadeen Shaker, 'International Reaction to Morsi's Removal Range from Glee to Censure', *AhramOnline*, 4 July 2013. Available at <https://english.ahram.org.eg/NewsContent/2/8/75725/World/Region/International-reactions-to-Morsis-removal-range-fr.aspx> (last accessed 23 October 2022).

100 'UAE Leaders Congratulate the Egyptian President', *Khaleej Times*, 4 July 2013.

101 'Amir Congratulates New Egyptian Interim President – Kuwait on the Side of Egyptian People: FM', *Kuwait Times*, 4 July 2013.

102 Patrick Werr, 'UAE Offers Egypt $3 Billion Support, Saudis $5 Billion', *Reuters*, 9 July 2013. Available at <https://www.reuters.com/article/us-egypt-protests-loan/uae-offers-egypt-3-billion-support-saudis-5-billion-idUSBRE9680H020130709> (last accessed 23 October 2022); and 'Kuwait Offers $4 bn Aid Package to Egypt: Minister', *Agence France Presse – English*, 10 July 2013.

103 'Statement by President Barack Obama on Egypt', The White House, 3 July 2013. Available at <https://obamawhitehouse.archives.gov/the-press-office/2013/07/03/statement-president-barack-obama-egypt> (last accessed 23 October 2022).

104 Kevin Cirilli, 'McCain: It Was a Coup, Suspend Aid to Egypt', *Politico*, 7 July 2013. Available at <https://www.politico.com/blogs/politico-now/2013/07/mccain-it-was-a-coup-suspend-aid-to-egypt-167699> (last accessed 23 October

2022). Less than week later, Senator Rand Paul introduced an amendment to end military aid to Egypt. It was defeated, however. See Burgess Everett, 'Paul's Attempt to Cut Egypt Aid Killed', *Politico*, 31 July 2013. Available at <https://www.politico.com/story/2013/07/egypt-aid-rand-paul-094980> (last accessed 23 October 2022). Although Obama did not suspend aid, he did delay the shipment of four F-16 fighter jets to Egypt several weeks later, in a signal of growing displeasure at the course of events.

105   Ran Dagoni, 'Israel Fears US May Suspend Egyptian Aid: Israel Is Concerned that Cutting US Aid to Egypt because of a Military Coup Could Jeopardize the Peace Treaty', *Globes*, 4 July 2013. Available at <https://en.globes.co.il/en/artic le-1000859492> (last accessed 23 October 2022).

106   'Israel Urges US Not to Freeze Egypt Aid: Report', *AFP*, 9 July 2013. Available at <https://www.foxnews.com/world/israel-urges-us-not-to-freeze-egypt-aid -report> (last accessed 23 October 2022).

107   Ibid. Netanyahu 'ordered his ministers to stay silent on the unfolding political crisis in Egypt'. AIPAC also urged US senators to continue funding Egypt after the coup, in a letter addressed to the chair and ranking member of the Foreign Relations Committee. The letter was read on the Senate floor on 31 July 2013. See Ali Gharib, 'Should We Cut Off Egypt Aid? Ask AIPAC', *The Daily Beast*, 2 August 2013. Available at <https://www.thedailybeast.com/should-we-cut -off-egypt-aid-ask-aipac?ref=scroll> (last accessed 23 October 2022).

108   Kareem Fahim and Rick Gladstone, 'Egypt Vows to End Sit-ins by Supporters of Deposed President', *New York Times*, 31 July 2013. Available at <https://www.nytimes.com/2013/08/01/world/middleeast/egypt.html> (last accessed 23 October 2022).

109   'All According to Plan: The Rabʿa Massacre and Mass Killings of Protesters in Egypt', Human Rights Watch, 12 August 2014. Available at <https://www .hrw.org/report/2014/08/12/all-according-plan/raba-massacre-and-mass-killin gs-protesters-egypt> (last accessed 23 October 2022).

110   Other officials had earlier reported that forty-two police and army personnel had been killed.

111   'Remarks by the President on the Situation in Egypt', 15 August 2013. Available at <https://obamawhitehouse.archives.gov/the-press-office/2013/08/15/rema rks-president-situation-egypt> (last accessed 23 October 2022).

112   Obama's reaction to the violence in Egypt came after concerted efforts by the international community to mediate between the Muslim Brotherhood and Morsi supporters and the interim government. Many high-profile diplomats travelled to Cairo in July and August to meet with Egyptian officials and Muslim Brotherhood leaders, including Morsi himself, in prison. This included

the EU's foreign policy chief Catherine Ashton, the State Department's deputy secretary William Burns, the Qatari, Emirati and German foreign ministers, and an African Union delegation led by former Malian president Alpha Oumar Konaré. Obama also dispatched Senators John McCain and Lindsay Graham to Egypt with the goal of averting violence and restoring democratic politics to the country.

113   'Saudi King Backs Egypt's Rulers against "Terrorism"', *Reuters*, 16 August 2013. Available at <https://www.reuters.com/article/us-egypt-protests-saudi /saudi-king-backs-egypts-rulers-against-terrorism-idUSBRE97F0P320130816> (last accessed 23 October 2022).

114   Rod Nordland, 'Saudi Arabia Promises to Aid Egypt's Regime', *New York Times*, 19 August 2013. Available at <https://www.nytimes.com/2013/08/20/ world/middleeast/saudi-arabia-vows-to-back-egypts-rulers.html> (last accessed 23 October 2022). See also, 'Arabs Ready to Cover Cuts in Egypt Foreign Aid: Saudi', *AFP*, 19 August 2013. Available at <https://www.foxnews .com/world/arabs-ready-to-cover-cuts-in-egypt-foreign-aid-saudi> (last accessed 23 October 2022).

115   Interview, Nabil Fahmy, Cairo, Egypt, 28 December 2018.

116   The evidence for this is overwhelming. International diplomats descended on Cairo soon after the coup in an attempt to manage the crisis and avert violence. Reporting about McCain and Graham's efforts to negotiate a peaceful settlement, the *New York Times* noted that 'the Egyptians brushed them off . . . All of the efforts of the United Stated government, all the cajoling, the veiled threats, the high-level envoys from Washington and the 17 personal phone calls by Defense Secretary Chuck Hagel, failed to forestall the worst political bloodletting in modern Egyptian history. The generals in Cairo felt free to ignore the Americans first on the prisoner release [McCain and Graham had called on the interim government to release several Muslim Brotherhood members] and then on the statement, in a cold-eyed calculation that they would not pay a significant cost – a conclusion bolstered when President Obama responded by cancelling a joint military exercise but not $1.5 billion in annual aid.' David D. Kirkpatrick, Peter Baker and Michael R. Gordon, 'How American Hopes for a Deal in Egypt Were Undercut', *New York Times*, 17 August 2013. After the massacre, there were renewed and even louder calls in the US for sanctioning Egypt's generals.

117   Edmund Sanders, 'Israel Walks Fine Line on Egypt Turmoil', *Los Angeles Times*, 19 August 2013. Available at <https://www.latimes.com/world/la-xpm-2013 -aug-19-la-fg-wn-israel-egypt-turmoil-20130819-story.html> (last accessed 23 October 2022). See also, 'Debate over Egypt Aid Splits Supporters of Israel', *The Forward*, 30 August 2013, 1.

118   Edith M. Lederer, 'UN Calls for 'Maximum Restraint' in Egypt', *AP*, 15 August 2013. Available at <https://apnews.com/article/74c92458d38c4d4f953500acb 636f1db> (last accessed 23 October 2022). See also, Steven Erlanger, 'European Union Sets Emergency Session on Suspending Aid to Egypt', *New York Times*, 19 August 2013. Available at <https://www.nytimes.com/2013/08/20/world /middleeast/european-union-sets-emergency-session-on-suspending-aid-to-egy pt.html?pagewanted=all> (last accessed 23 October 2022).

119   Jodi Rudoren, 'Israel Escalating Efforts to Shape Allies' Strategy', *New York Times*, 18 August 2013. Available at <https://www.nytimes.com/2013/08/19 /world/middleeast/israel-puts-more-urgency-on-shaping-allies-actions.html?pa gewanted=all> (last accessed 23 October 2022).

120   Ibid.

121   'Egypt Got $23 Billion in Aid from Gulf in 18 Months – Minister', *Reuters*, 2 March 2015. Available at <https://uk.reuters.com/article/uk-egypt-invest ment-gulf/egypt-got-23-billion-in-aid-from-gulf-in-18-months-minister-idUK KBN0LY0UT20150302> (last accessed summer 2019).

122   'What was Pledged at Egypt's Investment Conference?' *Atlantic Council*, 17 March 2015. Available at <https://www.atlanticcouncil.org/blogs/mena source/what-was-pledged-at-egypt-s-investment-conference/> (last accessed 23 October 2022).

123   Brian Rohan and Sarah El Deeb, 'Egypt Basks in World Support at Investor Conference', *AP*, 15 March 2015. Available at <https://apnews.com/article/ac 7a6f6cef8540979d79fa309510749f> (last accessed 23 October 2022).

124   It is nearly impossible to accurately assess the extent to which these commit-ments of aid and investment were realised. Saudi Arabia and the other Gulf states have a history of large promises of aid and investment and delivering much smaller amounts, which are also often delayed.

125   'Saudi King Signs Aid Deals Worth $24 Billion', *Economist*, 11 April 2016. Available at <http://country.eiu.com/article.aspx?articleid=1794120563> (last accessed 23 October 2022).

126   'Saudi Arabia to Supply Egypt with 700,000 Tonnes of Petroleum Products a Month', *Reuters*, April 11, 2016. Available at <https://www.reuters.com/artic le/egypt-saudi-oil/saudi-arabia-to-supply-egypt-with-700000-tonnes-of-petrole um-products-a-month-idUSL5N17E1VH> (last accessed 23 October 2022).

127   Ali Abdelaty, 'Egypt, Saudi Arabia Sign 60 Billion Saudi Riyal Investment Fund Pact', *Reuters*, 9 April 2016. Available at <https://www.reuters.com/article/us -egypt-saudi-idUSKCN0X60VQ> (last accessed 23 October 2022).

128   Declan Walsh, 'Egypt Gives Saudi Arabia 2 Islands in a Show of Gratitude', *New York Times*, 16 April 2016. Available at <https://www.nytimes.com/2016/04

/11/world/middleeast/egypt-gives-saudi-arabia-2-islands-in-a-show-of-gratitu
de.html> (last accessed 23 October 2022).

129   John Dennehy, 'UAE and Egypt Launch $20 Billion Joint Investment Platform',
The National, 14 November 2019. Available at <https://www.thenationalne
ws.com/uae/government/uae-and-egypt-launch-20bn-joint-investment-platfo
rm-1.937533> (last accessed 23 October 2022). See also Abdel Latif Wahba,
'Egypt, UAE to Set Up $20 Billion Joint Investment Platform', *Bloomberg*,
14 November 2019. Available at <https://www.bloomberg.com/news/artic
les/2019-11-14/egypt-u-a-e-to-set-up-20b-joint-investment-platform>   (last
accessed summer 2019). It was not clear how much progress had been made on
the UAE–Egypt joint investment platform by 2021.

130   'Investment Bottlenecks to Be Removed', *Saudi Gazette*, 27 November 2018.
Available at <https://saudigazette.com.sa/article/548999/SAUDI-ARABIA
/Investment-bottlenecks-to-be-removed> (last accessed 23 October 2022);
'Saudi–Egyptian Business Council Encourages Further Cooperation', *Asharq
Al-Awsat*, 25 February 2019. Available at <https://english.aawsat.com/home
/article/1607191/saudi-egyptian-business-council-encourages-further-cooper
ation> (last accessed 23 October 2022); 'Saudi Arabia's Economic Investments
in Egypt Run Deep', *Arab News*, 5 March 2018. Available at <https://www
.arabnews.com/node/1259251/saudi-arabia> (last accessed 23 October 2022).
There are also claims that Saudi Arabia is the single largest foreign investor in the
country, although there are similar Emirati claims.

131   David Butter, 'Egypt and the Gulf: Allies and Rivals', Chatham House, 20 April
2020, 12–13. Available at <https://www.chathamhouse.org/sites/default/files/
CHHJ8102-Egypt-and-Gulf-RP-WEB_0.pdf> (last accessed 23 October 2022).

132   Ibid.

133   '92 milyar duwlar d'am khaleeji lil Qahira munthu thawrat 25 yanayyir' [92 billion dollars of Gulf support to Cairo since the 25 January revolution), *Al Qabas*,
20 March 2019. Available at <https://alqabas.com/article/647244-92> (last
accessed 23 October 2022). Both *AhramOnline* and the Atlantic Council subsequently reported the US$92 billion figure after the 2015 Sharm El Sheikh con-
ference. See 'Egypt Signed Final Investment Deals Worth $33 Bn at Conference:
Salman', *AhramOnline*, 15 March 2015. Available at <http://english.ahram
.org.eg/NewsContent/3/162/125291/Business/EEDC-/Egypt-signed-inal-in
vestment-deals-worth--bn-at-c.aspx> (last accessed 23 October 2022); and 'One
Year On: The Economy Under Sisi', *Atlantic Council*, 9 June 2015. Available
at <https://www.atlanticcouncil.org/blogs/menasource/one-year-on-the-econ
omy-under-sisi/> (last accessed 23 October 2022).

134   Of course, this figure is an estimate and as stated earlier, it is often the case that

Saudi and other Gulf promises of aid and investment are either not realised, delayed or overvalued. The point is that Egypt has received massive and unprecedented amounts of economic support in the form of aid, investment and subsidised fuel from Saudi Arabia, the UAE and Kuwait since the coup. The political intent of this should be obvious. Moreover, the figures estimated above do not include additional forms of financial support. For example, Egypt received additional economic assistance from the Gulf states with the purchase of twenty-four French Rafale fighter jets in 2015. 'Saudi Arabia, UAE, Kuwait pumped US$19.5 billion into the Egyptian central bank which enabled French lending institutions to finance Cairo's Rafale fighter purchase,' according to *Defense World*. 'A banking source in London contacted by defenseworld.net said this is perhaps the first time an arms deal which resembles a large industrial investment has been worked out.' See 'Saudi, UAE, Kuwait Helped Finance Egypt's Rafale Buy', *Defense World.Net*, 17 February 2015. Available at <https://www.defense world.net/news/12196/Saudi__UAE__Kuwait_Helped_Finance_Egypt___s _Rafale_Buy#.YQK6BRNKjjA> (last accessed summer 2019). Egypt has also received smaller amounts of aid from the UAE for lobbying efforts in the US and spyware technology that are also not accounted for in these figures. See Zaid Jilani, 'The UAE Secretly Picked Up the Tab for the Egyptian Dictatorship's D.C. Lobbying', *The Intercept*, 4 October 2017. Available at <https://theinter cept.com/2017/10/04/egypt-lobbying-uae-otaiba-trump-sisi/> (last accessed 23 October 2022); and 'UAE Transfers Internet Surveillance System Bought from French Company to Egypt: Télérama', *Mada Masr*, 5 July 2017. Available at <https://www.madamasr.com/en/2017/07/05/news/u/uae-transfers-intern et-surveillance-system-bought-from-french-company-to-egypt-telerama/> (last accessed 23 October 2022).

135 Jason Brownlee, *Democracy Prevention: The Politics of the US–Egyptian Alliance* (New York: Cambridge University Press, 2012).

136 Saudi Arabia committed US$15 billion of investments and central bank deposits while Abu Dhabi's investment and holding company ADQ committed to purchase US$2 billion worth of Egyptian state-held stakes in publicly listed companies. Following the 2021 resolution of the 'GCC crisis' and warming relations between Doha and Cairo, Qatar also pledged an additional US$5 billion worth of investments in the Egyptian economy, increasing the total amount of Gulf money pledged to Egypt during 2022 to a jaw-dropping US$22 billion. See Dominic Dudley, 'Rich Gulf States Line Up to Offer Egypt Billions of Dollars', *Forbes*, 30 March 2022. Available at <https://www.forbes.com/sites/dominic dudley/2022/03/30/rich-gulf-states-line-up-to-offer-egypt-billions-of-dollars/ ?sh=61f415ce7da3> (last accessed 23 October 2022).

9

AL-QAIDA'S FAILURE IN THE FERTILE CRESCENT

Cole Bunzel

The US-led invasion of Iraq in 2003 and the uprising in neighbouring Syria in 2011 presented unique opportunities for Sunni jihadi militants. The invasion and occupation of Iraq created a security vacuum that the jihadis were quick to fill. Eight years later, the protest movement in Syria, which started as a call for dignity and political representation, likewise created the insecure conditions that the jihadis were able to exploit. Al-Qaida affiliates quickly arose in both countries, giving the impression that al-Qaida benefitted considerably from these security vacuums. This perception, however, is for the most part unfounded.

To be sure, al-Qaida did succeed in establishing an official presence in each of these countries, thus enhancing al-Qaida's brand and raising its international profile. The main jihadi force in Iraq, Abu Mus'ab al-Zarqawi's Jama'at al-Tawhid wa'l-Jihad, rebranded as al-Qaida in Mesopotamia in 2004. Nine years later, in 2013, the leading jihadi group in Syria, Abu Muhammad al-Jawlani's Jabhat al-Nusra, declared its loyalty to al-Qaida. However, in each of these cases the role actually played by al-Qaida in the local affiliate was limited in both extent and duration. The leaders of these affiliates were not dispatched by the senior al-Qaida leadership based in the Afghanistan/Pakistan region, or what is commonly known as al-Qaida central. These groups were not established at the behest of al-Qaida but rather declared their affiliation later on. Once the affiliation was declared, the leaders of the affiliates largely pursued their own agendas, never showing much deference to al-Qaida's leaders. Furthermore, neither affiliate remained long in the al-Qaida fold. In 2006, al-Zarqawi's al-Qaida in Mesopotamia transformed itself into the Islamic State of Iraq, which enjoyed a more tenuous link to al-Qaida that was finally severed with announcement of the Islamic State of Iraq and al-Sham (ISIS) in 2013. Similarly, in 2016–17, al-Jawlani's Jabhat al-Nusra gradually evolved into the group known as Hay'at Tahrir al-Sham, the formation of which marked a decisive breaking of ties with al-Qaida. In each of these cases al-Qaida opposed the independent drift of the affiliate, yet the affiliate proceeded on its course anyway.

Upon closer examination, al-Qaida's record in Iraq and Syria is one of abysmal failure. Not only did al-Qaida fail to exercise influence over its affiliates in the Fertile Crescent, it lost control of them entirely, its orders being defied in humiliating fashion. Nonetheless, the perception that al-Qaida benefitted from the unrest in Iraq and Syria has lingered. For instance, between 2006 and 2013, the Islamic State of Iraq was still commonly referred to, in government and media circles, as 'al-Qaida in Iraq', creating the impression of a deep and significant connection to al-Qaida central. Similarly, though Jabhat al-Nusra had transformed itself into Hay'at Tahrir al-Sham by early 2017, some government sources and media outlets would continue to identify it as al-Qaida or 'al-Qaida-linked'. All of this was to give al-Qaida far too much credit. In order to show the true nature and extent of al-Qaida's relationship with these groups, the following traces the making and unmaking of al-Qaida affiliates in these countries, highlighting al-Qaida's failure to shape a new regional order in the Fertile Crescent.

The *al-Qaida* in al-Qaida in Iraq

In the month before the March 2003 invasion of Iraq, Osama bin Laden released an audio statement calling on the people of Iraq to resist the impending American invasion and to draw the US into a long war.[1] All those who cooperated with the invaders, he said, are apostates whose blood is to be considered licit. But bin Laden was thinking larger than Iraq at the time. In his mind the Iraq resistance was to lead to the overthrow of the region's many 'oppressive and apostate ruling regimes in thrall to America'.

From an undisclosed location, bin Laden was hoping, by the power of his words, to inspire an uprising in Iraq that would propel a larger reconfiguration of the Middle East's political landscape. The problem was that al-Qaida was not in Iraq at the time. It was another jihadi leader, the Jordanian Abu Mus'ab al-Zarqawi, who was lying in wait for the Americans there and who would spearhead the local jihadi opposition. And it was Zarqawi who was responsible for devising and implementing the strategy that the jihadis in Iraq would pursue. As will be seen, this was a sectarian strategy focused on attacking Iraqi Shi'a, whom Zarqawi and his comrades perceived not only as heretics but also as collaborators of the Americans. While al-Qaida signalled its acceptance of this strategy at the beginning, it never seems to have wholeheartedly embraced it. The backdrop to this dispute between al-Qaida and Zarqawi is an ideological division in the jihadi movement that goes back years.

Zarqawi, it must be understood, was not a member of al-Qaida at the time that he formulated his Shi'a-focused strategy for Iraq, though he had had some dealings with al-Qaida before. In 1999, he was released from prison in Jordan and promptly left for Afghanistan, where he formed a relationship with some al-Qaida members but did not pledge *bay'a* (the contract of allegiance) to bin Laden. In coordination with a senior al-Qaida official named Sayf al-'Adl, he set up a training camp in Herat, in the far west of the country. The distance from the al-Qaida leadership based around Kandahar was deliberate. As al-'Adl would later write, Zarqawi and al-Qaida were not on the same page ideologically. In an essay published in 2005, he cited what al-Qaida deemed Zarqawi's 'extremist views' (*ara' mutashaddida*) on matters of theology (*'aqida*), including such matters as association and dissociation (*al-wala' wa'l-bara'*) and excommunication (*takfir*).[2] This was a reference to Zarqawi's strict adherence to Salafism, the purist movement in Sunni Islam associated with religious thought of Ibn Taymiyya (d. 1328) and his heirs in the Wahhabi movement that emerged in the Arabian Peninsula in the eighteenth century. Zarqawi was a student of the Palestinian-Jordanian jihadi scholar Abu Muhammad al-Maqdisi, who played a leading role in developing a more Salafi – that is, more purist and exclusivist – version of jihadism. The Salafi doctrine, particularly as developed by al-Maqdisi, emphasised the duties of separating from Muslims seen as deviant and of excommunicating those considered to have committed acts of unbelief. This was a more rigid and exclusionary form of Sunni jihadism than the one represented by al-Qaida, a group that sought to appeal to the global community of Muslims, or the *umma*, at large, not just to a small subset of Salafis.[3]

Nonetheless, al-'Adl thought it a good idea to win Zarqawi to al-Qaida's side as much as possible. He therefore helped procure the resources for Zarqawi's training camp, which the Jordanian operated with some of his followers from 1999 until 2001. The events of 9/11 would bring a swift end to Zarqawi's Afghan activities.[4]

Following the US invasion of Afghanistan in October 2001, Zarqawi and some his followers fled to Iran, where they decided on Iraq as their next destination. Iraq, they determined, would sooner or later be the target of a US military campaign, and so it behoved them to prepare the groundwork for an insurgency. In 2002, with the help of the Kurdish jihadi group Ansar al-Islam, Zarqawi entered northern Iraq, from where he would go on to found Jama'at al-Tawhid wa'l-Jihad (The Group of God's Oneness and Jihad).[5] The latter was active in Iraq from at least August 2003, but only announced its existence in April 2004.[6] After attacking the Jordanian embassy and UN headquarters in Baghdad, it turned its attention to the Iraqi Shi'a. In late August 2003, it bombed the Imam 'Ali Mosque in Najaf, killing the Ayatollah Muhammad Baqir al-Hakim and dozens more Shi'ite worshippers. And in spring 2004, it targeted Shi'ite civilians en masse in Baghdad and Karbala during the 'Ashura holiday. All of this was a preview of more atrocities against the Shi'a to come.

The targeting of the Shi'a was the central plank of Zarqawi's strategy, one that he outlined in a long letter addressed to the leaders of al-Qaida in February 2004.[7] In the letter Zarqawi argued that only by instigating a civil war between Sunnis and Shi'a in Iraq could the jihadis achieve their objective of attaining power. The Shi'a, he wrote, were not only heretical in their beliefs but were also a devious and cunning enemy. They were plotting to take control of the country and intended to take revenge on the Sunnis upon the Americans' departure. Therefore, the danger of the Shi'a was greater than that of the Americans. Only by striking them and 'dragging them into the arena of sectarian war', thereby exposing their true nature, would the jihadis be able to rally the Sunnis of Iraq to their cause.

Zarqawi's letter was more than a strategic document, however. It was also a proposal. Towards the end of it, he proposed a merger with al-Qaida on the condition that the latter give its blessing to the strategy as he outlined. He wrote:

> This is our vision as we have explained it, and this is our path as we have illuminated it. If you agree to it and adopt it as your method and your path, and if you are convinced by the idea of fighting the apostate sects, then we are your ready soldiers. We shall act under your banner and submit to your command. Indeed, we will pledge *bay'a* openly and in public.

As is clear from what followed, al-Qaida responded in the affirmative.

In October 2004, Zarqawi released an audio statement pledging *bay'a* to bin Laden, noting that al-Qaida had endorsed its strategic vision. 'Our noble brothers in al-Qaida', he said, 'have comprehended the strategy of Jama'at al-Tawhid wa'l-Jihad in Mesopotamia, the land of the caliphs, and their hearts opened to our method therein.'[8] Henceforward, Zarqawi's group would be known as al-Qaida in Mesopotamia (Tanzim al-Qaʻida fi Bilad al-Rafidayn). Zarqawi was thus keen to make his alliance with al-Qaida conditional, and to make the condition of his *bayʻa* public. The message he was broadcasting was to the effect that we are joining al-Qaida, but it is on our terms and we are following the strategy that we have outlined.

Why Zarqawi would seek to join his group to al-Qaida in the first place is less clear, particularly given the ideological divergence between himself and bin Laden. Zarqawi's motives in this regard probably had more to do with enhancing the status of his group, thus gaining access to more resources and recruits, than with anything else.[9] In summer 2003, he submitted a request to al-Qaida for 'money and supplies' through an intermediary.[10] Al-Qaida, for its part, was also interested in enhancing its brand. By agreeing to Zarqawi's strategy, it was rewarded with an official franchise in the heart of the Middle East, and one that was waging war against al-Qaida's chief enemy in the Americans. Perhaps al-Qaida's leaders thought that by formalising a relationship with him they could reshape Zarqawi's efforts in a direction more to their liking. If that is the case, they were sorely mistaken.

It was not long before tensions between al-Qaida and its new Iraqi affiliate became apparent. The first sign could be seen in a July 2005 letter from Ayman al-Zawahiri, the deputy leader of al-Qaida at the time, to Zarqawi, in which Zawahiri called into question the strategy that al-Qaida had purportedly agreed to.[11] While cordial in tone, the letter was in substance highly critical, urging Zarqawi to cease his attacks on Shiʻa civilians and to refrain from acts of extreme violence such as gruesome beheadings. All of this, Zawahiri argued, was counterproductive in that it alienated the great masses of Sunni Muslims whose support was indispensable. In his view the focus ought to be on expelling the Americans. He cast doubt on the permissibility of attacking Shiʻa civilians, saying that ordinary Shiʻa should be excused their errant beliefs on account of ignorance. The letter must have come as quite a shock to Zarqawi, given that Zawahiri was criticising a strategy that it had apparently signed off on. Zarqawi's response appears to have been to ignore the al-Qaida deputy leader.

Later that year, in December, the al-Qaida official and ideologue 'Atiyyat Allah al-Libi sent Zarqawi another admonishing letter.[12] Referring to

Zawahiri's earlier missive, al-Libi urged Zarqawi to send envoys to Waziristan and to refrain from taking major steps without consulting the al-Qaida leadership. He expressed frustration with the current absence of communication between al-Qaida in Mesopotamia and al-Qaida central, referring to the 'current disruption and loss of communication'.

From the two letters, it appears that there was little if any communication between Zarqawi and al-Qaida at this time. Zarqawi's group may have been operating under the al-Qaida banner, but there is hardly any evidence that al-Qaida was able to shape or modify its behaviour. Zarqawi never appears to have subordinated himself or his forces to al-Qaida in a meaningful way.

In January 2006, Zarqawi set in motion a process that would lead to the official dissolution of al-Qaida in Mesopotamia. This began with the formation of an umbrella organisation called the Mujahidin Shura Council, which brought together five other jihadi groups in Iraq with Zarqawi's. A few months later, he described the Mujahidin Shura Council as 'the starting point for establishing an Islamic state'.[13] In June, Zarqawi was killed in a US airstrike, but the state that he foretold was soon announced. In October 2006, the successor to the Mujahidin Shura Council announced the establishment of the Islamic State of Iraq (Dawlat al-'Iraq al-Islamiyya). As would later be revealed, al-Qaida had no part in this development, neither having approved of it nor having been consulted about it. In 2014, Zawahiri explained all of this in an audio message detailing al-Qaida's history with the Islamic State of Iraq.[14] The Islamic State of Iraq did profess its loyalty to al-Qaida in private, however, he averred.

In the years that followed, al-Qaida groused about the Islamic State of Iraq's lack of deference and willingness to communicate. In the two years following the Islamic State of Iraq's announcement, al-Qaida's leaders sent messages to the group asking for updates and complaining about the absence of communication. Sayf al-'Adl, in a November 2007 letter to Abu Hamza al-Muhajir, the Islamic State of Iraq's second in command, urged his correspondent to send letters to the al-Qaida leadership providing updates on conditions in Iraq, noting that al-Qaida was still awaiting responses to its previous requests. In March 2008, Zawahiri repeated the request in another letter to Abu Hamza.[15] So bad was the state of communication that Zawahiri included al-'Adl's earlier letter because he was unsure that it had been received.

In his 2014 audio statement, Zawahiri cited some correspondence between the two groups,[16] so there was at least some communication. But the degree of cooperation between the two sides never seems to have amounted to much. In early 2011, the American al-Qaida spokesman Adam Gahdan wrote to bin Laden expressing his view that al-Qaida should officially cut ties with the Islamic State of Iraq. He complained that what ties there were 'have been effectively severed for a number of years'. Failing to dissociate from the Islamic State of Iraq, he warned, would 'damage the reputation' of al-Qaida, citing the Islamic State of Iraq's targeting of mosques and other policies out of line with al-Qaida's stated positions.[17] Ironically, the American government and media still referred to the Islamic State of Iraq as al-Qaida in Iraq during this time, giving the misleading impression that al-Qaida was very much involved in the Iraqi group's affairs.[18] As it happened, Gahdan would soon be proved right in his assessment of where things stood.

Losing the Islamic State of Iraq

What brought matters to a head was a public dispute in 2013 between the Islamic State of Iraq and what it considered to be its Syrian subsidiary, Jabhat al-Nusra.[19] In late 2011, the leader of the Islamic State of Iraq, Abu Bakr al-Baghdadi, dispatched a contingent of fighters to northern Syria to take advantage of the developing security vacuum there. In January 2012, the fighters, led by the Syrian Abu Muhammad al-Jawlani, announced the formation of Jabhat al-Nusra (The Support Front), which said nothing of any connection to al-Qaida or the Islamic State of Iraq, presenting itself as a mainly Syrian organisation.[20] Over the course of the next year, as Jabhat al-Nusra grew in size and popularity, al-Baghdadi sensed that he was losing control over al-Jawlani's group. This led him to announce, on 9 April 2013, the dissolution of Jabhat al-Nusra. Explaining that the latter was merely a front for the Islamic State of Iraq, he announced the expansion of the Islamic State of Iraq to the land of greater Syria, or al-Sham, thus retitling his group – or 'state' – as the Islamic State of Iraq and al-Sham (al-Dawla al-Islamiyya fi 'l-'Iraq wa'l-Sham, ISIS).[21] The next day, on 10 April, al-Jawlani released a statement of his own rejecting al-Baghdadi's claim to have dissolved Jabhat al-Nusra, affirming that his group would continue to exist. In doing so, he 'reaffirmed' his *bay'a* to al-Qaida leader Zawahiri, thus appealing to an ostensibly higher authority than al-Baghdadi.[22]

As the two groups struggled for control of the jihadi scene in Syria, Zawahiri, now the head of al-Qaida, sent a letter to al-Baghdadi and al-Jawlani attempting to settle the dispute. Dated 23 May 2013, Zawahiri's letter faulted both leaders for having taken important steps without his approval

– Baghdadi's announcement of the Islamic State of Iraq and al-Sham, and al-Jawlani's announcement of his affiliation with al-Qaida, which was supposed to have remained secret. Overall, however, the letter was more favourable to al-Jawlani. Zawahiri ruled that the Islamic State of Iraq and al-Sham ought to revert back to being the Islamic State of Iraq and to operate only in Iraq, and he ruled that Jabhat al-Nusra was to be 'an independent branch' of al-Qaida whose jurisdiction is Syria. Looking ahead, he decreed that each leader was to remain in his post for one more year only, whereafter the al-Qaida leadership would determine whether he should remain or be replaced.[23]

While al-Jawlani embraced his new status as the leader of an independent al-Qaida affiliate, al-Baghdadi refused to accept Zawahiri's verdict. In an audio statement released in June, he declared that the Islamic State of Iraq and al-Sham was here to stay, citing a series of unspecified 'legal and methodological objections' with Zawahiri's decision.[24] Days later, Abu Muhammad al-'Adnani, the official speaker of ISIS, elaborated seven of these objections in a long audio message. These centred around the idea that Jabhat al-Nusra's leaders were illegitimate defectors who should not be rewarded for spurning al-Baghdadi's authority, and that the order to divide the mujahidin of Iraq and al-Sham amounted to an order to commit a sin (*ma'siya*).[25]

Another point of contention, related to the legitimacy of Zawahiri's ruling, concerned the history of relations between the Islamic State of Iraq and al-Qaida. The question was whether the Islamic State of Iraq was at one point an al-Qaida affiliate and so obligated to heed Zawahiri's commands, or whether it was an independent emirate from its founding in 2006. In May 2014, Zawahiri released a statement, complete with quotations of old correspondence, intended to prove that the Islamic State of Iraq was indeed 'a branch subservient to the Qa'idat al-Jihad group'.[26] Quoting old correspondence, he sought to prove that the Islamic State of Iraq had pledged *bay'a* to al-Qaida, but the best piece of evidence that Zawahiri was able to marshal was a letter asking al-Qaida if it should renew its *bay'a* in private after bin Laden's death in 2011. A representative of the Islamic State of Iraq wrote to an al-Qaida official, Abu Yahya al-Libi, asking, 'Should the State renew its *bay'a* openly, or keep it secret as was known and observed previously?' To Zawahiri this may have seemed like conclusive evidence, but to the Islamic State it was not. There was no letter from the leaders of the Islamic State of Iraq pledging *bay'a* to bin Laden or Zawahiri, leaving enough room for ISIS to argue that there had never been a *bay'a*.

Thus Al-'Adnani shot back at Zawahiri in a statement disputing his claim.[27] 'The State', he said, 'is not a subsidiary branch of al-Qaida, nor has it ever been so . . . It is not valid for an emirate or a state to pledge *bay'a* to an organisation.' While it is true, he conceded, that the Islamic State of Iraq had professed its 'loyalty' (*wala*) to al-Qaida's leadership in private, this did not establish it as an affiliate. Out of respect, he said, the Islamic State of Iraq heeded al-Qaida's instructions when it came to policy outside Iraq – for example, not attacking the Shi'a in Iran. But inside Iraq, it ignored al-Qaida's commands, as in its refusal to cease attacks against the Iraqi Shi'a. ISIS was thus under no obligation to obey Zawahiri in the matter concerning Syria and Jabhat al-Nusra.

In his statement, al-'Adnani raised another issue that would come to dominate the growing rivalry between al-Qaida and ISIS, namely their differences over ideology. Al-'Adnani accused al-Qaida under Zawahiri of having changed its methodology (*manhaj*), calling on him to correct his *manhaj* by taking a clearer stance on such issues as the Shi'a, President Mohamed Morsi of Egypt and regional militaries. Zawahiri's al-Qaida, according to al-'Adnani, was hesitant to pronounce *takfir* on the Shi'a, Morsi, and the Egyptian, Pakistani, Afghan, Tunisian, Libyan and Yemeni armies, among others. Al-'Adnani's attack marked a new turn. Henceforward, ISIS would portray al-Qaida's leaders and supporters as Murji'ites, a theological term meaning those who postpone judgments of *takfir*. In this way, ISIS was presenting Zawahiri's al-Qaida as fundamentally different from bin Laden's. 'The dispute between the Islamic State and the leadership of the al-Qaida organisation is a methodological dispute,' al-'Adnani stated. 'This is the issue, and not who has *bay'a* to whom.' In other words, the issue of ideology was more important than the issue of *bay'a*. In response, al-Qaida would begin to cast ISIS as a group of Kharijites, the early Islamic sect distinguished by extremism in *takfir*.[28] While both sides portrayed the ideological rift as a recent development, in reality differences in ideology could be traced back to the days of Zarqawi and earlier. Zarqawi's group was always more Salafi in orientation than al-Qaida, while al-Qaida always laid far more emphasis on pan-Islamic appeal.

A few months later, in June, ISIS took the step of declaring itself the revived caliphate, shortening its name to the Islamic State (al-Dawla al-Islamiyya). In announcing the caliphate, al-'Adnani maintained that all jihadi groups – including al-Qaida – were thereby dissolved, being obligated to join the caliphate. Addressing the 'soldiers of groups and organisations', he stated,

'The legitimacy of your groups and organisations is void.' All were expected, indeed required, to pledge *bay'a* to the leader of the Islamic State as caliph.[29] Thus, in the span of just over a year, the Islamic State had gone from contesting al-Qaida's claim to authority over it to asserting its own authority over al-Qaida. Many jihadi groups around the world, of course, including al-Qaida, rejected the absolutist claims of the new 'caliphate'.

Losing Jabhat al-Nusra

Having officially lost the Islamic State of Iraq in 2013–14, al-Qaida could perhaps console itself with the fact that it had established an official presence in Syria in the form of Jabhat al-Nusra. However, it was not long before al-Qaida began to lose its grip over al-Jawlani's group as well. In mid-2016, after more than a year of rumours that a break with al-Qaida was in the offing, Jabhat al-Nusra announced that it was leaving al-Qaida and rebranding.[30] The announcement was choreographed to show that the move had the full support and approval of al-Qaida, but it soon emerged that Zawahiri was not on board.[31]

On 28 July 2016, al-Jawlani appeared in a short video announcing the end of Jabhat al-Nusra and the formation of a new group, Jabhat Fath al-Sham (The Front for the Conquest of al-Sham), which was to have no connection to any foreign entity – that is, no ties to al-Qaida.[32] The stated goal of the new group was to establish God's religion and to unite the various mujahid factions in Syria. Indeed, the main reason al-Jawlani sought to rebrand was that Jabhat al-Nusra's status as an al-Qaida affiliate was making it difficult to unite the various rebel groups under his command. Some of these groups were worried that affiliating with Jabhat al-Nusra would expose them to US aerial attack; those that received funds from neighbouring states worried that it would jeopardise their funding streams. By rebranding as Jabhat Fath al-Sham, the leadership of Jabhat al-Nusra thought it might be able to allay these and similar concerns.

Al-Jawlani's video address was preceded by a short statement by an al-Qaida official giving al-Jawlani the green light.[33] The official, an Egyptian named Abu al-Khayr al-Masri, was in Syria at the time and had the role of al-Qaida's chief liaison with the Jabhat al-Nusra. In the statement, he indicated that Jabhat al-Nusra was free to do as it saw fit. 'We instruct the leadership of Jabhat al-Nusra to go forward according to what will preserve the welfare of Islam and the Muslims and protect the jihad of the people of al-Sham,' he said.

'We urge them to take the appropriate steps in this regard.' In his statement, Abu al-Khayr alluded to a recent audio address by Zawahiri that seemed to suggest a path forward for Jabhat al-Nusra independent of al-Qaida. Zawahiri had stated, concerning Jabhat al-Nusra's link to al-Qaida, that 'organisational affiliation will never be, God willing, an obstacle' to the unity of the mujahidin in al-Sham. If the mujahidin were to come together to form 'a mujahid, right-guided Islamic government that spreads justice, extends consultation, restores rights, helps the downtrodden, and revives jihad', then al-Qaida would not stand in the way.[34] By alluding to this statement, Abu al-Khayr was channelling the authority of Zawahiri. The entire affair was orchestrated so as to show that al-Qaida and Jabhat al-Nusra were in agreement regarding what was taking place.

The Jabhat Fath al-Sham project did not play out as anticipated, however, as many Syrian Islamist rebel formations resisted the unification efforts of the rebranded group. In late January 2017, Jabhat Fath al-Sham, together with four other similarly hardline groups, rebranded again when it announced the formation of Hay'at Tahrir al-Sham (The Committee for the Liberation of al-Sham, HTS).[35] HTS would take a more aggressive approach to effecting unity than its predecessor, seeking to control the rebel scene by force of arms if necessary. And it would place more emphasis on governance and administration than its predecessors, even as the Bashar al-Assad regime reasserted control over territory in northern Syria and the rebellion became increasingly confined to the province of Idlib. In November 2017, HTS announced the establishment of 'The Salvation Government' (Hukumat al-Inqadh) as the governing body in Idlib Province.

Shortly after the announcement of HTS, it emerged that all was not well between al-Qaida and its former affiliate. On 8 February 2017, two former Jabhat al-Nusra officials made clear in a statement that they had nothing to do with HTS, saying, 'We no longer have any organisational link to this new formation.'[36] One of these men was a Jordanian named Sami al-'Uraydi, who had served as Jabhat al-Nusra's senior most religious authority. On the same day, al-'Uraydi posted a comment on the Telegram messenger platform pointing to problems between HTS and al-Qaida.[37] The comment read: 'Among the greatest forms of disobedience is disobedience to the mother organisation; after it raised them as children, they disobeyed it when one of them started learning to speak.' Al-'Uraydi, it appeared, was accusing Jabhat al-Nusra, or one of its successor organisations, of disobeying al-Qaida. 'Uraydi had tweeted these exact same words back in 2015 when he was condemning ISIS's disobedience of al-Qaida.[38]

Details of what had taken place between al-Jawlani's group and al-Qaida soon began to leak from jihadi sources online. One of these sources was the jihadi scholar Abu Muhammad al-Maqdisi, mentioned above as a teacher of Zarqawi's. On 14 February 2017, al-Maqdisi wrote an essay asserting that Zawahiri had not approved of Jabhat al-Nusra's separation from al-Qaida.[39] Back in July 2016, he explained, a senior member of Jabhat al-Nusra wrote to him (that is, al-Maqdisi) seeking his support for the coming breaking of ties, claiming that the break was only to be 'superficial and nominal, not real', and that the move had the support of 'the majority of the deputies' of Zawahiri. In reality, al-Maqdisi continued, al-Qaida's leadership did not agree with the split, and 'when news of the rejection came, they [Jabhat al-Nusra's leaders] did not fulfil their promise to retreat from the superficial step, as they claimed and promised that they would. Rather they stayed the course until they made it a real breaking of ties.' In the coming months, more authoritative sources would confirm the main lines of al-Maqdisi's account.

The full story of what transpired did not emerge until the fall of that year. It was revealed as part of a written back and forth between al-'Uraydi and a senior HTS official named Abu 'Abdallah al-Shami (aka 'Abd al-Rahim 'Atun). The starting point for their exchange was criticism of HTS by Zawahiri. In April 2017, Zawahiri berated HTS in an audio message for focusing on administering territory when it ought to be preparing for a long campaign of guerilla warfare.[40] In a longer and even more critical audio message, released on 4 October 2017, he accused HTS of playing into the hands of the US by leaving al-Qaida and making jihad in Syria a national struggle.[41] America's objective, he said, is to divide the jihadis in Syria and elsewhere and to turn their global jihad into various national ones. He excoriated those who would renege on their *bay'as* with such excuses as 'we wish to escape bombardment' and 'the foreign backers have made it a condition' that we do so. In neither of these statements did Zawahiri refer to HTS by name, but it was perfectly clear whom he was criticising.

About a week after the second statement, on 13 October, Abu 'Abdallah al-Shami published a long response to Zawahiri in a closed forum online.[42] The response was leaked, however, reaching al-'Uraydi and others and thus leading to the back and forth. Recounting the history of Jabhat al-Nusra's development into HTS, al-Shami claimed that Jabhat al-Nusra's leaders had done nothing wrong, at one point declaring, 'We did not violate the *bay'a* or the compact, and we proceeded in a manner consistent with the Sharia and the organisation. We are not responsible for the problems that occurred.' The problems, he claimed, were 'organisational' ones bound up in the 'structure' of al-Qaida. And a particular problem was the lack of any contact with Zawahiri for an extended period – nearly three years.

For two years and ten months, al-Shami revealed, Zawahiri was incommunicado for reasons to do with his security, re-establishing contact with his deputies only just before the announcement of Jabhat Fath al-Sham, in July 2016. During this period, Jabhat al-Nusra's main al-Qaida contact was Abu al-Khayr al-Masri, who was released from Iranian detention sometime in 2015 as part of a prisoner exchange with Iran.[43] Abu al-Khayr, who presented himself as Zawahiri's chief deputy, arrived in Syria along with a number of other al-Qaida members. Also as part of the exchange, two senior al-Qaida members, Abu Muhammad al-Masri and Sayf al-'Adl, were released from Iranian detention but prohibited from leaving Iran.[44] As al-Shami explained, Abu al-Khayr al-Masri, Abu Muhammad al-Masri and Sayf al-'Adl proceeded to form a leadership council for making important decisions during Zawahiri's absence.

It was against this backdrop that the leadership of Jabhat al-Nusra met with Abu al-Khayr, in mid-2016, to discuss the possibility of rebranding Jabhat al-Nusra. According to al-Shami, the proposal put forward by al-Jawlani was for Jabhat al-Nusra to change its name and announce an apparent breaking of ties (*fakk al-irtibat*) with al-Qaida; the rebranded group would maintain its al-Qaida affiliation in secret. Then, if the unity was achieved with the other rebel groups in Syria, the breaking of ties would become real. In other words, the rebranding as Jabhat Fath al-Sham was intended to obscure the relationship with al-Qaida while setting the stage for a possible actual split with al-Qaida. To this Abu al-Khayr agreed, as did the majority of Jabhat al-Nusra's leadership. Back in Iran, Abu Muhammad al-Masri and Sayf al-'Adl rejected the manoeuvre when they learned of it. Two-thirds of the al-Qaida leadership council was thus against the move, but Abu al-Khayr instructed al-Jawlani to proceed with the rebranding regardless. Just before the announcement of Jabhat Fath al-Sham, al-Jawlani learned that contact had been re-established, and so he wrote to him explaining the idea for Jabhat Fath al-Sham.

Following the announcement, Zawahiri wrote to al-Jawlani to express his disapproval of what had happened, explaining that he considered the rebranding a real breaking of ties and thus a breach of the *bay'a*. Al-Jawlani believed that Zawahiri had been misinformed, but no amount of pleading would change his position. Finally, according to al-Shami, the leadership of Jabhat Fath al-Sham, convinced that the pursuit of unity in Syria was a legal obligation (*wajib shar'i*), proceeded to form Hay'at Tahrir al-Sham in accordance with (so they believed) the original proposal given to Abu al-Khayr. The second part of the proposal, as will be recalled, provided that the achievement of unity would consummate the separation from al-Qaida. HTS, then, was to be understood as not belonging to al-Qaida at all.

Days after al-Shami's account was published online, al-'Uraydi began writing a series of 'testimonies' on his Telegram channel in response.[45] Al-'Uraydi did not dispute the basic factual framework that al-Shami had laid out concerning al-Jawlani's group and al-Qaida. For instance, he described the formation of HTS as 'the complete breaking of ties' (*fakk al-irtibat al-kulli*) with al-Qaida as opposed to the superficial break that occurred with the announcement of Jabhat Fath al-Sham. What al-'Uraydi took issue with was al-Shami's argument that al-Jawlani and his allies had done nothing wrong. For al-'Uraydi, what al-Jawlani had done following the re-establishment of contact with Zawahiri was an act of insubordination and a violation of the *bay'a*. 'What', al-'Uraydi asked, 'is the difference between what you have done and what al-Baghdadi did?'

In making his case, al-'Uraydi provided some additional details that he claimed al-Shami had omitted. The first was that Abu al-Khayr had made a promise to a number of men in Jabhat al-Nusra, in the lead up to the announcement of Jabhat Fath al-Sham, that if Zawahiri were to reject the move then he would 'work to create sixty or seventy al-Qaida's' in Syria. In other words, if Zawahiri were to object to what had happened then he would work to restore the status quo ante – an open affiliation with al-Qaida. The second detail concerned the contents of Zawahiri's letter to al-Jawlani that was received shortly after the rebranding as Jabhat Fath al-Sham. According to al-'Uraydi, in the letter Zawahiri described what had taken place as an act of 'disobedience' (*ma'siya*) and ordered him to return to the way things were before the announcement of Jabhat Fath al-Sham, explaining that the decision to release an affiliate from al-Qaida required the consent of al-Qaida's Shura Council. Upon learning this, according to al-'Uraydi, Abu al-Khayr ceased to give his blessing to the process underway, that is, the superficial and then total break with al-Qaida. In sum, al-'Uraydi emphasised, in the second half of 2016, those opposed to Jabhat al-Nusra's rebranding included Zawahiri and two of his deputies (Abu Muhammad al-Masri and Sayf al-'Adl), while the other deputy (Abu al-Khayr) had withdrawn his support in deference to Zawahiri. Nonetheless, al-Jawlani went on to create HTS, not even informing Abu al-Khayr beforehand. (Abu al-Khayr would die in a US drone strike shortly thereafter, in February 2017.)

In the month after al-'Uraydi's 'testimonies' were published online, HTS grew weary of the chorus of abuse being heaped on it by the al-Qaida loyalists in Syria. On 27 November, it arrested a number of them, including al-'Uraydi. In a statement, HTS described them as 'the leaders of dissension' (*ru'us al-fitna*), accusing them of spreading lies and misconceptions and explaining that they would be tried in court.[46] Though the men would soon be released, the escalation of the conflict prompted al-Qaida to release a new audio message by Zawahiri.[47]

Zawahiri's message appeared the very next day. In it the al-Qaida leader criticised HTS for the first time in explicit terms. In a statement lasting more than thirty minutes, he underscored the importance of *bay'a*s and his disapproval of what he considered Jabhat al-Nusra's breach of the *bay'a* to him as the leader of al-Qaida. He said:

> Here I would like to stress definitively that we did not release anyone from the *bay'a* to us . . . not Jabhat al-Nusra or anyone else, and we did not accept that Jabhat al-Nusra's *bay'a* be secret. The *bay'a* between us and everyone who pledges *bay'a* to us is a binding pact that must not be violated and that must be observed.

The terms of a potential future break between al-Qaida and Jabhat al-Nusra, he went on, had been made clear many times. Zawahiri had described two conditions: (1) the unification of the mujahidin in al-Sham and (2) the establishment of an Islamic government in al-Sham with an imam chosen by its people. Neither of these conditions obtained. Zawahiri accused the leaders of Jabhat al-Nusra of opportunism and hypocrisy. Jabhat al-Nusra had shown loyalty to al-Qaida when it suited its interest in staving off the threat of ISIS. But as soon as that had receded there began talk of breaking ties and plotting to get out of the *bay'a*. Addressing al-Jawlani and his men, he asked, 'Did not you denounce al-Badri [that is, al-Baghdadi] and his gang as illegitimate on the grounds that they violated the *bay'a* to al-Qaida? How, then, can you permit for yourselves what you prohibited for others?' For Zawahiri, ISIS and Jabhat al-Nusra had committed the same sin of unlawfully exiting al-Qaida.

A few months after this row between HTS and al-Qaida, the al-Qaida loyalists in Syria started to operate under the new name of Tanzim Hurras al-Din (The Organization of the Guardians of the Religion).[48] Widely seen as al-Qaida's new Syrian affiliate, Hurras al-Din is led by an al-Qaida veteran named Abu Hammam al-Shami (aka Faruq al-Suri), a former general military official of Jabhat al-Nusra who spent time in Afghanistan and Iraq and is said to have pledged *bay'a* to Osama bin Laden in person.[49] The group has mainly concentrated on fighting the Assad regime using guerrilla-style tactics, and has forged alliances with other rebel groups in the Idlib area. With a force of no more than a few thousand fighters at the height of its strength, Hurras al-Din has never posed a serious challenge to HTS for supremacy in north-west Syria. For a time, HTS was tolerant of the new al-Qaida-linked outfit, but in mid-2020 it changed tack and cracked down on the group, closing its bases and detaining its leaders.[50] Some leaders, including al-Shami and al-'Uraydi, remain at large, while other have been killed in US drone strikes.[51] The HTS leadership appeared to have reached the conclusion that with a massive influx of Turkish forces into the area, as well the beginning of joint Turkish–Russian patrols, it was necessary to assert control over all military activity in the area of its putative sovereignty. Doing so would also show the international community that HTS was a credible partner willing and able to suppress al-Qaida-linked jihadis. Since mid-2020, Hurras al-Din has claimed only a handful of attacks and its media activities have nearly ceased altogether.

As all of this shows, HTS, when it was announced in January 2017, was not an affiliate of al-Qaida. This should have been clear to all observers by November of that year, when Zawahiri publicly berated HTS for abandoning al-Qaida. The US government and media, however, were slow to acknowledge what had taken place. In May 2018, the US State Department amended its terrorist designation of Jabhat al-Nusra to include the name Hay'at Tahrir al-Sham, denying that this amounted to a change in the group's relationship with al-Qaida.[52] Nathan Sales, the State Department's coordinator for counterterrorism, said that 'today's designation serves notice that the United States is not fooled by this al-Qa'ida affiliate's attempt to rebrand itself.' This view was mistaken. Jabhat al-Nusra's attempt to rebrand as Jabhat Fath al-Sham, with a secret al-Qaida affiliation, was the attempt to fool the US. The formation of HTS was not a repeat of this exercise. Al-Qaida was not being cunning and deceptive; it had been outmanoeuvred. More than a year later, in September 2019, the State Department made its first designation of Hurras al-Din, correctly describing it as 'an al-Qaida affiliate in Syria'.[53] However, it still did not recognise a change in HTS's status. Confusingly, Sales stated: 'Al-Qa'ida in Syria . . . encompasses the Nusrah Front, Hayat Tahrir al-Sham, and Hurras al-Din.'[54] Later that month, the *New York Times* added to the confusion when it described HTS as 'the larger Qaeda-linked organization' in comparison with Hurras al-Din.[55] This was almost two years after Zawahiri's speech condemning HTS for abandoning al-Qaida. Other news outlets likewise have continued to refer to HTS as linked to al-Qaida, a practice that recalls the way the press and others identified the Islamic State of Iraq as al-Qaida in Iraq for years when al-Qaida had next to no influence over the Iraqi group.

To be sure, the confusion is understandable given the complicated manner in which Jabhat al-Nusra developed into HTS, as well as the fact that most of the public debate over what happened is available only in Arabic. Still, to attribute influence over HTS to al-Qaida remains highly misleading.

Conclusion

In the first two decades of the 2000s, al-Qaida succeeded in establishing nominal control over two of the main Sunni jihadi groups in the Fertile Crescent: Abu Mus'ab al-Zarqawi's Jama'at al-Tawhid wa'l-Jihad, which became al-Qaida in Mesopotamia in 2004, and Abu Muhammad al-Jawlani's Jabhat al-Nusra, which declared its loyalty to al-Qaida in 2013 after having begun as an extension of the Islamic State of Iraq. In each of these cases, as has been seen, the level of control exercised by al-Qaida was limited and the relationship did not endure. By 2017, al-Qaida in Mesopotamia and Jabhat al-Nusra had morphed into the Islamic State and Hay'at Tahrir al-Sham. This outcome may not have been preordained, but two factors were working against a more meaningful and a lasting affiliation. The first was strategic and ideological disagreement, the second logistical and organisational deficiency.

In the case of al-Qaida in Mesopotamia, the divergence with al-Qaida over strategy was visible early on. Zarqawi conditioned his swearing of allegiance to bin Laden on the latter's agreement to his Shi'a-focused sectarian strategy, but al-Qaida was never fully on board, as was seen from Zawahiri's critical letter to Zarqawi. Zawahiri's intervention did not dispose Zarqawi to display any kind of deference to al-Qaida's leaders. Rather he undertook to create the Islamic State of Iraq, a project that, as he must have known, was to weaken al-Qaida's hold over his group. Al-Qaida was not consulted regarding its establishment.

Throughout this process, al-Qaida's efforts to maintain correspondence with Zarqawi and his lieutenants proved unsuccessful, either because of a lack of interest on the part of Zarqawi or because of logistical hurdles, or both. Far away in the Afghanistan–Pakistan region, all that al-Qaida's leaders could do was write letters and try to get them to Iraq via couriers. There was no way of ensuring that the letters would reach their destination, or that the orders therein would be obeyed. The same state of affairs – little to no communication – obtained during the Islamic State of Iraq. In 2013, when Zawahiri finally tried to assert his authority over the Iraqi group amid the dispute between ISIS and Jabhat al-Nusra, ISIS, unsurprisingly, would have none of it. Zawahiri, far afield, had overplayed his hand.

Jabhat al-Nusra also saw its relationship with al-Qaida break down over differences of strategy, though unlike in the case of Zarqawi's group these were not bound up in ideological disagreement.[56] In order to expand his influence over a greater part of the Syrian rebel scene, al-Jawlani believed it necessary to cut ties with al-Qaida, or at least to make Jabhat al-Nusra's relationship with al-Qaida secret. This, he believed, was consistent with Zawahiri's public statements to the effect that al-Qaida would never stand in the way of unifying the opposition and that Jabhat al-Nusra could leave al-Qaida when unity was achieved and an Islamic government established. As it turned out, Zawahiri did not mean to say that Jabhat al-Nusra should seek to leave al-Qaida and pursue a unity coalition. He was thinking in the longer term of how a separation from al-Qaida might play out. He did not desire that the Syrian group form an Islamic government in a small patch of territory, as would happen in Idlib. Such a project was bound to fail, he believed, and the jihadis ought to be preparing for guerrilla warfare instead.

The problem was that Zawahiri did not have the ability to communicate his objections to Jabhat al-Nusra until after it had started the process of transforming itself into HTS. Zawahiri had been off the grid for nearly three years, and when al-Jawlani learned of his objections he concluded that it was too late to stop, and so defied Zawahiri's command. While communication with senior al-Qaida leaders was better in the case of Jabhat al-Nusra than in the case of al-Qaida in Mesopotamia and its successors – largely because Zawahiri's chief deputy, Abu al-Khayr al-Masri, relocated to Syria in 2015 – the fact that Zawahiri could not be reached for nearly three years proved a major problem. Having been told by Abu al-Khayr that it was free to act as if it were leaving al-Qaida, and then possibly actually leave the organisation in the event of a unity agreement with the larger armed opposition, Jabhat al-Nusra was then told by Zawahiri that it had to reverse course. Much like al-Baghdadi in 2013, however, al-Jawlani in 2016 determined that the man far away in the Afghanistan–Pakistan region did not really have any authority over him. In justifying al-Jawlani's decision, his supporter Abu 'Abdallah al-Shami complained of the difficulties in trying to coordinate with al-Qaida, including the confusion over Abu al-Khayr's role as deputy, Zawahiri's long absence, and the slow pace of communication once contact was re-established. In other words, according to al-Shami, al-Qaida did not have its act together – it was dysfunctional.

In both cases, it is hard to avoid concluding that the local affiliate approached its relationship to al-Qaida in a spirit of opportunism. The affiliates drew close to al-Qaida when the relationship served their interests, and they ignored and abandoned al-Qaida when it no longer did. This explains Zarqawi's rebranding as al-Qaida when it seemed that would bring in more men and resources, and his successor's defiance of Zawahiri during the dispute with Jabhat al-Nusra. The same holds for al-Jawlani's declaration of loyalty to al-Qaida when he needed help against ISIS, and his decision later to ignore Zawahiri's orders and go on to form HTS. In both cases, the concerns of the affiliate took precedence over those of the mother organisation.

Since the rise of ISIS beginning in 2013, some terrorism scholars have remarked on al-Qaida's impressive resiliency in the face of the Islamic State challenge.[57] As they note, most of al-Qaida's affiliates, including al-Qaida in the Arabian Peninsula in Yemen, al-Shabaab in Somalia, and al-Qaida in the Islamic Maghreb in North Africa, did not jump ship and join the Islamic State. But ought this really to be interpreted as a sign of al-Qaida's enduring strength and organisational coherence? Perhaps the affiliates simply find it advantageous to remain with al-Qaida for the time being. Some of these may be more loyal to al-Qaida than others – al-Qaida in the Arabian Peninsula probably being the most loyal – but most are unlikely to bend to al-Qaida's will in matters seen as existential to the affiliate. If the history of al-Qaida's branches in the Fertile Crescent is any guide, al-Qaida will have a hard time asserting itself over its affiliates, particularly in the event of strategic and/or ideological differences. As one scholar observed some years ago, al-Qaida's apparent 'resilience . . . should not mask its internal dysfunction and failures'.[58] As the foregoing has shown, al-Qaida showed plenty of dysfunction in Iraq and Syria over the past two decades, and it failed to set the strategic agenda for its affiliates in either country.

Notes

1 Osama bin Laden, 'Risala ila ikhwanina 'l-Muslimin fi 'l-'Iraq', February 2003, in Osama bin Laden, *Majmu' rasa'il wa-tawjihat al-shaykh al-mujahid Usama ibn Ladin*, Nukhbat al-I'lam al-Jihadi, 2015, 482–6. Available at <https://www.ji hadica.com/wp-content/uploads/2020/02/Majmu-rasail-wa-tawjihat.pdf> (last accessed 29 October 2022).

2 Sayf al-'Adl, *Tajribati ma'a Abi Mus'ab al-Zarqawi*, Minbar al-Tawhid wa'l-Jihad, n.d., 3–4. Available at <https://www.jihadica.com/wp-content/uploads /2020/02/Tajrubati.pdf> (last accessed 29 October 2022).

3 For more on Zarqawi's brand of jihadism, see Cole Bunzel, 'From Paper State to Caliphate: The Ideology of the Islamic State', Brookings Institution, The Brookings Project on US Relations with the Islamic World, March 2015, 7–14.

4 For more on Zarqawi's activities during this period, see Nellie Lahoud, 'Metamorphosis: From al-Tawhid wa-al-Jihad to Dawlat al-Khilafa (2003–2014)', in *The Group that Calls Itself a State: Understanding the Evolution and Challenges of the Islamic State*, The Combatting Terrorism Center at Westpoint, December 2014, 10–12; Brian H. Fishman, *The Master Plan: ISIS, al-Qaeda, and the Jihadi Strategy for Final Victory* (New Haven, CT: Yale University Press, 2016), 16–23.

5 Fishman, *The Master Plan*, 21–7.

6 Lahoud, 'Metamorphosis: From al-Tawhid wa-al-Jihad to Dawlat al-Khilafa (2003–2014)', 12.

7 Abu Mus'ab al-Zarqawi, Letter to Osama bin Laden and Ayman al-Zawahiri. Available at <https://web.archive.org/web/20040401133349/http:/www.cpa -iraq.org/arabic/transcripts/20040212_zarqawi_full-arabic.html> (last accessed 29 October 2022). For a partial translation, see Gilles Kepel and Jean-Pierre Milelli, eds, *Al Qaeda in Its Own Words* (Cambridge: The Belknap Press, 2008), 251–67.

8 Zarqawi, 'Bayan al-bay'a li-Tanzim al-Qa'ida bi-qiyadat al-shaykh Usama ibn Ladin', 17 October, 2014, in *Kalimat mudi'a*, Shabakat al-Buraq al-Islamiyya, June 2006, 174–6. Available at <https://www.jihadica.com/wp-content/uploa ds/2020/01/kalimat-mudia.pdf> (last accessed 29 October 2022).

9 Barak Mendelsohn, *The al-Qaeda Franchise: The Expansion of al-Qaeda and Its Consequences* (New York: Oxford University Press, 2016), 118.

10 Fishman, *The Master Plan*, 46.

11 Ayman al-Zawahiri, Letter to Zarqawi, 16 July 2015. Available at <https://ctc .usma.edu/app/uploads/2013/10/Zawahiris-Letter-to-Zarqawi-Original.pdf> (last accessed 29 October 2022). For a translation, see Laura Mansfield, *His Own*

Words: Translation and Analysis of the Writings of Dr. Ayman Al Zawahiri (n.pl.: TLG Publications, 2006), 250–79.

12 'Atiyyat Allah al-Libi, Letter to Zarqawi, December 2015. Available at <https://ctc.usma.edu/app/uploads/2013/10/Atiyahs-Letter-to-Zarqawi-Original.pdf> (last accessed 17 November 2022).

13 Abu Mus'ab al-Suri, 'Hadha balagh lil-nas', 24 April 2006, in *Kalimat mudi'a*, 515–24, 523.

14 Ayman al-Zawahiri, 'Shahada li-haqn dima' al-mujahidin bi'l-Sham', Mu'assasat al-Sahab, 2 May 2014. Available at <https://ia802207.us.archive.org/24/items/shehadaemam/shehada.pdf> (last accecssed 29 October 2022).

15 Bunzel, *From Paper State to Caliphate*, 21–2.

16 Al-Zawahiri, 'Shahada li-haqn dima' al-mujahidin bi'l-Sham'.

17 Adam Gahdan, Letter to Osama bin Laden, January 2011, 7–9. Available at <https://www.jihadica.com/wp-content/uploads/2012/05/SOCOM-2012-0000004-Orig.pdf> (last accessed 29 October 2022).

18 See, for instance, 'Terrorist Designation of Ibrahim Awwad Ibrahim Ali al-Badri', US Department of State, 4 October 2011. Available at <https://2009-2017.state.gov/r/pa/prs/ps/2011/10/174971.htm> (last accessed 29 October 2022); Michael S. Schmidt and Eric Schmitt, 'Leaving Iraq, U.S. Fears New Surge of Qaeda Terror', *New York Times*, 5 November 2011. Available at <https://www.nytimes.com/2011/11/06/world/middleeast/leaving-iraq-us-fears-new-surge-of-qaeda-terror.html> (last accessed 20 October 2022).

19 For more on this history, see Bunzel, *From Paper State to Caliphate*, 25–30.

20 Abu Muhammad al-Jawlani, 'al-I'lan 'an Jabhat al-Nusra', 2012. Available at <https://www.jihadica.com/wp-content/uploads/2020/02/ilan.pdf> (last accessed 29 October 2022).

21 Abu Bakr al-Baghdadi, 'Wa-bashshir al-mu'minin', Mu'assasat al-Furqan, 9 April 2013. Available at <https://ia800406.us.archive.org/15/items/w_bsher_1/tcJN8J.pdf> (last accessed 17 November 2022).

22 Abu Muhammad al-Jawlani, 'Kalima sawtiyya lil-fatih Abi Muhammad al-Jawlani', Mu'assasat al-Manara al-Bayda', 10 April 2013. Available at <https://ia601700.us.archive.org/21/items/gabhaalnosra/02.mp3> (last accessed 29 October 2022).

23 Ayman al-Zawahiri, Letter to Abu Bakr al-Baghdadi and Abu Muhammad al-Jawlani, 23 May 2013. Available at <https://www.aljazeera.net/file/get/64c64867-0eb8-4368-a1fd-13c7afbc9aa3> (last accessed 29 October 2022).

24 Abu Bakr al-Baghdadi, 'Baqiya fi 'l-'Iraq wa'l-Sham', Mu'assasat al-Furqan, 15 June 2013. Available at <https://www.jihadica.com/wp-content/uploads/2020/02/baqiya.pdf> (last accessed 29 October 2022).

25 Abu Muhammad al-Jawlani, 'Fa-dharhum wa-ma yaftarun', Mu'assasat al-Furqan,

19 June 2013. Available at <https://www.jihadica.com/wp-content/uploads/2020/02/fa-dharhum.pdf> (last accessed 29 October 2022).

26 Ayman al-Zawahiri, 'Shahada li-haqn dima' al-mujahidin bi'l-Sham'.

27 Abu Muhammad al-'Adnani, "Udhran amir al-Qa'ida', Mu'assasat al-Furqan, 11 May 2014. Available at <https://www.jihadica.com/wp-content/uploads/2020/02/udhran.pdf> (last accessed 29 October 2022).

28 See, for instance, Ayman al-Zawahiri, 'al-Sham amana fi a'naqikum', Mu'assasat al-Sahab, 14 January 2016. Available at <https://www.jihadica.com/wp-content/uploads/2020/02/al-Sham-amana.pdf> (last accessed 29 October 2022).

29 Abu Muhammad al-'Adnani, 'Hadha wa'd Allah', Mu'assasat al-Furqan, 29 June 2014. Available at <https://www.jihadica.com/wp-content/uploads/2020/02/Hadha-wad-Allah.pdf> (last accessed 29 October 2022).

30 For one of the early rumours, see Mariam Karouny, 'Insight – Syria's Nusra Front May Leave Qaeda to Form New Entity', *Reuters*, 3 March 2015. Available at <https://www.reuters.com/article/uk-mideast-crisis-nusra-insight/insight-syrias-nusra-front-may-leave-qaeda-to-form-new-entity-idUKKBN0M00G620150304> (last accessed 21 November 2022).

31 For more on this history, see Charles Lister, 'How al-Qa'ida Lost Control of Its Syrian Affiliate: The Inside Story', *CTC Sentinel* 11, no. 2 (February 2018): 1–9; Charles Lister, 'The Syria Effect: Al-Qaeda Fractures', *Current Trends in Islamist Ideology*, Hudson Institute, 11 December 2019. Available at <https://www.hudson.org/national-security-defense/the-syria-effect-al-qaeda-fractures> (last accessed 29 October 2022); Aymen Jawad Al-Tamimi, 'From Jabhat al-Nusra to Hay'at Tahrir al-Sham: Evolution, Approach and Future', Konrad Adenauer Stiftung/Al-Nahrain Center for Strategic Studies, June 2018.

32 Abu Muhammad al-Jawlani, 'I'lan tashkil Jabhat Fath al-Sham', 28 July 2016. Available at <https://www.jihadica.com/wp-content/uploads/2016/09/Ilan-tashkil-Jabhat-Fath-al-Sham.pdf> (last accessed 29 October 2022).

33 Ahmad Hasan Abu al-Khayr al-Masri, 'Kalima sawtiyya', Mu'assasat al-Manara al-Bayda', 28 July 2016. Available at <https://www.jihadica.com/wp-content/uploads/2016/09/kalima-sawtiyya.pdf> (last accessed 29 October 2022).

34 Ayman al-Zawahiri, 'Infiru lil-Sham', Mu'assasat al-Sahab, 8 May 2016. Available at <https://www.jihadica.com/wp-content/uploads/2016/09/infiru-lil-sham.pdf> (last accessed 29 October 2022).

35 'Bayan tashkil Hay'at Tahrir al-Sham', 28 January 2017. Available at <https://www.jihadica.com/wp-content/uploads/2017/03/bayan-tashkil-Hayat-Tahrir-al-Sham.pdf> (last accessed 29 October 2022).

36 Telegram post by Warith al-Zarqawi (@walzarqa), 8 February 2017. Available at <https://www.jihadica.com/wp-content/uploads/2017/05/al-Uraydi-resignation.png> (last accessed 29 October 2022).

37 Telegram post by Sami al-'Uraydi (@Sami_Al_Aridi), 8 February 2017. Available at <https://www.jihadica.com/wp-content/uploads/2017/05/al-Uraydi-ququ .png> (last accessed 29 October 2022).

38 Tweet by Sami al-'Uraydi (@sami_oride), 30 September 2015. Available at <https://www.jihadica.com/wp-content/uploads/2020/02/sami-tweet-Septem ber-2015.png> (last accessed 29 October 2022).

39 Abu Muhammad al-Maqdisi, 'Mulahazat 'ala ta'qibat fadilat al-Shaykh Abi 'Abdallah al-Shami', 14 February 2017. Available at <https://www.jihadica .com/wp-content/uploads/2017/03/mulahazat-ala-taqibat.pdf> (last accessed 29 October 2022).

40 Ayman al-Zawahiri, 'al-Sham lan tarka'a illa lillah', Mu'assasat al-Sahab, 23 April 2017. Available at <https://www.jihadica.com/wp-content/uploads/2020/02 /al-Sham-lan-tarkaa-illa-lillah.pdf> (last accessed 29 October 2022).

41 Ayman al-Zawahiri, 'Sa-nuqatilukum hatta la takuna fitna bi-idhn Allah', Mu'assasat al-Sahab, 4 October 2017. Available at <https://www.jihadica.com /wp-content/uploads/2020/02/sa-nuqatilukum-hatta-la-takuna-fitna.pdf> (last accessed 29 October 2022).

42 Abu 'Abdallah al-Shami, 'Raddan 'ala kalimat al-Zawahiri', 29 November 2017. Available at <https://www.jihadica.com/wp-content/uploads/2020/02/raddan -ala-kalimat-al-Zawahiri.pdf> (last accessed 29 October 2022); in this document al-Shami reproduces his response to Zawahiri from the month prior.

43 Rukmini Callimachi and Eric Schmitt, 'Iran Released Top Members of Al Qaeda in Trade', *New York Times*, 17 September 2015. Available at <https://www.ny times.com/2015/09/18/world/middleeast/iran-released-top-members-of-al-qae da-in-a-trade.html> (last accessed 29 October 2022).

44 The names are redacted in the text published by al-Shami, but they are made clear in al-'Uraydi's response.

45 Sami al-'Uraydi, 'Silsilat lillah thumma lil-tarikh: shahadat hawl fakk al-irtibat bayn Jabhat al-Nusra wa-tanzim al-Qa'ida', 15–20 October 2017. Available at <https://www.jihadica.com/wp-content/uploads/2020/02/lillah-thumma-lil -tarikh.pdf> (last accessed 29 October 2022). For more on these 'testimonies', see Tore Hamming, 'What We Learned from Sami al-'Uraydi's Testimony Concerning Abu Abdallah al-Shami', *Jihadica*, 24 October 2017. Available at <https://www.jihadica.com/what-we-learned-from-sami-al-uraydis-testimony -concerning-abu-abdullah-al-shami/> (last accessed 29 October 2022).

46 Hay'at Tahrir al-Sham, 'Wa-lil-qada' kalimat al-fasl', 27 November 2017. Available at <https://www.jihadica.com/wp-content/uploads/2020/02/HTS-st atemen-on-ruus-al-fitna.jpeg> (last accessed 29 October 2022).

47 Ayman al-Zawahiri, 'Fa'l-nuqatilhum bunyana marsusan', Mu'assasat al-Sahab,

28 November 2020. The speed with which this was released suggests it was recorded well in advance and was to be released only if the confrontation between HTS and the al-Qaida loyalists came to a head.

48 The first statement by Hurras al-Din was released on 27 February 2018. See Tanzim Hurras al-Din, 'Anqidhu fustat al-Muslimin', 27 February 2018. Available at <https://www.jihadica.com/wp-content/uploads/2020/02/Anqid hu-fustat-al-Muslimin.pdf> (last accessed 29 October 2022). On Hurras al-Din, including its relations with HTS, see Aaron Zelin, 'Huras al-Din: The Overlooked al-Qaeda Group in Syria', The Washington Institute for Near East Policy, 24 September 2019. Available at <https://www.washingtoninstitute.org/policy-analy sis/huras-al-din-overlooked-al-qaeda-group-syria> (last accessed 29 October 2022).

49 For his biography, see 'Shahadat qubayl intiha' muhlat al-mubahala: shahadat al-qa'id Abi Hammam al-Suri', Mu'assasat al-Basira, March 2014. Available at <https://www.jihadica.com/wp-content/uploads/2020/02/silsilat-shahadat-qu bayl-al-mubahala.pdf> (last accessed 29 October 2022).

50 Al-Muraqib, 'Striving for Hegemony: The HTS Crackdown on al-Qaida and Friends in Northwest Syria', *Jihadica*, 15 September 2020. Available at <https:// www.jihadica.com/striving-for-hegemony-the-hts-crackdown-on-al-qaida-and -friends-in-northwest-syria/> (last accessed 29 October 2022).

51 Those killed include Abu Julaybib al-Urduni (aka Iyyad al-Tubasi) in late 2018, Abu Khallad al-Muhandis (aka Sari Shihab) in August 2019, Abu Khadija al-Urduni (aka Bilal Khuraysat) in December 2019, Abu 'l-Qassam al-Urduni (aka Khalid al-'Aruri) in June 2020, and Abu Muhammad al-Sudani in October 2020.

52 'Amendments to the Terrorist Designation of al-Nusrah Front', US Department of State, 31 May 2018. Available at <https://2017-2021.state.gov/amendments -to-the-terrorist-designations-of-al-nusrah-front/index.html> (last accessed 17 November 2022). See further Charles Lister, 'US Officials Just Mislabeled a Syrian Terror Group as al Qaeda. Worse, They're Missing a Far Bigger Threat', *Defense One*, 1 June 2018. Available at <https://www.defenseone.com/ideas/20 18/06/us-officials-just-mislabeled-syrian-group-al-qaeda-worse-theyre-missing -far-bigger-threat/148656/> (last accessed 29 October 2022).

53 'Modernization of Executive Order 13224', US Department of State, 10 September 2019. Available at <https://2017-2021.state.gov/modernization -of-executive-order-13224/index.html> (last accessed 17 November 2022).

54 Nathan Sales, 'Keeping the Pressure on al-Qaida', US Department of State, 12 September 2019. Available at <https://web.archive.org/web/20190920100 917/https://www.state.gov/keeping-the-pressure-on-al-qaida/> (last accessed 21 November 2022).

55 Eric Schmitt, 'U.S. Sees Rising Threat in the West from Qaeda Branch in Syria', *New York Times*, 29 September 2019.

56 Some jihadi critics of HTS, especially Abu Muhammad al-Maqdisi, have accused the group of ideological deviation – of diluting (*tamyiʿ*) the Islamic creed by associating with Muslim Brotherhood-style Islamists. Al-Qaida's leaders, however, have avoided such arguments. See Cole Bunzel, 'Diluting Jihad: Tahrir al-Sham and the Concerns of Abu Muhammad al-Maqdisi', *Jihadica*, 29 March 2017. Available at <https://www.jihadica.com/diluting-jihad/> (last accessed 29 October 2022).

57 See, for instance, Daveed Gartenstein-Ross and Nathaniel Barr, 'How al-Qaeda Survived the Islamic State Challenge', *Current Trends in Islamist Ideology* 21 (2017): 50–68.

58 Anthony N. Celso, 'Al Qaeda's Post-bin Laden Resurgence: The Paradox of Resilience and Failure', *Mediterranean Quarterly* 25, no. 2 (2014): 33–47, 47.

10

SALAFI POLITICS AMID THE CHAOS: REVOLUTION AT HOME AND REVOLUTION ABROAD?

Valeria Resta and Francesco Cavatorta

Introduction

S alafi politics and ideology have been a central preoccupation of scholars and policymakers since the September 2001 attacks on the US. The ideological tenets of al-Qaida were immersed in Salafi religious understanding and practices and, since then, works on Salafism have increased considerably. Much of the scholarly attention has focused on the growing phenomenon of Jihadi-Salafism, a very specific, and in fact rather novel, form of Salafi practice and politics.[1] The arrival of the Islamic State in the summer of 2014 saw a considerable increase in the number of studies on the relationship between politics, Salafi doctrine and violence.[2] Some of these studies broached the issue of how its political project fits with the established norms of the international state system. Richard Nielsen's study was most notable among them, arguing that the Islamic State's doctrine on the international system rejects the notion of state sovereignty and is therefore incompatible with the Westphalian state system that has been in place for centuries.[3] According to Nielsen, 'Daesh's existence poses a fundamental challenge to international order' and he dismisses the notion that if Daesh were to hold territory for a long period of time – thereby creating an embryonic caliphate – it would eventually accept basic international norms and recognise the sovereignty of other states. In short, Jihadi-Salafism is ideologically opposed to the Westphalian system because its reading of religious precepts prevents it from doing so and it is therefore inevitably driven to dismantle it in favour of

261

clearer divisions between believers and non-believers in two distinct political camps.

Given the political relevance of Jihadi-Salafism and its concrete manifestation in the Islamic State's and al-Qaida's survival, it is understandable that much attention has been dedicated to this phenomenon. However, this, together with its military defeat, should not detract from exploring other forms of Salafism, which have received less attention, but are equally important to analyse because they offer a very different picture of the relationship between Salafism and politics, including international relations, and because they attract many more followers in sheer numerical terms than Jihadi-Salafism. As Wiktorowicz makes clear in his seminal 2006 article, there are two other branches of Salafism when it comes to how Salafis should understand and 'live' the relationship between politics – broadly speaking – and religion: the quietists and the 'politicos'.[4] Although Wiktorowicz's classification has come under scrutiny for its rigidity, it remains a useful starting point.[5]

While the quietists refrain from intervening in institutional politics and reject the idea of forming political parties to advance their objectives, preferring instead to focus exclusively on religious education and proselytising, the politicos have chosen the route of institutional politics through the creation of political parties.[6] This chapter is concerned with the way in which politicos across the Arab world have dealt with the issue of foreign policy and international relations to examine how and why they differ from their jihadi counterparts and what the implications are in a political arena where they compete with both Islamist and non-Islamist parties. Although there have been several studies examining the new politics of Salafism and the positions of Salafi parties on social and economic issues, we know very little about what Salafis stand for when it comes to international relations.[7] The ways in which Salafi politicos think about foreign policy and international politics more broadly can also shed light on the degree of institutionalisation of Salafi parties and their potential pragmatism.[8] Although Islamist parties have demonstrated their pragmatism and commitment to democratic mechanisms, the same cannot be said about Salafi parties. Thus, exploring further their political preferences on crucial issues of international politics can lead us to better understand whether and how they have integrated notions of compromise and inclusion into pluralistic political systems. While almost all politicos have retreated from institutional politics due to the retrenchment of authoritarian rule and the emergence of civil conflicts, their role on the Arab political scene may be over or limited only temporarily.

Salafism in the Wake of the Arab Uprisings

Although the consequences of the Arab uprisings have yet to be fully understood and their dynamics entirely worked out, there are a number of elements that stand out in their aftermath. A notable aspect of post-uprising politics is the politicisation of Salafism. Most studies on Salafism before the uprisings emphasised either its violent nature, which terrorist groups perpetrate both nationally and internationally, or its quietist one, embodied in associations engaged in *daw'a* (proselitysing) and charitable work. Politicised Salafists were few and far between. It follows that their beliefs about the necessity of being engaged in institutional politics to promote and defend their political objectives were marginal within the wider movement. Aside from participating in elections and institutional politics in Kuwait, Salafi parties did not exist anywhere else across the Arab world before 2011.[9] Following the uprisings and faced with the prospect of not having their views heard in a liberalising and suddenly pluralistic political scene, Salafis in Tunisia, Egypt and Yemen founded political parties and participated – or attempted to participate in the case of Yemen – in the new institutions being devised to replace authoritarian rule. Although the Salafi political-institutional experience was short-lived and the return of authoritarian rule, as well as the chaos of botched transitions, drove many Salafis back into quietism, the experience of Salafi parties as competitive political actors deserves to be analysed for at least three reasons.[10]

First, Salafis might seize future opportunities to participate in electoral politics and therefore build on the experiences of the immediate post-2011 period. Examining what they stood for in post-uprising free elections might provide a useful guide on what to expect and how pragmatic – or not – they might be. Second, the views and policy preferences they set forth might diverge considerably from the ones that other Salafis promote and the failure to institutionalise their parties does not mean that such views no longer exist, making Salafism heterogeneous and more complex than usually assumed, particularly in policymaking circles. Analysing their programmes still reveals the fissures and debates at the heart of Salafi politics in the region. As the journalist Mustafa Salama argues, 'being a Salafi does not boil down to a set of specific political preferences' that every Salafi shares.[11] This has profound implications for the debate over Islamism more generally, which still 'suffers' from the pre-conceived ideas that emerged in the late 1980s and early 1990s about its supposedly unchanging authoritarian nature and ideological inflexibility. Third, the policy preferences that politicised Salafis subscribe to and offered to the electorate can shed light on the potential for ideological change within Salafism and how this might compare with changes that took place within the more mainstream Muslim Brotherhood-inspired Islamist parties.

Participation in elections demands that political parties compete with each other in the electoral market to convince voters to cast ballots in their favour, and Salafi parties across the region did indeed take elections seriously, drawing up electoral manifestos and presenting policy proposals and priorities to the electorate. This chapter examines the political programmes of a number of Salafi parties in Tunisia, Egypt and Kuwait to outline their policy positions on what kind of foreign policies their countries should pursue and what kind of international order should be established.

Theory

When looking at how Salafis view international politics and how they relate to the dominant Westphalian model, it is inevitable to reprise what mainstream Islamists have had to say over time about the topic. For a long time, Islamism in the Arab world was at its core a transnational project devoted to challenging the Westphalian state system. Building on Arab nationalism and its notions of anti-imperialism and Arab unity, Islamists saw the strictures of the Arab state as an obstacle to be removed because genuine citizenship, according to religious precepts, could only be realised in the context of all the faithful living under the same political authority. Already in the late 1920s the Muslim Brotherhood had 'among its original objectives . . . the construction of a central and sovereign Islamic state aimed at uniting the entire Muslim population (*umma*) under the single rule of the caliphate'.[12] This objective suggested a two-pronged strategy would be pursued. First, religious affiliation could and should be employed to mobilise against colonial powers, be it in Egypt or elsewhere in the region. This was accomplished to considerable effect. Second, liberation from colonial rule would finally permit the rise of a unified Arab world able to change the rules of the international game. This, however, did not occur and the second part of the strategy never materialised because different parts of the Arab world experienced divergent paths of liberation at different times, therefore giving rise to independent nation states.

The ruling elites of these new independent states had to secure their rule, and in doing so they had to re-imagine national narratives that would be promoted through the institutions of the nation state, leaving ideas about regional political unity somewhat at the margins.[13] Although Arab nationalism promoted unity in theory and pan-Arabism was indeed a powerful political movement for several decades after decolonisation, the differences between post-independence states was too great to lead to the creation of a single political authority. There were attempts at creating a union between Egypt and Syria and Egypt and Libya, but these experiments failed quite spectacularly. Over a rather short period of time, national and nationalistic dynamics prevailed despite periodic calls for Arab unity around international issues like the Arab–Israeli conflict. 'Unity' began to simply mean collaboration and coordination, not actual political unification. Eventually, even the notion of Arab brotherhood and collaboration in the international system failed to materialise, as the peace agreement between Egypt and Israel very clearly showed.

When Islamism surpassed Arab nationalism as the most popular ideological framework across the region, it attempted to revitalise the discourse of political unity, substituting religious affiliation for ethnicity and language. However, the entrenchment of the nation state system at the regional level was too deep to be genuinely challenged and Islamist movements in different countries tended to develop national political programmes, concentrating on national political issues and speaking of unity, again, as 'collaboration' rather than political unification. This nationalist turn of Islamist parties, thinkers and leaders should not suggest that the appeal of their ideology had suddenly rejected its international dimension and its drive towards the caliphate. The broad appeal of such a political objective remained, but it had to contend with the reality within which Islamist movements and their leaders had to operate.

In this respect, the inclusion-moderation hypothesis is quite useful to explain how most mainstream Islamists came to accept the Westphalian model despite having railed against it for decades. In order to be accepted into the broader political game through increasing participation and 'contamination' with other political currents, over time Islamists moderated their most radical stances when it came to the value of democratic institutions, the acceptance of a neo-liberal market economy, the inevitability of social pluralism in a complex society and the permanence of the nation state as the most significant actor in the international system.[14] As Adraoui makes clear, Islamist leaders like Ghannouchi 'present the Islamist vision as evolving from an intransigent ideology to a nationalized project incorporating significant parts of the Westphalian system, leading notably to a new theorization of borders and the caliphate'.[15] In fact, Tunisian Islamists, much like their Moroccan counterparts for instance, came to view the nation state as the inevitable locus of politics and quite explicitly came to reject the idea of a radical transformation of the international system. This more pragmatic attitude developed over time and had a profound impact on the type of foreign policy that Islamists would implement once in power. It followed that their reluctant acceptance of the regional Westphalian system generated much fewer radical demands in the international arena. Although the anti-imperialist rhetoric remained, their actions contradicted it and diverged from what was expected from them. From the Moroccan Justice and Development Party (PJD) abandoning their opposition to the kingdom's dealings with Israel to the Egyptian Brotherhood actively playing the mediating role that Mubarak had played in the conflict between Hamas and Israel, empirical findings confirm that 'moderation' had occurred once governmental responsibilities were thrust on Islamist movements. The Tunisian Islamists of Ennahda also had to significantly moderate their more radical foreign policy positions, confirming that rhetorical commitment to a turn towards the East, notably the Gulf, and the rejection of Westernisation would not be implemented in practice.[16]

As a number of scholars highlighted, Muslim Brotherhood-inspired political parties across the Arab world did go through a process of political moderation. Although some scholars problematise the division between moderates and radicals, there is no denying that Islamist parties eliminated their most radical positions and policy preferences from their ideological and programmatic arsenal.[17] As El-Ghobashy points out in her analysis of the Egyptian Muslim Brotherhood, a genuine 'metamorphosis' took place, which led these parties to embrace concepts and practices that had been alien to them.[18] Unsurprisingly, Islamists' positions on the basics of the international system changed over time as well.

It is at this juncture that the emergence of politicised Salafism becomes important insofar as one of the primary motivations for Salafis to create political parties in the aftermath of the fall of authoritarian regimes in Egypt, Yemen and Tunisia was to compete with mainstream Islamist parties. The latter were believed to have 'sold out' the Islamist political project by advocating for and participating in democratic practices and by shedding the project of its most radical stances.[19] According to the politicos within the Salafi family, failing to play the institutional game would inevitably lead to policy choices in contrast with religious precepts. To prevent this from occurring and to continue fostering the radical character of the Islamist project, Salafis needed to set up political parties to compete in the pluralistic elections following the uprisings despite maintaining that democracy was not a system to which they subscribed.[20] This argument proved convincing and several Salafi parties were created as the genuine Islamic alternative.[21] Once set up, they formulated and defended demands that Muslim Brotherhood-inspired Islamist parties had abandoned over time during their process of moderation. Thus, the rejection of the most radical policy stances on the part of what one might call mainstream Islamists favoured the rise of Salafis who sought to capitalise on what was perceived as an ideological betrayal on the part of Muslim Brotherhood-inspired parties. The logic of electoral competition kicked in and Salafi parties picked candidates, ran campaigns, built party structures and presented a political programme to ensure that their views and preferences would be represented.

This was a major turning point for the broad Salafi family and, according to some scholars, the very act of participating in democratic elections and institutions led the Salafis to inevitably being caught up in the inclusion-moderation process.[22] Although they were rhetorically and ideologically opposed to democracy, they participated in it, granting, implicitly, legitimacy to the system. In addition, they were 'forced' to play the game of daily 'politicking' and through this they had to learn how to strategise and compromise to attract support and 'get things done'. The routinisation of such behaviour is precisely what leads to moderation over time insofar as radical political actors realise that their ideological rigidity is not conducive to greater popular support and to the necessary compromises with other political movements. For this reason, some talked about the ikhwanisation of the Salafis to capture the inevitability of moderation through participation.[23] In short, the same process that led to the moderation of the Muslim Brotherhood and the political movements it inspired would characterise Salafi parties as well. It is interesting to note that it is not only scholars who believe in this process of ikhwanisation, but leading political figures within Islamism itself. Rachid Ghannouchi tried for a number of years to bring 'radical Salafis' into the tent of democratic Tunisia, arguing that they were young and somewhat hot-headed, but that participation and institutionalisation rather than repression would eventually turn them into supporters, however critical, of the post-uprising Tunisian system.[24] Ghannouchi's belief was only partly born out in practice, with some Salafis deciding to participate in electoral politics through the creation of political parties, while many others chose either critical quietism or violence to subvert democracy at home and fighting for the Islamic State abroad.

Given that Salafis' decision to enter politics was partly based on the desire to outflank the Muslim Brotherhood, it would be reasonable to expect that their policy preferences and objectives would diverge from those of mainstream Islamists. When it comes to Salafis' foreign policy positions and their broader understanding of the international system, the expectation is that they would position themselves as the 'true' bearers of Islamism, advocating for the return of the caliphate and a more confrontational foreign policy against the dominant world powers. This confrontation would not only lead to the dismantling of Western political imperialism, which for Islamists of all persuasions is most notable in Palestine, but also to the questioning of existing alliances and the international economic order, where international financial institutions are perceived to be the structures through which the West's domination of the Arab world is carried out in practice. Expecting such confrontational language would confirm that they did indeed position themselves as an alternative to mainstream Islamist parties in terms of foreign policy objectives and, simultaneously, as an alternative to Jihadi-Salafism in the way in which such objectives should be achieved because politicised Salafis would seek a popular mandate for their policies rather than committing violence.

Data

This study of Salafis' positions in the field of foreign policy is based on party manifestos presented to potential voters during parliamentary election campaigns. The working sample analysed here includes eight documents accounting for Salafi parties operating in Kuwait, Tunisia and Egypt.

For Kuwait, the party included in the analysis is al-Tajammu' al-Islami al-Salafi (the Salafi Islamic Gathering, SIG),[25] which is part of the broader al-Jama'a al-Salafiyya, the Salafi community, that also includes charity and proselytising networks. For Tunisia, political Salafism is represented by al-Jabhat al-Islah al-Islamiyya al-Tunisiyya (Tunisian Islamic Reform Front) which was founded and legalised in 2012 – after the founding elections for the Constitutional Assembly – with the aim of challenging the monopoly of Ennahda, a moderate Islamist party,[26] within the Islamist camp. Finally, the Salafi parties considered for the case of Egypt are al-Fadyla (the Virtue party), al-Asala (the Authenticity Party), al-Nour (the Party of Light) and al-Banna' wa al-Tanmiyya (the Building and Development Party). All of these parties constituted themselves in 2011 with the aim of defending Egyptian identity from secular and liberal parties as well as challenging the Muslim Brotherhood.[27] The first three parties originate from the al-Daw'a al-Salafiyya movement, the latter from al-Gama'a al-Islamiyya, an ultra-conservative Salafi movement that used to employ violence and was responsible for Anwar al-Sadat's assassination in 1981. Despite such 'genetic' differences, the parties ran in two separate coalitions, blurring the boundaries of their backgrounds. In fact, for opportunistic reasons, al-Nour, al-Asala and al-Banna' wa al-Tanmiyya ran under the Islamist Bloc coalition, while al-Fadyla chose to stay with the Democratic Alliance, the electoral coalition led by the Muslim Brotherhood's Freedom and Justice Party.[28]

The political parties included in this analysis display great variation both in terms of age and electoral success. The Kuwaiti al-Tajammu' al-Islami al-Salafi is the oldest political Salafi organisation, active and participating in parliamentary politics since the early 1980s.[29] In contrast, all Egyptian Salafi parties but one were banned in the aftermath of the 2013 military coup that ended participatory politics. The only exception is al-Nour, which managed to survive under al-Sisi's rule, although its role was heavily downsized and went from holding 111 seats in the previous legislature to eleven after the 2015 parliamentary elections. In Tunisia, Jabhat al-Islah has operated without interruption since 2012, but in light of its poor electoral showings, it never managed to enter parliament, and did not participate in the 2019 parliamentary elections when some of its members joined al-Karama, a heterodox coalition of populists, disgruntled leftists and Salafis. The coalition gained almost 6 per cent of the votes and twenty-one seats (out of 217).

In light of the short-lived experience of almost all the parties surveyed, only two (al-Tajammu' al-Islami al-Salafi and al-Nour) are represented with more than one election-year party manifesto. This leaves little room for studying programmatic changes in party positions over time. Nonetheless, the dataset is still helpful for examining Salafis' policy positions in the field of foreign policy and for comparing possible intra-party system and cross-country patterns of similarities and differences.

When it comes to their electoral manifestos, the documents vary significantly in structure and length. The 2008 electoral programme of al-Tajammu' al-Islami al-Salafi, for example, consists of a three-page document structured around the fifteen priorities the party identified, and for which measures of intervention are offered. These include clear Salafi priorities such as the implementation of sharia (which is, in fact, the first priority), the problem of housing, and high prices, women's rights, healthcare and youth, along with country-specific issues, such as the presence of foreign workers. This structure did not change significantly for the 2016 legislative elections. In this case, the party presented a nine-point programme reiterating the previous one with one noticeable change: women's rights were dropped while national unity and more detailed economic proposals for getting the Kuwaiti economy back on track were added. The Egyptian al-Nour's 2012 manifesto is thirty-two pages long and is largely concerned with culture and identity, the economy, health care and education, leaving relatively little room for international issues. Al-Nour's electoral programme for the 2015 parliamentary elections is instead only two pages long and is subdivided into nine sections that succinctly deal with different aspects of policymaking. Considerable attention to identity issues and the role of religion in the new political system characterise al-Banna' wa al-Tanmiyya's twenty-page programme, in which institutional concerns are prioritised. Al-Asala, by contrast, presented a one-page document laying out ten main goals so broad that they are impossible to disagree with (surprisingly, implementation of sharia is not among them). Finally, al-Fadyla presented a nineteen-page programme divided into eleven chapters, where education – at all levels and fields, especially the technical and scientific ones – is prioritised and discussed in greater detail than other policy issues. In Tunisia, al-Jabhat al-Islah presented a three-page manifesto, articulated into succinct points divided into the political, economic, social and cultural spheres, which follow a relatively rich description of the nature of the party.

Findings

The first important and already telling finding is the little attention Salafi parties devote to international affairs and foreign policy. In fact, in all of the surveyed party manifestos, foreign relations occupy a considerably smaller portion than all other topics. For instance, in al-Nour's thirty-two-page party manifesto, only one page is devoted to foreign policy, while education, for instance, takes up eight pages.

A second important empirical finding that emerges from the analysis is the great cross-country variation of foreign policy proposals. In Kuwait, for example, foreign policy is almost absent from al-Tajammu' al-Islami al-Salafi's party manifestos. In the party manifesto for the 2008 elections, the party devoted a section to 'human rights and international issues' in which it stated that Islam had to be the umbrella for security and peace across the world. It discusses how non-Muslims in Muslim countries are to be treated with kindness and compassion, and specifies that terrorism is prohibited and that international decisions and legal covenants are to be respected. In the 2016 party manifesto, the international dimension basically disappeared to the point that the only reference to it can be traced to a mention of the UN, inasmuch as the party advocated the use of UN funds allocated for the recovery of the Kuwaiti economy in the aftermath of the Iraqi invasion. Compared with Kuwait's Salafi party, Salafis in Egypt gave more thought to foreign relations. In this respect, the common thread linking all Egyptian Salafi parties is the call to restore Egypt's leading role in the regional and international arenas.

All of the parties surveyed lament the deterioration of Egypt's international standing during Mubarak's authoritarian rule. Al-Nour and al-Fadyla attribute this deterioration to the subordination of foreign policy to domestic concerns, ascribable to the ruling elite's focus on maintaining political and economic power. In al-Fadyla's reading, the restoration of Egypt's leading international role is a duty that comes with the cultural and political leverage of the country, both regionally and internationally. The party's proposal to 'make Egypt great again' is articulated into two distinct sections: one on Arab/regional politics and one on foreign policy. For the party, the elaboration of an 'Arab politics' that stands autonomous from the broader field of international politics is justified (if not prescribed) by the country's cultural, mediatic and political role within the Arab world, which entrusts Egypt the responsibility to protect 'the whole Arab nation', first and foremost from 'Zionist imperialism'. Programmatically, this entails the restoration of Egyptian sovereignty over the whole of Sinai; ensuring Palestinians' national rights; working to ensure the participation of Palestinian representatives in all decision making processes aimed at solving the Middle East crisis; working to support and unite all Arab, Islamic and international forces fighting for national liberation, social progress and religious unity and against colonialism and Zionism; and the creation of a multi-level Arab, Islamic front aimed at achieving a unitary Arab movement. The concerns informing al-Fadyla's 'Arab politics' are also present in the section devoted to foreign policy, further highlighting its importance in the party's larger policy framework. In general terms, the party calls for international peace based on justice and for cooperation aimed at improving human welfare.

This would be accomplished through the adoption of a foreign policy supporting anti-colonialism and anti-Zionism, while serving Egypt's strategic interests at the Arab, Islamic and international levels. In this sense, the party deems it necessary to forge closer ties with other Muslim-majority countries to curb the influence of great powers in the region with the aim of preserving national independence. Interestingly, al-Fadyla, advocates a stronger but renewed partnership with the US, conditional on a change in Washington's position towards Israel's settler colonialism and the Palestinian cause. Strengthening the relationship with the EU is also mentioned, as the party is aware of the fact that security on both sides of the Mediterranean has to be pursued through a unified framework of action.

Some of the issues raised by al-Fadyla find support among Egypt's other Salafi parties. This is the case for the call for greater autonomy among the Nile basin countries and the configuration of Egypt's international network along Arab, Islamic and African lines, in which foreign policy should be aimed at achieving full independence from foreign interference so as to preserve the country's national interests in the region. Furthermore, a general reassessment of Egypt's system of alliances in light of the principle of fairness and equity is also promoted by al-Banna' wa al-Tanmiyya party. More specifically, the party calls for respecting signed and ratified treaties and international conventions, provided they accord with religious principles and serve the people's interests through their elected representatives.

Another interesting finding about Egyptian Salafi parties is that support for the Palestinian cause is not uniform. While this is strongly advocated by al-Asala, in addition to al-Fadyla, and depicted as 'a central cause' and a 'religious duty' for Egypt by al-Banna' wa al-Tanmiyya, the Palestinian issue is completely absent in al-Nour's manifesto, even though the party envisages the pursuit of a foreign policy that achieves the interests of Muslim countries and the economic integration of the Arab and the Islamic world. In the party's 2011 manifesto, al-Nour stated that Egypt's foreign policy should support its national interests and security. It is only in al-Nour's 2015 party manifesto that the Palestinian cause is mentioned and enjoys the 'full support' of the party. Indeed, this is the only substantive point spelled out in the realm of international politics. The remaining two lines devoted to foreign policy call for the establishment of balanced foreign relations based on mutual respect and the achievement of common interests and for fruitful, constructive cooperation in the Arab, Islamic and African regional arenas, along with restoring the image of Egypt in the region and internationally. Another policy proposal that does not find its place in the programmes of Egypt's other Salafi parties is al-Nour's call to carry out 'international relations' with actors below the level of the nation state, which should not be the sole and privileged framework for international politics. Rather, al-Nour suggests entrusting 'the peoples of the region', suggesting that the party might interact with non-state actors.

The foreign policy proposals the Tunisian party al-Jabhat al-Islah puts forth are, for their part, in line with those proposed by its Egyptian counterparts. The party calls for Muslim unity in one state by 'eradicating artificial borders', the liberation of all oppressed Muslims – first and foremost the Palestinians – along with opposition to all forms of Zionism and strengthening international cooperation in a framework of mutual respect.

Discussion

Salafi parties' foreign policy proposals, as formulated in their party manifestos, do not prove to be as groundbreaking and radical as one might have assumed in light of Salafi proclamations over the course of the last decades. A number of themes emerge from the main findings that invalidate the hypothesis that Salafi parties' foreign policy proposals follow the same line as their jihadi counterparts. First is the very limited space that foreign policy and international politics occupy in the different documents. This is understandable. The party manifestos examined here were drawn up after the 2011 uprisings and were meant to attract voters for the founding elections. This had two implications that can explain why Salafi parties have largely overlooked foreign policy: (1) the uprisings had their roots in socio-economic concerns.[30] All parties competing in those elections needed to address economic and social issues in order to capture votes; and (2) the essence of the founding elections imposed on parties the need to propose to voters an idea of state and society that was totally different from the authoritarian past, leading them to focus on domestic transformations in spheres such as the economy, the place of religion in society or the delivery of essential services such as education or health care because of their 'proximity' to voters' priorities. Moreover, this ideological and programmatic enterprise had to be done in very little time. For Salafis plunged into the electoral arena quickly and for the first time, this was truly a stress test. Up to that moment, Salafis did not have any experience of politicking, and they had even less confidence in their economic vision and preferences, which had been absent from their concerns and internal debates.[31] Marginalising foreign policy made sense from a pragmatic perspective. This is a clear indication that once parties begin to institutionalise and compete in elections, they tend to gravitate around issues that voters prioritise. This is the case even for parties that can be described as strongly ideological, such as the Salafis. It is not surprising that other issues dominate their thinking and electoral programmes, no matter how incoherent or unattainable such policies might be. As in many other parts of the world, foreign policy and international issues are not particularly salient for the electorate, especially during founding elections when the political system's entire institutional set-up must be considered and pressing socio-economic needs must be addressed. Salafi parties are no exception, even in a region where foreign interference has deep roots and is profoundly felt.[32]

A second important and more concrete theme, as expected, addresses the transnational dimension of Salafism, and by extension its internationalist drive. With the exception of al-Tajammu's manifesto, pan-Arabism and pan-Islamism are present in all the political programmes. Nonetheless, these catchwords are formulated in a way that make them unsuitable to constitute a real alternative to the international status quo. In addition, they do not characterise a veritable Salafi foreign policy. On the one hand, the theme of pan-Arabism was born as a secular and leftist one and is now common to all parties, making it more of a shared ideal that every party can hang its hat on. On the other hand, in the aftermath of Ben Ali and Mubarak's departures, all the transitional parties, including the Salafis, called for the recuperation of national Islamic roots and the restoration of privileged relations with Muslim countries as an indication of 'redemption' from the imposition of secularism that characterised the Tunisian and Egyptian authoritarian regimes before 2011. This also suggests 'redemption' from the cultural and – most importantly – economic subjugation to the liberal paradigm of Western countries that was inherent in the exercise of power of local dictators. It follows that there does not seem to be anything particularly Salafi nor radical in signalling support for pan-Arabism and pan-Islamism. In this context, support for the Palestinian cause, which many Salafi parties deem a core issue in their international outlook, is far from being a uniquely Salafi concern. Quite the contrary, according to Arab Barometer survey data, the wider public, along with all other political parties, consider this among the most important topics in the realm of international politics.

In fact, for the collective imaginary of the region and, to an extent, beyond it, the Palestinian cause embodies Western – first and foremost US – oppression via Israel. In this sense, the framing of support for the Palestinian struggle owes much to Marxist jargon and resembles to what the anti-imperialist left posits.[33] Salafi foreign politics could have been distinct from the other political actors only if pan-Arabism, pan-Islamism and support for the Palestinian cause resulted in 'rocking the boat' of the international order by, for example, rejecting extant privileged partnerships (that is, the US for Egypt and France for Tunisia) or withdrawing national membership in international institutions, such as the UN, that proved incapable of preserving the interests of Arab citizens. However, Salafists' manifest intention to respect the covenants and existing treaties signals that this was not the case. The language and reasons employed to justify the potential withdrawal from treaties and covenants is so broad and undetermined that it seems to have been adopted precisely to avoid actually having to make such radical decisions. In a way, this is quite reassuring for the international community because it points to the political pragmatism of such parties. Although it is true that the policies in the manifestos might not tie the party down to a specific behaviour once in power, they are a clear suggestion that Salafi politicians are aware of the constraints of electoral politics and of the international position their countries find themselves in. Furthermore, and even more significantly, these policy positions place great distance between Salafi politicos and Jihadi-Salafis, whose preferences and actions are clearly intended to subvert the regional and international order. For those looking for nuance and complexity within Salafism, this is further empirical confirmation of the existence of such complexity. The most eloquent example of this pragmatism is al-Nour's commitment not to withdraw from extant agreements, including the controversial 1979 peace treaty with Israel, which has always been regarded in Islamist circles and beyond as an Arab capitulation to the Israeli–American axis.

A third theme emerging from the analysis is the attempt to reconcile a discourse of Arab/Islamic unity with the ease with which Salafis have accepted national state structures and institutions and how prevalent distinct national interests are in their programmes. Although it might be too strong to argue that only lip service is paid to principles of Islamic and Arab unity, it is quite clear from the manifestos that Salafi parties do not intend to challenge the Westphalian order and are not shy about their insistence on national interests, although at times they also mention broader Arab ones. This is due to a degree of ideological pragmatism and to a rather clear understanding of the institutions within which they have to operate. The clearest example of such

276 | VALERIA RESTA AND FRANCESCO CAVATORTA

ideological pragmatism and how it influences what parties include in their programmes is Kuwait's al-Tajammu, which does not even entertain notions of pan-Arabism and focuses instead on policies that might be beneficial to Kuwait alone. This might be surprising for Salafism, which has a strong trans-national dimension, but is much less the case when one examines Kuwaiti history. The Iraqi invasion of 1990 did not do much to attract Kuwaitis to the ideas of pan-Arabism or pan-Islamism. A similar trend is visible in Tunisia. Although the Tunisian al-Jabhat al-Islah maintains that state borders across the Arab world are artificial impediments to the unification of the Arab people, its electoral programme prioritises ensuring Tunisia's sovereignty, speaks about national identity and calls for its defence and genuine 'implementation' within the state. For its part, the Egyptian al-Banna' wa al-Tanmiyya sees the weaken-ing of loyalty and allegiance to the nation as one of Egypt's biggest problems and devotes an entire section to this theme, along with state building based on popular sovereignty and institutions 'that stand against military interference in politics'. Finally, al-Nour speaks about the renewal of the Egyptian state and the construction of a political regime made up of institutions capable of legitimately representing the Egyptian community. With regard to Egyptian Salafis, it is difficult to escape the conclusion that rather than genuine pan-Arabism or pan-Islamism, they see international politics as the realm where Arab unity is realised through Egypt's cultural and political leadership. In a sense this speaks to the legacy of Nasserism, whereby Egyptian exceptionalism is meant to lead the Arab world under the guise of unity. This confirms yet again how difficult it is for Salafis to escape the different historical paths of the countries they operate in, much like their Islamist counterparts had expe-rienced in previous decades. In short, all of this reveals that Salafi parties are quite at ease within state structures, once considered *jahili* ('pre-Islamic' and therefore illegitimate), and all parties in this analysis do not question the state order and are instead committed to preserving it.

The pragmatism of Salafi parties is due to their position in and under-standing of the political systems and the national institutions within which they operate. This, in turn, explains the great cross-country variation observed. In this vein, al-Tajammu's indifference towards foreign policy can be explained by the fact that this realm is considered the emir's prerogative, with parliament having little say in the matter, and the party just having come to terms with leaving aside the issue of the unification of the Islamic *umma*. Similarly, al-Nour's attitude towards the Palestinian cause and the US can be attributed to changed internal political conditions. Last, but not least, the limited opportunities of gaining seats pushed many members of the Tunisian Jabhat to run in coalition with other movements of different ideological persuasions, thereby compromising on some of its political objectives, including the foundational aspects of Salafi foreign policy.

Conclusion

Decades of quietism and repudiation of politics did not mean that Salafis were naïve electoral players once they finally decided to engage in politics – quite the contrary. The limited experience they have accumulated thus far in institutional politics has turned them into pragmatic political entrepreneurs and differentiates them from their jihadi counterparts. Wiktorowicz earlier argued that despite their different relationship with politics, all Salafis intend to create a genuine Islamic state where religious law determines the framework within which political, social and economic relationships take place. This might indeed still be the case even after Salafi parties actually participated in the nascent institutions of democratising systems in Egypt and Tunisia after the 2011 uprisings. However, one must be mindful about the way in which Salafis actually try to bring about such an Islamic state because the instruments of action have repercussions on how they understand the 'content' and nature of such a state. The analysis of how Salafi parties have dealt with foreign policy issues and international politics more broadly demonstrates the actual complexity of Salafism and the pragmatism of these parties even on matters where one might imagine greater proximity with their jihadi counterparts.[34] In reality, it took little time for them to realise that, after the uprisings, they had to attract voters to implement what they had preached up to that moment and needed to outline policies accordingly. They realised quite quickly that 'rocking the boat' was much harder than adjusting to the political and social pluralism that suddenly emerged in their countries. From this perspective, in light of the limited time they had available inside the institutions of the state, it can be said that the trajectory of politicised Salafis might be regarded, paradoxically, as one of the fastest examples of inclusion-moderation yet. This is clear even on foreign policy matters where one might have expected the adoption of much more radical positions given that Salafis decided to participate in institutional politics, in part, to counter the growth of the Muslim Brotherhood (in Egypt) and Ennahda (in Tunisia) and their supposed 'selling-out'. The harsh rhetoric one finds in Jihadi-Salafi circles about foreign policy objectives and the instruments of struggle through which they should be realised is virtually absent from Salafi manifestos and declarations. It is difficult to determine whether such a 'moderate' approach, embodied in the emphasis on maintaining extant state structures and the international order, owes more to inner ideological reflections or to a decision to send reassuring signals to other players in the transitional game – both domestic and international. In any case, what transpires is their commitment to abandon some of the more radical and unrealistic foreign policy issues – such as the unification of the Islamic *umma* – in favour of others that are believed to be more attainable, such as confirming (Egypt) or inscribing (Tunisia) sharia among the sources of legislation, or a greater role for religious teaching in school curricula. What can be easily detected thus far is that with regard to their objectives, Salafi political parties are not very different from mainstream Islamist ones, and this might explain why Jihadi-Salafism continues to be a seductive alternative for young Salafis disillusioned with the status quo and with the declining radicalism of elected politicians.

Notes

1 Joas Wagemakers, 'A "Purist Jihadi-Salafi": The Ideology of Abu Muhammad al-Maqdisi', *British Journal of Middle Eastern Studies* 36 no. 2 (2009): 281–97; Brian Fishman, *The Master Plan: ISIS, Al Qaeda and the Jihadi Strategy for Final Victory* (New Haven, CT: Yale University Press, 2016); Shiraz Maher, *Salafi-Jihadism: The History of an Idea* (Oxford: Oxford University Press, 2016); Aaron Zelin, *Your Sons Are at Your Service: Tunisia's Missionaries of Jihad* (New York: Columbia University Press, 2020).

2 Michael Weiss and Hassan Hassan, *ISIS: Inside the Army of Terror* (New York: Phaidon Press, 2015); Joby Warrick, *Black Flags: The Rise of ISIS* (New York: Anchor Books, 2016); Fawaz Gerges, *ISIS: A History* (Princeton: Princeton University Press, 2016).

3 Richard Nielsen, 'Does the Islamic State Believe in Sovereignty', in Marc Lynch, ed., *Islamism in the IS Age*, POMEPS Studies 12 (2015): 28–30.

4 Quintan Wiktorowicz, 'Anatomy of the Salafi Movement', *Studies in Conflict & Terrorism* 29, no. 3 (2006): 207–40.

5 Joas Wagemakers, 'Revisiting Wiktorowicz: Categorising and Defining the Branches of Salafism', in Francesco Cavatorta and Fabio Merone, eds, *Salafism after the Arab Awakening: Contending with People's Power* (London: Hurst & Co., 2017), 7–24.

6 For the quietists, see Roel Meijer, *Global Salafism: Islam's New Religious*

Movement (London: Hurst & Co., 2009); for the politicos, see Khalil al-Anani and Maszlee Malik, 'Pious Way to Politics: The Rise of Political Salafism in Post-Mubarak Egypt', *Digest of Middle East Studies* 22 no. 1 (2013): 57–73.

7   Marc Lynch, 'The new Salafi Politics', POMEPS Studies 2, October 2012. Available at <https://pomeps.org/arab-uprisings-the-new-salafi-politics> (last accessed 24 October 2022); Eberhard Kienle, 'Nouveaux régimes, vieilles politiques? Réponses islamistes aux défis économiques et sociaux', *Critique Internationale* 61, no. 4 (2013): 85–103; Francesco Cavatorta and Valeria Resta, 'Beyond Quietism: Party Institutionalization, Salafism and the Economy', *Politics & Religion* 13, no. 4 (2020): 796–817.

8   Bjørn Utvik, 'The Ikhwanization of the Salafis: Piety in the Politics of Egypt and Kuwait', *Middle East Critique* 23, no. 1 (2014): 5–27.

9   Steve Monroe, 'Salafis in Parliament: Democratic Attitudes and Party Politics in the Gulf', *Middle East Journal* 66, no. 3 (2012): 409–24.

10 Laurent Bonnefoy, 'Quietist Salafis, the Arab Spring and the Politicization Process', in Francesco Cavatorta and Fabio Merone, eds, *Salafism after the Arab Awakening: Contending with People's Power* (London: Hurst & Co., 2017), 205–18.

11 Christian Caryl, 'The Salafi Moment', *Foreign Policy*, 12 September 2012, 109.

12 Mohamed-Ali Adraoui, 'Borders and Sovereignty in Islamist and Jihadist Thought: Past and Present', *International Affairs* 93(4) (2017): 917–35, 918.

13 Roger Owen, *State, Power and Politics in the Making of the Modern Middle East* (Abingdon: Routledge, 1992).

14 Mona El-Ghobashy, 'The Metemorphosis of the Egyptian Muslim Brothers', *International Journal of Middle East Studies* 37, no. 3 (2005): 373–95; Jillian Schwedler, 'Can Islamists Become Moderates? Rethinking the Inclusion-Moderation Hypothesis', *World Politics* 63, no. 2 (2011): 347–76; Francesco Cavatorta and Fabio Merone, 'Moderation through Exclusion? The Journey of the Tunisian *Ennahda* from Fundamentalist to Conservative Party', *Democratization* 20, no. 5 (2013): 857–75; Sumita Pahwa, 'Pathways of Islamist Adaptation: The Egyptian Muslim Brothers' Lessons for Inclusion Moderation Theory', *Democratization* 24, no. 6 (2017): 1066–84.

15 Adraoui, 'Borders and Sovereignty in Islamist and Jihadist Thought'.

16 Maryam Ben Salem, 'The Foreign Policy of Tunisia's Ennahdha: Constancy and Changes', in Mohamed-Ali Adraoui, ed., *The Foreign Policy of Islamist Political Parties* (Edinburgh: Edinburgh University Press, 2018), 47–69

17 Jillian Schwedler, *Faith in Moderation: Islamist Parties in Jordan and Yemen* (Cambridge: Cambridge University Press, 2006).

18 El-Ghobashy, 'The Metemorphosis of the Egyptian Muslim Brothers'.

19 Fabio Merone, 'Enduring Class Struggle in Tunisia: The Fight for Identity beyond Political Islam', *British Journal of Middle Eastern Studies* 42, no. 1 (2015): 74–87.

20 Emmanuel Karagiannis, 'The Rise of Electoral Salafism in Egypt and Tunisia: The Use of Democracy as a Master Frame', *Journal of North African Studies* 24, no. 2 (2019): 207–25.

21 Khalil al-Anani, 'Unpacking the Sacred Canopy: Egypt's Salafis between Religion and Politics', in Francesco Cavatorta and Fabio Merone (eds.) *Salafism after the Arab Awakening: Contending with People's Power* (London: Hurst & Co., 2017), 25–42.

22 Utvik, 'The Ikhwanization of the Salafis'; Francesco Cavatorta, 'Salafism, Liberalism and Democratic Learning in Tunisia', *Journal of North African Studies* 20, no. 5 (2015): 770–83.

23 Utvik, 'The Ikhwanization of the Salafis'.

24 Zelin, *Your Sons Are at Your Service*.

25 In line with other scholars, we refer to al-Tajammu' al-Islami al-Salafi as a Salafi party, although in Kuwait parties are simply tolerated but not formally legal. See Hendrik Kraetzschmar and Paola Rivetti, eds, *Islamists and the Politics of the Arab Uprisings: Governance, Pluralisation and Contention* (Edinburgh: Edinburgh University Press, 2018); Monroe, 'Salafis in Parliament'; Zoltan Pall, 'Do Salafi Parties Represent a Contradiction in Terms? The Development and Fragmentation of Kuwait's Salafi Islamic Group', in Francesco Cavatorta and Lise Storm, eds, *Political Parties in the Arab World: Continuity and Change* (Edinburgh: Edinburgh University Press, 2018), 100–24. For this reason, Salafi parties, like all the others operating in Kuwait, are also referred to as proto-parties. See Hendrik Kraetzschmar, 'In the Shadow of Legality: Proto-parties and Participatory Politics in the Emirate of Kuwait', in Francesco Cavatorta and Lise Storm, eds, *Political Parties in the Arab World: Continuity and Change* (Edinburgh: Edinburgh University Press, 2018): 230–51.

26 Up to 2016, Ennahda party members defined their party as having an 'Islamic inspiration', rather than as an Islamic or Islamist party (Interview with Ajmi Lourimi, Tunis 2012). Since 2016, the party has labelled itself as the party of Muslim democrats. See Rachid Ghannouchi, 'From Political Islam to Muslim Democracy', *Foreign Affairs* 95, no. 5 (2016): 58–67.

27 Al-Anani and Malik, 'Pious Way to Politics'.

28 Jerome Drevon, 'The Constrained Institutionalization of Diverging Islamist Strategies: The Jihadis, the Muslim Brotherhood, and the Salafis between Two Aborted Egyptian Revolutions', *Mediterranean Politics* 22, no. 1 (2017): 16–34.

29 Zoltan Pall, *Salafism in Lebanon: Local and Transnational Movements* (Cambridge: Cambridge University Press, 2018).

30 Gilbert Achcar, *The People Want: A Radical Exploration of the Arab Uprising* (Los Angeles: University of California Press, 2013); Andrea Teti et al., *The Arab Uprisings in Egypt, Jordan and Tunisia: Social, Political and Economic Transformations* (London: Palgrave, 2018).

31 Cavatorta and Resta, 'Beyond Quietism'.

32 Sean Yom, *From Resilience to Revolution: How Foreign Interventions Destabilize the Middle East* (New York: Columbia University Press, 2015).

33 Valeria Resta, 'Leftist Parties in the Arab Region Before and After the Arab Uprisings: Unrequited Love?' in Francesco Cavatorta and Lise Storm, eds, *Political Parties in the Arabic World: Continuity and Change* (Edinburgh: Edinburgh University Press, 2018), 21–48.

34 Stéphane Lacroix, 'Egypt's Pragmatic Salafis: The Politics of Hizb al-Nour', Carnegie Endowment for International Peace, November 2016. Available at <https://carnegieendowment.org/2016/11/01/egypt-s-pragmatic-salafis-politics -of-hizb-al-nour-pub-64902> (last accessed 24 October 2022).

SELECT BIBLIOGRAPHY

Abboud, Samer N. *Syria: Hot Spots in Global Politics*, second edn. Cambridge: Polity Press, 2018.

Achcar, Gilbert. *The People Want: A Radical Exploration of the Arab Uprising*. Los Angeles: University of California Press, 2013.

Adraoui, Mohamed-Ali. 'Borders and Sovereignty in Islamist and Jihadist Thought: Past and Present'. *International Affairs* 93, no. 4 (July 2017): 917–35.

Aktürk, Şener. 'Türkiye'nin Rusya Ile İlişkilerinin Yükselişi ve Gerilemesi, 1992–2015, Neorealist Bir Değerlendirme'. In *Kuşku Ile Komşuluk, Türkiye ve Rusya İlişkilerinde Değişen Dinamikler*, edited by Gencer Özcan, Evren Balta and Burç Beşgül, 129–45. Istanbul: İletisim, 2017.

Al Faisal bin Abdul Aziz Al Saud, Turki. 'Saudi Arabia's Foreign Policy'. *Middle East Policy* 20, no. 4 (2013): 37–44.

Al-Eriani, Kamilia. 'Mourning the Death of a State to Enliven It: Notes on the "Weak" Yemeni State'. *International Journal of Cultural Studies* 23, no. 2 (2020): 227–44.

Allison, Roy. 'Russia and Syria: Explaining Alignment with a Regime in Crisis'. *International Affairs* 89, no. 4 (July 2013): 795–823.

Allsopp, Harriet. *The Kurds of Syria: Political Parties and Identities in the Middle East*. London: I. B. Tauris, 2014.

Al-Rasheed, Madawi, ed. *Salman's Legacy: The Dilemmas of a New Era in Saudi Arabia*. New York: Oxford University Press, 2018.

Al-Tamimi, Aymen Jawad. 'From Jabhat Al-Nusra to Hay'at Tahrir al-Sham: Evolution, Approach and Future'. Konrad-Adenauer Stiftung/al-Nahrain Center for Strategic Studies, 2018, 10–11.

Amnesty International. 'Israel's Apartheid against Palestinians: Cruel System of Domination and a Crime against Humanity', 1 February 2022.

Amour, Philipp. 'Israel, the Arab Spring, and the Unfolding Regional Order in the Middle East: A Strategic Assessment'. *British Journal of Middle Eastern Studies* 44, no. 3 (2017): 293–309.

al-Anani, Khalil. 'Unpacking the Sacred Canopy: Egypt's Salafis between Religion and Politics'. In *Salafism After the Arab Awakening: Contending with People's Power*, edited by Francesco Cavatorta and Fabio Merone, 25–42. London: Hurst & Co., 2017.

al-Anani, Khalil and Maszlee Malik. 'Pious Way to Politics: The Rise of Political Salafism in Post-Mubarak Egypt'. *Digest of Middle East Studies* 22, no. 1 (2013): 57–73.

Anderson, Lisa. 'Is There a Future for American Universities in the Middle East?' *Foreign Affairs*, 22 March 2019.

Aras, Bülent and Emirhan Yorulmazlar. 'Mideast Geopolitics: The Struggle for a New Order'. *Middle East Policy* 24, no. 2 (2017): 57–69.

Aras, N. Ela Gökalp and Zeynep Şahin Mencütek. 'The International Migration and Foreign Policy Nexus: The Case of Syrian Refugee Crisis and Turkey'. *Migration Letters* 12, no. 3 (2015): 193–208.

Ardemagni, Eleonora. 'UAE's Foreign Policy: From Militias in the Rimland to Straits Diplomacy'. *Sada*. Carnegie Endowment for International Peace, 28 October 2021.

Ataç, C. Akça. 'Pax Ottomanica No More! The "Peace" Discourse in Turkish Foreign Policy in the Post-Davutoğlu Era and the Prolonged Syrian Crisis'. *Digest of Middle East Studies* 28, no. 1 (2019): 48–69.

Atwan, Abdel Bari. *Islamic State: The Digital Caliphate*. Berkeley: University of California Press, 2015.

Aydıntaşbaş, Asli and Cinzia Bianco. 'Useful Enemies: How the Turkey–UAE Rivalry Is Remaking the Middle East'. European Council on Foreign Relations, 15 March 2021.

Ayoob, Mohammed. 'Subaltern Realism Meets the Arab World'. In *Routledge Handbook of International Relations in the Middle East*, edited by Shahram Akbarzadeh, 59–68. London: Routledge, 2019.

Baabood, Abdullah. 'Omani Perspectives on the Peace Process in Yemen'. Berghof Foundation, 7 June 2021.

Badeau, John S. *The American Approach to the Arab World*. New York: Published for the Council on Foreign Relations by Harper & Row, 1968.

Bank, André and Roy Karadag. 'The "Ankara Moment": The Politics of Turkey's Regional Power in the Middle East, 2007–11'. *Third World Quarterly* 34, no. 2 (2013): 287–304.

Baron, Adam. 'Foreign and Domestic Influences in the War in Yemen'. PWP Conflict Studies. Blacksburg, VA: Virginia Tech Publishing, 2019.

Bar-Siman-Tov, Yaacov. 'Security Regimes: Mediating between War and Peace in the Arab–Israeli Conflict'. In *Regional Security Regimes: Israel and Its Neighbors*, edited by Efraim Inbar, 33–55. Albany: State University of New York Press, 1995.

Barzegar, Kayhan and Abdolrasool Divsallar. 'Political Rationality in Iranian Foreign Policy'. *The Washington Quarterly* 40, no. 1 (Spring 2017): 39–53.

Başol, Dünya. 'Arab Spring and Israeli Security: The New Threats'. *Alternative Politics* 3, no. 3 (2011): 509–46.

Bassiouni, Mahmoud Cherif, Nigel Rodley, Badria Al-Awadhi, Philippe Kirsch and Mahnoush H Arsanjani. 'Report of the Bahrain Independent Commission of Inquiry'. Bahrain Independent Commission of Inquiry, 23 November 2011.

Bayat, Asef. 'Islam and Democracy: The Perverse Charm of an Irrelevant Question'. In *Making Islam Democratic: Social Movements and the Post-Islamist Turn*, 1–15. Stanford: Stanford University Press, 2007.

———. *Revolution without Revolutionaries: Making Sense of the Arab Spring*. Stanford: Stanford University Press, 2017.

Baycar, Hamdullah. 'Rapprochement Spree: Abu Dhabi Recalibrates Relations with Ankara'. *Sada*. Carnegie Endowment for International Peace, 16 December 2021.

Beck, Martin. 'Israel: Regional Politics in a Highly Fragmented Region'. In *Regional Leadership in the Global System: Ideas, Interests and Strategies of Regional Powers*, edited by Daniel Flemes, 127–48. London: Routledge, 2010.

———. 'The Concept of Regional Power as Applied to the Middle East'. In *Regional Powers in the Middle East: New Constellations after the Arab Revolts*, edited by Henner Fürtig, 1–20. New York: Palgrave Macmillan, 2014.

———. 'The End of Regional Middle Eastern Exceptionalism? The Arab League and the Gulf Cooperation Council after the Arab Uprisings'. *Democracy and Security* 11, no. 2 (2015): 190–207.

———. '"Watching and Waiting" and "Much Ado About Nothing"? Making Sense of the Israeli Response to the Arab Uprisings'. *Palgrave Communications* 2, no. 1 (2016): 160–79.

Beck, Martin and Thomas Richter. 'Fluctuating Regional (Dis-)Order in the Post-Arab Uprising Middle East'. *Global Policy* 11, no. 1 (2020): 68–74.

Becker, Howard. *Outsiders: Studies in the Sociology of Deviance*. New York: Free Press, 2018.

Bekdil, Burak. 'Turkey's Double Game with ISIS'. *Middle East Quarterly* 22, no. 3 (Summer 2015): 1–8.

Benjamin, Medea. *Drone Warfare: Killing by Remote Control*. London: Verso Books, 2013.

Berti, Benedetta. 'Israel and the Arab Spring: Understanding Attitudes and Responses to the "New Middle East"'. In *The West and the Muslim Brotherhood after the Arab Spring*, edited by Lorenzo Vidino, 130–47. Al Mesbar Studies & Research Center and The Foreign Policy Research Institute, 2013.

Biçakci, A. Salih. 'Sway on a Tightrope: The Development of a Mutualistic Relationship between Turkey and DAESH'. *Uluslararası İlişkiler Dergisi* 16, no. 62 (June 2019): 101–33.

Black, Ian. 'Just Below the Surface: Israel, the Arab Gulf States and the Limits of Cooperation'. LSE Middle East Centre Report. LSE Middle East Centre, March 2019.

Blumi, Isa. *Destroying Yemen: What Chaos in Arabia Tells Us about the World*. Oakland, CA: University of California Press, 2018.

Bonnefoy, Laurent. 'Quietist Salafis, the Arab Spring and the Politicisation Process'. In *Salafism After the Arab Awakening: Contending with People's Power*, edited by Francesco Cavatorta and Fabio Melone, 205–18. London: Hurst & Co., 2017.

Boserup, Rasmus, Waleed Hazbun, Karim Makdisi and Helle Malmvig. 'Introduction'. In *New Conflict Dynamics: Between Regional Autonomy and Intervention in the Middle East and North Africa*, edited by Rasmus Boserup, Waleed Hazbun, Karim Makdisi and Helle Malmvig, 7–16. Copenhagen: Danish Institute for International Studies, 2017.

Boucek, Christopher and Marina Ottaway, eds. *Yemen on the Brink*. Washington DC: Carnegie Endowment for International Peace, 2010.

Brandt, Marieke. *Tribes and Politics in Yemen: A History of the Houthi Conflict*. Oxford: Oxford University Press, 2017.

Brown, Nathan. Tracking the "Arab Spring": Egypt's Failed Transition'. *Journal of Democracy* 24, no. 4 (2013): 45–58.

Brownlee, Jason. *Democracy Prevention: The Politics of the US–Egyptian Alliance*. New York: Cambridge University Press, 2012.

Brzezinski, Zbigniew. *Strategic Vision: America and the Crisis of Global Power*. New York: Basic Books, 2012.

Bull, Hedley. *The Anarchical Society: A Study of Order in World Politics*. London: Macmillan, 1977.

Bull, Hedley, Stanley Hoffmann and Andrew Hurrell. *The Anarchical Society: A Study of Order in World Politics*, fourth edn. Basingstoke: Palgrave Macmillan, 2012.

Bull, Hedley Norman and Adam Watson, eds. *The Expansion of International Society*. New York: Oxford University Press, 1984.

Bunzel, Cole. 'From Paper State to Caliphate: The Ideology of the Islamic State (The Brookings Project on US Relations with the Islamic World No. 19)'. Brookings, March 2015.

Burns, William J. 'An End to Magical Thinking in the Middle East'. *The Atlantic*, 8 December 2019.

Butter, David. 'Egypt and the Gulf: Allies and Rivals'. Chatham House, 20 April 2020.

Buzan, Barry. 'Culture and International Society'. *International Affairs* 86, no. 1 (2010): 1–25.

Buzan, Barry and Ana Gonzalez-Pelaez, eds. *International Society and the Middle East: English School Theory at the Regional Level*. Basingstoke: Palgrave Macmillan, 2009.

Byman, Daniel. 'Sectarianism Afflicts the New Middle East'. *Survival* 56, no. 1 (January 2014): 79–100.

Carapico, Sheila. 'Yemen between Revolution and Counter-terrorism'. In *Why Yemen Matters: A Society in Transition*, edited by Helen Lackner, 29–49. London: Saqi, 2014.

Caryl, Christian. 'The Salafi Moment'. *Foreign Policy*, 12 September 2012.

Cavatorta, Francesco. 'Salafism, Liberalism, and Democratic Learning in Tunisia'. *The Journal of North African Studies* 20, no. 5 (October 2015): 770–83.

Cavatorta, Francesco and Fabio Merone. 'Moderation through Exclusion? The Journey of the Tunisian Ennahda from Fundamentalist to Conservative Party'. *Democratization* 20, no. 5 (August 2013): 857–75.

———, eds. *Salafism After the Arab Awakening: Contending with People's Power*. London: Hurst & Co., 2017.

Cavatorta, Francesco and Valeria Resta. 'Beyond Quietism: Party Institutionalisation, Salafism, and the Economy'. *Politics and Religion* 13, no. 4 (December 2020): 796–817.

Celso, Anthony N. 'Al Qaeda's Post-Bin Laden Resurgence: The Paradox of Resilience and Failure'. *Mediterranean Quarterly* 25, no. 2 (June 2014): 33–47.

Chandler, David. *Empire in Denial: The Politics of State-building*. London: Pluto Press, 2006.

———. *Statebuilding and Intervention: Policies, Practices and Paradigms*. Abingdon: Routledge, 2014.

Çiçek, Cuma, and Vahap Coşkun. *Dolmabahçe'den Günümüze Çözüm Süreci: Başarısızlığı Anlamak ve Yeni Bir Yol Bulmak*. Ankara: Barış Vakfı, 2016.

Clark, Victoria. *Yemen: Dancing on the Heads of Snakes*. New Haven, CT: Yale University Press, 2010.

Clausen, Maria-Louise. 'Justifying Military Intervention: Yemen as a Failed State'. *Third World Quarterly* 40, no. 3 (March 2019): 488–502.

Cockburn, Patrick. 'Whose Side Is Turkey On?' *London Review of Books* 36, no. 1 (November 2014).

——. *The Rise of Islamic State: ISIS and the New Sunni Revolution*. New York: Verso, 2015.

Cornell, Svante E. 'What Drives Turkish Foreign Policy?' *Middle East Quarterly* 19, no. 1 (January 2012): 13–24.

Crowley, P. J. *Red Line: American Foreign Policy in a Time of Fractured Politics and Failing States*. Lanham, MD: Roman & Littlefield, 2017.

Daher, Joseph. 'The Dynamics and Evolution of UAE–Syria Relations: Between Expectations and Obstacles'. Technical Report. European University Institute, 2019.

Davidson, Christopher M. *Abu Dhabi: Oil and Beyond*. London: Hurst & Co., 2009.

Del Sarto, Raffaella A., Helle Malmvig and Eduard Soler i lecha. 'Interregnum: The Regional Order in the Middle East and North Africa after 2011'. MENARA Final Reports, 28 February 2019.

Demir, Idris, ed. *Turkey's Foreign Policy Towards the Middle East: Under the Shadow of the Arab Spring*. Newcastle-upon-Tyne: Cambridge Scholars Publishing, 2017.

Demirtaş, Birgül. 'Turkish–Syrian Relations: From Friend "Esad" to Enemy "Esed"'. *Middle East Policy* 20, no. 1 (2013): 111–20.

Dessì, Andrea and Lorenzo Kamel. 'The Gaza Equation: The Regional Dimension of a Local Conflict'. MENARA Working Papers, September 2018.

Diwan, Kristin Smith. 'The New Rules of Monarchy in the Gulf'. *Lawfare*, 3 September 2017.

Drevon, Jerome. 'The Constrained Institutionalization of Diverging Islamist Strategies: The Jihadis, the Muslim Brotherhood, and the Salafis between Two Aborted Egyptian Revolutions'. *Mediterranean Politics* 22, no. 1 (January 2017): 16–34.

Egeli, Sıtkı. 'Dost-Düşman-Dost Döngüsü ve Türkiye-Rusya Askeri Rekabetinin Dönüşümü'. In *Kuşku ile Komşuluk, Türkiye ve Rusya İlişkilerinde Değişen Dinamikler*, edited by Gencer Özcan, Evren Balta and Burç Beşgül, 163–80. Istanbul: İletişim, 2017.

Ehteshami, Anoushiravan. 'Saudi Arabia as a Resurgent Regional Power'. *The International Spectator* 53, no. 4 (October 2018): 75–94.

El Husseini, Rola. 'Hezbollah and the Axis of Refusal: Hamas, Iran and Syria'. *Third World Quarterly* 31, no. 5 (July 2010): 803–15.

El-Ghobashy, Mona. 'The Metamorphosis of the Egyptian Muslim Brothers'. *International Journal of Middle East Studies* 37, no. 3 (2005): 373–95.

Elmasry, Mohamad. 'Unpacking Anti-Muslim Brotherhood Discourse'. *Jadaliyya* 28 (June 2013).

El-Shazly, Nadia and Raymond Hinnebusch. 'The Challenge of Security in the Post-Gulf War Middle East System'. In *The Foreign Policies of Middle East States*, edited by Raymond A. Hinnebusch and Anoushiravan Ehteshami, 71–90. Boulder, CO: Lynne Rienner, 2002.

Fakhro, Elham. 'Selling Normalization in the Gulf'. *Middle East Report Online*, 23 June 2021.

Falk, Richard. 'Rethinking the Arab Spring: Uprisings, Counterrevolution, Chaos and Global Reverberations'. *Third World Quarterly* 37, no. 12 (2016): 2322–34.

Farouk, Yasmine. 'More than Money: Post-Mubarak Egypt, Saudi Arabia, and the Gulf'. Gulf Research Center, April 2014, 1–21.

Fawcett, Louise. 'Regional Leadership? Understanding Power and Transformation in the Middle East'. In *Regional Powers and Regional Orders*, edited by Nadine Godehardt and Dirk Nabers, 155–70. London: Routledge, 2011.

——, ed. *International Relations of the Middle East*, third edn. Oxford: Oxford University Press, 2013.

——. 'Iran and the Regionalization of (in)Security'. *International Politics* 52, no. 5 (September 2015): 646–56.

——. 'Regionalizing Security in the Middle East: Connecting the Regional and the Global'. In *Regional Insecurity after the Arab Uprisings: Narratives of Security and Threat*, edited by Elizabeth Monier, 40–57. London: Palgrave Macmillan, 2015.

——. 'States and Sovereignty in the Middle East: Myths and Realities'. *International Affairs* 93, no. 4 (2017): 789–807.

Filkins, Dexter. 'A Saudi Prince's Quest to Remake the Middle East'. *The New Yorker*, 2 April 2018.

Fishman, Brian. *The Master Plan: ISIS, Al Qaeda, and the Jihadi Strategy for Final Victory*. New Haven, CT: Yale University Press, 2016.

Fraihat, Ibrahim. *Unfinished Revolutions: Yemen, Libya, and Tunisia after the Arab Spring*. New Haven, CT: Yale University Press, 2016.

Freer, Courtney. 'From Co-Optation to Crackdown: Gulf States' Reactions to the Rise of the Muslim Brotherhood during the Arab Spring'. In *The Qatar Crisis*, edited by Marc Lynch, 68–73. Project on Middle East Political Science (POMEPS) Briefing 31, October 2017.

Freer, Courtney Jean. *Rentier Islamism: The Influence of the Muslim Brotherhood in Gulf Monarchies*. New York: Oxford University Press, 2018.

Fromherz, Allen James. *Qatar: A Modern History*. London: I. B. Tauris, 2012.

Ganesan, Janani. 'Decoding the Current War in Syria: The WikiLeaks Files'. *Versobooks.Com* (blog), 31 August 2015.

Gartenstein-Ross, Daveed and Nathaniel Barr. 'How al-Qaeda Survived the Islamic State Challenge'. *Current Trends in Islamist Ideology* 21 (2017): 50–68.

Gause, F. Gregory. 'The Middle East Academic Community and the "Winter of Arab Discontent": Why Did We Miss It?' In *Seismic Shift: Understanding Change in the Middle East*, edited by Ellen Laipson, 11–28. Washington DC: Stimson Center, 2011.

———. 'Beyond Sectarianism: The New Middle East Cold War'. Brookings Doha Center Analysis Paper, July 2014.

———. 'Donald Trump and the Middle East'. In *Chaos in the Liberal Order: The Trump Presidency and International Politics in the Twenty-first Century*, edited by Robert Jervis, Francis J. Gavin, Joshua Rovner and Dianne N. Labross, 273–86. New York: Columbia University Press, 2018.

Gerges, Fawaz A. *ISIS: A History*. Princeton: Princeton University Press, 2017.

Ghani, Ashraf and Clare Lockhart. *Fixing Failed States: A Framework for Rebuilding a Fractured World*. Oxford: Oxford University Press, 2009.

Ghannouchi, Rached. 'From Political Islam to Muslim Democracy: The Ennahda Party and the Future of Tunisia'. *Foreign Affairs* 95, no. 5 (October 2016).

Goddard, Stacie E. and Daniel H. Nexon. 'The Dynamics of Global Power Politics: A Framework for Analysis'. *Journal of Global Security Studies* 1, no. 1 (February 2016): 4–18.

Goldberg, Jeffrey. 'The Obama Doctrine'. *The Atlantic*, April 2016.

Goodarzi, Jubin. 'Iran: Syria as the First Line of Defence'. *The Regional Struggle for Syria* edited by Julien Barnes-Dacey and Daniel Levy, 25–31. London: European Council on Foreign Relations, 2013.

Goodarzi, Jubin M. *Syria and Iran: Diplomatic Alliance and Power Politics in the Middle East*. London: I. B. Tauris, 2006.

Gulbrandsen, Anders. 'Bridging the Gulf: Qatari Business Diplomacy and Conflict Mediation'. Masters Dissertation, Georgetown University, 2010.

Gunter, Michael M. *Out of Nowhere: The Kurds of Syria in Peace and War*. London: Hurst & Co., 2014.

Haferlach, Lisa and Dilek Kurban. 'Lessons Learnt from the EU–Turkey Refugee Agreement in Guiding EU Migration Partnerships with Origin and Transit Countries'. *Global Policy* 8, no. 4 (2017): 85–93.

Hansen, Suzy. *Notes on a Foreign Country: An American Abroad in a Post-American World*. New York: Farar, Straus & Giroux, 2017.

Harchaoui, Jalel and Mohamed-Essaïd Lazib. 'Proxy War Dynamics in Libya'. PWP Conflict Studies, 2019.

Harknett, Richard J. and Jeffrey A. VanDenBerg. 'Alignment Theory and Interrelated Threats: Jordan and the Persian Gulf Crisis'. *Security Studies* 6, no. 3 (Spring 1997): 112–53.

Hashemi, Nader and Danny Postel, eds. *Sectarianization: Mapping the New Politics of the Middle East*. New York: Oxford University Press, 2017.

Hawthorne, Amy and Andrew Miller. 'Q&A – "Why Did Egyptian Democratization Fail?" Fourteen Experts Respond'. Project on Middle East Democracy, 21 January 2021.

Hazbun, Waleed. 'The Uses of Modernization Theory: American Foreign Policy and Mythmaking in the Arab World'. In *American Studies Encounters the Middle East*, edited by Marwan Kraidy and Alex Lubins, 175–206. Chapel Hill: University of North Carolina Press, 2016.

———. 'Regional Powers and the Production of Insecurity in the Middle East'. MENARA Working Papers, no. 11, September 2018, 20.

———. 'Reimagining US Engagement with a Turbulent Middle East'. *Middle East Report* 294 (Spring 2020).

Hehir, Aidan. 'The Myth of the Failed State and the War on Terror: A Challenge to the Conventional Wisdom'. *Journal of Intervention and Statebuilding* 1, no. 3 (November 2007): 307–32; and in *Statebuilding and Intervention: Policies Practices and Paradigms*, edited by David Chandler, 72–98. London: Routledge, 2009.

Heller, Mark. 'Israel: Extra-regional Foundations of a Regional Power Manqué'. In *Regional Powers and Regional Orders*, edited by Nadine Godehardt and Dirk Nabers, 229–40. London: Routledge, 2011.

———. 'Israel as a Regional Power: Prospects and Problems'. In *Regional Powers in the Middle East: New Constellations after the Arab Revolts*, edited by Henner Fürtig, 163–74. New York: Palgrave Macmillan, 2014.

Henriksen, Dag and Ann Karin Larssen, eds. *Political Rationale and International Consequences of the War in Libya*. Oxford: Oxford University Press, 2016.

Heydemann, Steven and Emelie Chace-Donahue. 'Sovereignty Verus Sectarianism: Contested Norms and the Logic of Regional Conflict in the Greater Levant'. *Uluslararası İlişkiler / International Relations* 15, no. 60 (2018): 5–19.

Hilu Pinto, Paolo Gabriel. 'The Shattered Nation: The Sectarianization of the Syrian Conflict'. In *Sectarianization: Mapping the New Politics of the Middle East*, edited by Nader Hashemi and Daniel Postel, 123–42. Oxford: Oxford University Press, 2017.

Hinnebusch, Raymond. *The Foreign Policies of Middle East States*. Boulder, CO: Lynne Rienner Publishers, 2002.

———. 'Syria: Defying the Hegemon'. In *The Iraq War: Causes and Consequences*, edited by Rick Fawn and Raymond Hinnebusch, 129–47. Boulder, CO: Lynne Rienner Publishers, 2006.

———. 'Order and Change in the Middle East: A Neo-Gramscian Twist on the International Society Approach'. In *International Society and the Middle East*:

English School Theory at the Regional Level, edited by Barry Buzan and Ana Gonzalez-Pelaez, 201–25. Basingstoke: Palgrave Macmillan, 2009.

———. 'Back to Enmity: Turkey–Syria Relations since the Syrian Uprising'. *Orient, Journal of German Orient Institute* 56, no. 1 (2015): 14–22.

———. *The International Politics of the Middle East*. Manchester: Manchester University Press, 2015.

———. 'Historical Context of State Formation in the Middle East: Structure and Agency'. In *The Routledge Handbook to the Middle East and North African State and States System*, edited by Raymond Hinnebusch and Jasmine K. Gani, 21–39. Abingdon and New York: Routledge, 2019.

———. 'The Arab Uprising and Regional Power Struggle'. In *The Routledge Handbook of International Relations in the Middle East*, edited by Shahram Akbarzadeh, 110–24. Abingdon and New York: Routledge, 2019.

———. 'War in the Middle East'. In *The Routledge Handbook to the Middle East and North African State and States System*, edited by Raymond Hinnebusch and Jasmine K. Gani, 354–74: Abingdon and New York: Routledge, 2019.

Human Rights Watch. 'All According to Plan: The Rab'a Massacre and Mass Killings of Protesters in Egypt', 12 August 2014.

Ibrahim, Raslan. 'Primary and Secondary Institutions in Regional International Society: Sovereignty and the League of Arab States'. In *International Organization in the Anarchical Society*, edited by Cornelia Navari and Tonny Brems Knudsen, 293–319. Cham: Palgrave Macmillan, 2019.

Ikenberry, G. John. *America Unrivaled: The Future of the Balance of Power*. Ithaca, NY: Cornell University Press, 2002.

Inbar, Efraim, ed. *Regional Security Regimes: Israel and Its Neighbors*. Albany: State University of New York Press, 1995.

———. 'The Strategic Implications for Israel'. In *The Arab Spring, Democracy and Security: Domestic and International Ramifications*, edited by Efraim Inbar, 145–65. London: Routledge, 2013.

Inbar, Efraim and Shmuel Sandler. 'The Changing Israeli Strategic Equation: Toward a Security Regime'. *Review of International Studies* 21, no. 1 (1995): 41–59.

International Crisis Group. 'Averting an ISIS Resurgence in Iraq and Syria', 11 October 2019.

———. 'Fleshing Out the Libya Ceasefire Agreement', 4 November 2020.

Isaac, Sally Khalifa. 'A Resurgence in Arab Regional Institutions? The Cases of the Arab League and the Gulf Cooperation Council Post-2011'. In *Regional Insecurity after the Arab Uprisings: Narratives of Security and Threat*, edited by Elizabeth Monier, 151–67. Basingstoke: Palgrave Macmillan, 2015.

Jacoby, Tami Amanda. 'The Season's Pendulum: Arab Spring Politics and Israeli

Security'. In *Regional Insecurity after the Arab Uprisings: Narratives of Security and Threat*, edited by Elizabeth Monier, 168–86. Basingstoke: Palgrave Macmillan, 2015.

Jebnoun, Noureddine. 'Introduction: Rethinking the Paradigm of "Durable" and "Stable" Authoritarianism in the Middle East'. In *Modern Middle East Authoritarianism*, edited by Noureddine Jebnoun, Mehrdad Kia and Mimi Kirk, 1–24. Abingdon: Routledge, 2013.

Jervis, Robert. *Perception and Misperception in International Politics: New Edition*. Princeton: Princeton University Press, 1976.

———. 'Unipolarity: A Structural Perspective'. *World Politics* 61, no. 1 (2009): 188–213.

Jones, Clive and Yoel Guzansky. 'Israel's Relations with the Gulf States: Toward the Emergence of a Tacit Security Regime?' *Contemporary Security Policy* 38, no. 3 (2017): 398–419.

Jones, Clive and Beverley Milton-Edwards. 'Missing the "Devils" We Knew? Israel and Political Islam Amid the Arab Awakening'. *International Affairs* 89, no. 2 (2013): 399–415.

Jones, Marc Owen. *Political Repression in Bahrain*. Cambridge: Cambridge University Press, 2020.

Jones, Marc Owen and Ala'a Shehabi, eds. *Barhrain's Uprising: Resistance and Repression in the Gulf*. London: Zed Books, 2015.

Kamrava, Mehran. *Troubled Waters: Insecurity in the Persian Gulf*. New York: Cornell University Press, 2018.

Kappel, Robert. 'Israel: The Partial Regional Power in the Middle East'. In *Regional Powers in the Middle East: New Constellations after the Arab Revolts*, edited by Henner Fürtig, 145–61. New York: Palgrave Macmillan, 2014.

Kapstein, Ethan B. and Michael Mastanduno, eds. *Unipolar Politics: Realism and State Strategies after the Cold War*. New York: Columbia University Press, 1999.

Karagiannis, Emmanuel. 'The Rise of Electoral Salafism in Egypt and Tunisia: The Use of Democracy as a Master Frame'. *Journal of North African Studies* 24, no. 2 (March 2019): 207–25.

Kepel, Gilles and Jean-Pierre Milelli, eds. *Al Qaeda in Its Own Words*. Cambridge, MA: Belknap Press of Harvard University Press, 2008.

Khatib, Lina. 'Syria, Saudi Arabia, the U.A.E. and Qatar: The "Sectarianization" of the Syrian Conflict and Undermining of Democratization in the Region'. *British Journal of Middle Eastern Studies* 46, no. 3 (May 2019): 385–403.

Kienle, Eberhard. *Contemporary Syria: Liberalization Between Cold War and Peace*. London: I. B. Tauris, 1994.

————. 'Nouveaux régimes, vieilles politiques? Réponses islamistes aux défis économiques et sociaux'. Translated by Delphine Ettinger. *Critique internationale* 61, no. 4 (2013): 85–103.

Kirkpatrick, David D. *Into the Hands of the Soldiers: Freedom and Chaos in Egypt and the Middle East*. New York: Viking, 2018.

Klieman, Aaron. 'The Israel–Jordan Tacit Security Regime'. In *Regional Security Regimes: Israel and Its Neighbors*, edited by Efraim Inbar, 127–50. Albany: State University of New York Press, 1995.

Korotayev, Andrey, Kira Meshcherina and Alisa Shishkina. 'A Wave of Global Sociopolitical Destabilization of the 2010s: A Quantitative Analysis'. *Democracy and Security* 14, no. 4 (2018): 331–57.

Kraetzschmar, Hendrik. 'In the Shadow of Legality: Proto-parties and Participatory Politics in the Emirate of Kuwait'. In *Political Parties in the Arab World: Continuity and Change*, edited by Francesco Cavatorta and Lise Storm, 230–51. Edinburgh: Edinburgh University Press, 2018.

Kraetzschmar, Hendrik and Paola Rivetti, eds. *Islamists and the Politics of the Arab Uprisings: Governance, Pluralisation and Contention*. Edinburgh: Edinburgh University Press, 2018.

Krane, Jim. *Dubai: The Story of the World's Fastest City*. London: Atlantic Books, 2009.

Krieg, Andreas, ed. *Divided Gulf: The Anatomy of a Crisis*. Singapore: Palgrave Macmillan, 2018.

Kuschnitzki, Judit. 'The Establishment and Positioning of Al-Rashad: A Case Study of Political Salafism in Yemen'. In *Salafism After the Arab Awakening: Contending with People's Power*, edited by Francesco Cavatorta and Fabio Merone, 99–118. London: Hurst & Co., 2017.

Lackner, Helen, ed. *Why Yemen Matters: A Society in Transition*. London: Saqi, 2014.

————. *Yemen in Crisis: Autocracy, Neo-Liberalism and the Disintegration of a State*. London: Saqi Books, 2017.

Lacroix, Stéphane. 'Sheikhs and Politicians: Inside the New Egyptian Salafism'. Brookings Doha Center, Policy Briefing, 11 June 2012.

————. 'Egypt's Pragmatic Salafis: The Politics of Hizb al-Nour'. Carnegie Endowment for International Peace, 1 November 2016.

Lahoud, Nelly. 'Metamorphosis: From al-Tawhid wa-al-Jihad to Dawlat al-Khilafa (2003–2014)'. In *The Group That Calls Itself a State: Understanding the Evolution and Challenges of the Islamic State*, edited by Nelly Lahoud, Bryan Price, Daniel Milton and Muhammad al-'Ubaydi, 8–26. The Combatting Terrorism Center at West Point, December 2014.

Laipson, Ellen, ed. *Seismic Shift: Understanding Change in the Middle East*. Washington DC: Stimson Center, 2011.

Lake, David A. 'Regional Hierarchy: Authority and Local International Order'. *Review of International Studies* 35 (2009): 35–58.

Laruelle, Marlene, ed. 'Russia's Policy in Syria and the Middle East'. Central Asia Program, Institute for European, Russian, and Eurasian Studies, January 2019.

Lassen, Christina. 'A Changing Regional Order: The Arab Uprisings, the West and the BRICS'. In Issam Fares Institute for Public Policy and International Affairs Working Paper Series, vol. 18, 2013.

Lebow, Richard Ned. *The Tragic Vision of Politics: Ethics, Interests and Orders*. Cambridge: Cambridge University Press, 2003.

Lecha, Soler, Silvia Colombo Eduard, Lorenzo Kamel and Jordi Quero, eds. 'Re-conceptualizing Orders in the Mena Region: The Analytical Framework of the Menara Project', November 2016.

Levine, Daniel J. 'After Tragedy: Melodrama and the Rhetoric of Realism'. *Journal of International Political Theory* 15, no. 3 (2018): 316–31.

Liik, Kadri and Ellie Geranmayeh. 'The New Power Couple: Russia and Iran in the Middle East'. European Council of Foreign Relations, 13 September 2016.

Lister, Charles. 'How al-Qaida Lost Control of Its Syrian Affiliate: The Inside Story'. *CTC Sentinel* 11, no. 2 (2018): 1–9.

——. 'The Syria Effect: Al-Qaeda Fractures'. *Current Trends in Islamist Ideology*, Hudson Institute, 11 December 2019.

Lüleci-Sula, Çağla and Ismail Erkam Sula. 'Migration Management in Turkey'. *Uluslararası İlişkiler/International Relations* 18, no. 72 (2021): 1–18.

Lund, Aron. 'A Turning Point in Aleppo'. *Diwan*. Carnegie Middle East Center, 1 December 2016.

——. 'From Cold War to Civil War: 75 Years of Russian–Syrian Relations'. Swedish Institute of International Affairs, July 2019.

Lundgren, Magnus. 'Meditation in Syria: Initiatives, Strategies, and Obstacles, 2011–2016'. *Contemporary Security Policy* 37, no. 2 (2016): 273–88.

Lynch, Marc. 'Obama and the Middle East: Rightsizing the U.S. Role'. *Foreign Affairs* 94, no. 5, September/October 2015.

——. *The New Arab Wars: Uprisings and Anarchy in the Middle East*. New York: Public Affairs, 2016.

——. 'The New Arab Order: Power and Violence in today's Middle East'. *Foreign Affairs* 97, no. 5 (October 2018).

Lynch, Marc and Curtis R. Ryan. 'Introduction'. *PS: Political Science & Politics* 50, no. 3 (July 2017): 643–6.

Maddy-Weitzman, Bruce. *The Crystallization of the Arab State System, 1945–1954*. Syracuse: Syracuse University Press, 1993.

Magen, Amichai. 'Comparative Assessment of Israel's Foreign Policy Response to the "Arab Spring"'. *Journal of European Integration* 37, no. 1 (2015): 113–33.

Mahdi, Waleed F. 'Echoes of a Scream: US Drones and Articulations of the Houthi Sarkha Slogan in Yemen'. In *Cultural Production and Social Movements After the Arab Spring: Nationalism, Politics and Transnational Identity*, edited by Eid Mohamed and Ayman El Desouky, 205–21. London: I. B. Tauris, 2021.

Maher, Shiraz. *Salafi-Jihadism: The History of an Idea*. New York: Oxford University Press, 2016.

Makdisi, Karim. 'Intervention and the Arab Uprisings: From Transformation to Maintenance of Regional Order'. In *New Conflict Dynamics. Between Regional Autonomy and Intervention in the Middle East and North Africa*, edited by Rasmus Boserup, Waleed Hazbun, Karim Makdisi and Helle Malmvig, 93–107. Copenhagen: Danish Institute for International Studies, 2017.

Makdisi, Karim, Waleed Hazbun, Sabiha Senyücel Gündoğar and Gülşah Dark. 'Regional Order from the Outside In: External Intervention, Regional Actors, Conflicts and Agenda in the MENA Region. MENARA Concept Papers 5 (November 2017).

Malley, Robert. 'The Unwanted Wars: Why the Middle East is More Combustible Than Ever'. *Foreign Affairs* 98, no. 6 (November/December 2019).

Malmvig, Helle. 'Power, Identity and Securitization in Middle East: Regional Order after the Arab Uprisings'. *Mediterranean Politics* 19, no. 1 (2014): 145–8.

von Maltzahn, Nadia. *The Syria–Iran Axis: Cultural Diplomacy and International Relations in the Middle East*. London: I. B. Tauris, 2013.

Mansfield, Laura. *His Own Words: Translation and Analysis of the Writings of Dr. Ayman Al Zawahiri*. N. pl.: TLG Publications, 2006.

Mansour, Imad. 'The Domestic Sources of Regional Orders: Explaining Instability in the Middle East'. PhD Dissertation, McGill University, 2009.

Masoud, Tarek. 'Egyptian Democracy: Smothered in the Cradle, or Stillborn?' *The Brown Journal of World Affairs* 20, no. 2 (Spring/Summer 2014): 3–17.

Mead, Walter Russell. 'The Jacksonian Revolt: American Populism and the Liberal Order', *Foreign Affairs* 96, no. 2 (March/April 2017): 2–7.

Mearsheimer, John J. *The Tragedy of Great Power Politics*. New York: W. W. Norton & Co., 2001.

Meijer, Roel. *Global Salafism: Islam's New Religious Movement*. London: Hurst & Co., 2009.

Mendelsohn, Barak. *The al-Qaeda Franchise: The Expansion of al-Qaeda and Its Consequences*. New York: Oxford University Press, 2016.

Merone, Fabio. 'Enduring Class Struggle in Tunisia: The Fight for Identity beyond Political Islam'. *British Journal of Middle Eastern Studies* 42, no. 1 (January 2015): 74–87.

Merton, Robert K. 'Insiders and Outsiders: A Chapter in the Sociology of Knowledge'. *American Journal of Sociology* 78, no. 1 (1972): 9–47.

Mervin, Sabrina, ed. *The Shi'a Worlds and Iran*. London: Saqi, 2010.

Miller, Andrew. 'The End of the Middle East's Primacy in U.S. Foreign Policy'. *Texas National Security Review*, 13 February 2020.

Miller, Benjamin. *States, Nations, and the Great Powers: The Sources of Regional War and Peace*. Cambridge: Cambridge University Press, 2007.

Miller, Rory. *Desert Kingdoms to Global Powers: The Rise of the Arab Gulf*. New Haven, CT: Yale University Press, 2016.

Mohamed, Eid and Ayman A. El-Desouky, eds. *Cultural Production and Social Movements after the Arab Spring: Nationalism, Politics, and Transnational Identity*. London: I. B. Tauris, 2021.

Monier, Elizabeth. 'The Arabness of Middle East Regionalism: The Arab Spring and Competition for Discursive Hegemony between Egypt, Iran and Turkey'. *Contemporary Politics* 20, no. 4 (2014): 421–34.

Monroe, Steve L. 'Salafis in Parliament: Democratic Attitudes and Party Politics in the Gulf'. *Middle East Journal* 66, no. 3 (2012): 409–24.

Murden, Simon W. 'The Secondary Institutions of the Middle Eastern Regional Interstate Society'. In *International Society and the Middle East: English School Theory at the Regional Level*, edited by Barry Buzan and Ana Gonzalez-Pelaez, 117–39. Basingstoke: Palgrave Macmillan, 2009.

Nas, Çiğdem. 'The EU's Approach to the Syrian Crisis: Turkey as a Partner?' *Uluslararası İlişkiler* 16, no. 62 (2019): 45–64.

Nielsen, Richard A. 'Does the Islamic State Believe in Sovereignty'. In *Islam in the IS Age*, edited by Marc Lynch, 28–30. POMEPS Studies 12, 2015.

Niva, Steve. 'Disappearing Violence: JSOC and the Pentagon's New Cartography of Networked Warfare'. *Security Dialogue* 44, no. 3 (2013): 185–202.

Orkaby, Asher. 'The 1964 Israeli Airlift to Yemen and the Expansion of Weapons Diplomacy'. *Diplomacy & Statecraft* 26, no. 4 (October 2015): 659–77.

Owen, Roger. *State, Power and Politics in the Making of the Modern Middle East*. Abingdon: Routledge, 1992 and 2004.

Özcan, Gencer. 'If The Crisis Is What We Make of It: Turkey and the Uprisings in Syria'. In *Analyzing Foreign Policy in Turkey*, edited by Fuat Aksu and Helin Sarı, 178–98. Cambridge: Cambridge Scholars Publishing, 2017.

———. 'Rusya'nın Suriye Bunalımına Müdahalesi ve Türkiye'. *Kuşku İle Komşuluk, Türkiye ve Rusya İlişkilerinde Değişen Dinamikler*, edited by Gencer Özcan, Evren Balta and Burç Beşgül, 269–98. Istanbul: İletişim, 2017.

Pahwa, Sumita. 'Pathways of Islamist Adaptation: The Egyptian Muslim Brothers' Lessons for Inclusion Moderation Theory'. *Democratization* 24, no. 6 (September 2017): 1066–84.

Pall, Zoltan. 'Do Salafi Parties Represent a Contradiction in Terms? The Development and Fragmentation of Kuwait's Salafi Islamic Group'. In *Political Parties in the Arab World: Continuity and Change*, edited by Francesco Cavatorta and Lise Storm, 100–24. Edinburgh: Edinburgh University Press, 2018.

Pall, Zoltan. *Salafism in Lebanon: Local and Transnational* Movements. Cambridge: Cambridge University Press, 2018.

Peleg, Ilan. 'Israel and the Arab Spring: The Victory of Anxiety'. In *The Arab Spring: Change and Resistance in the Middle East*, edited by Mark Haas and David Lesch, 174–94. Boulder, CO: Westview Press, 2013.

Petti, Matthew and Trita Parsi. 'No Clean Hands: The Interventions of Middle Eastern Powers, 2010–2020'. Quincy Paper, 19 July 2021.

Phillips, Christopher. 'Sectarianism and Conflict in Syria'. *Third World Quarterly* 36, no. 2 (February 2015): 357–76.

———. *The Battle for Syria: International Rivalry in the New Middle East*. New Haven, CT: Yale University Press, 2018.

Podeh, Elie. 'Israel and the Arab Peace Initiative, 2002–2014: A Plausible Missed Opportunity'. *Middle East Journal* 68, no. 4 (2014): 584–603.

———. *Chances for Peace: Missed Opportunities in the Arab–Israeli Conflict*. Austin: University of Texas Press, 2015.

———. 'Saudi Arabia and Israel: From Secret to Public Engagement, 1948–2018'. *The Middle East Journal* 72, no. 4 (2018): 563–86.

Porter, Ross. 'Tricking Time, Overthrowing a Regime: Reining in the Future in the Yemeni Youth Revolution'. *The Cambridge Journal of Anthropology* 34, no. 1 (March 2016): 58–71.

———. 'Freedom, Power and the Crisis of Politics in Revolutionary Yemen'. *Middle East Critique* 26, no. 3 (July 2017): 265–81.

———. 'Security against the State in Revolutionary Yemen'. *Cultural Anthropology* 35, no. 2 (May 2020): 204–10.

Quandt, William B. *Peace Process: American Diplomacy and the Arab–Israeli Conflict since 1967*. Berkeley: University of California Press, 2005.

Quero, Jordi and Eduard Soler Lecha. 'Regional Order and Regional Powers in the Middle East and North Africa'. In *Political Change in the Middle East and North Africa: After the Arab Spring*, edited by Inmaculada Szmolka, 257–80. Edinburgh: Edinburgh University Press, 2017.

Rabi, Uzi and Chelsi Mueller. 'The Gulf Arab States and Israel since 1967: From "No Negotiation" to Tacit Cooperation'. *British Journal of Middle Eastern Studies* 44, no. 4 (October 2017): 576–92.

Rengger, Nicholas. *International Relations, Political Theory and the Problem of Order: Beyond International Relations Theory?* London: Routledge, 2000.

Resta, Valeria. 'Leftist Parties in the Arab Region before and after the Arab Uprisings:

"Unrequited Love"?' In *Political Parties in the Arab World: Continuity and Change*, edited by Francesco Cavatorta and Lise Storm, 21–48. Edinburgh: Edinburgh University Press, 2018.

Rhodes, Ben. *The World as It Is: A Memoir of the Obama White House*. New York: Random House Publishing Group, 2018.

Rice, Condoleezza. *No Higher Honor: A Memoir of My Years in Washington*. New York: Crown Publishers, 2011.

Rickli, Jean-Marc. 'The Political Rationale and Implications of the United Arab Emirates' Military Involvement in Libya'. In *Political Rationale and International Consequences of the War in Libya*, edited by Dag Henriksen and Ann Karin Larsen, 134–54. Oxford: Oxford University Press, 2016.

Rishmawi, Mervat. 'The League of Arab States in the Wake of the "Arab Spring"'. Cairo Institute for Human Rights Studies, 2013.

Roberts, David B. 'Qatar and the UAE: Exploring Divergent Responses to the Arab Spring'. *Middle East Journal* 71, no. 4 (2017): 544–62.

Rondeaux, Candace, Oliver Imhof and Jack Margolin. 'The Abu Dhabi Express: Analyzing the Wagner Group's Libya Logistics Pipeline & Operations'. *New America*, November 2021.

Rózsa, Erzsébet. 'Geo-Strategic Consequences of the Arab Spring'. *PapersIEMed* 19, June 2013.

Rüma, İnan and Mitat Çelikpala. 'Russian and Turkish Foreign Policy Activism in the Syrian Theatre'. *Uluslararası İlişkiler Dergisi* 16, no. 62 (June 2019): 65–84.

Ryan, Curtis. 'The New Arab Cold War and the Struggle for Syria'. *Middle East Report* 262 (2012): 28–31.

Salem, Maryam Ben. 'The Foreign Policy of Tunisia's Ennahdha: Constancy and Changes'. In *The Foreign Policy of Islamist Political Parties: Ideology in Practice*, edited by Mohamed-Ali Adraoui, 47–69. Edinburgh: Edinburgh University Press, 2018.

Salem, Paul. 'The Middle East in 2015 and Beyond: Trends and Drivers'. The Middle East Institute (MEI) Policy Focus Series, 2014.

——. 'Working toward a Stable Regional Order'. *The Annals of the American Academy of Political and Social Science* 668, no. 1 (2016): 36–52.

Salisbury, Peter. 'Risk Perception and Appetite in UAE Foreign and National Security Policy'. Chatham House, July 2020.

Salloukh, Bassel F. 'Overlapping Contests and Middle East International Relations: The Return of the Weak Arab State'. *PS: Political Science and Politics* 50, no. 3 (July 2017): 660–3.

Sandler, Shmuel. 'The Arab Spring, Democracy and Security'. In *The Arab Spring*,

Democracy and Security: Domestic and International Ramifications, edited by Efraim Inbar, 128–44. London: Routledge, 2013.

Sarı Karademir, Burcu. 'A Dance of Entanglement: US–Turkish Relations in the Context of the Syrian Conflict'. *Uluslararası İlişkiler Dergisi* 16, no. 62 (June 2019): 27–43.

Scahill, Jeremy. *Dirty Wars: The World Is a Battlefield*. New York: Nation Books, 2013.

Schonmann, Noa. 'Fortitude at Stake: The Accidental Crisis in American–Israeli Relations, August 1958'. *Israel Affairs* 23, no. 4 (2017): 626–49.

Schwedler, Jillian. *Faith in Moderation: Islamist Parties in Jordan and Yemen*. Cambridge: Cambridge University Press, 2006.

Schwedler, Jillian. 'Can Islamists Become Moderates? Rethinking the Inclusion-Moderation Hypothesis'. *World Politics* 63, no. 2 (April 2011): 347–76.

Schweller, Randall L. 'Why Trump Now: A Third-Image Explanation'. In *Chaos in the Liberal Order: The Trump Presidency and International Politics in the Twenty-first Century*, edited by Robert Jervis, Francis J. Gavin, Joshua Rovner and Dianne N. Labross, 22–39. New York: Columbia University Press, 2018.

Seale, Patrick. *The Struggle for Syria: A Study of Post-War Arab Politics, 1945–1958*. New Haven, CT: Yale University Press, 1987.

Sela, Avraham. 'The Vicissitudes of the Arab States System: From Its Emergence to the Arab Spring'. *India Quarterly* 73, no. 2 (2017): 145–79.

Şenyuva, Özgehan and Çiğdem Üstün. 'A Deal to End "the" Deal: Why the Refugee Agreement Is a Threat to Turkey–EU Relations'. The German Marshall Fund for the United States, 2016, 4.

Shehabi, Ala'a and Marc Owen Jones, eds. *Bahrain's Uprising: Resistance and Repression in the Gulf*. London: Zed Books, 2015.

Shlaim, Avi. 'Israeli Interference in Internal Arab Politics: The Case of Lebanon'. In *The Politics of Arab Integration*, edited by Giacomo Luciani and Ghassan Salame, 232–55. London: Croom Helm, 1988.

———. 'Israel, Palestine, and the Arab Uprisings'. In *The New Middle East: Protest and Revolution in the Arab World*, edited by Fawaz Gerges, 380–401. Cambridge: Cambridge University Press, 2013.

Singh, Amrit. 'Death by Drone: Civilian Harm Caused by US Targeted Killings in Yemen'. Open Society Justice Initiative and Mwatana Organization for Human Rights, 2015.

Smith, Simon C. *Britain's Revival and Fall in the Gulf: Kuwait, Bahrain, Qatar, and the Trucial States, 1950–71*. Abingdon: Routledge, 2004.

Stein, Ewan. 'An Uncivil Partnership: Egypt's Jama'a Islamiyya and the State after the "Jihad"'. *Third World Quarterly* 32, no. 5 (2011): 863–81.

———. 'Ideological Codependency and Regional Order: Iran, Syria, and the Axis of Refusal'. *Political Science* 50, no. 3 (2017): 676–80.

———. 'Historical Sociology and Middle East International Relations.' In *The Routledge Handbook of International Relations in the Middle East*, edited by Shahram Akbarzadeh, 46–58. Abingdon and New York: Routledge, 2019.

Susser, Asher. 'The "Arab Spring": Competing Analytical Paradigms'. *Bustan: The Middle East Book Review* 3, no. 2 (2012): 109–30.

———. 'Israel's Place in a Changing Regional Order (1948–2013)'. *Israel Studies* 19, no. 2 (2014): 218–38.

Taştekin, Fehim. *Karanlık çöktüğünde: IŞİD: din adına şiddetin dünü ve bugünü.* Istanbul: Doğan Kitap, 2016.

———. *Rojava: Kürtlerin Zamanı.* Istanbul: İletişim Yayınları, 2017.

Teti, Andrea, Pamela Abbott and Francesco Cavatorta. *The Arab Uprisings in Egypt, Jordan and Tunisia: Social, Political and Economic Transformations.* London: Palgrave, 2017.

Tibi, Bassam. 'The Middle East Torn between Rival Choices: Islamism, International Security and Democratic Peace'. In *Regional Insecurity after the Arab Uprisings: Narratives of Security and Threat*, edited by Elizabeth Monier, 204–23. Basingstoke: Palgrave Macmillan, 2015.

Totten, Michael, David Schenker and Hussain Abdul-Hussain. 'Arab Spring or Islamist Winter? Three Views'. *World Affairs* 174, no. 5 (2012): 23–42.

Trenin, Dmitri. *What Is Russia Up To in the Middle East?* Cambridge: Polity Press, 2018.

Tür, Özlem and Mehmet Akif Kumral. 'Paradoxes in Turkey's Syria Policy: Analyzing the Critical Episode of Agenda Building'. *New Perspectives on Turkey* 55 (November 2016): 107–32.

Ulrichsen, Kristian Coates. *The Gulf States in International Political Economy.* Basingstoke: Palgrave Macmillan, 2015.

———, ed. *The Changing Security Dynamics of the Persian Gulf.* Oxford: Oxford University Press, 2018.

———. *Qatar and the Gulf Crisis.* Oxford: Oxford University Press, 2020.

United Nations Development Programme. 'Assessing the Impact of War in Yemen: Pathways for Recovery', 23 November 2021.

Utvik, Bjørn Olav. 'The Ikhwanization of the Salafis: Piety in the Politics of Egypt and Kuwait'. *Middle East Critique* 23, no. 1 (January 2014): 5–27.

Wagemakers, Joas. 'A Purist Jihadi-Salafi: The Ideology of Abu Muhammad al-Maqdisi'. *British Journal of Middle Eastern Studies* 36, no. 2 (August 2009): 281–97.

———. 'Revisiting Wiktorowicz: Categorising and Defining the Branches of Salafism'.

In *Salafism After the Arab Awakening: Contending with People's Power*, edited by Francesco Cavatorta and Fabio Merone, 7–24. London: Hurst & Co., 2017.

Walt, Stephen M. 'Alliances in a Unipolar World'. *World Politics* 61, no. 1 (2009): 86–120.

———. 'The End of the American Era'. *The National Interest* 116 (2011): 6–16.

Warrick, Joby. *Black Flags: The Rise of ISIS*. New York: Anchor Books, 2016.

Wedeen, Lisa. *Peripheral Visions: Publics, Power, and Performance in Yemen*. Chicago: University of Chicago Press, 2008.

Wehrey, Frederic. *The Burning Shores: Inside the Battle for the New Libya*. New York: Farrar, Straus and Giroux, 2018.

Weiss, Michael and Hassan Hassan. *ISIS: Inside the Army of Terror*. New York: Phaidon Press; New York: Simon and Schuster, 2016.

Wendt, Alexander. *Social Theory of International Politics*. Cambridge: Cambridge University Press, 1999.

Wiktorowicz, Quintan. 'Anatomy of the Salafi Movement'. *Studies in Conflict & Terrorism* 29, no. 3 (May 2006): 207–39.

Williams, William Appleman. *The Tragedy of American Diplomacy*. New York: Delta Books, 1962.

Winter, Stefan. *A History of the 'Alawis: From Medieval Aleppo to the Turkish Republic*. Princeton: Princeton University Press, 2016.

Wohlforth, William C. 'The Stability of a Unipolar World'. *International Security* 24, no. 1 (1999): 5–41.

Woodward, Susan L. *The Ideology of Failed States: Why Intervention Fails*. Cambridge: Cambridge University Press, 2017.

Worth, Robert F. 'Mohammed Bin Zayed's Dark Vision of the Middle East's Future'. *The New York Times*, 9 January 2020.

Wright, Thomas. *All Measures Short of War*. New Haven, CT: Yale University Press, 2017.

Wrong, Dennis. *The Problem of Order: What Unites and Divides Society*. New York: The Free Press, 1994.

Yahya, Maha. 'Refugees in the Making of an Arab Regional Disorder'. Carnegie Endowment for International Peace, 2015.

Yalçınkaya, Haldun. 'Foreign Fighters of ISIS and Their Threat: The Experience of Turkey (2014–2016)'. *Uluslararası İlişkiler* 14, no. 53 (2017): 23–43.

Yassin-Kassab, Robin and Leila Al-Shami. *Burning Country: Syrians in Revolution and War*. London: Pluto Press, 2016.

Yom, Sean. 'US Foreign Policy in the Middle East: The Logic of Hegemonic Retreat'. *Global Policy* 11, no. 1 (2020): 75–83.

Yom, Sean L. *From Resilience to Revolution: How Foreign Interventions Destabilize the Middle East*. New York: Columbia University Press, 2015.

Young, Karen E. 'The Interventionist Turn in Gulf States' Foreign Policies'. The Arab Gulf States Institute in Washington, 1 June 2016.

Youngs, Richard. 'Impasse in Euro-Gulf Relations'. Foundation for International Relations and Foreign Dialogue (FRIDE) Working Paper 80, April 2009.

Zartman, William. 'States, Boundaries and Sovereignty in the Middle East: Unsteady but Unchanging'. *International Affairs* 93, no. 4 (2017): 937–48.

Zelin, Aaron Y. *Your Sons Are at Your Service: Tunisia's Missionaries of Jihad*. New York: Columbia University Press, 2020.

INDEX

Printed in the USA
CPSIA information can be obtained
at www.ICGtesting.com
JSHW011504200524
63496JS00011B/469